Art and Value

Historical Materialism
Book Series

The titles published in this series are listed at *brill.com/hm*

Art and Value

*Art's Economic Exceptionalism in Classical,
Neoclassical and Marxist Economics*

By

Dave Beech

BRILL

LEIDEN | BOSTON

Library of Congress Cataloging-in-Publication Data

Beech, Dave.
  Art and value : art's economic exceptionalism in classical, neoclassical and Marxist economics / By Dave
Beech.
    pages cm. — (Historical materialism book series ; volume 94)
  Includes bibliographical references and index.
    ISBN 978-90-04-28814-0 (hardback : alk. paper) — ISBN 978-90-04-28815-7 (e-book) 1. Art--Economic
aspects. I. Title.

  N8600.B425 2015
  338.4'77—dc23

                                                                                        2014047089

This publication has been typeset in the multilingual "Brill" typeface. With over 5,100 characters covering
Latin, IPA, Greek, and Cyrillic, this typeface is especially suitable for use in the humanities.
For more information, please see www.brill.com/brill-typeface.

ISSN 1570-1522
ISBN 978-90-04-28814-0 (hardback)
ISBN 978-90-04-28815-7 (e-book)

This book is printed on acid-free paper.

MIX
Paper from
responsible sources
FSC
www.fsc.org   FSC® C109576

Printed by Printforce, the Netherlands

Dedicated to Cat and Presley

∵

Contents

Acknowledgements

This book began in 2006 as a study of the Marxist theories of reification, commodification, recuperation and spectacle, which is to say precisely those concepts that Marxism has devised to understand the relationship between art and capitalism. My plan for the extra time that I would have to spend at home due to the imminent birth of my son was to write a book when he slept. Eighteen months later I had two sheets of A4 and a more realistic idea of fatherhood. The first full draft of the book was a series of studies, examining art's economy through its relationship to technology, skill, beauty, ideology, and globalisation. Since each chapter deserved a book length study of its own, the draft was abandoned almost as soon as it was completed. The second full draft was a series of critiques that revealed the *limits* of capital, mainstream economics, cultural economics, and Western Marxism. Both of these early drafts were tested in reduced form at various conferences and I would like to thank the participants of these in drawing my attention to the shortfalls of my own project and to the potential misunderstandings that would likely result from publishing a critique of the established wisdom on art's relationship to capitalism without providing a fresh theorisation. I am grateful to the participants of the symposium held by postgraduate students at the Slade School of Art in 2011. My short paper, entitled 'Art's Antagonism to Economics', was criticised from the audience by Peter Osborne, which led me to extend the scope of the book. I also benefited from comments made in response to the Marxism in Culture lecture I gave at UCL in 2011 entitled 'Art and Economics', my paper entitled 'Art, Merchant Capital and Finance Capital' at the Historical Materialism conference in 2011, and a series of discussions held at Chelsea College of Art & Design by the Contemporary Marxism Group between 2010 and 2013. The arguments within the book were improved as a result of points raised by participants, panel members and audiences at these events.

I am grateful to all those who made comments on early drafts: Mark Hutchinson, Kim Charnley, Alex Fletcher, Andrew Kliman, and Jeff Wall. I am indebted to the anonymous reviewers of the first draft of the book who made valuable suggestions for improvements and pointed out errors in the text. Mel Jordan and Andy Hewitt – fellow members of the art collective Freee – have maintained a supportive critical engagement with the arguments of the book throughout its long development. Finally, my wife Cat and son Presley, to whom this book is dedicated, have reminded me every day of the values that are at the heart of this book, even when researching it and writing it meant that I had to betray those values temporarily while I withdrew into a world made entirely of books.

A condensed version of the chapters on 'Art and Merchant Capital' and 'Art and Finance Capital' was delivered as a paper at the Historical Materialism Conference in 2011. An early and shorter version of the chapter 'On the Absence of a Marxist Economics of Art' was delivered as a paper at the Association of Art Historians conference in 2012. A short version of the chapters 'Art and Exceptionalism in Classical Economics' and 'Art and Exceptionalism in Neo-Classical Economics' was delivered as a paper as part of the Eminent Visiting Artists Lecture Series at the University of British Columbia, Vancouver in 2013. A summary of the historical development of the concept of economic exceptionalism was presented at the 'Questions of Value' symposium at the Nottingham Contemporary in March 2013 and at Queen Mary, University of London Drama Department Seminars in May 2013.

Introduction

There has been an extraordinary convergence of mainstream economics and Marxist cultural analysis. Both assert in the most ardent terms that art is, always has been, or has recently become nothing but a commodity. In 2010, the economist Clare McAndrew said, 'the reality is that art is produced, bought, and sold by individuals and institutions working within an economic framework inescapable from material and market constraints'.[1] Five years earlier, Marxist art historian Julian Stallabrass claimed, 'artists are snug in the market's lap'.[2] Tyler Cowen, a neoliberal economist writing in 1998, insisted, 'artists are subject to economic constraints, just as other businessmen are'.[3] Extending the historical frame further, the German philosopher Theodor Adorno, one of the pioneers of the Marxist theory of art's incorporation by capitalism, writing in the 1930s, argued that '[c]ultural entities typical of the culture industry are no longer *also* commodities, they are commodities through and through'.[4] Nothing can be achieved by denying that art has been transformed by developments ushered in by capitalist society. Art has often adopted not only the technological innovations of capitalism but also its latest forms of management, marketing and values, not to mention the visual styles of advertising, popular culture and administration. None of this has gone unnoticed by commentators on the apparently cosy relationship between art and capitalism but what has been neglected is the difference between art's cultural, social and political incorporation by capitalism, on the one hand, and its economic incorporation, on the other.

My starting point is not the simple fact of the agreement between left and right that artworks are commodities like any other, but the specific differences of tone with which this consensus is expressed. There is a marked contrast to be observed, for example, between asserting that art has been incorporated by capitalism by virtue of the social and subjective hold that capitalism has over artists, and that the art market has commodified art. There is also a difference between arguing that artworks are commodities insofar as they are exchanged in the marketplace and arguing, for instance, that artists such as 'Beethoven and Michelangelo, who sold their artworks for a profit, were entrepreneurs

---

1 McAndrew 2010a, p. 19.
2 Stallabrass 2004a, p. 200.
3 Cowen 1998, p. 2.
4 Adorno 1991, p. 100.

and capitalists'.[5] Likewise, it is one thing to say that art museums increasingly belong to the economic sector of the tourist industry and quite another to say that artists 'brand' themselves by making work of a recognisable kind, two distinct arguments that often appear together as if the 'professionalisation' of the arts is simply applied across the board. Despite apparent agreement, also, we should not conflate the argument that there is an oversupply of artistic labour with the overabundant existence of artistic 'dark matter', that is to say, 'the vast zone of cultural activity'[6] that does not pass through the art market, partly because the concept of 'oversupply' assumes a market determined by the consumer (in this case: the employer of wage labour) whereas the art world's 'dark matter' is deliberately and conscientiously 'makeshift, amateur, informal, unofficial, autonomous, activist, non-institutional, self-organized'.[7] These differences of explanation are not just differences of emphasis, I want to suggest, but are symptoms of the lack of evidence of the economic transformation of artistic production by commodity exchange.

Each exponent of the theory of art's commodification appears to reserve a place for opponents as claiming that art is a special vocation independent of the motives and mechanisms of market forces. Stallabrass unearths evidence of this ideology in statements made by wealthy collectors, powerful curators and celebrity artists, all of whom have a vested interest in art appearing to be independent of the market. Similarly, Cowen sets himself off from wide spectrums of 'cultural pessimists', primarily leftists, aesthetes and romantics, who 'typically believe that the market economy corrupts culture'.[8] Clearly, opponents do not always sit in the place they have been allotted: Stallabrass is a left-wing writer who believes that the market economy corrupts culture but he nonetheless argues that art is in fact widely incorporated by the marketplace, while Cowen is a pro-marketeer who does not believe that art is corrupted by the market, not because he believes the ideology that art exists in some special sphere above market considerations but because he subscribes to the belief that markets promote liberty, freedom and creativity. My critique of the various theories of the commodification of art does not stem from a belief that art is too elevated to be analysed economically or that artists are too passionate about art to be swayed by financial self-interest. My method, in this book, is not to interrogate the structure of the arguments for or against the validity of the observation that the contemporary art market has become a powerful force

---

5   Cowen 1998, p. 3.
6   Sholette 2011, p. 45.
7   Sholette 2011, p. 1.
8   Cowen 1998, p. 9.

within the discourses and practices of the studio, or to provide a theoretical judgement on the romantic and idealist projection of the artist as a deeply individual producer who cannot be corrupted by the market. My intention is to pay close attention to the various competing *mechanisms* stated or implied by the various theories of art's production, distribution and consumption of art in capitalism. Market mechanisms are certainly present in the art world, but other mechanisms are also present. I will not assume that market mechanisms will always dominate over discursive mechanisms or state mechanisms or scholastic mechanisms. The question of whether market mechanisms succeed or fail to make their presence felt in art must remain open, pending the analysis of the success and failure of counter-mechanisms that art's institutions develop to protect art from the perceived threat of commercialisation, marketisation and commodification.

This book is a detailed assessment of the claim that art production coincides with capitalist commodity production. My study consists of an analysis of the arguments given within the various bodies of literature that make up the two broad traditions of the economics of art and the Western Marxist analysis of art's relationship to capitalism. However, I am neither an economist nor a Marxologist. I am an artist. This means, of course, that I am precisely the kind of individual within the art world meddling in cultural economics that Ruth Towse bemoans with the phrase 'Save us from the amateurs!'[9] In large part the purpose of this book can be characterised in direct opposition to this technocratic slogan. Although my counter-slogan might well read 'Save us from the experts!' I have certainly not followed the tradition of the gentleman amateur aesthete who feels justified in expressing his opinion on all matters. I have, on the contrary, attempted to learn as much about economics as possible without the acquisition of that knowledge converting me into an expert. In other words, I have taken every opportunity I could find to use my knowledge and experience as a critical artist to unpick the certainties of economics, especially as these have been uncritically applied to art. Also, I have tackled the tradition of Western Marxism without subscribing to its central assumptions about art's relationship to capitalism. No doubt I have made mistakes in my attempt to take on the analysis of art's economics in both these traditions, but at the same time I hope that my critique is sufficiently engaged with them to go beyond pedestrian complaints and raise some new questions.

I am not the first artist to attempt to address art's relationship to capitalism. Among my predecessors it is essential to highlight the importance of Bertolt

---

9   Towse 2002, p. 153.

Brecht, who wrote about art's transformation by the rise of capitalist mass culture. Asger Jorn, the avant-garde Danish artist who was a founding member of COBRA and the Situationist International, wrote 'Value and Economy' in 1961, which was simultaneously a critique of the application of exchange value to art and an anti-Stalinist rejection of dominant Marxist theories of art and production. In the mid-1970s in New York, a generation of artists including Sarah Charlesworth, Adrian Piper, Mel Ramsden and Ian Burn, and a related group based in Coventry, including Terry Atkinson, Mike Baldwin and David Bainbridge, reflected extensively on the effects of the developing market for contemporary avant-garde art. 'While it may once have seemed an exaggeration of economic determinism to regard works of art as "merely" commodities in an economic exchange', Ian Burn wrote in 1975, 'it is now pretty plain that our entire lives have become so extensively constituted in these terms that we cannot any longer pretend otherwise'.[10] Burn, here, in part registers the somewhat shocking revelation that Conceptual Art, which was not only avant-garde but typically consisted of works such as photocopies and printed texts that lacked all the recognisable qualities of luxury trade, had begun to fetch the kinds of prices that had previously been reserved for unique paintings and sculpture. At the same time, Burn's topical observations are reinforced by knowledge of debates in Marxist aesthetics from the 1930s, bringing theory and practice together in a mutually supporting exchange. It is not what Cowen would call 'market optimists' that Burn confronts, but two diametrically opposed and yet equally naive positions: economic determinism and market denial. We will see variations of these positions resurface time and time again throughout this book, with arguments for the benefits of market forces on art vying with arguments that art suffers at the hands of market mechanisms; and arguments insisting that art has been commodified competing with arguments that it is impossible to commodify art. Mel Ramsden, writing on the same subject at the same time, confesses that he leans 'perilously close to the foibles of economic determinism' in arguing that 'the adventuristic art of the 1970s ... [has] become a function of the market-system'.[11] Burn's analysis of art's transformation by business and 'a market so powerful that even the most iconoclastic work can be comfortably celebrated'[12] is more finely grained than the bald assertion of art's general recuperation and commodification. He understands the significance, for instance, of 'the fact that artists' time has never been commodified'.[13] Burn

---

10   Burn in Alberro and Stimson 1999, p. 320.
11   Ramsden 1975, p. 66.
12   Burn in Alberro and Stimson 1999, p. 325.
13   Burn in Alberro and Stimson 1999, p. 322.

also recognises that art is not brought under the power of capital by subjecting it to the standard procedures of productivity, management and mechanisation: 'So we intuitively achieve the corporate spirit of bureaucratic organization without any of its overt structures',[14] he says. Such anomalies, and others besides, are the itches that this book is determined to scratch.

How are we to determine whether and in what way art has been affected by capitalism? No doubt capitalist society has penetrated art in numerous ways, as artists respond to changes in modern urban living, new technology, the growth of pop culture, the existence of private affluence and public squalor, and so on and so forth. Cheap global travel and instant global communication have transformed the isolated bohemian artist into an international networker, and the increased quantity of galleries, museums, curators and collectors, added to the accelerated speed with which information about artists circulates, means that the long suffering artist who once found success only after death is now picked up by the market and the art museum shortly after graduating. The many ways in which art and artists have adjusted to capitalist society require special study, but I shall neglect all those that have nothing to say about whether art corresponds to the capitalist mode of production. Both the nature of the capitalist mode of production and its relationship to the pre-capitalist mode of production was elucidated during the Marxist debates on the transition from feudalism to capitalism in the 1950s and the Brenner debate in the 1970s.[15] These debates, which did not put any emphasis on the fate of art, have an enormous bearing on the question of art's economic and political ontology, if we pursue the Marxist analysis of art's mode of production.

The various arts of painting, sculpture, poetry and theatre predate this transition, but the period between the fourteenth century and the end of the sixteenth century in which feudalism collapses and capitalism emerges coincides with the epochal transformation of the Renaissance which ended the guild system's domination and replaced the artisan with the individual *artificer*. Painters, sculptors and architects from the beginning of the thirteenth century, first in sculpture but beginning in painting with Giotto's naturalism, produce works that, in Arnold Hauser's words, become 'un-Gothic', 'unmetaphysical', 'unsymbolical' and 'unceremonial'.[16] We can add 'unaristocratic' and 'un-rural'. Not only does the class character of patronage begin to slide from aristocracy to bourgeoisie, but also by the end of the period of transition a new economic

---

14   Burn in Alberro and Stimson 1999, p. 325.
15   See Hilton 1976, and Aston and Philpin 1985.
16   Hauser 1992, p. 27.

relationship altogether arises, in which collectors, art dealers and speculation in the trading of artworks make their first appearance.

If, prior to the transition from feudalism to capitalism, painters and sculptors belong to the guild and produce handicrafts for clients and patrons, by the end of the transition painters and sculptors were producing works independently of the consumer and in a personal style. There is a *prima facie* case for concluding that art, like other forms of production, was transformed by the rise of capitalism, and many Marxist art theories take this for granted, but we need to look more closely at the details of the transition in order to establish art's relationship to it. This was the era in which merchants, no longer pedlars going from town to town, accumulated wealth and power in the major cities, and which therefore refuted the physiocratic idea that all wealth derives from land and ushers in the economic theory – and policies – of mercantilism.

The first wave of the transition debate was inaugurated by an exchange between Maurice Dobb and Paul Sweezy after Sweezy took issue with Dobb's definition of feudalism and his theory of its decline. Sweezy believed that Dobb placed too much emphasis on the internal contradictions of feudal society in order to explain its downfall, claiming that the development of towns and cities independent of feudal lords established an external power, the marketplace, which eventually challenged feudalism and ushered in capitalism. Such questions do not impinge on the study of art's relationship to the transition. What matters more, I would suggest, is the nature of the transition itself and its result. In particular, the transition between feudalism and capitalism must be able to distinguish accurately between the two social systems, and this is vital for our inquiry into whether art goes through the same metamorphosis. This is possible because the controversy, which focused primarily on the causes and agents of the emergence of capitalism, did not involve any dispute over the character of capitalism itself that Dobb presented. As a method for identifying capitalism, his analysis of the mode of production, derived from Marx, has not been bettered.

In his classic 'Studies in the Development of Capitalism', first published in 1947, Dobb distinguished the capitalist mode of production from pre-capitalist modes of production according to 'the way in which the means of production were owned and to the social relations between men which resulted from their connections with the process of production'.[17] Money and profit, as well as markets, capital and 'the acquisitive use of money'[18] all preceded capitalism. 'Thus capitalism was not simply a system of production for the market – a

---

17   Dobb 1950, p. 7.
18   Dobb 1950, p. 8.

system of commodity production as Marx termed it – but a system under which labour power has "itself became a commodity" and was bought and sold on the market like any other object of exchange'.[19] In particular, Dobb targets the commonly held view that capitalism was brought about through the introduction and extension of free markets, commodity exchange and enterprise. Merchants had obtained profits from the exchange of commodities through markets for centuries before the advent of capitalism. Dobb says, 'the existence of trade and of money-lending and the presence of a specialized class of merchants or financiers ... does not suffice to constitute a capitalist society'.[20] Robert Brenner picked this theme up in his own contribution to the transition debate, rejecting what he called the 'commercialization model'. Brenner argued that this theory has its origin in Adam Smith and that it is at fault because it fails to distinguish adequately between 'wealth' and 'capital'.[21] Brenner explains: 'If expansion through trade and investment did not bring with it the transition to capitalist social-productive relations – manifested in the full emergence of labour power as a commodity – there could be no capital accumulation on an extended scale'.[22]

Following Marx, Dobb defines capitalism 'neither in a spirit or enterprise nor in the use of money to finance a series of exchange transactions with the object of gain, but in a particular mode of production'.[23] What sets off capitalism is not that these isolated pockets of capitalistic behaviour spread to the point of being dominant, but that production is subordinated to capital through the commodification of labour. Marx defined the mode of production as consisting of the forces of production (primarily the state of technological capability) and the relations of production. Since the capitalist mode of production is not determined by technological developments, it is the social relations of production, principally the division between a class of non-labouring owners and a class of non-owner labourers, that sets capitalism apart. Surplus is not unique to capitalism. It is the form in which surplus is extracted that differentiates modes of production. The capitalist mode of production is characterised by the relationship between the capitalist and the wage labourer. This is why Dobb dates the birth of capitalism in the latter half of the sixteenth century, with 'the subordination of domestic handicraftsmen, working in their own

---

19   Dobb 1950, p. 7.
20   Dobb 1950, p. 8.
21   See Brenner 1977.
22   Brenner 1977, pp. 26–7.
23   Dobb 1950, p. 7.

homes, to a capitalist on the so-called "putting-out system";[24] in which merchants, who had previously dealt in raw materials and finished articles, drop off raw materials to handicraft workers at their homes and return to pick up finished articles for sale. Whether merchants turned into capitalist producers, or producers turned into capitalist merchants, clearly, capitalism was initially based on extant technologies, established economic forms (wage labour and trade), and familiar commodities (textiles, shoes, locks, guns, etc.), or, as Marx put it, the putting out system does not bring about 'the overthrow of the old mode of production, but rather preserves it and uses it as its premise'.[25] None of the individual elements of the capitalist mode of production are novel, but the social organisation of them is unprecedented. 'We must look for the opening of the capitalist period only when changes in the mode of production occur, in the sense of a direct subordination of the producer to a capitalist',[26] Dobb says.

Instead of theorising art's relationship to capitalism through the concepts of commodification, culture industry, spectacle and real subsumption, all of which have a superficial ring of truth, the key to understanding art's relationship to capitalism must be derived from questioning whether art has gone through the transition from feudalism to capitalism. This may not provide the whole account of how art has been penetrated by capitalist society, but it must be the foundation of any adequate account of the exceptional economics of art and for any politics of art within and against capitalism. Following Dobb this means examining the mode of production of art, rather than being distracted by impressionistic perceptions of art's deep involvement in the market, its close proximity to corporate capitalism, its globalisation and its conspicuous super profits. To examine art's mode of production is to pay close attention, primarily, to its social relations of production, not its modes of consumption, distribution, exchange and circulation. If we make the mistake of 'following the money', the assessment of art's economics will be drawn away from the mode of production and lead to erroneous conclusions drawn from the way that capitalist society is capable of turning anything into a commodity that can be exchanged for profit. The existence of art dealers, collectors, auction houses and art asset managers does not say anything about art's mode of production. If it seems reasonable to believe that dealers, collectors and so on have an influence on artists, or if the assumption that artists, like any other commodity producer, will be incentivised by market demand seems to be justified, the relationship between art and capitalism can appear to be cosy. However, what

---

24   Dobb 1950, p. 18.
25   Marx 1959, p. 393.
26   Dobb 1950, p. 17.

the transition debates indicate is that the question of whether art conforms to the capitalist mode of production cannot be determined simply by observing certain capitalistic elements at work in the production or circulation of art but depends entirely on whether art embodies the social relations in which the capitalist subjugates production through the ownership of the means of production and the payment of wages to purchase labour power.

When I speak of art's relationship to the capitalist mode of production, it is this that I have in mind. What is more, the clarity of the contrast that Dobb draws between the capitalist mode of production and independent handicraft production that preceded it, is not only helpful in identifying the capitalist mode of production but also, it seems to me, in identifying artistic production, typically, as not conforming to the capitalist mode of production: 'It is clear that such a definition [of the capitalist mode of production] excludes the system of independent handicraft production where the craftsman owned his own petty implements of production and undertook the sale of his own wares'.[27] Dobb explains that simple commodity production 'differed from the crafts undertaken on a feudal estate only to the extent that the craftsman was making his wares for sale on a market and not making them as an obligation of service for a lord',[28] adding that there was nothing 'about this mode of production that made it capitalistic: even though the craftsman took apprentices and employed a journeyman or two to help him'.[29] Now, insofar as the independent handicraft producer sold his own products, and produced them specifically for sale, it is clear that he was a commodity producer. The artist is also a commodity producer today insofar as she owns her own 'petty implements' and, unlike the wage labourer, continues to own the product she produces. However, since the independent craftsman was neither a capitalist nor a wage labourer, and handicraft production does not conform to the capitalist mode of production, then the artist can be a commodity producer without this fact suggesting by any means that the artist has been economically transformed by the capitalist mode of production. Thus, the evident 'commodification' of art is not proof that art has become capitalistic. In fact, the concept of commodification was coined by Western Marxists specifically to account for the fate of art within capitalism, just as the notion of the 'Culture Industry', developed by the Frankfurt School, has been a persuasive force in establishing the belief among Marxists and the left generally that art sits firmly, if uncomfortably, within the capitalist mode of production. However, the concept of commodification fails

---

27   Dobb 1950, p. 7.
28   Dobb 1950, p. 71.
29   Dobb 1950, pp. 71–2.

to distinguish between 'simple commodity production'[30] and 'capitalist commodity production' and the concept of the Culture Industry applies to art only by ignoring the unchanged mode of production (specifically the social relations of production) of art from its precapitalist handicraft form.

For mainstream economists various new concepts have been used to bring art within standard or near standard economic analysis, including the concept of 'human capital', developed first by Gary Becker, in which education and training are seen, rather than simply as acquiring knowledge and skill, as a peculiar kind of 'capital' owned by the worker to be realised in the labour market (so that going to galleries can be seen as one of the 'investments' that artists 'profit' from when they make their own informed work), and the neoclassical concept of 'opportunity cost', in which apparently costless goods, such as taking a walk or drawing a picture for your own amusement, are shown to have a 'price' equivalent to the best alternative, such as what one might have earned or what society might have gained if one had not, as we say, 'taken the time off'. Each of these arguments presupposes a specific configuration of the relationship between artworks, institutions, artists and society as a whole. I will examine the consequences of placing the emphasis variously on one aspect rather than all the others, tracking the differences between examining the economy of art through artworks, on the one hand, or the choices of artists, on the other, or through the ways that art's institutions mediate the artist's relationship to capital or consumerist society infiltrates the beliefs and actions of artists and collectors. Throughout this study, for reasons that will become clearer later on, I will not ask whether art is or is not economic, or whether art is or is not exchanged as a commodity, but in what ways precisely art is subjected to or remains free from economic rationality and how exactly art enters or resists commodification. The best way to test art's relationship to economics and the marketplace, I will argue, is through an examination of the mechanisms by which decisions on art are made.

There are certain anomalies in the economics of art that need to be addressed. Although the Conceptual artists of the mid-1970s would not be persuaded that art could somehow remain independent of the market, art's mode of production remained largely untouched by industrialisation and the transformation of handicraft into wage labour that was the bedrock of capitalist commodity production. Burn, for instance, was aware that 'both my labor and means of production remain my own property and I sell only the product of my labor'.[31] What Burn refers to, here, is the fact that, insofar as the artist tends

---

30   Dobb 1950, p. 71.
31   Burn in Alberro and Stimson 1999, p. 321.

not to be paid a wage and owns both the means of production and the product that she produces, then no productive capitalist plays any direct role within the production of art. Since capitalists have not only taken ownership of already existing production but have transformed production through mechanisation, the division of labour and the scientific organisation of production, the absence of the productive capitalist from artistic production might imply that artistic labour can or ought to remain free from capitalist procedures. This is not borne out by experience, according to Burn. Despite art's unusual *de facto* economic independence, Burn argues, artists have adopted 'an intensely capitalistic mode of production'.[32] This may not be true of all artists, but certainly it is safe to say that many of the most successful artists have taken on certain capitalist practices or, perhaps we could say, artists have learned from capitalists about how to run their studios, use marketing, produce their works more efficiently, and a range of other techniques. Market mechanisms do not intervene in artistic production in the typical way that they do with the production of commodities for the market, and yet, Burn admits, it would 'be sheer lunacy for me to maintain that my market relations are just incidental'.[33] Artists, it seems, have done just what capitalism would have wanted them to do without any capitalist ever having to manage them. Although this odd form of capitalism might immediately raise the question *why* artists would subject themselves to the capitalist mode of production if they were not economically obliged to do so, the more promising question is *how* capitalism has been actively incorporated into artistic practices. Instead of turning our attention towards the choices that individual artists have made in 'going commercial' or 'being cynical', the study of how capitalism has infiltrated art despite art's actual mode of production remaining almost entirely unaffected by the capitalist mode of production means paying attention to the full variety of social mechanisms active in art's production and reproduction.

First, I want to caution that it is vital to understand the transmission of capitalist techniques into artistic production alongside the maintenance of techniques belonging to pre-capitalist artistic production and the transmission of techniques drawn from science, scholarship, entertainment, political activism, everyday life and other practices. Second, I want to propose that the best way to gauge the impact of capitalism on art is to analyse the processes by which capitalist techniques have been incorporated into art. There is a highly significant difference between the incorporation of capitalist methods through market mechanisms and the incorporation of the same methods

---

32   Burn in Alberro and Stimson 1999, p. 320.
33   Burn in Alberro and Stimson 1999, p. 325.

through non-market mechanisms such as studying business textbooks. If market mechanisms are not directly involved in the production of art, then through what mechanisms has capitalism transformed artistic production? Burn says that artists have 'internalized'[34] the capitalist mode of production and 'the bureaucratic method':[35]

> [i]t is hard for me to be blind to the fact that what has happened to recent art closely parallels the entrenchment of the giant multinational corporations. But, I want to restate, this has been achieved primarily on tacit agreements and not on the typically overt bureaucratic techniques – proving once more how little surveillance a system like this requires once the principles have been internalized and everyone has 'like-minded' interests.[36]

So, if art 'parallels' global corporations, it is not because art operates through the same mechanisms and techniques, but through other social forces, here described as 'tacit agreements'. Burn also links artistic innovation with marketable novelty, saying 'the market capitalizes on "innovation" for its own sake, strictly as a profit maximizing factor',[37] and then adds: 'I am certainly self-consciously familiar with how "high art" has been rhetorically infected with the need to innovate and personally aware of being made to feel the pressure to innovate, on pain of extinction'.[38] The internalisation of market incentives, it seems, is not something that the artist always does alone, and might do reluctantly or under duress. Rather than focusing our attention entirely on the apparent result – that art has been commodified regardless of how this has been achieved – it is important to explain the various processes through which artists adapt the production of art according to capitalist society and therefore how art encounters capital, markets, consumers, and so forth. If artists have 'internalised' capitalist techniques, then the result – namely, art's commodification – has come about through non-market mechanisms. There is, therefore, a conflict between the result and the process of the historical incorporation of art within capitalism: paradoxically, art has been commodified without being commodified.

---

34   Ibid.
35   Ibid.
36   Burn in Alberro and Stimson 1999, p. 326.
37   Burn in Alberro and Stimson 1999, p. 324.
38   Burn in Alberro and Stimson 1999, p. 325.

The art historian Paul Wood, in his study of the relationship between art and the economic concept of the commodity, argues that '[f]rom the point of view of an analysis of art and culture, Marx's most significant comments on the commodity occur in section 4 of chapter 1, titled "The Fetishism of Commodities"'.[39] This selective reading of Marx follows the pattern set by Lukács and Adorno, which I will discuss at length in Chapter 7, 'On the Absence of a Marxist Economics of Art'. For Western Marxists since the 1920s the concept of commodity fetishism – and related concepts such as reification and spectacle – has been the key to understanding the relationship between art and capitalism. Marx's discussion of commodity fetishism is the seemingly natural place to start a Marxist analysis of art's relationship to capitalism because it concerns the cultural life of the commodity, including its meanings, our beliefs about commodities, its mysteries, secrets and appearances. In the concept of the commodity, Wood says, 'Marx mapped the route from an economic category to intensive features of our experience'.[40] However, Wood adds, a 'case can be made for modern art's having been forced onto its characteristic terrain of subjectivity, expression, authenticity, and abstraction because of the absolute sway of the commodity in the historical experience of modernity'.[41] This is because, as Étienne Balibar points out, 'fetishism is not a subjective phenomenon or a false perception of reality... It constitutes, rather, the way in which reality... cannot but appear'.[42] Georg Lukács said the 'fetishistic illusions enveloping all phenomena in capitalist society succeed in concealing reality',[43] and that the 'historical legitimation of modernism derives from the fact that the distortion of human nature... is an inevitable product of capitalist society'.[44] If a society organised around commodity exchange necessarily generates 'fetishistic illusions' and these illusions become attached to art, then perhaps in the concept of commodity fetishism we have a method for understanding the riddle of art being commodified without being commodified. But we need to ask *how exactly* the artwork takes on the enigmatic character of the commodity. What, if any, are the *mechanisms* that conscript art to the fetishism of commodities if art has not been brought under the capitalist mode of production?

---

39   Wood in Nelson and Shiff 1996, p. 388.
40   Wood in Nelson and Shiff 1996, p. 392.
41   Wood in Nelson and Shiff 1996, p. 388.
42   Balibar 1995, p. 60.
43   Lukács 1971, p. 14.
44   Lukács 1979, p. 75.

Wood summarises art's complex relationship to the capitalist economy:

> It seems clearer than ever that art is one form of commodity production in a wider field of cultural commodity production. What remains open to debate, however, is the extent to which the meanings generated by the resulting products can accrue added value. That is, the extent to which they can retain and articulate critical distance from the commodity system at large; or whether the 'drag' of embeddedness at the economic level in the circuits of production, exchange, and consumption vitiates the possibility of distance at the level of the imaginative-symbolic.[45]

This is, in effect, a boiled down version of Adorno's argument. Its two components, the commodification of art and art's interpretative independence from commodification, are antagonistic to one another. If art's commodification is taken as standard then art's critical independence from market society, which is non-standard, cannot be explained by art's imputed commodification. Market forces discipline commodities so that they are subject to 'consumer sovereignty', but art's commodification appears to permit the artist to be a critical author rather than a commodity producer meeting the demands of the marketplace. The precondition for commodity fetishism is the reorganisation of social production according to the principle of capital accumulation. Commodities do not enter into the capitalist mode of production through the machinations of commodity fetishism; commodity fetishism is the result of the social fragmentation brought about by specialisation, the division of labour and the relationship between the wage labourer and the products they produce. Commodity fetishism, therefore, cannot attach artworks to capitalism without raising the question of art's anomalous and incomplete process of commodification. A more feasible argument, it seems to me, would be to explain art's critical independence – the very possibility of art's critique of commodity society – as being rooted in its anomalous and paradoxical relationship to the capitalist mode of production, namely art's commodification without commodification. It is worth noting, here, that from the point of view of the capitalist mode of production in general, the most significant comments on the commodity made by Marx are not restricted to the chapter on commodity fetishism and it is to Marx's comprehensive analysis of the capitalist mode of production that we need to turn in order to locate art's relationship to capitalism.

Saying that society *as a whole* generates fetishistic illusions (which means that nothing escapes from commodity fetishism) is, among other things, to

---

45   Wood in Nelson and Shiff 1996, pp. 404–5.

claim that those practices that are not reorganised by capitalism, such as art practice, are brought into line by other means. Non-market mechanisms, such as sociological or ideological processes, perhaps, must be at work. Lukács's concept of 'reification' is a perfect example of a theory which proposes that capitalism extends itself through non-market mechanisms, insofar as reification carried the content of Marx's theory of 'commodity fetishism' through processes that were primarily subjective, intellectual, experiential or aesthetic. Wood approaches this difficulty by tying one to the other.

> Even if it is allowed that modern art had been able to preserve a measure of truth in its expressed content by a strategic withdrawal from the terrain of the commodity, still the damage was done at a deeper level. For as art withdrew from the particularity of the world of commodities as depicted subject, its own being in the world as putatively spiritual product ('creation') was being undercut by the increasing commodification of the art object itself. The commodification of spirit made no exception for art.[46]

Wood does not feel the need to prove the statement that the art object had been commodified, presumably because this argument had been made many times since the 1930s and the evidence of art's economic transactions through the art market and auction houses is overwhelming. Wood explains that 'modern art has been fundamentally and doubly marked by commodification',[47] first through the depiction and thematisation of the world of commodities and marketing, including the subjective effects of commodity culture on consumers, and second, insofar as 'the productive system of art in the modern period itself became commodified'.[48]

> Just as the widespread shift from depiction to expression in effect concealed commodification as a principal subject of modern art, so the intensified rhetoric of autonomy concealed commodification as one of its conditions.[49]

Wood's knot of commodification, in which something not dissimilar to independent handicraft production confronts the commodities that result from it, can only be untied, I believe, by paying as much attention to the *means* as

---

46   Wood in Nelson and Shiff 1996, p. 397.
47   Wood in Nelson and Shiff 1996, p. 382.
48   Ibid.
49   Ibid.

the *ends* of commodification. Wood draws the conclusion that art has been commodified despite everything, but he presents this assertion as a magical resolution of a rather stubborn difficulty. Throughout this book I will refuse to settle for the kind of abstract argument that resolves such problems with a philosophical flourish or a dialectical inversion.

Another highly visible theoretical example of how Marxists have imagined capitalism being extended into art, and other practices, through non-market mechanisms is the concept of 'real subsumption'. Antonio Negri, back in the 1970s, argued that with 'the real subsumption of society by capital, everything that is produced-circulated-consumed is a mere cog in the wheel of the reproduction of the already existent'.[50] Stewart Martin accepts the current received wisdom from post-Fordist theory that capitalism no longer operates in the old ways according to the economics of material production and argues, therefore, that within a 'cultural capitalism', there has been 'a creeping subsumption of life'.[51] Real subsumption is the name given to the processes by which social practices, not limited to productive practices but extending to domestic and intimate activities, appear to be shaped by the capitalist mode of production. Negri explains:

> Subsumption is an ugly concept. It is a Marxian term that describes the relationship between capital and society. It is important, however, to make a distinction between two kinds of subsumption: the formal and the real. At a given moment in the development of capitalism, the forms of production that had nothing to do with capital (forms of agricultural production, of fishing, or craft manufacture) were subsumed; they were incorporated and reorganized by the incipient capitalist hegemony when the structure of big factories, first textiles then cars, began to organize the whole of society. This type of subsumption is known as formal subsumption. It is the formal aspect of capital that includes the various productive activities.
>
> Real subsumption, on the other hand, is a hegemony of capital without limits. Here the form of capitalist production has intervened in and occupied every space of society. Society itself has been converted into a factory.[52]

---

50   Negri 1991, p. xxxvii.
51   Martin 2009, p. 482.
52   Negri 2003, p. 105.

This has become orthodoxy for the contemporary theory of real subsumption, although, strictly speaking, Negri runs Marx's distinction of formal and real subsumption together (the first corresponding to the economic subsumption of production; the latter consisting of the reorganisation of production – textile mills, factories and so on – to establish a specifically capitalist mode of production) under the heading of 'formal subsumption' and saves the concept of 'real subsumption' for the additional 'phase' in which capitalism takes over social life generally.

If the theory of real subsumption is valid, then it would go a long way to explaining how it is possible for art to be commodified without being commodified, because art could be subsumed by capitalism without capitalists formally subsuming artistic practice through ownership of its means of production, the payment of wages to the producers of art, and the realisation of surplus value through sales on the market. I do not wish to refute the claim that capitalist techniques enter the production, distribution and consumption of art through non-economic processes and non-market mechanisms. However, in lieu of a full reassessment of the deployment of the concept of real subsumption in the Marxist explanation of art's anomalous commodification, which I will provide in Part 2 of this book, it is vital to understand that Marx refers exclusively to the *formal and real subsumption of labour under capital*. Marx does not write about the subsumption of society, nor of any other abstractions. And the significance of this, in my view, is that for Marx subsumption is a *mechanism* through which capital exerts its power, first by purchasing labour power and then by reorganising production according to its own specific needs, through the division of labour, the use of mechanisation and so forth. At no point do any of the other theorists of art's real subsumption claim that artistic *labour* has been subsumed by capital. In fact, the point of the theory of real subsumption, as it stands today, is that it bypasses the formal subsumption of labour. The theorists of real subsumption ask a more general and abstract question, namely, whether art has been subsumed. This leaves the location of art's subsumption entirely open. Are artworks subsumed, or have artists been subsumed? Have art's institutions been subsumed, and can institutions of counter subsumption be built? Such questions might prove to be fertile grounds for further research, but they must first overcome a fundamental indeterminacy. How does the real subsumption of art explain how art is or is not transformed by the processes of industrialisation, centralisation, technologisation, the division of labour and the conscious application of science that characterises the capitalist mode of production? As soon as we posit subsumption in general rather than the subsumption of labour by capital then, it appears to me, the mechanism by which capital takes hold of society is lost. These lines of inquiry will be pursued in detail in Part 2 of this book.

The concept of real subsumption not only acts as a broker between non-market mechanisms and the capitalist mode of production, it also closes the gap between economics and philosophy. In Peter Osborne's assessment, Adorno and Horkheimer 'use the idea of subsumption to read Marx through Kant, thereby reducing subsumption to ... the general logic of equivalence of an instrumental rationality that also – indeed, primarily – characterises administration'.[53] Osborne explains:

> it is more plausible to think of art's integration into the culture industry in terms of a change in the character of its formal subsumption, as a result of changes in the political economy and technologies of cultural production more generally. For example, there is both a greater differentiation of market sectors and a greater integration of cultural functions (art, fashion, mass culture, advertising, design, tourism) within the cultural industry than hitherto. Autonomous art clearly functions, structurally, as research and development for other branches of the culture industry; it is analogous to the way in which formal experimentation was conceived as laboratory work within late Soviet constructivism. This is one systemic functionalisation of autonomous art within the culture industry. While it has certainly changed the conditions of artistic production, it has not negated the possibility of autonomous works. On the contrary, it aspires to them. (Autonomy obtains only at the level of the individual work; functionalisation at the level of whole).[54]

Osborne runs several ideas together here, referring to integration and functionalisation as synonyms or near synonyms for subsumption, and talking about the changing 'conditions of artistic production', which reads as a hybrid of the social and cultural *context* of production cross fertilised with actual changes in the *economics* of art. When he refers to changes in the 'technologies of cultural production', Osborne argues that art has been transformed according to the capitalist mode of production through artists adopting tools that have been developed for capitalist production. Osborne ties Wood's knot even tighter with the result that the separation of the economic and the non-economic, and the distinction between market mechanisms and non-market mechanisms, becomes either impossible or ill advised. The point seems, on the contrary, to proceed on the assumption of the indistinguishable combination of the social and the economic – closer to a conception of 'political economy'

---

53   Osborne 2007, p. 110.
54   Osborne 2007, p. 111.

rather than neoclassical 'economics' – in which economic goals are pursued through social means (such as legislation, education and culture) while social goals are pursued through economic means (such as reducing the power of the unions through unemployment). If it is possible for art to be fundamentally and extensively reconfigured by capitalism without having its economic relations converted into those of the capitalist mode of production then, it appears, the study of art's economic relations is not only a red herring but might well be damaging insofar as proof of art's non-compliance with the capitalist mode of production could get capitalism off the hook for the ways in which it has made art a standardised, spectacular, commercialised, industrialised global business.

What does it matter, we might ask, if art has been incorporated by capitalism socially or culturally rather than economically? Is not the result the same? If social mechanisms rather than economic mechanisms were responsible for art's apparent commodification, then we would be justified in talking about art's commodification without commodification. That is to say, art is economically exceptional but is not, as a result, free from capitalist society in general. What is more, it is possible for art to have remained economically unchanged by the development of the capitalist mode of production and for artists to sell their works through the art market, employ assistants and use modern technology. While the latter are important, and worthy of studies of their own, this book does not explore many of the ways in which art operates within capitalism but focuses entirely on art's relationship to capital and labour. E.P. Thompson once criticised Marx for studying capital instead of capitalism, leaving out the historical and social processes in order to focus on the logic of accumulation.[55] In the Marxist examination of art's relationship to capitalism, however, we find the opposite situation, in which the social analysis of art's relationship to capitalism has completely overshadowed any attempt to understand art's relationship to capital. This book seeks to set this straight and argues that art's economic exceptionalism, in particular art's unusual relationship to capital and the capitalist mode of production, ought not to be overlooked in the mainstream economist's haste to establish art as susceptible to economic analysis, or in the Marxist condemnation of art's marketisation and capitalism's colonisation of art. By and large, the Marxist principle of establishing an economic analysis from which a politics is derived appears to have been suspended in the case of art and aesthetics. Articulating a more precise relationship between art and capital, therefore, has political implications. Art's relationship with capital can be analysed with more precision than art's relationship to capitalism, as the latter can be understood not only

---

55   Thompson 1995, pp. 80–2.

as the society corresponding to the capitalist mode of production but also as the society of the spectacle, the society of control, liquid modernity, the affluent society, consumer society and the post-industrial society, among others. That is to say, capitalism has been understood through its distinctive cultures, technologies, social relations, forms of power, styles of living and so on, and all of these suggest different *relations between art and capitalism*. What this book does is seek to establish art's relationship to capitalism through an analysis of art's relationship to capital. My point is not to show that art *ought* to be treated as exceptional, or that art is exceptional in some other non-economic sense, but merely to demonstrate that art actually is *economically exceptional*. The possibility of a Marxist economic analysis of art that is capable of distinguishing artistic production from capitalist commodity production is not to be confused with romantic anti-capitalist arguments. The economic case for the economic exceptionalism of art (and certain other goods) must be developed from an economic analysis of art's production, circulation and finance.

Diedrich Diederichsen's 'On (Surplus) Value in Art', from 2008, contains some considered economic analyses of art based firmly in the Marxist tradition. It is a very short and deliberately provocative essay in three parts, exploring the meaning of the German term *Mehrwert*, which Marx used and which is conventionally translated as 'surplus value'. Diederichsen explores the concept of surplus value exclusively in relation to art, which is unique in the history of Marxism and Marxology. He deliberately crashes the two legacies of Marxism together not just thematically but methodologically. The text is a stylistic montage of poetic play and analytic theorems, starting with the almost scandalous gesture of conflating Marx's technical use of *Mehrwert* with the colloquial German use of the word, the latter introduced as shedding light on the former. The first part of the book applies the prosaic meaning of *Mehrwert* to art, asking where the 'payoff' is. He characterises this 'payoff' in terms of the concept of a punch line, which he links not only to telling jokes but advertising, branding and the need for legitimation. Popular culture is organised around such payoffs but art is too, he says, only in a specific mode. Diederichsen coins the term 'artistic *Mehrwert*' which refers to the difference between art and other things. Is something extra required of something for it to belong legitimately to the category of art? Artistic *Mehrwert* is what distinguishes art, 'what makes something art',[56] as he says, meaning the quality, or merit, that constitutes art as a 'bonus realm', as something special or different. Its relationship to economic surplus value is, therefore, rather unusual. On the one hand, Diederichsen says, '*Mehrwert* is the daily bread and butter of the capitalist economy', and artistic

---

56   Diederichsen 2008, p. 24.

Mehrwert, by contrast, is more like a ' "bonus" that is accorded the status of an exception'.[57] However, this exception to the norm is something required of art, Diederichsen argues. Art 'must *always* generate *Mehrwert*, just like capitalism and capitalists'.[58] Diederichsen may be right to associate art with surplus (the difference between a readymade and the object before it is nominated as art appears as some kind of surplus) but his argument that this is akin to capitalist surplus is made on the basis of a pun. Diederichsen neglects the fact that there are two kinds of surplus value, 'absolute surplus value' and 'relative surplus value', which I will discuss at length in Chapter 7. What is more, Diederichsen fails to explain how art produces surplus value without the element, necessary in the Marxist analysis of capitalist accumulation, of surplus labour. Surplus labour and therefore surplus value cannot be obtained without the existence of the capitalist-worker relation. Only wage labourers produce surplus value, because it is only under conditions in which labour is the commodity for sale that surplus labour is possible.

At one point Diederichsen argues that the production of new 'fresh' works by artists amounts to 'variable capital including *Mehrarbeit* [or surplus labor]',[59] as if a worker could provide surplus labour outside the relationship between wage labourer and capitalist. He adds that the production of fresh works is always done 'on the basis of an already existing reputation and knowledge (constant capital)',[60] which completes the transference of the entire capitalist mode of production into the body of the artist. Diederichsen's economics of art reads like a Dada poem made out of cuttings from *Capital Volume I*. Diederichsen's distinction between price and value gets fuzzy at times, his application of the Marxist formula of 'socially average labour time' to art is awkward to say the least, his treatment of knowledge as 'constant capital' and seasonal production as 'variable capital' is inept, and the assertion that performative art produces more surplus value because it consists of 'living labour' is idiotic. His reference to 'artistic labour power' has, at best, a sonic relation to Marx's concept of labour power. If Negri is right to say that art encounters capital not at the point of production, but through the art market's systems of distribution, which shows that art is economically exceptional (coming into contact with merchant capital and investment capital but never with productive capital) then Diederichsen's hunt for surplus value in artworks, art education, the artist's lifestyle, and so on, is facing in the wrong direction.

57   Diederichsen 2008, p. 21.
58   Diederichsen 2008, p. 22.
59   Diederichsen 2008, p. 37.
60   Ibid.

Diederichsen, therefore, does not provide the missing chapter on the Marxist economic analysis of art.

One of the themes of Diedrichsen's book is art's exceptionalism. He repeatedly refers to art's economics as exceptional but blends the idea of economic exceptionalism with the colloquial use of the word as something having special merit. He speaks, for instance, of 'the normality of the exceptionalism that determines the everyday life of art'.[61] Diederichsen mixes this dialectics of exceptionalism with mundane uses of the word, in phrases such as 'exceptional returns',[62] when describing the high prices that artworks can fetch. At the same time, he coins new apparently technical phrases that contain the word, including the 'everyday aspect of artistic exceptionalism', a "domesticated" exceptionalism' and 'the double exceptionalism of speculation', none of which are explained. In Part 1 of this book I will provide a comprehensive reading of the concept of art's economic exceptionalism throughout the literature of mainstream economics and in Part 2 I will extend this study to a Marxist theory of art's economic exceptionalism. This amounts to what I am calling art's exceptionalism reassessed, which boils down to a shift from a theory of art's exceptionalism based on prices and consumer behaviour to a theory of art's exceptionalism based on artistic production and art's relationship to capital.

My aim, in this book, is to develop a schema for a new economic analysis of art's economic exceptionalism. I will test the mainstream argument that art operates as a near standard commodity within the art market and as an asset in the finance economy. I will also re-examine the Marxist theory of art's commodification. This book confirms neither tradition and builds a case, instead, for art's *economic exceptionalism*. This term is modern, but the concept was developed as early as the eighteenth century with reference to rare and unique goods such as antiques and rare wines. Both the concept and the phrase have fallen into misuse within mainstream[63] economics and no theory of economic

---

61   Diederichsen 2008, p. 39.

62   Diederichsen 2008, p. 46.

63   Paul Samuelson coined the term 'mainstream economics' in his textbook on economics. He used it to refer to the brand of economics taught in the universities. I use the term 'mainstream economics' to refer to both classical and neoclassical economics, which form the basis of textbooks on economics today. Marx's three volumes of *Capital* do not fully belong to the classical economic mainstream because they form a *critique* of political economy, and are, at best, marginal to the textbooks on academic economic knowledge. Throughout this book the term 'mainstream economics' therefore refers not only to what is currently the dominant economic ideology of neoliberalism, but also its neoclassical rivals. Mainstream economics has an orthodox wing (Chicago School economics, following Milton Friedman) and several heterodox wings (which includes a wider range of

exceptionalism has ever been developed. Marxists have never applied the concept of economic exceptionalism to art in any systematic way, for reasons that
I will explain in Chapter 7. Consequently, this is the first book-length study
of economic exceptionalism as it can be traced across classical, neoclassical
and Marxist economics. In presenting this study, I hope to achieve two related
objectives: to provide a new basis for the economics of art, and to develop a
coherent theory of economic exceptionalism in general using art as a lens
through which exceptionalism can be understood. This book also contains the
first ever account of a Marxist theory of art's economic exceptionalism, developing the argument that art is exceptional specifically to the capitalist mode
of production. Art's economic exceptionalism – that is to say, art's anomalous,
incomplete and paradoxical commodification – explains art's incorporation into capitalism as the very basis of art's independence from capitalism,
because it shows that art has not been fully transformed by the capitalist mode
of production. By and large products are converted into commodities through
the imposition of market mechanisms, but this has not occurred in the case of
art, and other mechanisms need to be substituted for economic ones. What are
the non-economic mechanisms and processes that bring art within the orbit
of commodity exchange? The answer to this question is not only the basis of
any adequate understanding of the relationship between art and capitalism,
but also the basis of art's political engagement with society. What is more, any
policies for art's funding or organisation, including any political campaigns
to defend art, art education and art's institutions from the anonymous profit-
seeking incentives of market forces and the instrumentalisation of art by the
state, if they are not to be normative projections onto art, must be based on the
actual exceptional economics of art.

In this book I will address the complexity and contestation of economics by
examining a wide selection of the economic literature from classicism, neoclassicism, welfare economics and the Marxist critique of political economy.
There is not only one economics of art. Since the arts are not economically
unified, the economic analysis of one sector cannot stand in for the economic
analysis of another. Different disciplines within the arts, including theatre, literature and the visual arts, have different modes of production, distribution
and consumption. There is a labour market for film and the theatre (actors

_____

economic positions including several strains of 'imperfect market' economics by
Galbraith, Stiglitz, Robinson, Sraffa and others). Keynesianism currently belongs to the
heterodox category of mainstream economics. My use of the term 'mainstream economics' is not intended to be generalising in any way, but preserves its internal divisions while
insisting on the fundamental distinction between mainstream economics and Marxism.

are wage labourers) and an industry of specialists who support production (consisting also of wage labourers), but poets, novelists and visual artists tend not to be wage labourers. There is also a mass market for the cinema, theatre, poetry and novels, with individuals purchasing tickets or books directly, while the visual arts can often be consumed for free not only in public museums but also in the commercial galleries that exhibit works for sale. Art also consists of freely distributed zines, badges, posters and street performances, as well as videos produced specifically to be viewed on YouTube, works that no longer exist except in documentary photographs, works produced in remote locations that are best viewed in books or online, net-art, protest art, public art and participatory events that continue to exist only in the form of conversation and shared actions. As an artist who works collaboratively and critically within the public sphere, often including published or commercially printed materials, my conception of art is not restricted to the 'orthodox choice of objects of study, along with [an] unquestioned reliance on the largely unexamined category of "art" '[64] typical of the mainstream economics of art. My analysis leans towards an analysis of what is known as 'visual art', partly because this draws on my experience and partly because the exceptional economics of visual art was recognised by classical economists – and is therefore the basis of the formation of the concept of art's economic exceptionalism – and furthermore because visual art is more exceptional to the capitalist economy than film, the theatre, music and literary publishing.

In discussing visual art, therefore, I do not presume, for instance, that art always involves the production of objects, or that an individual artist always produces it. Nor do I identify art with the range of goods sanctioned by the art market or the national and international public institutions of art. A great deal of art is produced without commercial or critical success, and this must be accorded a proportionate role within the economics of art. Following the money leads to a biased economics of art as well as a reduced conception of art deserving of economic analysis. The economic analysis of art should not be limited to just great art or just failed art, to just art in the marketplace or art in the public sector. Art does not become economic by being sold (costs make them economic regardless of sales) and therefore no adequate economic analysis of art can be restricted to the art market or to types of art – most conspicuously paintings, prints and sculptures – that happen to sell. The economics of art must not be restricted to the encounters between art and money, either in the market or through the state, but must incorporate all the free labour that

---

64   Jonathan Harris in Hauser 1999, p. xii.

goes into artistic production, the whole range of ways in which art is consumed for free, the values that compete with economic value in decisions made within the art world, and the pejorative use of terms like 'commercial' and 'selling out' in the assessment of art. What I want to insist on is that the legendary economic irrationalism of artists and the social demand that art be accessible to all for free are economic factors in their own right and, if they can be ratified by the analysis of art's production and consumption, have to be central to the economics of art. If artists are unbusinesslike and the consumption of art is not determined by the ability to pay, then art has developed a tense relationship to economic practice and theory. Hence, this book is an attempt to study the *economic basis* for the tension between art and economics. I will provide the fullest account to date of art's economic exceptionalism as it is evidenced at every stage of art's economic transactions as well as how it has been – or can be – articulated in classical, neoclassical and Marxist economics.

The principle of art's economic exceptionalism is expressed in the founding texts of economics and is referred to consistently until the end of the nineteenth century. When economics underwent a revolution after 1870, and its classical phase was replaced with neoclassical doctrine, the argument for art's economic exceptionalism almost entirely disappeared. However, what I show is that a new theory of art's economic exceptionalism can be developed specifically in relation to neoclassical economics, something that has never previously been attempted. While classical economists typically observed the existence of economic exceptionalism without analysing its fundamental logic, neoclassical economists typically deny its existence in dogmatic fashion. Neither developed a substantive theory of economic exceptionalism. For this reason I have had to piece together a theory from fragments dotted throughout the literature. I do this in three distinct ways. First, in the case of classical economics, I assemble a theory of economic exceptionalism from passing remarks, qualifying clauses, anecdotal evidence and puzzling observations found in the writing of Smith, Ricardo, Mill and others. Second, in the case of neoclassical economics – for which there are no such casual references to exceptionalism – I have identified the key neoclassical doctrines to which the economy of art can be shown to be anomalous. Third, in the case of Marxist economics, I extrapolate an analysis of art's economic exceptionalism from a study of the capitalist mode of production in the three volumes of *Capital*, the *Grundrisse* and the *Contribution to a Critique of Political Economy*. This book therefore contains the most comprehensive history of economic exceptionalism to date, an extension of the concept of exceptionalism appropriate to contemporary mainstream economics, and a reassessment of exceptionalism through the Marxist critique of political economy.

Marxist economics has the tools to go further than mainstream economics in theorising art's economic exceptionalism. Marxism is the only economic tradition with any record in distinguishing between capitalist and non-capitalist production. Consequently, a Marxist economic analysis of art is uniquely able to identify artistic production as not conforming to the capitalist mode of production and therefore to extend the concept of art's economic exceptionalism to interrogate not only art's economic performance but its relationship to capitalism. Nevertheless, it would be entirely false to claim that Marxism has pioneered the theory of art's economic exceptionalism. On the contrary, the history of Marxism's engagement with art has gone in the opposite direction, pioneering the analysis of art's commodification, industrialisation, commercialisation, spectacularisation and incorporation. Current developments within Marxist theory build on the very foundations that have prevented Marxism from drawing on its classical roots to theorise art's economic exceptionalism. Western Marxist concepts like reification and Culture Industry remain at the heart of contemporary Marxist thinking on art, particularly in its sociological and philosophical heartlands. Marxist economics survives, but no Marxist economist has tackled the specific question of the economics of art. On top of this, classical Marxist economics has been criticised within Marxism itself as out of touch with historical changes in capitalism since the 1960s.

My intention throughout this book is to explore art's relationship to capitalism without relying on the established sociological methods of Western Marxism that have supported the claim that art has been incorporated into capitalism *without providing any economic proof* that artistic production has been transformed into capitalist commodity production. My method, here, is to establish art's relationship to capitalism through an analysis of its relation to capital. I draw on Marxism's classical roots, particularly the three volumes of *Capital*, to investigate the economics of art. The claims made by Western Marxism about art's commodification within the Culture Industry, I will argue, need to be measured against the actual economic conditions of artistic practice, which exhibit the characteristics of commodification without having been transformed by the process of commodification through the imposition of economic mechanisms in production. Of course, artists and artworks encounter money in various forms, but capital in the strict sense, we will see, plays an extremely limited role, and in the majority of cases no role at all, in the production and circulation of art. While mainstream economists and Western Marxists are happy to assert that art is a commodity like any other, the pioneers of classical economics and the Marxist economic analysis of art demonstrates not only that art is economically exceptional but, in the case of the latter, that it is exceptional to the capitalist mode of production in particular.

The primary objection to the claim that art is economically exceptional within mainstream economics today is based on the observation that art is patently economic. The error, here, is not the assertion itself, which is undeniable. Art is economic. Even art that fails to sell must inevitably incur costs to the artist in purchasing raw materials, studio rent, and the cost of an education or, at the very least, time. And many of these transactions will necessarily be standard commodity exchanges. The market for canvas is not economically exceptional, the purchase of video cameras is no different for an artist than anybody else, and the rents for artists' studios are fixed by the same mechanisms as all other rents (including real estate prices, regulations, subsidies and other factors). The error in denying art's economic exceptionalism by pointing out that art is palpably economic is the assumption that if art is economic then it cannot be economically exceptional. Economic exceptionalism has never designated something outside or beyond economics. Classical economists argued that art exhibited non-standard patterns of pricing, due to limits placed on augmenting supply, such as the death of the artist. Economic exceptionalism is an economic phenomenon.

Art is economically exceptional but it remains economic. Art is expensive, artists spend money and time producing works, studios are rented, galleries make profits, art investments increase and decrease in value, museums obtain funds and employ the tools of marketing, millions of people worldwide are employed in the arts and art is an enormous global business. However, the fact that art is economic does not in any way prove that art is economically standard. Anomalies need to be explained. Key anomalies include the following: art is not a standard capitalist commodity, artists are not wage labourers and, when they are commercially successful, artists are not standard entrepreneurs. If such anomalies can be established as empirically verifiable or theoretically robust, then art's economic exceptionalism must be incorporated into the assessment of art's relationship to capitalism and art's status within Cultural Economics. The assumption that art can be studied according to the standard Marxist or mainstream economic methods, or that art is not significantly different from standard commodities, markets and industries can only be determined by an economic analysis of art's relation to capital. If, as I argue, art is economically exceptional, then much of the literature on art's economics and art's place within capitalism will have to be fundamentally reviewed.

Art's exceptionalism is not an economic argument for art's autonomy. Since Adorno argues that art's commodification is the precondition for art's autonomy – that is, art's liberation from church, state and tradition – a separate case would have to be made that art's economic exceptionalism (particularly in the strong sense that art does not conform to the capitalist mode of commodity production) is or is not grounds for art's self-determination. No such argument is developed in this book, and no assumption that any such argument follows from the economic analysis of art is made. Nor should art's exceptionalism be understood as a claim that art or artists are somehow unaffected by capitalism, either through rugged independence of mind or privileged independence of means. Opting out of capitalism as a society is impossible, but many practices and forms of exchange within capitalism are not capitalistic in the strict sense of being engaged in for exchange, that is, to accumulate wealth. Art, this book argues, is one such practice. Central to the argument in this book is the claim that art is bound up with capitalism but does not conform to the capitalist mode of commodity production. Art's economic exceptionalism, therefore, is not an effect of the artist's heroic will power, unworldly irrationality or flamboyant lifestyle. Exceptionalism is not ideal or romantic but actual and supported by analysis of the economic facts.

Étienne Balibar and Pierre Macherey, writing in 1974, said that Marxism has always been preoccupied with two questions in relation to literature and art.[65] The first is the ontology of art and aesthetics understood as an inquiry into its ideological character, and the second is the 'class position' of the author and the text. They back this up by drawing on Marx and Engels's writings on Balzac and Lenin's writings on Tolstoy. They could have added Trotsky's writings on Futurist literature, or Plekhanov on French theatre. Note, however, that Balibar and Macherey are accurate in their description of the content of this early treatment of art by Marxists. Not one of them examined art using the methods of Marx's critique of political economy. What art is and how it relates to capitalism has been one of the abiding concerns of Marxist thinking, but the answer has never been sought in an economic analysis of art's production and consumption. On the contrary, it has been a staple of the Marxist interpretation and explanation of art to ask questions about whether the artist is a worker, an entrepreneur, a manager and so on, but chiefly through an ideological analysis of her 'class position' as expressed in the text, not in her actual economic relations. Marxism has a reputation for 'economic reductionism' but, in fact, Marxism has consistently and vociferously protected art from economics. Marxist writers are among the most prominent theorists of art's 'autonomy' –

---

65   Balibar and Macherey 1974, reprinted in Young 1981 pp. 79–100.

its independence from both state control and market forces. And, of course, this is entirely consistent with the central tenets of a tradition founded on the *critique* of political economy.

Stewart Martin has sewn the two together by saying that 'artistic communism', which has its roots in German Romantic philosophy after Kant, proposes art as 'the realization of freedom'.[66] Rather than tracking the circulation of art objects from producers to consumers via dealers, and all the rest of art's dealings with the world of trade and profit, Marxists have turned to art as a kind of anticipation of communism: 'Autonomy or self-determination seeks the unconditioned or absolute, and the absolute is revealed in art'.[67] In building a Marxist economic analysis of art I am not in dispute with the commitment to 'artistic communism'. Rather, I am convinced that the analysis of the economics of art ought to be the basis of it. The antagonism to capital which 'artistic communism' calls forth, I will argue, is evident in art's economic exceptionalism as it might be reassessed through Marxist economic theory. But, paradoxically, arguing for the Marxist economic analysis of art is not what Marxists do, so I am breaking with Marxism in the very act of returning to Marx's analysis of *Capital*.

This book is divided into two parts. The first consists of an assessment of the record of mainstream economics in developing an economics of art's economic exceptionalism. The second consists of an assessment of the record of the Marxist aesthetic tradition followed by a Marxist economic analysis of art. This division is partly methodological and partly a result of the persistent chasm between the two traditions. It is impossible to make a coherent and unified assessment of both traditions simultaneously without perpetually running up against incommensurable assumptions and conflicting methods. And yet no adequate account of the literature on the economics of art can be derived from one tradition alone. Eventually this book presents a Marxist economics of art, but the questions and issues by which such a theory must be judged include those raised within mainstream economics. The confrontation between a Marxist critique of political economy and a mainstream economics of art is not the horizon of the study of art and value. What runs through the book, instead, is the antagonism between questions of quality in art and questions of price in economics and market forces. What I attempt is a double interrogation of art and value, combining a detailed study of (a) *the economic preconditions for art's practices of value attribution* with (b) the analysis of *the economic consequences of artworks being attributed value through*

---

66   Martin 2009, p. 484.
67   Ibid.

non-market mechanisms. While each on its own can produce many important insights and valid observations, any argument that is not based on both must be one-dimensional. In this restricted sense it is evident, as this book attempts to demonstrate, that both mainstream economics and Western Marxism have understood art's relationship to capitalism only one-dimensionally.

The analysis of art in terms of the standard functions of self-regulated markets and their mechanisms for allocating resources according to demand comes up against serious obstacles in the case of art, and economists have been aware of these obstacles since the inauguration of classical economic theory. I will assess a selection of key responses to these obstacles in Chapter 1, beginning with an assessment of the argument that economics is incapable of incorporating aesthetic value in its calculations, and finishing with two conspicuous arguments that economics and market forces are preferable to bureaucracy, the rule of experts and the elitism of taste. In Chapter 2 I will trace the analysis of art in classical economics, which is dominated by the assumption of art's economic exceptionalism. In Chapter 3, I will examine the absence of the concept of economic exceptionalism within neoclassical economics and make a new case for several distinctively neoclassical theories of exceptionalism. Chapter 4 looks at the fate of exceptionalism after 1945, with the introduction of welfare economics and the welfare state to subsidise art, while Chapter 5 examines the arguments and policies that came to challenge the welfare consensus after 1966. Having tracked the theories of art in classical, neoclassical and welfare economics, Chapter 6 introduces the Marxist critique of the mainstream economic tradition in a way that suggests a complete re-evaluation of the concept of economic exceptionalism. Chapter 7 asks why there has never been a Marxist economic analysis of art despite the fact that Marx's three volumes of *Capital* offer a toolbox for doing just that. Chapters 8, 9 and 10 apply Marx's analysis of productive capital, merchant capital and finance capital to the economics of art. Chapter 11 examines whether Marx's analysis of capitalism has become outdated by recent developments within capitalism and the theory of capitalism. Finally, the conclusion provides, for the first time, a coherent theory of economic exceptionalism as it applies to art.

PART 1

Art and Economics

∴

CHAPTER 1

Art, Value and Economics

Hubert Llewellyn Smith, the Chief Economic Advisor to the UK government between 1919 and 1926 and Chairman of the British Institute of Industrial Art between 1920 and 1925, and holder of numerous other posts besides,[1] wrote an obscure[2] book in 1924 called *The Economic Laws of Art Production*,[3] which argued that value in art eludes the discipline of economics. Nobody before Llewellyn Smith had produced a book-length study of the economics of art. John Ruskin had published his book *Unto This Last* in 1862, which protested against political economy as a science, principally for its abdication of 'social affection'.[4] Despite Ruskin's prominence as an art critic, watercolourist and the first Slade Professor of Fine Art, he formulates not one element of an economics of art in this book or any other. Rather, Ruskin's critique of economics follows the romantic tramlines of vitalism and communal wellbeing, casting economics as sterile and deathly, while arguing in favour of its unspecified rival, which he claims is built on 'powers of love, of joy, and of admiration'.[5] Llewellyn Smith, who Roger Backhouse lists among a handful of 'drivers' of welfare reform, did not follow Ruskin's lead, even if there are echoes of Ruskinian values in Llewellyn Smith's insistence that art cannot be adequately accounted for within existing economic doctrine. Unlike Ruskin, who had argued that economics was inadequate for the analysis of any worthwhile human endeavour, Llewellyn Smith neither dismissed the whole of economics as a science nor disputed the possibility of an economics of art. Nevertheless, fundamental modifications were required. Significantly, Llewellyn Smith does not exploit the shortfall between exchange value and the values of art to dismiss economic analysis. Instead he calls for a more specific and nuanced economic study of artistic production that expands the concept of value, albeit in an evidently fanciful manner. Hence, his subtitle suggests economic work to be done: *An Essay towards the Construction of a Missing Chapter on Economics.*

---

1 Llewellyn Smith is best known as the Director of the Consultative Committee for the *New Survey of London Life and Labour* undertaken in 1928 (see Gazeley 2003, p. 79).
2 No reference has been made to this book in the growing literature on Cultural Economics and the book is not mentioned in Llewellyn Smith's obituary. See Beveridge 1946.
3 Llewellyn Smith 1924.
4 Ruskin 1985, p. 167.
5 Ruskin 1985, p. 222.

Llewellyn Smith argued neither that art is immune from economics altogether nor that standard economic theory has already developed laws adequate to the study of the production of art. Although neoclassical economists
built their study of economic activity around a calculus of pleasure and pain,
he argued, the question of quality eludes economic analysis. Their 'crude
notion of utility', he said, 'is far from adequate for the purpose of the economic
analysis of art'.[6] Llewellyn Smith perceived the economics of art to be radically different from the economics of standard goods insofar as questions of
quality cannot be driven out of an economics of art without serious negative
consequences.

> We are here at the parting of the ways between the economics of quan-
> tity and of quality, since the notion of the graduation of human desires
> according to quality brings us into the region of ethical considerations,
> and very near to the hotly contested question of the relations between
> Art and Morals.[7]

Overstating his case, Llewellyn Smith's point of departure, nevertheless, identifies a fundamental question for any economics of art: can market forces (his
'economics of quantity') feasibly be expected to perform as a mechanism for
allocating resources to the arts on merit (his 'economics of quality')? So long
as the answer is assumed to be negative, Llewellyn Smith's question is the
overriding problem that the welfare economics of art sets out to solve, giving
rise to the Arts Council in the UK in 1946 (see Chapter 4) and the National
Endowment for the Arts in the USA in 1966 (see Chapter 5). Like the welfare
economists after him, Llewellyn Smith builds a case for an economics of art
that is not merely the application of economic doctrine to the arts sector. His
quest is to contrive an economics capable of evaluating the specific imperatives of artistic production.

Llewellyn Smith puts some daylight between standard economic practices
and the production of art by contrasting the best aims of producers supplying
a market with the minimum requirements for an artist producing a work of art.

> It is essential to the idea of a work of art not only that it should supply
> a human demand, or even that it should aim at supplying it in the best

---

6   Llewellyn Smith 1924, p. 18.
7   Llewellyn Smith 1924, p. 19.

possible way, but also that the desire which it aims at fulfilling should be worthy of being fulfilled.[8]

While market forces ask suppliers only to provide what customers demand, or at best to meet demand with the highest possible standards, this, according to Llewellyn Smith, falls miserably short of the principles underlying artistic practice. If artists do not merely supply what the market demands, or give consumers what they want, but are driven, instead, by considerations of quality and purpose beyond those for which others are willing to pay, then the producers of art are not motivated and incentivised in the way that typical commodity producers are. The science of economics, which has developed to understand, explain and predict activities governed by the mechanisms of supply and demand, will necessarily be inadequate in attending to the production and consumption of art, if artists do not attempt to supply what their collectors demand. Here, among other things, Llewellyn Smith confronts the doctrine of consumer sovereignty and calls it into question.

In the 1970s Tibor Scitovsky made a similar distinction without Llewellyn Smith's moral inflation, saying that we 'need to reclassify satisfactions according to some principle which will separate the economic from non-economic'.[9] When we wash, dress and take care of the house, for instance, he says, we satisfy ourselves in a way that is 'beyond the range of the economic accounts'.[10] But the difference between the economic and non-economic is not based on the difference between self-satisfaction and satisfactions derived from others. The consumption of goods and services provided by others, he says,

> may or may not be economic satisfactions, depending on whether or not they go through the market and acquire a market value in the process. Passage through the market is the criterion: whatever passes through the market belongs in the realm of economics.[11]

Scitovsky adds that labour itself 'which produces market goods may be an economic activity, but the satisfaction the worker himself gets out of his work is not an economic good'.[12] In another instance of production that is simultaneously economic and non-economic, Scitovsky says that artists are generally cut

---

8   Llewellyn Smith 1924, pp. 18–19.
9   Scitovsky 1992, p. 80.
10   Scitovsky 1992, p. 81.
11   Ibid.
12   Scitovsky 1992, p. 90.

off from demand, 'often not producing what the consumer wants'.[13] Therefore 'one of the producers to whom consumers relinquish initiative is the artist'.[14] He explains:

> we attach the weight of future generations to the specialist's judgment. This, of course, outweighs that of this single present generation. Hence the feeling that artists should not prostitute their art to please the consumer's passing fancy and make more money.[15]

Although Scitovsky romanticises the artist no less than Llewellyn Smith, his distinction between the economic and the non-economic helps to clarify the complex relationship between art and its non-market circulation, including the values that reside there. Even artworks that have passed through the market, we might say, extending Scitovsky's argument, can circulate within non-market and non-economic social environments and require, in these contexts, the kind of non-economic value that Llewellyn Smith glorifies.

Llewellyn Smith makes the positive case for the independence of art and artists from the marketplace when he says that the desires that art fulfils ought to be worthy of being fulfilled. The negative case is perhaps more familiar today, evident in the widely used concept of 'selling out'. Not selling out is the labour of preserving art's value against art's price in general and the tastes of market demand in particular. Selling out is not only the sale of one's work for money, but involves the sale of one's independence. That is to say, if an artist sets out from the start to be a commercial artist driven by the market, then the sale of works cannot be described as selling out. Englebert Humperdinck never sold out. Nor has Mark Kostabi. In music it was only the rock 'n' roll rebels, hippy rock groups, radical punk bands and wholesome indie bands who 'sold out', because they originally set themselves up as wild, alternative, independent, and so on. In art it is only the avant-gardists, independents and radicals who sell out. What you sell when you 'sell out' is not the work but the values that previously set the work apart. Strictly speaking, therefore, artists do not sell out when collectors finally come round to recognise the value of their works, but only when the artist modifies their own work to meet a demand that had previously been rejected. Llewellyn Smith highlights the tension between the production of art and the production of commodities for sale in terms that nowadays appear overblown but which do not contradict the contemporary

---

13   Scitovsky 1992, p. 275.
14   Ibid.
15   Scitovsky 1992, p. 277.

concern about selling out: 'one of the most important criteria which determines the rank of a work of art is the degree of nobility of the function which it
aims at performing'.[16] Let us say, more moderately, that the values attached to
art (and other non-economic or not primarily economic activities), including
questions of quality that discriminate between individual works, are not only
independent of their price but are regarded (by the communities that judge
such works) to be more important than their market value. Selling out occurs
when market value impinges on these more important values. Llewellyn Smith
therefore argues that what distinguishes art from other luxuries is that the
commodity is not merely desired or demanded by consumers but that the
desire or demand itself has value.

Llewellyn Smith expresses the discrepancy between artistic production and
the production of commodities geared entirely towards consumer demand
in a highly charged idiom of ethical certainties and cultural values that strike
the reader today as offensively elitist. It would be possible to reject Llewellyn
Smith's entire campaign for an economics of art, since it is designed specifically to address questions of value and quality as nothing but an expression
of the ideological and normative narrow interests of minority culture. What
appears unwarranted is the manner of his indexing of quality to art, as if art
has a monopoly on value. The danger of a defence of art against market value
is that the value that it attempts to preserve is solidified as an invariable of art
that is absent from non-art. As such, the possibility of bad art appears to be a
contradiction in terms, and the transformation of art by the art market appears
to be either impossible or can occur only by abolishing art. This is because the
values that are attached to art and which are not reducible to market value
necessarily take on a kind of absolute, abstract and universal character in order
to perform the function of the sturdy foundation of the argument. A cultural
hierarchy that derives from the social and historical contingencies of a particular cultural settlement therefore is crystallised as a timeless and necessary
distinction with which to identify art and endorse its values against those of
commerce. A worthy campaign to confront the limits of economics is therefore cased in privilege, bias and elitism because the defence of values in art is
transposed into the glorification of art as the noble exemplification of value in
culture and human endeavour generally.

There is another difficulty lurking within Llewellyn Smith's approach. As
much as Llewellyn Smith might warn against the inability of economic concepts and market forces to appreciate the full value of art, mainstream economists will complain that Llewellyn Smith has made the error of constructing

---

16   Llewellyn Smith 1924, p. 19.

a *normative economics*. Llewellyn Smith's confrontation with economics thus ties together the question of art's economic exceptionalism with the doctrinal methodological distinction between normative and positive economics. Arguments that resources ought to be allocated to certain activities might be perfectly acceptable within political discourse, moral campaigns and religious activism, but such statements are not scientific according to the established economic doctrine, albeit a doctrine that promotes what Ben Fine and Dimitris Milonakis call 'economics imperialism'.[17] While the distinction between normative and positive economics is philosophically questionable,[18] there is a methodological divide within the discipline that stubbornly resists detailed intellectual scrutiny. It goes without saying that Llewellyn Smith's book falls on the officially discredited side of the split. But the methodological problems go deeper than the mainstream injunction against normative economics. His intuition that economics misses something vital in the aesthetic evaluation of art is not developed into a cogent alternative theory of value, which is why he only calls for an additional chapter to economics rather than something stronger. Given that his objections to the application of standard economic mechanisms and market values to art cannot be successful without a fundamental transformation of economics, the additional chapter is bound to appear erroneous to the fundamentally unchallenged doctrine it supplements. What Llewellyn Smith fails to do, it seems to me, is to spell out adequately just how art is actually valued.

Llewellyn Smith's aesthetic hyperboles sound, to our ears, like nostalgia for a golden age of aesthetic high principal. We need to transpose his argument by examining how values are attributed to contemporary art today. And the evaluation of art is, if anything, uncertain. Without anticipating the precise form of the uncertainty of artistic judgements, let us say that the values attached to art are typically subject to disagreement. This is why we say that art is subjective. That is to say, two viewers can agree on the facts – this is a work by such and such, of a certain size, with certain colours, perhaps, or made of certain materials – but they cannot agree on whether or not it is good, beautiful, and so on. Paul Wood raises the question of the indeterminacy of judgements in art in his exchange with Alex Callinicos, saying 'I find his writing [on modern art] marked by a certainty which comes from the deployment of a political perspective as a kind of template'.[19] Certainty is a kind of pox on artistic judgement, and this is why Llewellyn Smith's defence of artistic judgement is self-defeating. One can value art very highly and very deeply or value particular

---

17   Fine and Milonakis 2009a.
18   See House 2001, Putnam 2002, Bhaskar 2008.
19   Callinicos and Wood 1992, p. 125.

artworks with intensity and commitment, while simultaneously holding that this value cannot – and *should* not – be enforced or established once and for all. In colloquial terms, we say art's values, like love, are 'felt' rather than known. Leo Steinberg endorses indeterminacy in the judgement of art because 'all given criteria of judgement are seasonal' and that 'other criteria are perpetually brought into play by new forms and fresh thought'.[20] He concludes his erudite essay on Picasso's last nude drawings with the statement, 'these are tentative approximations'[21] not as a display of academic caution but as a recognition of the provisionality of artistic interpretation and judgement. In the words of Stephen Moore, 'Steinberg's vigilance' consists in the acknowledgement of 'provisionality'.[22]

Conventionally within art we explain the divergence of opinion of two judgements of art in Humean terms. Discussion reaches that point where, as he says, all of a sudden and imperceptibly 'the usual copulations of propositions, *is*, and *is not* ... [are replaced with] an *ought*, or an *ought not*.[23] In the Humean universe, all values seem to be brought to facts through prejudice, bias, taste and preference. As such, Hume presupposes a divide between subject and object, and the philosopher becomes a border guard for it, alerting us when the subject trespasses on the territory of the object world governed by facts, what is and is not. Artworks, which are made by human beings, cannot be isolated from the subject in this way. For instance, the thickness of a line in a painting is not related primarily to standards of measurement (inch, centimetre, and so on) but to comparable lines (in art, culture, social life, nature, and so forth). Material properties in art have semiotic qualities (for example, whether the line is continuous or broken, heavy or faint, permanent or temporary, abstract or representational, geometrical or loose, made out of charcoal or people's bodies) but also values which they activate. The Humean mistake is to think that the various elements in the artwork are not already psychologically, socially and historically loaded, as if the 'facts' or material features of the artwork could be isolated from the disputes that they inevitably carry within them. History is embedded in the materiality of artworks. However, the values that saturate a work of art are never *known values* but always *contested values*.

'The urgent need to understand, to achieve a transparent reading, paradoxically requires delay and opacity',[24] Pierre Macherey says.

---

20   Steinberg 1972, p. viii.
21   Steinberg 1995, p. 119.
22   Moore 2008, p. 16.
23   Hume 1987, p. 469.
24   Macherey 1978, p. 38.

The writer, as a producer of a text, does not manufacture the materials with which he works. Neither does he stumble across them as spontaneously available wandering fragments, useful in the building of any sort of edifice; they are not neutral transparent components which have the grace to vanish, to disappear into the totality they contribute to, giving it substance and adopting its forms.[25]

Indeed, even the social causes 'that determine the existence of the work ... have a sort of specific weight, a peculiar power':[26]

Not because there is some absolute and transcendent logic of aesthetic facts, but because their real inscription in a history of forms means that they cannot be defined exclusively by their immediate function in a specific work.[27]

Just as literature and literary discourse, for Macherey, is 'a contestation of language',[28] we can say that the material properties of artworks – measurable magnitudes of stuff – are better understood as contestations of the material world and its measurements. Hence, the material elements of artworks themselves cannot be separated from values even when these values are necessarily subject to controversy and indeterminacy. This is why it is a fallacy to presuppose 'the active presence of a single meaning around which the work is diversely articulated'.[29]

To speak about the value of art or values in artworks is not to assert the kind of normative expressions of bias and preference that positivism rejects – that is, expressions of assent.[30] On the contrary, to speak of value in art is to *proceed without certainty*. That is to say, there is a palpable hesitancy in the manner by which values are harvested from artworks. Unlike the consumer, who expresses her preferences through acts of exchange, and unlike the populist philistine who apparently quips, 'I don't know much about art, but I know what I like', the competent art viewer speaks of value in art with a tone

25   Macherey 1978, pp. 41–2.

26   Macherey 1978, p. 42.

27   Ibid.

28   Macherey 1978, p. 61.

29   Macherey 1978, p. 76.

30   Alasdair MacIntyre says this tradition gives an account of all value judgements of the kind 'this is good' as meaning 'I approve of this; do so as well', or meaning 'hurrah for this!' (MacIntyre 1987, p. 12).

of *studied indeterminacy*. What is more, this hedging is itself a performative incarnation of value. A caricature of the dithering aesthete can be sketched in order to reveal its affiliation with power,[31] but there is something important in this indeterminacy. Classical pianists play the same scores time and time again but do not expect to sound the same each time, nor do they try to eliminate these subtle variations. Actors on stage, likewise, do not seek to reproduce or replicate performances day in day out, but are trained to be responsive to variations of performance. In contrast with scientific methodology,[32] replicating a procedure in painting, sculpture, installation, video, performance or any other type of art will always and necessarily produce divergent results. This is not because art is a less stringent[33] practice than science but because being stringent in art means attending to these variations.

---

31   Julian Stallabrass, for instance, lampoons the conspicuous indeterminacy with which values are held in the world of art, as if this indeterminacy were a mere shadow play, covering a much firmer kind of determination, namely private self-interest. There is a sociological argument, derived from Pierre Bourdieu, of which Stallabrass is familiar, which claims the display of indeterminacy conforms to a set of protocols from which the aesthete derives 'cultural capital'. This means that there is a price on indeterminacy in art. But it is possible for something to have a price as well as having a value, and the latter is not addressed by explaining the former.

32   Science proceeds on the assumption that experiments follow a methodology that can be replicated and, thereby, the results of the study can be tested by other scientists. Methodology in science, therefore, is meant to guarantee outcomes: if you follow these procedures with these instruments etc., then you will produce the same results. What methodology in science does, then, is convert quality into quantity. That is to say, materials and processes, which all have specific qualities, are abstracted or generalised under laboratory conditions, so that their interaction can be quantified. But this is not the case in art, where methodology and technique do not guarantee results. Following the same process in art will inevitably lead to significant variations as a result.

33   These two different kinds of stringency are also evident in the history of philosophy. A division runs through modern and contemporary philosophy between, to be very schematic about it, the Kantians and the Heideggerians, in a dispute over the relative merits of, for instance, knowledge versus feeling, or rationality versus experience, or truth versus rhetoric. Philosophy seems to be cut in two by the division within value itself. Simon Critchley explains: 'the best way of understanding the misunderstanding between opposed philosophical traditions [is] in terms of the model of "the two cultures". According to this model, analytic and Continental philosophy can be seen as expressions of opposed, indeed antagonistic, habits of thought – Benthamite empiricist-utilitarian and Coleridgean-hermeneutic-romantic – that make up the philosophical self-understanding of a specific culture'. Kantians, analytic philosophers and their allies are stringent about the coherence and consistency of arguments, whereas the Heideggerians, phenomenologists and their allies are stringent about the specificity of experience and the relation between the

Llewellyn Smith both recognises and suppresses the indeterminacy and hesitancy of art's version of stringency. In art, he says, 'the only possible unit of measurement is a human judgement and not a physical constant'.[34] Mainstream economists committed to the doctrine of consumer sovereignty will recognise, here, the cue for their own version of human judgement: consumer preferences. Hence, economists might regard the turn to 'human judgement' by Llewellyn Smith – a supposed escape route from economics – as the surest route into economics. However, there is a marked contrast between *judgements* and *preferences*. Both are individual and subjective, and neither can be taught by rote. Judgements, however, cannot be objectively assessed, and cannot be 'known' variables since they must be produced individually (albeit through social processes) and held subjectively (albeit within institutions that ratify some judgements and marginalise others). This is the broader significance of Llewellyn Smith's distinction between human judgements and physical constants. Llewellyn Smith has in mind a mode of consumption that is not accomplished simply by looking at the artwork that you have bought. The consumption of artworks requires the sort of judgement that can only be the result of self-exertion and, preferably, self-transformation. The consumption of art requires effort, self-exertion and self-transformation. What is lacking from the mere purchase of an artwork, therefore, is not simply *information*. Aesthetic experience is a form of experience through which the subject is formed and exemplified. This is why individuals who cannot experience art (namely, philistines) have historically been understood as something short of subjects in the full sense. Art is a prominent and dominant testing ground – and the reward – of a certain kind of subject. If we think of the judgement of art as a reflective process in which the subject is formed as capable of judgement – and therefore as someone who is judged by the judgements they make – then one cannot acquire art or the capacity to judge art without, in a strong sense, acquiring oneself through the labour of self-exertion and self-transformation. This is what I take to be the heart of

---

self and the world. The first, it might be said, is formalist and focuses on the truth, or *what can rightly be said* of the world, while the other is experiential and focuses on authenticity, or *how human beings inhabit* the world. 'Essentially', Critchley tells us, 'this is a dispute between the scientific conception of the world ... and the existential or "hermeneutic" experience of the world'. Analytic philosophy speaks technically, impersonally and formulates laws or logical proofs, whereas continental philosophy speaks in the first-person and often counts philosophical inquiry among the techniques of personal, moral, and political transformation. One is stringent about its conceptual formation; the other is stringent about the contingent formation of conceptual schemas.

34   Llewellyn Smith 1924, p. 28.

Llewellyn Smith's opposition of 'human judgement' and a 'physical constant' as it pertains to the limit of market value in relation to art.

Llewellyn Smith does not say that human judgements must contain indeterminacy and be expressed hesitantly, but his opposition between judgement and a physical constant implies that judgements are at least somewhat uncertain or subjective rather than measurable and objective. However, while Llewellyn Smith aims to distinguish human judgements from economic preferences, he also and immediately suppresses the disturbing aspects of human judgement by considering only the judgements of experts and only once such judgements have undergone a process of aggregation. Llewellyn Smith comes up with an eccentric and rather dubious thought experiment to aggregate human judgements of art. Suppose we could assemble 'an ideal jury of experts', he says, to determine the 'art value' of a given article. Faced with several works, he thinks, the jury would be able to 'rank' them.

> A competent judge should be able, without insuperable difficulty, to range the competing works roughly in order of artistic merit. If the works were submitted to a number of competent experts acting separately, the order of merit assigned by each would perhaps differ but slightly, so long as the judges were drawn from the same 'cultural area', and the conditions were sufficiently clear and detailed to ensure that the authors were aiming substantially at the same objective.[35]

'I use this purely hypothetical example of an ideal board of examiners', he says, 'merely as a vivid illustration of what I mean by the concept of "art-value"'.[36] Llewellyn Smith thus converts human judgement into art value through the mechanism of a jury of experts. This complacent scenario assumes too much consensus between the expert members of the panel, expecting them to belong to the same class of the same society of the same geographical region and to possess the same cultural background and taste. Values lose their indeterminacy, hesitancy and contentiousness so that they can be aggregated or homogenised into a consensus.

However, the role of experts in his mechanism raises problems of its own. Experts cannot be the only alternative to consumer sovereignty. Llewellyn Smith's solution to the problem of quality in art is populated by experts so that the judgements that they produce can be distinguished from those of aggregated consumers with their individual preferences. Such a distinction needs

---

35   Llewellyn Smith 1924, p. 29.
36   Llewellyn Smith 1924, p. 30.

to be made, but mainstream economists persuaded that markets are the most fair and efficient mechanism for allocating resources will justifiably regard the jury of experts as technically inferior to market mechanisms, as well as less democratic.[37] To be fair, Llewellyn Smith's jury of experts anticipates significant elements of the decision-making principles of the Arts Council and other arts bodies whose allocation of resources is determined by merit. However, one thing of which such institutions have consistently been accused is their lack of democracy, lack of representativeness, and preservation of elitism. The reason Llewellyn Smith turned to experts, it seems to me, was to distinguish judgements from preferences, as if the difference between them was that the former are more legitimate. However, what distinguishes judgements from preferences is not that one represents expert opinion and the other represents non-expert opinion. Judgements refer to quality independent of price while consumer preferences trade off quality for value for money. One may prefer an inferior product because of its price relative to a superior product, but one would not thereby judge the inferior product to be superior. It is clear, therefore, that the neoliberal economist William Grampp is blinded by doctrine when he says 'aesthetic value is a form of economic value just as every other form of value is'.[38]

Expertise is a false solution to the problem of judgement in art. Often today experts are deployed in the conversion of collective decision-making problems into administrative problems. Art raises specific difficulties with regard to this process, since there can be no experts on artistic judgement, no experts on pleasures and no experts on taste. Jürgen Habermas tells us the institutions of education, health, family and culture which 'formerly merely had to codify a canon that had taken shape in an unplanned, nature-like manner', is transformed by modernity's process of rationalisation which 'produces a universal pressure for legitimation in a sphere that was once distinguished precisely for its power of self-legitimation'.[39] In other words, the role of the expert in art is not only founded on the discrediting of traditional and customary modes of

---

37   It is an open question whether the minority who are wealthy enough to purchase art-
       works in the art market are preferable, from the point of view of democracy, to the minor-
       ity of experts who are assembled in juries to make judgements about art. Mainstream
       economists will argue that it is possible, however, to coordinate the two mechanisms.
       An economic argument can be made that expert opinions about quality in art can fil-
       ter through markets in the long run and they can influence consumer preferences; and
       another economic argument can be levelled against the idea that quality can be assessed
       independently of the majority of expressed preferences.
38   Grampp 1989, p. 21.
39   Habermas 1992, p. 71.

cultural authority, but also on the new requirement to justify values rationally (albeit in a form that short circuits that justification through the legitimated representative of authority). Expertise is a function of administration, not a genuine legitimation processes.

Nevertheless, Llewellyn Smith's suggestion that art-value can be assigned through judgement in a collective process of peer review, as we might put it today, is not completely ridiculous, especially if it consists of practitioners making judgments on each other rather than experts making decisions on behalf of citizens and consumers, or academics judging the value of handicrafts. More importantly, though, Llewellyn Smith's proposed mechanism for aggregating judgement is clearly not a market mechanism. It is, therefore, a hypothesis that sits right on the fault line of the confrontation between art and economics. Ruth Towse makes the same point from the opposite vantage point:

> One of the chief features of commercialised culture is the fact that it relies heavily upon market forces. This means that private entrepreneurs, who are in business to make profits, get to decide what creative work is produced and consumers, perhaps without having a lot of knowledge or experience of what is good art, decide what succeeds on the market through their choice of what to buy or attend. Many people in the arts deplore this principle, arguing that we need expert judgement to decide what is worthwhile art and government subsidy to finance it, because consumers are not well informed enough or willing to pay enough to sustain it through the market. Economists, however, regard consumer sovereignty – the belief that consumers are the best judges of their wants – as the main determining factor in consumption.[40]

Experts are opposed to consumers, here, as the representatives of two methods of collective decision-making. If, let us say, the jury of experts was assembled within a public institution and funded by tax revenues, then this will be seen by the advocates of free markets to be a process of funnelling the money of the majority (who would ordinarily show no preference for art) to pay for the culture of a minority (whose preference for art has the privilege of no longer having to be subject to market disciplines). But if markets are the best mechanism for allocating resources based on preferences expressed through purchases, it does not follow that they are the best mechanism for allocating resources based on judgements. Llewellyn Smith is clearly on to something, therefore, when he says that 'within the limits assigned the conception of

---

40   Towse 2010, p. 18.

art-value as a definitely measurable quantity *independent of exchange value* is of great importance'.[41] The mechanism needs to be different not only because the subjective element is different (judgement versus preference) but also because the anticipated outcome is different. While consumers typically respond to prices before deciding on what to purchase (thereby inevitably on average purchasing the goods that represent the best value, not always the finest goods), the question of quality in economics is not absent but is mediated by the realities of cost, competition and ability to pay. What Llewellyn Smith proposes with the concept of art-value is an evaluation of art purely in terms of the question of quality without such mediations and compromises as are routinely imposed by market forces.

Llewellyn Smith argues that so long as the best artworks are not necessarily those that sell at the highest prices, and so long as a significant proportion of important works cannot find purchasers in the art market, there remains a divide, we might say an antagonism, between art-value and the exchange value of art. Llewellyn Smith's 'missing chapter' from economics, which is an economics of art, is an economics of quality instead of an economics of quantity because the value of art, being independent of its market value, must be based on human judgement rather than consumer preferences. This, in turn, requires a mechanism based on the exchange of judgements and the development of a collective judgement, rather than the market mechanism that can only aggregate the individual choices of purchasers based on assessments of value for money. Foreshadowing those actual juries set up to administer the public subsidy of the arts and anticipating in a rough way the concept of 'merit good' developed by Richard Musgrave (see Chapter 4), Llewellyn Smith's hypothetical scenario has since become actual and widespread. In fact, today the existence of such expert juries is under threat not only from a shrinking welfare state but also from the growing presence of corporate and business leaders on the boards of public art institutions, replacing the kind of art experts that Llewellyn Smith had in mind with a variety of business and commercial experts. Despite the absolutism of Llewellyn Smith's conception of art's value, his reliance on experts, the self-defeating hope of aggregating judgement and the proposal of juries as the mechanism for arriving at collective assessments of art, his overriding concern with the quality of art against market forces cannot be entirely dismissed without underestimating art, overestimating markets, or both.

But art value cannot be said to have been victorious over market value in the recent history of art and the economic study of art. One way of thinking about

---

41   Llewellyn Smith 1924, p. 31 (emphasis added).

the failure of art value to hold off the incursions of market value is through Richard Cockett's three cycles of the rivalry between liberalism and the state between the 1760s and the 1980s,[42] in which liberalism usurped feudalism only to be displaced by the welfare state which was itself rolled back by neoliberalism. But these ideological shifts have not remained external to discourses about art, especially within debates on the economics of art. Hans Abbing, for instance, is an artist and economist who has diligently campaigned for any notion of value specific to art to be either rejected entirely as akin to a religious notion or, at the very least, subjected to the liberal and allegedly democratic checks and balances of market forces.

> Artists, art lovers and donors want to believe that economic value devalues and corrupts art and that only aesthetic value should matter... They side with one form of power, the cultural power of the well educated, while dismissing the economic power of not only the well-to-do but also the general masses.[43]

Two re-descriptions structure this argument. Education and knowledge are redescribed as cultural power, while wealth is re-described as economic power. Together these re-descriptions obscure the differences between knowledge and money, as well as the social mechanisms and modes of acquisition that they each require. What is more, Abbing phrases his comparison of what appears to be two types of power in terms of a social division including two elites and one popular constituency. While siding with the power of education, knowledge and the academic public sphere, he thinks, can only put the artist in touch with a cultural elite, dismissing the market not only cuts the artist off from the rich but also the masses. The fact that the masses, insofar as they encounter art 'in the flesh', so to speak, are more likely to do so through public museums rather than by directly purchasing art, does not give Abbing second thoughts about art's access to the masses through the marketplace. Also, Abbing associates academia and the markets through the concept of power, implicitly aligning himself with the neoliberal defence of market forces that has typically been characterised as the realm of individual choice opposed to the external command of rulers, dictators, administrators and bureaucrats. Power, according to the advocates of the free market, is a feature of social decision-making that market forces obliterate by handing over all decision-making to individual consumers. Abbing observes that the value of art tends

---

42   See Cockett 1995, p. 6.
43   Abbing 2002, p. 77.

to dominate discussion of art but compensates for this by contrasting what members of the art world 'want to believe' with the actual interests of rich and poor alike. Despite Abbing's own idealistic view of markets and commercial exchange, he spells out the antagonism between art and market forces with some clarity.

American art critic Dave Hickey, in an argument that is the perfect inverse of Llewellyn Smith, claims that the problem with art today is its domination by experts and academics (and the judgements they issue).[44] In what Grant Kester describes as 'the most widely read book among American art students'[45] in the 1990s, Hickey pitches beauty against social power and cultural academicism. Hickey's starting point is the widespread suspicion of the market within the art world, and the fact that beauty was associated with the market. Hickey 'canvassed artists and students, critics and curators, in public and in private – just to see what they would say'[46] about beauty. Rather than equating beauty with the 'subversive potential' of their own individual and inalienable visual pleasure, as the Ruskinian art critic would like, these art world know-it-alls were universally suspicious of beauty.

> If you broached the issue of beauty in the American art world of 1988, you could not incite a conversation about ... pleasure ... or even Bellini. You would instead ignite a conversation about the marketplace. That, at the time, was the 'signified' of beauty. If you said 'Beauty', they would say, 'The corruption of the market'.[47]

Ask an artist about beauty and she complains about the market. It is worth noting at this point that the link between beauty and the market that Hickey's interviewees appeared to spout automatically was not necessarily theoretically or academically imposed. Artists knew from experience that beauty was a feature of the art that the market demanded. Bureaucracy and academicism are brought into Hickey's explanation of artists' antipathy to beauty because he understands that art's own institutions (museums, university departments, magazines and so on) which provide an alternative support system which allows artists to opt out of the art market, are caricatured as nothing but the replication of the Académie Royale de Peinture et de Sculpture. In Hickey's view, beauty is a casualty of art's independence from the market. For the artists, on the other hand, beauty was suspicious precisely because of its association

---

44   See Hickey 2009.
45   Kester 2003, p. 11.
46   Hickey 2009, p. 3.
47   Hickey 2009, pp. 3–4.

with the market. 'Beauty sells',[48] they told him. Standard commodity producers would not complain that beauty sells, of course: such an insight would normally trigger the profitable production of marketable goods that were beautiful in the eyes of consumers. For the artists that Hickey spoke to, however, the market and the beauty it demanded and rewarded was to be rejected and resisted.

Hickey's revival of beauty is not a return to the academic regulation of the beautiful but, in the manner of Roger de Piles, seeks to undermine the academy with the promotion of a 'vernacular'[49] beauty. While most commentators have assessed the implications of Hickey's revival of beauty, leading to a minor industry of publishing on the virtues and vices of beauty, a smaller number have interpreted the politics of Hickey's advocacy of beauty against academia and the state. The basis of this second strand of commentary is Hickey's depiction of the contemporary art world as a hierarchical, bureaucratic, managerial academy in which, by the late 1980s,

> the ranks of 'art professionals' had swollen from a handful of dilettantes on the East Side of Manhattan into this massive civil service of PhDs and MFAs administering a monolithic system of interlocking patronage (which, in its constituents, resembles nothing so much as that of France in the early nineteenth century).[50]

The litany of negative associations (professionals, civil servants, administrators, patronage, monolithic system) is carefully orchestrated to persuade the reader that the art world has become the kind of conservative, reactionary, self-serving and pedantic system that prevailed when the Romantics, Realists and Modernists rejected orthodoxy and its institutions to establish art's independence from external authority. Amelia Jones contextualises the political scene of Hickey's project as follows:

> the book stages itself, rather self-contradictorily, as a radical corrective to so-called 'political correctness' (or PC) – the supposed hegemony of narrow-minded 'art professionals' who currently administer 'a monolithic system of interlocking patronage'. Hickey, then, strategically poses himself

---

48   Hickey 2009, p. 8.
49   Hickey 2009, p. 15.
50   Hickey 2009, p. 4.

as correcting what he characterizes as an egregious bureaucratization of art through academic discourses of identity and cultural politics.[51]

Social life plays the role of villain in his argument, reduced to the caricature of 'political correctness'. Not quite flirting with Thatcher's complete denial of the existence of society, the social appears in Hickey's argument exclusively as a negative force that constrains the individual. This is because Hickey wants the value of art, distilled in the value of beauty, to stand independently of the values of social life, community and all forms of collective decision-making or organisation. The academy represents power rather than knowledge, for Hickey, and its effects are bureaucratic, imposing its conclusions on citizens through norms, regulations and legislation. Jones, on the other hand, focuses on the way that the academy acts as a conduit for radical struggles such as the women's movement and civil rights, and sees the academy itself as a site of struggle in which the broader social issues must be brought to bear not only in research papers and the curriculum but in the organisation of its institutions. With Hickey and Jones, liberty confronts regulation.

Collapsing the post-modernist New York art scene into the historical scene of the founding moment of modernist autonomy, Hickey gives his alternative to the existing cultural order an heroic connotation. Using nothing but a stream of remote resemblances, Hickey gives the impression that the contemporary art world is governed by the kind of power native to the academies that had controlled the production of art, and the training of artists, since the seventeenth century. The academy, Hauser says, had 'at its disposal all the benefices that an artist can ever hope to receive, and all the instruments of power calculated to intimidate him'.[52] For two centuries the academy had enjoyed a monopoly on art education, commissions, titles, prizes, pensions and exhibitions, and although Hickey does not demonstrate that the 'massive civil service' of art professionals in NY held a similar monopoly on the livelihood of artists, the charge of interference retains a great deal of its historical power. Depressingly, today's art institutions appear to Hickey as no different from those set up to attach art to royal power and aristocratic patronage, or what Hauser, referring particularly to the French seventeenth-century model of academicism, calls 'the state organization of art production'[53] with its 'canon of artistic values'.[54]

---

51   Jones in Elliot, Caton and Rhyne 2002, p. 215.
52   Hauser 1992, p. 180.
53   Hauser 1992, p. 181.
54   Hauser 1992, p. 183.

If history has repeated itself, this time art is constrained not merely by the salon jury, the protocols of the academy and the aristocratic patronage they represented, but the combined force of late twentieth-century global capitalism and the capitalist state, in which

> powerful corporate, governmental, cultural and academic constituencies vied for power and tax-free dollars, each with its own self-perpetuating agenda and none with any vested interest in the subversive potential of visual pleasure.[55]

Art critics, art theorists, curators, professors and informed artists themselves are mingled with CEOs, bureaucrats and cultural gatekeepers (an alliance of the wealthy and powerful) in a conspiracy against art and the viewer. Art and the art viewer are threatened in this power play between two of the largest and most effective social forces the world has ever known (global corporations and the capitalist state), as well as the very institutions of art itself (museums, art schools and scholarship). In one sense the sheer scale of Hickey's assembled enemy appears preposterous, like the fantasy of a conspiracy theorist. In another sense, however, we would not expect anything less: art has always attracted the attention of the powerful and wealthy who attempt to turn art to their own advantage or to remodel art in their own image.

Within the historical framing that he provides – essentially a seventeenth-century absolutism – Hickey's endorsement of beauty strikes us as revolutionary since it has roots in a late eighteenth- or early nineteenth-century bourgeois conception of cultural individualism. But the comparison is not kind to Hickey on closer inspection. The reason the modernist assault on the academy appears revolutionary is that it belonged to the extended bourgeois reform of aristocratic society. As well as establishing new temporary institutions for the exhibition of modern art, such as the Salon des Refusés of the nineteenth century or the avant-garde cabarets of the early twentieth, the bourgeoisie also set up new institutions for art education, new scholarly disciplines such as art history, art criticism and aesthetic philosophy, as well as the introduction of new methods for funding art and new legal protections for artists such as Hogarth's copyright law. Hickey's advocacy of visual pleasure borrows its emancipatory affect from the historical origin of a set of bourgeois institutions that he re-describes, without irony, as aristocratic ones. The only bourgeois art institution that Hickey vindicates is the free market, including the art market. The presence of cultural and academic constituencies in his

---

55   Hickey 2009, p. 4.

list of established agents (that seek power and money rather than promote visual pleasure) is symptomatic of an outlook in which the obligation of art is to be experienced by individuals without the mediation of any institutions at all. Like a Romantic protestant, Hickey wants his religion without a church (particularly without a clergy); he wants the believer to have a direct and internal relationship to God. Hickey believes that 'visual pleasure' is a liberal aspiration that confounds bureaucracy (but not markets) because it belongs to individuals alone. Beauty is taken up by Hickey as 'the single direct route, without a detour through church or state, from the image to the individual'.[56]

There is a liberal radicalism to his argument that levels all opinions on art and therefore bursts the balloon of art's covert biases and overt privileges. In this regard, Hickey is the true adversary of Llewellyn Smith's moralising aesthetic judgement as well as his welfarist bureaucracy. For Hickey there is nothing to separate judgements from preferences except bogus claims to authority. What is lacking here, of course, is the exertion and self-transformation of the experience of art. Beauty, for Hickey, like consumer preferences, is ultimately already *known*, not by experts but by individuals themselves. When Hickey describes beauty as 'subversive' he has in mind a challenge to academic orthodoxy; not, for instance, the unravelling of habit, custom, education and ideology that inhabits the individual and which aesthetic exertion overcomes only through self-transformation. We get a clear indication of the politics of this position from the fact that Hickey explains his concept of beauty in relation to an excerpt from the American Declaration of Independence in which it is stated that 'whenever any Form of Government becomes destructive ... it is the Right of the People to alter or to abolish it'.[57] For Hickey, beauty represents the individual's unmediated and always legitimate evaluation of art and therefore both the redundancy of experts and the virtue of markets. If judgement expects more of the subject, visual pleasure protects the subject from pernicious external forces. The individual who takes visual pleasure from beauty is the antidote to the political subject: free already (without the revolutionary labour of freedom) and immune from power already (without the institutional safeguards of political organisations and the state). In other words, the aesthetic subject, as Terry Eagleton explains is the prototype of the bourgeois liberal individual. 'The construction of the modern notion of the aesthetic artefact is thus inseparable from the construction of the dominant ideological forms of modern class-society, and indeed from a whole new form of human subjectivity appropriate to that

56   Hickey 2009, p. 12.
57   Hickey 2009, p. 75.

social order'.[58] Max Horkheimer detected in this autonomous aesthetic individual the 'internalized repression' of a social power buried deep in the very
bodies and sensibilities of those over which it rules. The consumer of beauty,
then, insofar as he or she uncritically expresses social taste as his or her own
individual taste, is an unwitting carrier and agent of his or her own subjuga-
tion. That is to say, visual pleasure can only protect the subject from pernicious
external forces so long as these forces have not been internalised and become
the very basis of visual pleasure itself. Hence, Eagleton says, 'nothing could
strengthen power more than its diffusion through the unconscious textures
of everyday life'.[59] Unlike judgement, which Llewellyn Smith preserved by del-
egating to experts, visual pleasure cannot be entrusted to others. Here, then,
Llewellyn Smith's absolutist judgement confronts Hickey's relativistic pleasure
not only with rival conceptions of artistic subjectivity but also rival conceptions of the social relations necessary for that subject to thrive. Judgement contrasts graphically with consumer preference and therefore in Llewellyn Smith's
argument with market value and market mechanisms, but visual pleasure is
set up by Hickey against expertise and therefore authority and bureaucracy.
Consequently, Llewellyn Smith, who fears the threat of market forces against
quality in art, turns to a bureaucratic panel of experts to preserve art's integrity,
whereas Hickey, who fears the threat of academic inertia against the equal-
ity of pleasure in art, turns to the market in which consumers are free to find
visual pleasure in any product they regard as beautiful.

The same quarrel over collective and individual remedies to art's social
predicament is rolled out in the standoff between Jones and Hickey. Its terms
reflect the two opposing strategies of the nineteenth-century liberation from
the remnants of feudalism that began in Victorian Britain, under the head-
ings of Free Trade and Reform. Like Hickey, the Free Traders, such as Richard
Cobden, campaigned against state interference in the economy; rejected pro-
tectionism of all kinds, including tariffs and duties; and countenanced the
overthrow of aristocratic privilege with a new ideology of industry, thrift and
liberty. Like Jones, the 'Radicals', led in the UK by Jeremy Bentham, also known
as Reformers, involved themselves in legislation, paid close attention to language use, established institutions, attacked prejudice and bias wherever it
was to be found, and insinuated themselves into places of power, often oust-
ing privilege in the process. Despite this, it is one of the Victorian patriarchs,
not a Free Trader, whom Jones identifies most with Hickey's position. Hickey's
revival of beauty has its roots, she argues, in Ruskin, who said, 'every man knows

---

58   Eagleton 1990, p. 3.
59   Eagleton 1990, p. 44.

where and how beauty gives him pleasure'.[60] The Victorian critic of 'the science of getting rich'[61] agrees with the postmodern advocate of the art market on the subjective, individual and inalienable judgement of beauty. Ruskin has an inkling of something missed by Hickey (and overlooked by Jones), however, when he says that there are professions (he includes soldiers, pastors, physicians and lawyers, but he could have added many others) which are carried out by individuals who 'have a work to be done irrespective of fee – to be done even at any cost, or for quite the contrary of a fee'.[62] For Ruskin the market is not a safe haven for beauty. Ruskin lacks the populist enthusiasm that Hickey's *vernacular* beauty takes for granted, advising a parliamentary commission in 1857 that the benefits of civilising the masses with art has the disadvantage of spoiling the experience of art for the educated.[63] Jones brings the two together on account of a shared social myopia that expresses itself through a naturalised abstract notion of beauty. Hickey, therefore, not only hurls us back to Ruskin's 'heatedly romantic'[64] veneration of beauty, but also 'to the imperialist and exclusionary logic of cultural value that gave Ruskin and his contemporaries their social authority as arbiters of taste'.[65]

Arts's relationship to market forces and commodification is repackaged by Hickey through the opposition between pleasure and expertise, or liberty and regulation, and therefore through a dichotomous and antagonistic pairing of the individual and society. Liberalism is Hickey's commonsense.[66] John Stuart Mill said that 'the only part of the conduct of anyone, for which he is amenable to society, is that which concerns others'.[67] Individual liberty should not be

---

60   Ruskin quoted in Elliot, Caton and Rhyne 2002, p. 215.

61   Ruskin 1985, p. 180.

62   Ruskin 1985, p. 178.

63   See Bennett 1998, p. 111.

64   Jones in Elliot, Caton and Rhyne 2002, p. 215.

65   Jones in Elliot, Caton and Rhyne 2002, p. 216.

66   The key liberal virtues are tolerance, variety, choice and freedom from various kinds of authority including convention, conformity and the interference of government and the state. John Stuart Mill's individualism is the enemy of a list of vices that only have to be named to recruit the art world to the cause of liberty: narrowness, uniformity, persecution, intolerance, custom, public opinion, tyranny, standardisation, tradition, mediocrity, administration and regulation. The cornerstone of liberalism is John Locke's 'harm principle', adopted by Mill via Wilhelm von Humbolt, which states that no individual's freedom should be curtailed provided their actions do not infringe on the liberty of others. Mill puts it this way: 'the only purpose for which power can be rightfully exercised over any member of a civilized community, against his will, is to prevent harm to others'.

67   Mill 1945, p. 12.

interpreted as the freedom to do harm to others, and yet, at the same time, liberty depends on the suppression of the illiberal. The liberty of law-abiding citizens depends upon the coercive powers of the state (the police, the courts and the military) to restrict the liberty of harmful individuals. The aesthetic equivalent of the suppressed necessity of social threats against the individual within liberalism is the condemnation of modernism, avant-gardism, anti-art and the anti-aesthetic that Alexander Alberro identifies as the barely acknowledged precondition for the revival of beauty in contemporary art criticism and philosophy. Beauty can appear as the 'undisputed and universal bearer of a better society', Alberro says, only if we 'suspend the messiness of history in the hope of returning us to an idyllic and abstract past that knew of no internal tensions, disputes, and contradictions'.[68] The liberty of visual pleasure is predicated on regulating art discourse in such a way that the illiberal critique of beauty by philistine artists and their allies is made mute. If we think of the critical tradition of the avant-garde as epitomising the struggle by artists to liberate art, artists and art's publics from inherited cultural constraints, then the messy history that Alberro mentions is the *process of liberation* that the liberty of the individual art lover in the revival of beauty enjoys only as a *bequest*.

Hickey and Mill share a conception of liberty that contains no politics of liberation.[69] Hickey's opposition between the individual and society is static (the former perceived as a species of the consumer and the latter perceived as exemplified by those institutions and structures that populate themselves with official agents, experts and academics – that is to say, those very forces that economists routinely complain interfere with markets) and therefore does not call for collective social transformation but a simple choice by the individual.

---

68   Alberro 2004, p. 39.

69   As soon as individuals combine to organise themselves, liberals see nothing but a violent illiberal mob in the case of the dominated, or a powerful elite protecting its own privilege in the case of the dominant. Hence, Mill and the liberals do not defend the 'right of association' that the working class repeatedly fought for during the eighteenth and nineteenth centuries: to debate, organise and protest against the state. Individualism cannot explain industrial strikes, for instance. For each individual calculating their best interests, it would be better for others to strike while they continue to work. This is known as the free-rider problem, and individualist social theories cannot shake it off. As Barnes puts it, 'social agents interacting and communicating in a system ... [are] wholly unintelligible in terms of the postulates of individualism'. Just as liberals fail to account for the historical processes whereby collective agency brings about the social preconditions for individual liberty, Hickey rejects and ridicules the historical processes by which the viewer and artist alike are liberated from doctrine, custom, tradition and sedimented values.

There are, of course, forms of collective action and social decision-making that do not correspond to the liberal caricatures of mob rule and bureaucratic constraint.[70] 'What is lacking is dialogue', as Frank Michelman puts it, in his critique of Ronald Dworkin's liberal theory of law. Equally we find no endorsement of dialogue within Hickey's account of the relationship between art and value. Beauty speaks to us directly, he argues, and sequesters both beauty and art from dialogue, as well as targeting the dialogical exchange between scholars to clear the way for self-regulated commodity exchange. Llewellyn Smith had naively hoped that subjective judgements could approach consensus through a simple social mechanism. His expert panel of judges belonged to a 'method of determining art-value ... by the consensus of opinion of impartial and competent experts'.[71] Hickey, by contrast, cynically[72] rejects all mechanisms that mediate between individuals, including 'the patronage of our new "non-profit" institutions ... presumed to be untainted, redemptive, disinterested, taste free, and politically benign. Yeah, right'.[73] Hickey defends beauty by means of a defence of the marketplace for art. Thus, in an academicised and bureaucratised art world, Hickey claims that 'saying that the "art market is corrupt" is like saying that the cancer patient has a hangnail'.[74]

As an advocate of the individual's own inalienable sense of visual pleasure, Hickey might have been sensitive to the artist's independence from market demand, but instead he deliberately or naively mistakes the reference to the power of the market to corrupt art (by rewarding artists financially for producing work they would not otherwise produce) as a reference to the market not being *corrupting* but *corrupt*.[75] The corruption that the artists feared was the power of money to incentivise the production of art demanded by collectors rather than the kind of art that the artists judged to be worthwhile. Hickey cannot see any threat to artistic independence lurking within market

---

70   Michelman quoted in Botha et al. 2003 p. 244.

71   Llewellyn Smith 1924, p. 30.

72   I do not use the word 'cynic' here to exhibit my dislike of Hickey's opinion but simply to signify that he proceeds by identifying malicious motives behind the surface of apparently philanthropic actions.

73   Hickey 2009, p. 5.

74   Hickey 2009, p. 4.

75   Hickey, the talented writer, deliberately contorts the use of the word 'corrupt' in this passage, so that the evidence of corruption in government, administration and management appears to be misapplied to the market. In a straight comparison, surely bureaucratic institutions are likely to be more corrupt than free markets with their renowned checks and balances? If Hickey can transpose the complaint about the corrupting influence of the market into a debate on the market being itself corrupt, then he feels the argument can be turned on its head.

demand. Oddly, his utopia of the marketplace appears to contain no bargains, no trade offs, no compromises, only individuals who know what they want and use money to purchase it directly. Perhaps he assumes that artists only produce art for the money and therefore the market merely facilitates that aim. If so, then the market does not corrupt artists, incentivising them to make commodities demanded of them, but merely informs them about demand and therefore facilitates them in their aim of making money rather than art. What is more, it is clear from his antipathy to the kind of art produced under the conditions of postmodern academia that he welcomes the disciplining power of markets to punish artists who do not conform to what he imagines is the market demand for beauty. Artists who do not measure their achievements in terms of financial reward or by pleasing consumers are likely to see this utopian wish as a dystopian incarnation of market corruption. Also, Hickey does not raise the possibility that the tastes of wealthy collectors might not be synonymous with the hard won principles and standards of artists.[76] Instead he defines the artists' rejection of beauty, on account of its intimacy with the market, as a mark of aristocratic distinction: 'although their complaints usually are couched in the language of academic radicalism, they do not differ greatly from my grandmother's *haut bourgeois* prejudices against people "in trade"'.[77] Hickey gets his class analysis muddled up here. Prejudice against trade, that is to say traders or merchants, is a privilege of the gentry. Artists are not above merchants in the hierarchy of occupations but sit below traders, since artists are direct producers, that is to say, handicraft workers and skilled labourers. If artists reject trade it is not because they receive their income as landowners, rentiers and the inheritors of great fortunes and valuable estates. Artists reject markets because they aim to be independent producers, not because they pride themselves on being independent of production. There is a different politics that animates the rejection of beauty by artists who work with fidelity to the avant-garde, and this politics is not reducible to a silk stocking prejudice. Beauty in art bears the stigmata of market value and therefore the critique of beauty is not only the critique of market value as it is expressed most vividly in the art object but is also a negative expression of the preservation of the value of art and the values of the artist as an independent producer.

There is a liberalism in Hickey's argument that flattens out all opinions on art and therefore erodes institutional power and internalised elitism, but his

---

76   I do not mean to imply that it is impossible for collectors to have hard-won principles and standards. My point is to contrast the artist with the standard perception of the consumer, particularly the sovereignty of the consumer, whose preferences are under no pressure to raise themselves into hard-won principles and standards.

77   Hickey 2009, p. 8.

argument was made, it is important to remember, in the wake of President Reagan's goal to slash public funding to the arts by 50 percent.[78] With scant analysis and a great deal of rhetorical sleight of hand, Hickey markets his ideas to the reader – and the chief idea is that markets are the best possible mechanism for making collective decisions about art. His advocacy of the art market hangs on the twinning of consumer preference with the individual appreciation of beauty. Beauty, which in his hands is the expression of preference rather than the subject of judgement, is Hickey's cure for an administered art world. 'For more than four centuries', Hickey suggests, 'the idea of "making it beautiful" has been the keystone of our cultural vernacular'.[79] This is a very dubious statement.[80] Hickey perhaps has in mind the broken lineage that spans from

---

78 See DiMaggio 1996, pp. 65–7.

79 Hickey 2009, p. 12.

80 Hickey's friend Peter Schjeldahl refines the central point of the revival of beauty: 'There is something crazy about a culture in which the value of beauty becomes controversial' (Schjeldahl in Beckley and Schapiro 2001, p. 55). This idea has a ring of truth. If beauty is the experience of pleasure, visual or otherwise, then what sort of culture would deny us beauty other than one that is seriously flawed? Schjeldahl appeals to intuition rather than historical or sociological explanation that prevents him from understanding the long-standing concern about beauty's social effects. Pierre Bourdieu, the leading sociologist of culture in the twentieth century, argued, for instance, that beauty is valued precisely because it divides us. From a sociological point of view, it is the social distinction that gives beauty its pleasure. Saying something is beautiful is never innocent. There is an economy of pleasure attached to social hierarchies and symbolic power. If we feel that visual pleasure belongs to us and cannot be legislated by others, ought not to be judged by others and is, in this way, subjective and individual, this is because, Bourdieu argues, there is an interval between the acquisition of taste and the enjoyment of beauty, and therefore a systemic forgetting of the acquisition. Following Bourdieu's sociology of taste, therefore, we can transpose Schjeldahl's commonsense affirmation of beauty as follows: There is something pleasurable about beauty in a culture in which taste distinguishes oneself from those without education in a culture in which the acquisition of taste is forgotten and the individual therefore takes all the credit. Historically, as well as sociologically, there are good reasons to regard beauty as controversial. Jerome Stolnitz charts the rise and fall of the value of beauty in art and aesthetics. After the 'intermission of aesthetics . . . from the time of Plotinus to the eighteenth century' (Stolnitz 1961, p. 186), he says, 'the field of aesthetics was no longer organized around the concept of "beauty" and second, that "beauty" was no longer the sole nor even the chief value-category' (Stolnitz 1961, pp. 193–4). Since 'the concept of objective beauty seems to have become intractable [in the eighteenth century], attention was directed to its logical character, to explain why it had to be rejected' (Stolintz 1961, p. 196). Stolintz sums up the less than impressive history of the concept of beauty within aesthetic thought thus: 'The concept "beauty" commended itself to traditional thought because of the assumption that it had or could be given a

the Renaissance humanists and Vasari to the commitment to beauty promoted by Pater, Ruskin, Morris and the Pre-Raphaelites. Beauty, however, has never been promoted as blithely as it is in Hickey's consumerist liberal conservatism. Hickey's beauty, like consumer preferences, is ultimately already *known*, not by experts but by individuals themselves. Hickey's market utopia for art is matched by mainstream economists and is reflected also in the market dystopias of the critical tradition. Peter Bürger's *Theory of the Avant-Garde* shares many of the facts and evaluations of Hickey's account of the bureaucratisation of art through the establishment of modernism as dominant culture, saying 'the neo-avant-garde institutionalizes the *avant-garde as art* and thus negates genuinely avant-garde intentions'.[81] Hickey also echoes Andrea Fraser's argument that the trajectory of institutional critique in art between the 1960s and 1990s saw the critique of institutions become the institutionalisation of critique. Mark Rectanus writes about the 'convergence of interests among corporate cultural production, non-profit organizations and public institutions'.[82] Between 1971 and 1974, according to Neil Mulholland, 'the avant-garde was put under specialized protection'[83] by the Arts Council of Great Britain. Sarat Maharaj refers to the 'normalising of critique'[84] but also, interestingly, the methods by which artists like Georges Adéagbo and Zarina Bhimji enact 'a détournement of critique'.[85] Nina Möntmann, also retaining some hope, says 'the question is, how you can turn an institution that is increasingly taking over

---

determinate meaning and therefore a viable application to objects or to the properties of objects. After the xviiith century, this assumption is weakened or vitiated for many thinkers' (Stolintz 1961, pp. 203–4). And by the 1960s it was possible to say 'that "beautiful" seems now often to be valued pejoratively or invidiously' (Stolintz 1961, p. 185), not because artists or society had gone 'crazy' but because '[s]omething more and, implicitly, something better than beauty is appealed to (ibid.). Beauty signifies the market's potential corruption of art, therefore, because 'when a work is only beautiful, it is inoffensive, or it is in an orthodox style' (ibid.). Throughout its history, artists have consistently seen beauty as controversial. In this long view, therefore, there is something disturbing – not crazy perhaps but uncritical and lacking depth – about a culture in which the value of beauty is uncontroversial.

81   Bürger 1984, p. 58.

82   Rectanus 2002, p. 236.

83   Mulholland 2003, p. 15. How precarious was the *détente* between the avant-garde and the state is demonstrated by the fact that this period of convergence corresponded to Norbert Lynton's short stint as the Director of Exhibition for the Arts Council, given that he was appointed in 1970 and resigned in 1975.

84   Maharaj in Eigenheer 2007, p. 33.

85   Maharaj in Eigenheer 2007, p. 35.

corporate structures into an agent of emancipation'.[86] Although Hickey drains
art's institutions of all capacity for emancipation, including the *détournement* of critique, his enmity towards institutions recognises the fact that
art's institutions have lost some of their earlier revolutionary and reformist
character.

Hickey's embrace of the market through the flattened concept of beauty
as unmediated visual pleasure was anticipated by the forerunners of 'Young
British Art' in the late 1980s and early 1990s as the liberation from government
and critical scrutiny. This new generation of artists and writers clearly directed
their work at the market instead of dwindling state subsidies and circumspect
art theory. Andrew Renton, one of the leading curators and writers attached to
the new generation of British artists, said the 'early eighties taught us that there
was a market place for art'.[87] Renton's book, *Technique Anglaise*, co-edited with
the artist Liam Gillick,[88] shows how the balance of power in favour of the market in the 1980s transformed the perception and practices of contemporary art
in London for artists, critics and gallerists.[89] Karsten Schubert, a prominent
dealer of the period in London, went a step further: 'What we saw was that the
market in the Eighties totally undermined critical judgement and, in the process, a lot of stuff which in the past would not have been looked at, suddenly
you could look at'.[90] The dealer gives voice to what would become Hickey's
campaign against academia and informed judgement, a campaign with the
express aim of emancipating the individual's visual pleasures. Among those
individuals whose emancipation was so dear to Hickey in his endorsement
of the market against the academy were the collectors whose tastes had been
frustrated by the reign of 'critical judgement'. In effect, the case made both by
Hickey and Schubert is that in the 1980s the market took over the role from art's
discourses for evaluating art. Before the 1980s, state funding for the arts was

86   Möntmann 2006, p. 37.

87   Gillick and Renton 1991, p. 13.

88   Gillick, paradoxically, was the leading artist of *Technique Anglaise*, but engaged exten-
      sively in art theory and art criticism, while his work never abandoned the critique of
      markets, as many of his peers did. That none of the participants in *Technique Anglaise*
      inquired into the formation of this particular mode of being an artist in relation both to
      the markets and to critical discourse discredits them all.

89   Maureen Paley, a key London art dealer, said that the growth of the market in the
      Thatcherite 1980s coincided with the retraction of support from the public sector: 'The
      fact that there was no grant money around produced something positive. It didn't pro-
      duce a huge depression, but produced a positive sense that you can take matters into your
      own hands' (Gillick and Renton 1991, p. 25).

90   Gillick and Renton 1991, p. 15.

led in principle by the agenda set by academic and critical discourses (in the form of panels of experts, funding criteria and so on) – this was the economic basis for the power of the critic that Schubert celebrated overthrowing during the eighties boom. Hickey's argument does not refer to such historical contingencies but proceeds abstractly, intuitively and rhetorically, instead, which is why it reads as doctrinaire. His argument about beauty shoehorns Ruskin's opposition of aesthetics and theory into the standard defence of consumer sovereignty.

While for Llewellyn Smith the economics of art must be an economics of quality not quantity, putting values at the heart of the assessment of art through human judgement, Hickey opposes bureaucracy and academicism to the liberty and individualism of the marketplace. Llewellyn Smith argues that art-value must confront the market value of art as a necessarily inadequate measure of artistic quality, while Hickey celebrates the market as permitting the kind of visual pleasure that the academic discourses of artistic value condemn. Abbing splits value in two, as well, regarding the values of artists and others within the art world as myths, while treating market value as objective, scientific and rational. Art's 'myths' are an example of 'normative economics', for Abbing, that is to say, a set of claims made about how art *ought* to be independent of market forces, collectors and money, which shows itself in the various claims, made by artists and others in the art world, that art is not a business activity, artists are not driven by financial gain, and artworks are not commodities. 'As an artist', he says, 'I am convinced that money should not interfere with art. Being an artist I must relate to art, not to the market. I want to keep money out of my relationship with art'.[91] At the same time, he tells us, as an economist, 'I know that the use of money and markets has its advantages...Because art is so diverse, exchange in kind would certainly be less efficient than deals involving money'.[92] When Abbing speaks as an artist his account is drenched with strong feelings shielding vague justifications. He is *convinced* that money should not interfere with art (which points to those social forces that convinced him), and that he *must* relate to art rather than the market (which points to a threat perpetuated by art as a social power structure). Also, he *wants* to keep money at bay (which indicates that he has succeeded in being initiated in the belief system of the art world). He does not entertain the possibility that his deep convictions might be based on good, solid evidence for art's economic exceptionalism; and so he does not investigate art's specific economic conditions to verify his convictions. On the contrary, when Abbing

91   Abbing 2002, p. 37.
92   Ibid.

speaks as an economist his account is saturated with the rhetoric of scientific truth that is justified all the way down. He *knows* about the use of money and markets; they have *advantages* and they are *efficient*. Note the distinction between normative and positive coincides with the distinction between orthodox economic theory and challenges to that orthodoxy. In this, Abbing follows Gary Becker's 'extreme posture', in which 'as much of non-economic life as possible is explained by the economic approach. Whatever falls outside is deemed to be non-economic by virtue of being non-rational and unsystematic'.[93]

If art's antagonism to economics is not a 'taboo' but a clear-headed defence of art's value in relation to exchange value, or quality in relation to quantity; and if, for instance, art is not a standard business but a productive activity that is set up precisely and conscientiously to protect the art from consumer demand; then the formula for art's economic exceptionalism will have to be redrafted not in terms of myths, beliefs and other exotic forms of irrationality, but in terms of the ways in which art production and consumption do not correspond to the models of classical and neoclassical economics. There is, in fact, an established argument within the history of economics that confirms art's economic exceptionalism, but it exists only in fragments, and has been neglected and misunderstood. Advocacy for the market will have to be judged subsequent to a reconstruction of the lost theory of art's economic exceptionalism. The next chapter begins, therefore, by paying close attention to the first references to economic exceptionalism by the founders of political economy, and traces its development, including its increasingly close association with art, throughout the classical literature. Even though many of the assumptions of classical economics are later called into question in various ways, and therefore the classical theory of economic exceptionalism will have to be superseded, the general theory of economic exceptionalism that I will develop in the final chapter of the book has its historical roots in the anomalies and limits to classical doctrine that political economists acknowledged from the outset. Economic exceptionalism spans the economic and the non-economic, taking account of non-economic value and non-economic social mechanisms within the production and circulation of art. Insofar as art has been commodified without being commodified, the theory of economic exceptionalism is the key to understanding both the antagonism between art and capitalism as well as the basis of the uneasy *entente* between them.

---

93   Fine and Milonakis 2009a, p. 33.

CHAPTER 2

Art and Exceptionalism in Classical Economics

Statements by early economists referring directly to the economics of art are rare. In the sixteenth and seventeenth century the Mercantilists, who expressed the interests of merchants against landed privilege and artisan producers, including the defence of tariffs and state taxes on foreign trade, said very little about artisanal production and nothing about art. Since 'the problem of value could only be posed once the guild handicrafts had begun to give way to capitalist economy', the Mercantilists argued that wealth was produced through trade.[1] Merchants traded art during this period, but the production and circulation of art was still governed by guilds, academies, salons and patrons, not by trade. Marginal to the economy as a whole, and not corresponding to the dominant economic issues of the day, the Mercantilists had nothing specific to say about art. The Physiocrats, who in the eighteenth century developed an economic theory of agriculture as the source of rent and therefore wealth, regarded the production of goods as 'sterile'. Conflating industrial production with artisanal production and capitalist farming, the Physiocrats rejected them all as producing nothing new since, according to François Quesnay, industry is only a combining of raw material already in existence, and therefore is 'simply production of forms, and not a real production of wealth'.[2] At the end of the eighteenth century, however, art begins to be drawn into economic debates, albeit parenthetically or incidentally. Before the advent of political economy, it was well known that the prices of artworks, antiques and other rare goods bore little or no relation to costs of production, and that the price of a work could vary enormously over its lifetime. Only with classical economics does art begin to occupy a consistent, if necessarily marginal, place within economic thought. In fact, the theory of art's prices in classical economics is a theory of art's marginal place within economic doctrine and market forces. Classical price theory is not designed to explain how an artwork which cost the artist little or nothing to produce could sell for a king's ransom; consequently the classical economists developed a supplementary theory for these anomalous goods. That is to say, from Adam Smith to J.S. Mill, all economists made an exception within their theory of price for those goods, such as artworks and rare wines, which consistently fetched prices much higher than their costs

---

1 Rubin 1979, p. 64.
2 Quesnay quoted in Rubin 1979, p. 127.

© KONINKLIJKE BRILL NV, LEIDEN, 2015 | DOI 10.1163/9789004288157_004

of production. 'The single most consistent interest displayed by economists across the centuries', De Marchi tells us, 'has been in pricing, and the valuation of art has generally been considered problematic for economic analysis'.[3] It should not be assumed that economic laws are first established and that, later, exceptions to the laws are identified. That is to say, there is no time lag between the birth of economics and the acknowledgement of exceptions to economic laws. Cases of production and consumption that are not susceptible to the laws of supply and demand bring clarity to the account of the typical. Smith and others establish economic laws, in part, by showing what is exempt from them, and art is one of the key exceptions. Art's economic exceptionalism helps to define the field of economics as a social science.

Smith, like all the classical economists, identified a class of goods that cannot be brought under the standard price pattern of commodities produced for and exchanged in the self-regulated market. Ordinarily, supply is adjusted to meet demand in a self-regulated market economy, Smith says, through anonymous mechanisms that reward supply for expanding to existing demand and penalises suppliers for overproduction. The exchange value of a thing is a reflection of its 'real price',[4] according to Smith, which is 'the toil and trouble of acquiring it'.[5] Goods reach what Smith calls their 'natural price'[6] when the supply and demand are in equilibrium and therefore the commodity is sold 'precisely for what it is worth, or for what it really costs the person who brings it to market'). 'The natural price', Smith says, is 'the central price, to which the prices of all commodities are continually gravitating'.[7] Retailers attempting to sell commodities above their natural price in a free competitive market will, in principle, lose out as customers purchase the same goods from competitors selling the goods cheaper. However, natural prices are not actual prices. They are induced through market disciplines, hence prices are unnatural whenever market forces do not or cannot prevail. Smith identified a variety of anomalies, limits and manipulations of market forces, pointing out that prices can be kept above their natural price through 'accidents ... natural causes, and sometimes particular regulations of policy'.[8]

---

3 De Marchi and Goodwin 1999, p. 1.
4 Smith 2007, p. 20. The concept of 'real price' was coined by Quesnay, the leading Physiocrat economist.
5 Ibid.
6 Smith 2007, p. 36. The concept of 'natural price' was coined by Petty, the Mercantilist economist.
7 Smith 2007, p. 38.
8 Smith 2007, p. 39.

Smith lays out the foundation for his theory of economic exceptionalism during his exploration of the various circumstances in which market forces confront an artificial or natural limit.

> When the quantity of any commodity which is brought to market falls short of the effectual demand, all those who are willing to pay the whole value of the rent, wages, and profit, which must be paid in order to bring it thither, cannot be supplied with the quantity which they want. Rather than want it altogether, some of them will be willing to give more. A competition will immediately begin among them, and the market price will rise more or less above the natural price, according to either the greatness of the deficiency, or the wealth and wanton luxury of the competitors.[9]

Smith points out that high prices result from the granting of monopolies, to the anomalous prices that result from natural disasters, and to profitable secrets in manufacturing and trade as leading to or sustaining unnaturally high prices. By and large, according to Smith, the increased demand of scarce goods due to accidental circumstances is a temporary blip, and the artificially high prices due to the withholding of information can never be sustained for very long, while the benefits of monopoly can be sustained for as long as the regulation remains in place. Significantly, however, the prices of economically exceptional goods due to natural causes are permanently at odds with their natural value. There are some goods, Smith says, that must always be supplied below the level of demand. Smith gives the example of 'some vineyards in France of a peculiarly happy soil and situation' that routinely 'fall short of the effectual demand'[10] and which therefore yield prices well above their natural price. 'Such commodities may continue for whole centuries together to be sold at this high price'.[11] These unnaturally high prices are permanent because they are the result of a natural scarcity or natural monopoly. That is to say, if the supply of the commodity cannot be increased to fit to demand then there is no way of supply and demand bringing about an equilibrium in price, and rather than the price reflecting the costs of production, the price will soar as high as the purchasers can bear.

A monopoly, Smith says, 'has the same effect as a secret in trade or manufactures',[12] and is therefore temporary, but 'may last as long as the

---

9   Smith 2007, p. 37.
10   Smith 2007, p. 38.
11   Smith 2007, p. 40.
12   Ibid.

regulations of policy which give occasion to them'.[13] Monopolies elevate prices indefinitely but not permanently. As to the level that monopoly prices reach, Smith restates the formula for exceptionalism generally: 'The price of monopoly is upon every occasion the highest which can be got'.[14] While accidents, monopolies and secrets can bring about unnaturally high prices, it is only the effects of natural limitations on increasing the quantity of supply to meet demand that Smith regards as absolute, hence lasting forever. Not all wine prices are exceptional. Wine *per se* is not economically exceptional. A bottle of Vin de France is generic and therefore can be supplied by any region, which means that the market can price it in the standard way. Those vineyards that supply such 'good common wine', as Smith says, do not command extraordinary prices or high levels of rent. 'It is with such vineyards only, that the common land of the country can be brought into competition'.[15] The highest-grade wines from the best vineyards, however, are limited because of the specific qualities of the soil, drainage, climate and fertility. Smith is aware that the vested interests of established wine growers can be protected by laws 'to prevent the planting of new ones'[16] and thereby reduce the competition among suppliers so as to increase the competition among buyers, but he regards this anomaly as minor since 'this superior profit can last no longer than the laws which at present restrain the free cultivation of the vine'.[17] Nevertheless, Smith insists that a completely unregulated competition among wine growers cannot prevent differences of *terroirs* from which derive differences of flavour and quality 'peculiar to the produce of a few vineyards'.[18] Economic exceptionalism is observed and interpreted by Smith as an anomaly akin to but not identical with monopoly in which the mechanisms of supply and demand fail to bring about a natural price, because limited supply leads to competition among buyers resulting in prices limited only by the wealth and desire of individual consumers. Aggregate demand does not determine the prices of economically exceptional goods since there is no aggregate supply. Prices are determined in a fashion closer to an auction than a self-regulated market, with goods going to the highest bidders rather than finding an equilibrium price at which the goods can be supplied according to demand. The 'usual and natural proportion' of the 'rent and profit of wine' can 'take place only with regard to those

---

13   Ibid.
14   Ibid.
15   Smith 2007, p. 101.
16   Smith 2007, p. 100.
17   Smith 2007, p. 101.
18   Ibid.

vineyards which produce nothing but good common wine',[19] he says. But the prices of the best wines are not regulated by supply and demand in the standard way and their 'fashionableness and scarcity' as well as the 'extraordinary labour bestowed upon their cultivation' creates eager competition among the buyers, which 'raises their price above that of common wine'.[20] The example of wines from precious vineyards in France, therefore, is to be contrasted with 'the exorbitant price of the necessaries of life during the blockade of a town, or in a famine',[21] and the temporary competitive advantages obtained through 'secrets in manufactures' and 'secrets in trade' which 'can seldom be long kept',[22] because the high prices of economically exceptional goods are not based on the award of monopoly rights and *cannot be corrected by the free reign of supply and demand.* 'Such enhancements of the market price are evidently the effect of natural causes, which may hinder the effectual demand from ever being fully supplied, and which may continue, therefore, to operate for ever',[23] he says. Economic exceptionalism is not an example of monopoly, even if its high prices resemble those of monopolies, because exceptional goods cannot be brought under the laws of supply and demand by legislating against monopoly.

Smith's example of the French vineyard is the original motif that triggers and shapes the classical theory of economic exceptionalism. It recurs throughout the literature for over two hundred years. Smith returns to it himself when he says the 'sugar colonies possessed by European nations in the West Indies may be compared to those precious vineyards'.[24] Smith does not include art within his theory of economically exceptional goods. He refers to art, separately, when he discusses the distinction between productive and unproductive labour. 'There is one sort of labour which adds to the value of the subject upon which it is bestowed: there is another which has no such effect. The former, as it produces a value, may be called productive; the latter, unproductive labour', Smith writes. 'A man grows rich by employing a multitude of manufacturers: he grows poor, by maintaining a multitude of menial servants', he explains. There is a dual meaning to the word 'productive', one meaning productive of an outcome, and the other meaning productive of value, which Smith combines by observing that the costly menial servant fails to produce an outcome, while the labour of the industrial worker produces both commodities and

19   Ibid.
20   Smith 2007, p. 102.
21   Smith 2007, p. 37.
22   Smith 2007, p. 39.
23   Smith 2007, p. 40.
24   Smith 2007, p. 102.

profit. Hence, Smith says, 'the labour of the manufacturer fixes and realizes itself in some particular subject or vendible commodity'.[25] Smith associates menial servants with the head of state, under the same heading of unproductive labour, as well as 'all the officers both of justice and war' administering and executing state power, and adds, 'the whole army and navy, are unproductive labourers'.[26] Artists of various kinds are brought under the same heading as the professional middle classes: 'In the same class must be ranked, some both of the gravest and most important, and some of the most frivolous professions: churchmen, lawyers, physicians, men of letters of all kinds; players, buffoons, musicians, opera singers, opera dancers, &c'.[27] Absent from this list are painters, sculptors and printmakers, who produce vendible products. If Smith wishes to suggest that a profit cannot be made in hiring labourers who do not produce a commodity that outlives the labour, then he is mistaken. Partners in a legal firm certainly profit from the lawyers who work for them, and musicians, actors, singers and dancers certainly produce profits for theatre owners, promoters and impresarios. At the same time, those wage labourers who produce a vendible commodity, such as the gardener of a great estate, is unproductive (in the sense of not producing a profit) so long as the employer is the consumer of the product of labour. In art the two different inflections of productive labour do not coalesce, as Smith suggests, but split apart, as actors, singers, dancers and so forth are typically wage labourers who produce a profit for capitalists, whereas visual artists, even when they produce vendible products, are typically not paid wages at all and, when capitalists do profit from visual art, they do not produce profit through productive labour but through the sale of artistic products. Although Smith separates the two, issues connected to the theory of productive and unproductive labour will resurface periodically in the discussion of art's economic exceptionalism.

Jean-Baptiste Say in his *Treatise* of 1803 spells out Smith's theory of exceptionalism with reference to the natural limitations of the special vineyard: 'If the soil, capable of growing good wine, be very limited in extent, and the demand for such wine very brisk, the profit of the soil itself will be extravagantly high'.[28] Say extends Smith's conception of economic exceptionalism by including manufactured goods alongside those products limited by natural causes, but he also dilutes the theory by conflating exceptionalism with the super profits of monopolies, saying

---

25   Smith 1993, p. 212.
26   Ibid.
27   Smith 1993, p. 213.
28   Say 2007, p. 364.

there are some particular products, which nature or human institutions have subjected to monopoly, and thus prevented from being supplied in equal abundance with those of a similar description. Of this kind are the wines of particular and celebrated vineyards, the soil of which cannot be extended by the extended demand. So the postage of letters is, in most countries, charged at a monopoly rate.[29]

Say describes the high prices of sought after wines in terms of the same facts or observations as Smith but he explains the anomaly within a different framework, that of monopoly prices. Say's concern with monopoly and the high prices it obtains is connected to his campaign against all forms of artificially elevating prices above value. When a government imposes a wine tax 'which raises to 15 cents the bottle that would otherwise be sold for 10 cents', no value or utility is added to the wine and therefore all that takes place is the 'transfer of 5 cents per bottle from the hands of the producers or consumers of wine to those of the tax-gatherer'.[30] Mugging is of the same order, according to Say, who explains that no matter how hard or skilfully the mugger works to take ownership of goods belonging to another person, 'there results no production, but only a forcible transfer of wealth from one individual to another'.[31] Import duty, he argues, is a premium paid to the home manufacturer 'out of the consumer's pocket'.[32] In all these cases, and others besides,[33] Say concludes that the prices of goods are 'raised without any accession to their utility or intrinsic value'.[34] In this limited taxonomy of prices, therefore, the trade in fine wine and the high prices of sought after artworks count among 'the serious mischief of raising prices upon the consumers'.[35]

Say reduces Smith's acknowledgement of a range of limits to market forces to the unmodulated binary pair of competition and monopoly, in which the latter merely produces unproductive super profits through the imposition of monopoly prices, but he also lends what appears to be the concept of

---

29   Say 2007, p. 241.

30   Say 2007, p. 63.

31   Say 2007, p. 85.

32   Say 2007, p. 161.

33   Another two examples: first, when 'legislation is too complicated', he says, this 'holds out a great encouragement to fraud, by multiplying the chances of evasion, and very rarely adds to the solidity of title or of right' (Say 2007, p. 121); and second, 'chartered companies and incorporated trades', he says, are an 'exclusive privilege, a species of monopoly... which the consumer pays for, and of which the privileged persons derive all the benefit' (Say 2007, p. 176).

34   Say 2007, p. 63.

35   Say 2007, p. 162.

economic exceptionalism to another cause. He wants to argue that natural forces and land contribute to the production of value. Hence, he uses Smith's example of the vineyard as an illustration of an 'invariable maxim', namely, 'that the productive agency of land is possessed of value'.[36] Smith's argument that a vineyard will sell wine at a higher price if supply cannot be increased to meet demand has been relayed, here, as an argument that land, the wind and the sea, in addition to capital and labour, adds to wealth. Insofar as Say insists that natural agents contribute to the value of all products, then the claim that the soil contributes to the value of fine wine would render the apparently exceptional case of the vineyard as merely an outstanding example of the standard case of the production of value. This is why, in his formula, he speaks of 'the profit of the soil'. Whereas the wind or the sea can add value, he says, without being diminished and without preventing others from profiting from their power, the precious vineyard, like land in general, is 'susceptible of appropriation'.[37] While 'the indefinite latitude allowed to industry to occupy at will the unappropriated natural agents, opens a boundless prospect to the extension of her agency and production',[38] the precious vineyard is a *natural monopoly*. Since the field cannot be extended, any monopoly that the wine producer obtains is a result of the combination of a natural limit and the appropriation of that natural resource as private property. If the price of wine from precious vineyards is higher than inferior bottles, Say can attribute the difference partly to monopoly and partly to the earth. With either argument, or both, Say dissipates the anomalousness of Smith's example as merely an exaggerated version of the combination of 'the three great agents of production, industry, capital and natural agents'.[39]

Say is the first classical economist to extend the discussion of economic exceptionalism to include art. Principally he develops a novel explanation of the economics of art through an analysis of the exceptional producers of art. Say discussed art at some length, referring to painting and music in particular, in his chapter on 'immaterial labour'. Illustrating his concept of an 'immaterial product', Say describes a scene in which a doctor visits a sick person, prescribes a remedy and leaves a bill for his services 'without depositing any product'.[40] 'The industry of a musician or an actor yields a product of the same kind',[41] he adds, as well as mentioning 'the public functionary, the advocate or the judge'

---

36   Say 2007, p. 364.
37   Say 2007, p. 77.
38   Ibid.
39   Say 2007, p. 79.
40   Say 2007, p. 119.
41   Ibid.

and 'the talent of the painter'.[42] This echoes Smith's discussion of productive and unproductive labour and the distinction between labour that produces a vendible product and labour that does not. Say is aware of the unusual aspect of art that it is potentially both an immaterial product and a utility in itself to the artist or performer. 'In learning music, a man devotes to that study some small capital, some time and personal labour; all which together are the price paid for the pleasure of singing a new air or taking part in a concert'.[43] Say extends the argument, linking art with 'gaming, dancing and field-sports',[44] by observing that the 'amusement derived from them is instantly consumed by the persons who have created them',[45] explaining:

> When a man executes a painting, or makes an article of smith's or joiner's work for his amusement, he at the same time creates a durable product or value, and an immaterial product, viz., his personal amusement.[46]

Say also raises an important point regarding the relationship between capital and immaterial products like music. 'The nature of immaterial production makes it impossible ever to accumulate them',[47] he says. As a result some of the producers of immaterial products do not reap the rewards of their labour. The philosopher scientist suffers from the economics of immaterial labour, he says, insofar as 'he throws into circulation, in a moment, an immense stock of his product' but 'will receive a very inadequate portion of the value of the product, to which he has contributed'.[48] Say offers two compensations to the badly rewarded philosopher scientist. First, he points out that it is only in his capacity as a philosopher that he is inadequately recompensed, but that there is 'nothing to prevent him being at the same time a landed proprietor, capitalist or adventurer and possessed of other revenue in these different capacities'.[49] And second, he says, this injustice is recognised by every nation 'sufficiently enlightened to conceive of the immense benefit of scientific pursuits', resulting in the award of 'special favours and flattering distinctions, to indemnify the man of science, for the trifling profit derivable from his professional occupations'.[50]

---

42   Say 2007, p. 120.
43   Say 2007, p. 123.
44   Ibid.
45   Ibid.
46   Ibid.
47   Say 2007, p. 120.
48   Say 2007, p. 329.
49   Ibid.
50   Ibid.

We will see, when we discuss the economics of art in the second half of the twentieth century, that Say here anticipated two prominent themes of Cultural Economics, namely the phenomenon of artists holding 'second jobs' and their satisfaction with non-pecuniary rewards. Say, however, does not count artists among those who are not adequately remunerated for their immaterial labour.

Priests, for Say, like men of knowledge, are also 'very ill paid' even though the church 'requires in its ministers a long course of study and probation, and such study and probation necessarily call for an advance of capital'.[51] The situation of the priest appears to contradict the following thesis: 'When, besides expensive training, peculiar natural talent is required for a particular branch of industry, the supply is still more limited in proportion to the demand, and must consequently be better paid'.[52] While priests are badly paid, artists, for Say, are among such rare producers who are paid at a higher than average rate because of their talent:

> A great nation will probably contain but two or three artists capable of painting a superior picture, or modeling a beautiful statue; if such objects, then, be much in demand, those few can charge almost what they please; and, though much of the profit is but the return with interest of capital advanced in the acquisition of their art, yet the profit it brings leaves a very large surplus.[53]

Artworks and some other rare goods are recognised by Say as commanding high prices, but for the first time their rarity is explained not merely as a contingent consequence of their survival (in the way antiques and 'old master' paintings are rare) but because the immaterial precondition for their production (the capacity of the best artists) is rare. This presents a new theoretical component of the developing classical account of art's economic exceptionalism, and like Smith's vineyard, it will recur in modified forms throughout the literature.

There is one more insight that Say might be said to contribute to a theory of art's economic exceptionalism. Although he does not connect this with art at all, Say annexes consumption to the destruction of value, saying what is added by human exertion can be subtracted by human use. 'Value can be consumed, either long after its production, or at the very moment, and in the very act of

---

51   Say 2007, p. 327.
52   Ibid.
53   Say 2007, p. 328.

production, as in the case of the pleasure afforded by a concert, or theatrical exhibition'.[54] Say raises this point in order to distinguish between productive consumption and unproductive consumption, but at this preliminary stage of the argument he raises an interesting puzzle about artworks when he says that whatever 'cannot possibly lose its value is not liable to consumption'.[55] He has in mind such natural agents as land and the wind, the latter of which he regards as adding value to any product produced with a windmill[56] but which is not diminished by its use. However, it seems worth inquiring into whether paintings, sculptures and other non-perishable artworks do not flout the thesis that their consumption must entail the destruction of their value. Artworks are, in this sense, both consumed (in the sense of *enjoyed*) and not consumed (in the sense of remaining *undiminished*) by experiencing them. In Say's terms, does this mean that artworks are not commodities? 'A horse, an article of furniture, or a house when re-sold by the possessor, has been but partially consumed; there is still a residue of value, for which an equivalent is received in exchange on the re-sale',[57] he says, begging the question of whether artworks are partially consumed when they are resold. Certainly the fact that artworks are not entirely used up in their enjoyment is a necessary precondition for art fetching the kind of prices at auction that attracted the attention of economists in the first place. If artworks do not lose their value and are therefore 'not liable to consumption' then what kind of economic good are they? We will return to this question later.

As well as giving an outline of an economics of art, Say attends to the economics of luxuries. These are, in his words, 'the articles of least necessary consumption'.[58] The prices of 'superfluities' appear in Say's writing to be very fluid. A sudden urban upsurge in demand 'may raise the current considerably above the natural price', he says, 'or a change of fashion may again depress it infinitely below that point'.[59] With demand changing arbitrarily and unpredictably, due to the indulgent nature of its consumption and the fashions that govern the desire of its customers, Say goes on to argue that the producers of superfluities 'make the most scanty profits, and that their workmen are the

---

54   Say 2007, p. 388.
55   Ibid.
56   See Say 2007, p. 75.
57   Say 2007, p. 388.
58   Say 2007, p. 322.
59   Ibid.

worst paid'.[60] Given his opposition to consumers paying over the odds, it follows that Say does not prefer the situation of the luxury trade making super profits. It is evident that 'the price of the gewgaws may sometimes very liberally reward the labour and capital devoted to their production',[61] and that a 'hat maker has been known to make a fortune by a fancy hat', but Say wants to warn us that, 'taking all the profits made on superfluities, and deducting the value of goods remaining unsold, or, though sold, never paid for, we shall find that this class of products affords, on the whole, the scantiest profit. The most fashionable tradesmen are oftenest in the list of bankrupts'.[62] Today, there is growing evidence that artists, like luxury producers for Say, are among the worst paid of graduate workers and one of the most commonly observed facts about the prices of artworks is that they vary enormously depending on fashion. We will consider later whether art is a standard luxury, but it is clear that in his discussion of luxury, immaterial labour and talented labour, as well as his treatment of art prices as monopoly prices, Say made a very considerable contribution to the theory of art's economic exceptionalism.

David Ricardo's *On the Principles of Political Economy and Taxation* from 1817 develops Smith's argument that certain types of good are not regulated by supply and demand via the concept of 'monopoly price', which Say had used to characterise economic exceptionalism. 'Commodities are only at a monopoly price', Ricardo says, 'when by no possible device their quantity can be augmented; and when therefore, the competition is wholly on one side – amongst the buyers'.[63] Like Smith and Say before him, the thing that needs to be explained for Ricardo is the pricing patterns of certain anomalous goods. Ricardo's articulation of economic exceptionalism does not contradict Smith, whose account also contains reference both to scarcity and the absence of labour to increase supply, but Ricardo gives a different emphasis. Smith explained the high prices of fine wine as due to 'natural causes' while Ricardo puts his emphasis on the impossibility of *labour* to increase its supply. Say, like Smith, had played down the absence of labour in arguing that a limited supply with brisk demand will create prices above value. Ricardo, by contrast, immediately spells out that the scarcity that matters here is the kind that cannot be tackled with increasing quantities of supply through labour. While Smith, Say and Ricardo agree that the whole issue of the anomalous pricing of rare goods turns on the question of the possibility or impossibility of increasing the supply

---

60   Ibid.
61   Ibid.
62   Say 2007, p. 322.
63   Ricardo 1923, p. 165.

of certain goods, assuming demand is higher than supply, Ricardo understands the question of increasing quantities of goods exclusively in terms of labour.

Since labour is the source of value, the only circumstance in which scarcity rather than labour can determine the cost of something is if labour is absent in some necessary way. If no labour can increase the quantity of rare statues, scarce books and fine wine, then they will sell at a 'monopoly price'. The significance of the concept of 'monopoly price' for Ricardo is that it does not conform to his labour theory of value. Smith had developed a less sophisticated and less comprehensive labour theory of value. Say, on the other hand, had treated labour as only one of the factors contributing to value, alongside natural agents and capital. Ricardo, unlike Smith, says that the determination of value by labour time applies to 'such commodities only as can be increased in quantity by the exertion of human industry, and on the production of which competition operates without restraint'.[64] The 'monopoly price' of rare goods is the result of the absence of both. Only in such cases when quantities can be increased to meet supply with the application of labour can the labour theory of value operate. That such conditions are present in the vast majority of cases from the production of shoes to the harvesting of mussels does not alter the fact that exceptions exist. Ricardo's clarification that the labour theory of value only applies to the production of goods capable of reproduction gives a new significance to those scarce goods that cannot be supplied in greater numbers by increasing labour. Since Ricardo had produced the most coherent and detailed labour theory of value to date, those goods which were scarce because no labour could increase their quantity were exceptional not only to the laws of supply and demand in a general sense, as he understood them, but to the very foundation of his economic principles. 'Their value is wholly independent of the quantity of labour originally necessary to produce them, and varies with the varying wealth and inclinations of those who are desirous to possess them'.[65] Exceptional goods cannot be reproduced by labour in the quantities demanded but, as a consequence of this, are also set loose from labour as a measure of the values of goods in exchange. The resulting prices are set according to the contingencies of the competition between wealthy consumers and, therefore, such prices conform to no pattern or logic. Rare goods the quantities of which cannot be augmented by labour to match market demand cause 'competition amongst the purchasers [which depends] on their wealth, and their tastes and caprices'.[66]

---

64   Ricardo 1923, p. 3.
65   Ricardo 1923, p. 6.
66   Ricardo 1923, p. 165.

'Those peculiar wines', he says,

> which are produced in very limited quantity, and those works of art,
> which from their excellence or rarity, have acquired a fanciful value, will
> be exchanged for a very different quantity of the produce of ordinary
> labour, according as the society is rich or poor, as it possesses an abun-
> dance or scarcity of such produce, or as it may be in a rude or polished
> state. The exchangeable value therefore of a commodity which is at a
> monopoly price, is no where regulated by the cost of production.[67]

It goes without saying that scarce goods have a robust demand; goods that lack
demand are not counted as economically scarce. If it is only when the demand
of goods exceeds supply that they are counted as scarce, then there are two
possible economic consequences of scarcity: either supply is increased to meet
demand or a competition ensues between potential purchasers. The former is
standard, while the latter is exceptional. What is more, the former conforms
to Ricardo's labour theory of value while the latter does not. After spelling out
Smith's basic tenets of a labour theory of value, Ricardo says: 'That this is really
the foundation of the exchangeable value of all things, *excepting those which
cannot be increased by human industry*, is a doctrine of the utmost importance
in political economy'.[68] Ordinarily, in market exchanges, there is 'competition
among the sellers, as well as amongst the buyers',[69] Ricardo says, but there are
exceptions.

> This is not the case in the production of those rare wines, and those valu-
> able specimens of art, of which we have been speaking; their quantity
> cannot be increased, and their price is limited only by the extent of the
> power and will of the purchasers.[70]

Goods that 'cannot be increased by human industry' have prices that cannot
exchange according to the value of the labour required to reproduce them.[71]

The main armature of the theory of exceptionalism is assembled by 1817
through the combined and accumulated efforts of Smith, Say and Ricardo.
There are some goods that command unnaturally high prices that require an

---

67   Ibid.
68   Ibid (emphasis added).
69   Ibid.
70   Ibid.
71   Ibid.

explanation supplementary to the standard price theory. Smith outlines the key factors as the presence of a natural limit placed on supply that leads to competition among buyers, raising prices as high as the market can stand. Say adds manufactured goods to Smith's natural rarities and puts them all under the heading of monopoly prices, but also extends the discussion from rare goods to the rarity of talented producers. Ricardo reemphasises rare goods and returns to Smith's original formulation of exceptionalism only to refine it by putting the stress on the impossibility of augmenting supply through labour. None of the founders of the theory of economic exceptionalism argue that art, or other rare and unique goods, *ought* to be valued differently from ordinary commodities, that it is priceless or that 'the quid pro quo of a market transaction in art has destructive effects'.[72] On the contrary. Economic exceptionalism has a precise economic basis and is the result of strictly economic considerations based on the observation of anomalies to classical theory. None of these economists dwell for very long on the details and implications of economic exceptionalism, but each is satisfied that, once the exceptions are identified, the science of economics can proceed to study the ins and outs of standard price mechanisms. Like the concept of use value for the early classical economists, economic exceptionalism is referred to precisely in order to bracket it off as outside the purview of economic study. There is therefore a second level to art's economic exceptionalism. An economics of art is never fully developed within classical economics because art's prices and artistic labour do not help to explain and promote the laws of supply and demand on which economic science turned. However, it is in these passages on economic exceptionalism where art first becomes present in economics.

If, for Say and Ricardo, following Smith, artworks are commodities, they are not commodities like any other. In the decades to follow, the economic exceptionalism of art was refined but also rejected. In fact, the exceptionalism of economic exceptionalism was already called into question before Ricardo had given it its clearest account. Jean Charles Léonard Simonde de Sismondi did not theorise the exceptionalism of art and rare goods. Rather, he generalised exceptionalism's arbitrary monopoly prices as a normal but malignant result of industrial production. In this respect, Sismondi anticipates some aspects of the neoclassical and neoliberal argument that exceptionalism is outmoded in an oligopolistic economy. He originally published his *Nouveaux Principes d'Economie* in 1816, the year before Ricardo published his *Principles of Political Economy and Rent*. I did not include Sismondi's comments on economic exceptionalism within the period of the formation of the theory between 1774 and

---

72   Velthius 2007, p. 58.

1817 because Sismondi did not contribute to its formation. His commentary on the concept of economic exceptionalism is an expression of his resistance to industrialisation – he 'wanted to reverse the wheel of history and go back to the patriarchal economy of independent petty producers (craftsmen and peasants)'.[73] He extends the argument for 'monopoly' prices to market forces generally, describing the relation between big capital and small capital as a struggle that produces markets that tend to monopoly. However, the form and tone of his argument puts him closer to the Pre-Raphaelites and Romantic anti-capitalism than the theorists of 'perfect competition'. Sismondi is perturbed by the new class of 'proletarii', producing commodities on a mass scale, which 'encroaches on those kinds of business formerly known as master trades'.[74] Voicing the cause of master craftsmen, whose livelihoods were 'threatened with ruin',[75] Sismondi fails to theorise the economic exceptionalism of art and rare goods because he fears that industrialisation and its machinery are eroding their historical advantages. He speculates that an invention might be devised to overcome the limitations of climate and season. It appears to Sismondi that the natural limitations on supply which Smith identified with the high prices of wine from special vineyards in France might be completely overcome by modern methods of production, leading not only to the elimination of economic exceptionalism but also the traditions and ways of life of the artisan producer.

Combining Sismondi's arguments with those of Smith and Say, Thomas Malthus takes up the case of the French vineyard with its finite territory in his *Principles of Political Economy* from 1820. He provides an orthodox explanation of the high price of fine wine but, like Sismondi, speculates about a possible technological solution that would bring the exceptional case back in line with the standard price mechanisms of supply and demand.

> The produce of certain vineyards in France, which, from the peculiarity of their soil and situation, exclusively yield wine of a certain flavour, is sold, of course, at a price far exceeding the cost of production, including ordinary profits. And this is owing to the greatness of the competition for such wine, compared with the scantiness of its supply, which confines the use of it to so small a number of persons that they are able, and, rather than go without it, willing to give an excessively high price.[76]

---

73   Rubin 1979, p. 240.
74   Sismondi 1847, p. 198.
75   Sismondi 1847, p. 220.
76   Malthus 1836, p. 145.

While the price of such wine does not conform in a standard way to classical price theory – and is therefore exceptional – Malthus makes a proposal that suggests that the products of the special vineyards in France are not, in principle, permanently beyond the laws of supply and demand.

> But, if the fertility of these lands were increased so as very considerably to increase the produce, this produce might so fall in value as to diminish most essentially the excess of its price above the cost of production.[77]

Malthus does not appear to believe that such a solution to the economic exceptionalism of rare wine is imminently possible, but by speculating about it he implies that Smith's category of enhancements of price due to natural causes only appears to differ from monopoly prices generally because of a technical deficiency. Economic exceptionalism therefore appears to be permanent only under conditions of technological backwardness. Since the basis of economic exceptionalism is the impossibility to augment supply, Malthus overcomes the problem by imagining the unspecified means for increasing the fertility of the vineyard and thereby places it under the heading of monopoly by simply asking, 'but what if we could augment supply?' This is not an unreasonable question for an economist to ask, but the answer at least ought to include the possibility of the continued inability of the augmentation of supply for some period, or even the possibility that supply will never be able to match demand and therefore bring about an equilibrium price.

Malthus speculates also about the opposite scenario in which, instead of the prices of rare wine finding their equilibrium through science and technology increasing the fertility of vineyards, demand could escalate.

> The number of person, who might have a taste for scarce wines, and be desirous of entering into a competition for the purchase of them, might increase almost indefinitely, while the produce itself was decreasing; and its price, therefore, would have no other limit than the numbers, powers, and caprices of the competitors for it.[78]

As such, Malthus treats each element of Smith's example as a variable and examines the likely outcome of any of them changing independently of the others. What he does not do is reflect on the theoretical implications of the possibility of these variables not varying at all, that is to say, of the example

---

77   Ibid.
78   Malthus 1836, pp. 145–6.

as an anomaly to be explained with a supplementary non-standard theory of
the price of rare goods. What is more, Malthus appears to forget the case of
the special vineyard when he explains the concept of rent through the fertility
of land. First he observes that different parcels of land must be differentiated
according to their fertility. Then he argues that the fertility of a field can be
understood as 'its *power* of yielding a rent'.[79] After this, he asserts, 'no degree of
monopoly – no possible increase of external demand can essentially alter these
different *powers*'.[80] Malthus is right that no monopoly or extent of demand can
alter the fertility of a piece of land, except that Malthus himself argues that the
precious vineyard might increase the quantity of its supply to meet demand
through an increase in fertility, which, at least in part, would be brought about
as a response to demand. Notwithstanding this, Malthus is wrong if he believes
that therefore monopoly and the extent of demand cannot increase the rent of
the land or the price of the products of the land.

Malthus does not restrict himself to shaking the assumptions of Smith's
example of rare wines. He works over the recent debates on art, too. 'Superior
artists are paid high on account of the scanty supply of such skill, whether
occasioned by unusual labour or uncommon genius, or both',[81] Malthus says.
Here he follows Say rather than Ricardo, focusing on the rarity of labour rather
than the extraordinary high prices of unique artworks by old masters. Say had
spoken about both rare goods and rare labour, whereas Malthus does not give
a separate account of the prices of antiques, relics, paintings and sculptures.
What is more, Say chided Malthus for underestimating talent as a source of
wealth:

> What do you think of our talents? Do they not belong to the productive
> powers? Do we not draw revenues from them? Revenues more or less
> large in the same manner as we draw a greater revenue from an acre of
> good land than from an acre of heath? I know some admirable artists
> who have no other income than what they derive from their talents, and
> who yet live in opulence. According to you, they ought to be no richer
> than a dauber of signs.[82]

Not to be outdone, Malthus attempts to correct Say, who as we noted earlier had argued that one cannot accumulate immaterial products. Malthus

---

79   Malthus 1836, p. 141.
80   Ibid.
81   Malthus 1836, p. 221.
82   Say 1967, p. 81.

contends, on the contrary, 'it is quite impossible to deny that knowledge, talents, and personal qualities are capable of being accumulated'.[83] Malthus is right that such qualities can be accumulated but he is wrong that Say denied it. Say did not argue that knowledge and talent could not be accumulated; he argued that the immaterial products of knowledge and talent could not be accumulated. Malthus, therefore, despite all his efforts, contributed nothing new to the concept of economic exceptionalism or the economic analysis of art, though perhaps he is a pioneer of the conviction, common today among mainstream economists, that economic exceptionalism can be dissipated, overcome or normalised.

Nassau Senior, in his *Outline of the Science of Political Economy* from 1836, did not modify the principle of economic exceptionalism but added a significant new explanation for the exceptionalism of art.

> There are some commodities the results of agents no longer in existence, or acting at remote and uncertain periods, the supply of which cannot be increased, or cannot be reckoned upon. Antiques and relics belong to the first class, and all the very rare productions of Nature or Art, such as diamonds of extraordinary size, or pictures, or statues, of extraordinary beauty, to the second.[84]

The death of producers is a novel observation that adds to the list of empirical conditions under which classical economists understood the limitation of supply specific to economic exceptionalism. Since exceptionalism is based on the impossibility of augmenting the quantity of production through labour, Senior considers the economic effect of the death of certain producers whose production cannot be reproduced by others. However, something must be added to Senior's account of the death of the artist before it can rightly be considered as a condition for economic exceptionalism. The death of the artist must be economically significant. Abbing explains precisely the point that I have in mind: 'If the director of Shell dies today, tomorrow somebody will have taken his place; he is replaceable. But if Karel Appel dies, no more 'appels' will be produced'.[85] The death of the artist is only economically significant because of the Renaissance conception of art in which 'art is the creation of an autocratic personality [that is, the artist as genius]... based no longer on

---

83   Malthus 1836, p. 28.
84   Senior 1836, p. 169.
85   Abbing in Klamer 1996, p. 141.

an objective What but on a subjective How'.[86] A butcher or a plumber can pass on her skills and business to her children (hence, Jones & Son), but an artist after the Renaissance cannot. Death is therefore the equivalent in a certain kind of manufacturing to the natural limit of a vineyard in a certain kind of agriculture.

> The values of such commodities are subject to no definite rules, and depend altogether on the wealth and taste of the community. In common language they are said to bear a fancy price, that is, a price depending principally on the caprice or fashion of the day.[87]

Goods that bear a fancy price – a term that echoes Ricardo's phrase 'fanciful value' – are regarded by Senior as economically exceptional. This is why he says:

> In the following discussion we shall altogether omit such commodities, and confine our attention to those of which the supply is capable of increase, either regular, or sufficiently approaching to regularity, to admit of calculation.[88]

Standard goods, for Senior, are defined in terms that derive from exceptional ones, insofar as they also suffer from an obstacle to supply, namely the labour that produces it, and it is on this basis that he argues that the prices of standard goods express their costs of production.

While the circulation of artistic goods by dead artists is regarded by Senior as exceptional, he does not regard artistic labour as exceptional in any way. In fact, his introduction of the dead producer as a condition of economic exceptionalism can be accounted for in terms of his blindness to any exceptionalism in the work or sale of products by living artists.

> The means adopted by the painter and the actor are the same in kind. Each exercises his bodily organs, but the painter exercises them to distribute colours over a canvass, the actor to put himself into certain attitudes, and to utter certain sounds. The actor sells his exertions themselves. The painter sells not his exertions but the picture on which those exertions have been employed. The mode in which their exertions are

---

86   Hauser 1992, pp. 61–2.
87   Senior 1836, p. 169.
88   Ibid.

sold constitutes the only difference between the menial servants and the other labouring classes.[89]

Here Senior pays attention only to the modalities of labour – principally the difference between material labour, which produces a product, and immaterial labour, which does not (following the two arguments given by Smith in his definition of productive and unproductive labour). By focusing exclusively on the labour processes of artists, Senior fails to explain how living artists can fashion works that cost very little to produce and yet sell them for great sums. Presumably part of the reason why Senior neglects this exceptional aspect of artistic labour is that his conception of the economic exceptionalism of artworks is restricted to works resold in the secondary market.

Since he explains the high prices of artworks by drawing attention to the effects of the death of their producers, Senior does not appear to be able to account for the high prices of works by living artists. Nor is he consistently concerned with the rising prices of artworks. The sale of works by dead artists that fetch paltry sums is as exceptional to Senior as those that command exorbitant prices in comparison with their costs of production. By way of illustration, Senior suggests the following: 'The Boccaccio, which a few years ago sold for £2000, and after a year or two's interval for £700, may perhaps, in fifty years hence, be purchased for a shilling'.[90] This is odd because the price drops and drops, which is not exceptional in the terms set out by Smith, Say and Ricardo, as many standard second hand goods suffer the same fate in the marketplace. The point, typically, is to explain the opposite, that a painting by van Gogh, for example his portrait of Dr Gachet, might be worth a shilling in 1890, sell for 330 francs in 1897 and $82.5 million in 1990. However, Senior's point appears to be that no living artist could sustain himself or his practice by consistently selling paintings for a shilling, and yet the works of dead painters can exchange for consistently small amounts. So, while Senior's example of a Boccaccio selling for a shilling cannot be explained directly by Ricardo's labour theory of value, and is exceptional in that respect, this example blurs the boundary between exceptional and standard production because a commodity originally exchanged at an equilibrium or natural price can still, if resold, fetch values well below its original value. Hence, it is because of the specific way that Senior introduces the anomaly of the sales of artworks by dead artists to economic study, that he remains insensitive to the specific economic

---

89   Senior 1836, p. 150.
90   Senior 1836, p. 169.

circumstances of artistic labour and to the anomalous prices of artworks sold
by living artists.

Senior is alert to the semi-exceptionalism of works of art selling at vastly
reduced rates because of a conspicuous feature of artworks that distinguishes
them from standard commodities. Like Say, Senior observes that artworks are
not used up in their consumption.

> That almost all that is produced is destroyed is true; but we cannot admit
> that it is produced for the purpose of being destroyed. It is produced for
> the purpose of being made use of. Its destruction is an incident to its use,
> not only not intended, but, as far as possible, avoided. In fact, there are
> some things which seem unsusceptible of destruction except by acciden-
> tal injury. A statue in a gallery, or a medal, or a gem in a cabinet, may be
> preserved for centuries without apparent deterioration.[91]

Since 'the bulk of commodities are destroyed'[92] the case of artworks which
survive for very long periods while still being enjoyed – 'used' rather than 'consumed' in Senior's terminology – is anomalous, and this has economic consequences. While 'food and fuel, which perish in the very act of using them'[93]
must be sold at least at the cost of production in order for their producers
to subsist, goods that can be used without being consumed can be resold at
prices that are independent of their costs of production. The standard division
between consumable and durable goods is not sufficient to grasp the central
point that Senior makes here. Artworks are not simply durable goods, in the
sense that the use of them only consumes them over an extended period of
time. Artworks can be destroyed, they physically deteriorate and need to be
conserved, but unlike standard durable goods they do not materially depreci-
ate through the act of using them. Since Senior's particular version of the theory of economic exceptionalism focuses on the trade in works by dead artists,
the difference between artworks and standard durable goods is of particular
significance to him.

Distinguishing not between standard and exceptional goods but standard
and exceptional circumstances, Thomas De Quincey, in his book *The Logic
of Political Economy* (1845), said in 'ninety-nine cases out of a hundred'[94] it is
'difficulty of attainment' that determines price. In such standard circumstances,

---

91   Senior 1836, p. 151.
92   Ibid.
93   Ibid.
94   De Quincey 1863, p. 258.

he says, if a thing 'be, for your purposes, worth ten guineas, so that you would rather give ten guineas than lose it; yet, if the difficulty of producing it be only worth one guinea, one guinea is the price it will bear'.[95] Although his argument is sketchy and underdetermined, in the standard case of commodity exchange De Quincey follows classical doctrine by equating prices with costs of production. 'On the other hand, in the hundredth case', he says, 'we will suppose the circumstances reversed':

> You are in Lake Superior in a steamboat, making your way to an unsettled region 800 miles ahead of civilization, and consciously with no chance at all of purchasing any luxury whatsoever, little luxury or big luxury, for a space of ten years to come: one fellow-passenger, whom you will part with before sunset, has a powerful musical snuff-box; knowing by experience the power of such a toy over your own feelings, the magic with which at times it lulls your agitations of mind, you are vehemently desirous to purchase it. In the hour of leaving London you had forgot to do so, here is a final chance.[96]

The seller, De Quincey says, will not hear of the 'difficulty of attainment' as having 'any controlling power or mitigating agency'[97] in negotiations of price. So, although six guineas a piece in London or Paris, 'you pay sixty rather than lose it when the last knell of the clock has sounded which summons you to buy now or to forfeit for ever'.[98] So, De Quincey explains, whereas in the standard case, difficulty of attainment determines the price regardless of your personal higher estimation of its value, in the exceptional case, the situation is reversed, and the element which was active now becomes passive and the element which was passive now becomes active. He uses the analogy of a water pump in which two forces D and U are combined, so that when the 'practical compression of D being withdrawn, U springs up like water in a pump when released from the pressure of air'.[99] When 'difficulty of attainment (which here is the greatest possible viz., an impossibility)',[100] it 'creates, as it were, a perfect vacuum',[101] which causes the price to reach its highest limit.

---

95   Ibid.
96   Ibid.
97   Ibid.
98   De Quincey 1863, pp. 258–9.
99   De Quincey 1863, pp. 259–60.
100   De Quincey 1863, p. 260.
101   De Quincey 1863, p. 261.

Snuffboxes are not normally economically exceptional but in a remote location, far from the supply of snuffboxes, competition among suppliers is eliminated and therefore the price cannot be regulated by costs of production. De Quincey gives another example of an economically exceptional price of a snuffbox, in a footnote, in the form of an extended anecdote, in the style of a ghost story, in which a superior and gilded snuffbox that had once cost a thousand guineas could not find a buyer at any cost because of its history. This particular snuffbox Lord Nelson declined as a gift because 'this trinket was supposed to have caught in a fatal net of calamity all those whom it reached as proprietors'.[102] Here, again, a commodity that, in principle, can be supplied in increased quantities by labour in response to demand is, due to special circumstances, isolated from general supply and no longer subject to the laws of the market. In this instance, the 'perilous snuff-box'[103] becomes worthless despite its cost of production, charming qualities and expensive raw materials. An identical snuffbox might be worth a thousand guineas but this particular item does not belong to aggregate supply any more. Like a house that is impossible to sell because it was previously occupied by a serial killer, a commodity can be expelled from the market on an individual basis. No diminution in aggregate demand is necessary for the collapse of the price of such an individual item. And, perhaps, it is worth reminding ourselves of the similar situation that Senior highlights with his example of Boccaccio. Although Senior does not speak of an individual work by Boccaccio that dramatically sinks in value, the projected fall from grace of this individual artist is not connected to a general decline in the demand for artworks.

J.S. Mill, in his *Principles of Political Economy* from 1848, describes De Quincey's hypothetical example of buying a musical snuffbox in the wilderness as follows:

> This case, in which the value is wholly regulated by the necessities or desires of the purchaser, is the case of the strict and absolute monopoly; in which, the article being only obtainable from one person, he can exact any equivalent, short of the point at which no purchaser could be found.[104]

Mill regards De Quincey's example as illustrating one extreme of the relationship between demand and supply. The lowest limit is the cost of production, but 'the utility of a thing in the estimation of the purchaser, is the extreme

---

102   De Quincey 1863, p. 259.
103   Ibid.
104   Mill 1965, p. 464.

limit of its exchange value'.[105] The most that an individual will spend in order to consume a good is as high as the value of a commodity can ascend, he says. Ordinarily purchasers do not pay the highest value that they are willing to pay because 'peculiar circumstances are required to raise it so high'.[106] One such peculiar circumstance, according to Mill, is the case of the snuffbox on a steamboat in Lake Superior analysed by De Quincey. Mill agrees with De Quincey that the high price of the snuffbox remote from civilisation is determined entirely by the utility of the purchaser (and that the force of 'difficulty of attainment' is inert); but Mill adds the classic examples of economic exceptionalism:

> There are things of which it is physically impossible to increase the quantity beyond certain narrow limits. Such are those of wines which can be grown only in peculiar circumstances of soil, climate, and exposure. Such also are ancient sculptures; pictures by old masters; rare books or coins, or other articles of antiquarian curiosity.[107]

And, following De Quincey, Mill contrasts this with those products 'embracing the majority of all things that are bought and sold'[108] that can be attained through the expenditure of labour and capital.

Mill singles out 'things absolutely limited in quantity, such as ancient sculptures or pictures',[109] as not abiding by 'the Law of Value'.[110] 'Such commodities, no doubt, are exceptions',[111] Mill says. But, he goes on to say, 'the principle of the exception stretches wider, and embraces more cases, than might at first be supposed'.[112]

> There are but few commodities which are naturally and necessarily limited in supply. But any commodity whatever may be artificially so. Any commodity may be the subject of a monopoly: like tea, in this country, up to 1834; tobacco in France, opium in British India, at present. The price of a monopolized commodity is commonly supposed to be arbitrary; depending on the will of the monopolist, and limited only (as in Mr. De

---

105 Mill 1965, p. 462.
106 Ibid.
107 Ibid.
108 Mill 1965, p. 464.
109 Mill 1965, p. 465.
110 Mill 1965, p. 468.
111 Ibid.
112 Ibid.

Quincey's case of the musical box in the wilds of America) by the buyer's extreme estimate of its worth to himself.[113]

Mill, evidently, did not wish to divide economic exchange between standard cases and economically exceptional cases. Instead, he established a continuous gradient of patterns of exchange that altered with the conditions of supply and demand. Commodities of absolutely fixed supply were placed at one end, commodities with absolutely fixed demand at the other, with commodities produced in relation to varying supply and demand in the middle. It is in this context that Mill blurs the distinction between products that cannot be increased in number through labour and commodities that are restricted in supply for the express purpose of increasing their price. 'The monopolist can fix the value as high as he pleases, short of what the consumer either could not or would not pay; but he can only do so by limiting the supply'.[114] By suggesting that the monopolist actively limits supply, Mill plays down De Quincey's contribution (that limitations on supply can be geographical and relative as well as, for instance, geological and absolute), and plays up Say's conflation of economic exceptionalism with 'monopoly prices'.

With Mill the classical theory of economic exceptionalism comes to an end. Mill adds nothing to the theory and his version of it is a shadow of that which can be found in Ricardo and Senior. Even Smith's insights into the dual pressures of economically exceptional goods (that they cannot be supplied with the quantity demanded and therefore lead to competition among buyers), are superior to Mill's formulation. It is perhaps a reflection of the marginality of exceptionalism within classical doctrine that Mill's treatment of it can be so shoddy. No classical economist ever developed a coherent or substantial theory of economic exceptionalism and no debate was ever elaborated concerning differences of formulation. Classical economists consistently acknowledged that certain goods commanded unnatural prices and, although the list of such goods grew longer and expanded well beyond the natural rarities of Smith's original conception, the example of the French vineyard became a minor trope of the literature. Although Say's extension of the category of exceptional goods to include luxuries did a service to the debate, his classification of all varieties of price above value as a branch of monopoly was an error that has led to problems in distinguishing exceptionalism from other forms of limitation on self-regulated markets. However, he also develops for the first time a theory of immaterial labour that commands higher prices because of

---

113   Ibid.
114   Ibid.

the rarity of talented producers. Ricardo reasserts Smith's emphasis on the competition amongst buyers and adds that there is little or no competition among sellers for goods the quantity of which cannot be increased through labour. Senior coins the phrase 'fancy prices' to name the result of exceptionalism and extends Ricardo's observation of the impossibility of increasing supply through human industry by considering the economic consequences of the death of producers of antiques, relics, pictures and statues. Classical economists did not develop a comprehensive or coherent theory of economic exceptionalism. Nor did they use this phrase. For classicism, economic exceptionalism was nothing more than the observation that certain goods cannot be manufactured in the quantities demanded and that therefore prices cannot be regulated by the variation of supply in relation to demand. Whenever economists referred to art for almost two hundred years after 1770, they invariably took it that art was economically exceptional. But the development of a theory of exceptionalism, and therefore the possibility of an economic analysis of art as exceptional, was terminated at this stage by the displacement of classical economic doctrine by neoclassical economics. While the classical case for economic exceptionalism disappears within the new doctrine, the next chapter will examine the unacknowledged persistence of exceptionalism within neoclassical economics itself.

CHAPTER 3

Art and Exceptionalism in Neoclassical Economics

Classical economic doctrine was demoted from the pinnacle of the economic mainstream by the introduction of a new price theory in the 1870s that appeared to immunise economics from having to theorise economic exceptionalism. The new breed of economists, starting with Carl Wenger, Friedrich von Wieser and William Stanley Jevons, argued that prices are not determined by costs but utility, not supply but demand, and therefore are not objective but subjective. Two innovations in particular threaten the theory of economic exceptionalism inherited from classical theory. First, since prices are determined by utility according to neoclassical economics, there can be no distinction between natural and unnatural prices, as Smith understood those terms, and therefore the existence of 'fancy prices' or 'monopoly prices' appears not to be exceptional but standard. Second, the objective measure of value that is the basis of the standard price from which exceptional goods deviate, namely the labour theory of value, is replaced with a dynamic and incremental theory of price, known as marginalism, in which there is no standard price and therefore no exceptional price. The result is that neoclassical economists do not theorise economic exceptionalism; if art remains economically exceptional within neoclassicism itself, a new absent theory will have to be constructed from the material that excludes it.

Neoclassical economics is built around the principle of diminishing marginal utility, which was formulated by Friedrich von Wieser as follows:

> The value of commodities is derived wholly from their utility, but the utility they afford is not wholly convertible into value.... Nor ought it to be; the value should express, not the total utility, but only a part of it, 'the final degree of utility', as Jevons said, the 'marginal utility' (Grenznutzen) as we say.[1]

The value of a commodity, therefore, is determined by the benefit a consumer perceives to obtain from the last unit consumed. Alfred Marshall explains the principle behind marginal economics with a Pre-Raphaelite illustration:

---

1   Wieser 1891, p. 109.

© KONINKLIJKE BRILL NV, LEIDEN, 2015 | DOI 10.1163/9789004288157_005

> The simplest case of balance or equilibrium between desire and effort is found when a person satisfies one of his wants by his own direct work. When a boy picks blackberries for his own eating, the action of picking is probably itself pleasurable for a while; and for some time longer the pleasure of eating is more than enough to repay the trouble of picking. But after he has eaten a good deal, the desire for more diminishes...[2]

What is illustrated in this image is the constantly shifting and individual or subjective basis of value. This is summarised in Gossen's 'First Law' that states that an increase in the same kind of consumption yields pleasure continuously diminishing up to the point of satiety. Marginal utility initially increases in increments of diminishing magnitude and then, in principle, eventually decreases in increments of increasing magnitude. Wieser explains this curve of utility as follows:

> Assume that a man owns one good, and that the employment of it gives a utility equal to 10; and suppose that his holding gradually increases up to 11 goods, in the course of which the marginal utility decreases proportionally down to 0. The value of the stock at each point will be as follows:

Goods	1	2	3	4	5	6	7	8	9	10	11
	1×10	2×9	3×8	4×7	5×6	6×5	7×4	8×3	9×2	10×1	11×0
Utility	10	18	24	28	30	30	28	24	18	10	0

> *Here a regular decrease of the marginal utility, and, therefore, of the value of the single good, is seen to take place along with an increase of the supply, and further explanation is unnecessary. Each additional good brings with it a diminished increment of utility and must, therefore, bring only a diminished increment of value.*[3]

---

2   Marshall 1997, p. 147. De Quincey uses a similar example to illustrate a different theoretical point: 'In the vast forests of Canada, at intervals, wild strawberries may be gratuitously gathered by the ship-loads; yet such is the exhaustion of a stooping posture, and of a labour so monotonous, that everybody is soon glad to resign the service into mercenary hands' (De Quincey, 1863, p. 249).

3   Wieser 1893, pp. 27–8.

The commodity is only worth what the customer will pay to obtain one more increment of it, and therefore according to neoclassical theory prices are related not to some fixed measure of value but a changing scale of perceived utility.

It is because utility typically diminishes with increased units of a certain good that marginal theory is careful to link prices to quantities. 'There are some prices which no seller would accept, some which no one would refuse', Marshall says, in order to get to the nub of the question, namely that there 'are other intermediate prices which would be accepted for larger or smaller amounts by many or all of the sellers'.[4] The first unit of a particular commodity is said to yield more satisfaction, or utility, than subsequent units of the same commodity, reaching a point at which further units are perceived as worthless or even harmful. Marginal utility depends upon quantities already obtained. Since the utility of a commodity tends to diminish with increasing quantities of it, choices made by consumers are not based entirely on preference but also on relative values between different commodities. Roger Backhouse explains this with another fruit-based illustration:

> if an apple costs twice as much as a banana, the pleasure obtained from the last apple purchased must be twice as large as the pleasure of an additional banana. If it were less, the individual would give up an apple to get two extra bananas.[5]

Smith had illustrated classical price theory with the example of a beaver being worth two deer, saying that hunting beaver requires twice as much time as hunting deer. He says it is 'natural' that the produce of two days labour should be worth double that of the produce of one day's work. What the early marginalists want to add, here, is, first, that a household in possession of a beaver may regard a deer as worth more than an extra half beaver, and second, that the different consumers' preference for deer over beaver, perhaps, will increase the price of deer relative to beaver regardless of their respective labour costs. Marginalists object to the classical labour theory of value on the grounds that it is an 'essential corollary of this concept [that] value is unrelated to the subjective valuations which purchasers put upon a product'.[6] Steve Keen says, 'the neoclassical school argues that value, like beauty, is "in the eye of the beholder" – that utility is subjective, and that the price, even

---

4   Marshall 1997, p. 148.
5   Backhouse 2002, p. 169.
6   Keen 2011, p. 414.

in equilibrium, has to reflect the subjective value put upon the product by both the buyer and the seller'.[7]

Subjective value assessed at the margin is not only expressed in terms of quantities but also in terms of choices. Philip Wicksteed imagines a consumer choosing between possessing a book by Darwin or buying a Waterbury watch, or another consumer deciding whether to spend money on a fish supper or a cigar, and yet another asking: 'Do I prefer to *possess* a valuable picture or to *consume* so much a year in places at the opera?'[8] Such 'heterogeneous impulses and objects of desire or aversion which appeal to any individual',[9] he says, can be brought together on 'a general "scale of preferences" or "relative scale of estimates" on which all objects of desire or pursuit (positive or negative) find their place'.[10] Choices made at the margin are taken to be calculations, sometimes rough and sometimes irrational (Wicksteed talks about someone being in love with a house and therefore paying over the odds for it), of alternatives. 'If we secure this, how much of that must we pay for it, or what shall we sacrifice to it?' he says. The standard formula is given shortly afterwards: 'What alternatives shall we forgo?'[11] Value is tied up with subjective evaluations, as opposed to costs of production, through the concept of 'opportunity cost'. The doctrine of opportunity cost asserts that every choice has the hidden cost of opportunities not taken as a result of that choice. 'By devoting our efforts to any one task, we necessarily give up the opportunity of doing certain other things'.[12] These 'other things', that is to say *opportunities forgone*, are the 'costs' that result from choices. Costs can be pecuniary or non-pecuniary (spending a day in wage labour has the opportunity cost of spending the day with loved ones, and *vice versa*), but the doctrine introduces calculations that lead to the norm 'nothing is free', since, although it costs you no outlay to stay in bed all day, the opportunity cost is the amount you could have earned if you had chosen to work instead. The opportunity cost doctrine asserts that relative prices reflect foregone opportunities.

It is often said that the concept of opportunity cost is *implicit* within the writing of several early economists such as Johann Heinrich von Thünen,

7   Keen 2011, p. 415.
8   Wicksteed 1888, p. 137.
9   Wicksteed 1957, p. 32.
10   Wicksteed 1957, p. 33.
11   Wicksteed 1957, p. 21.
12   Green 1894, p. 222.

John Stuart Mill, Leon Walras and Adam Smith,[13] but the doctrine was not explicitly formulated before Friedrich von Wieser theorised 'alternative cost' between 1876 and 1914. Prices are nothing but the expression of opportunity costs, according to the Austrian School. Although, in many respects, Wicksteed's formulation of opportunity cost is less technically robust than Wieser's, James Buchanan regards it as more modern because it 'tied opportunity cost quite directly to choice'.[14] Between Wicksteed and Lionel Robbins, the most prominent advocate of the opportunity cost doctrine was H. Davenport, who formulated it in terms of 'displaced opportunity or foregone fact or sacrifice'.[15] So, the 'costs' of opportunity cost are not financial in any direct sense. For Wieser and the Austrian School, opportunity cost is not measured in money, but is, in fact, what money represents. This is why the doctrine can also be formulated thus: 'the unrealized flow of utility from the alternatives a choice displaces'.[16] 'The importance of the alternative cost doctrine to those who espoused it was that it demonstrated the fallacy of the "real cost" theories of value'.[17] After several decades of controversy, in which the Austrian subjective theory of cost competed with various objective theories of value,[18] mainstream economics has learned to incorporate the doctrine of opportunity cost into almost every variant of economic theory.

Despite the absence of an objective costs of production 'natural price', Wieser distinguishes between a 'natural monopoly' and a 'Cost Good', which

---

13   In a 'comment' on an article titled 'Opportunity Cost of Marriage' by Gary North, George Stigler states that North wrongly dates 'the beginning of the alternative cost theory as 1870. This date is wrong by at least a century: Smith used alternative cost routinely in 1776' (Stigler 1969, p. 863). James Buchanan, who was the greatest advocate of the opportunity cost doctrine in the second half of the twentieth century, confirms this by beginning his discussion of opportunity cost with a reference to Adam Smith's famous example of relative value (one beaver being exchanged for two deer) – see Buchanan 1999.

14   Buchanan 1969, p. 17.

15   Davenport 1968, p. 61.

16   Novemsky 2009, p. 553.

17   Blaug 1968, p. 492.

18   The dispute between the two schools had two phases, the first consisting of the rivalry between the original members of the Austrian school (Wieser, Böhm-Bawerk, Menger, Walras, Jevons) and the adherents of classical theory (principally Marshall at the time). In 1872 Marshall reviewed Jevons's book *Political Economy in the Academy*, in which he chastised the Austrian's 'marginal utility' theory as dressing up a well-known but minor point. This inaugurated a major and long-lasting debate. For an introduction to the issues within the dispute see Backhouse 2002, pp. 166–84. The second phase was played out principally by Gottfried Haberler and Jacob Viner. This dispute is reviewed by Jarolsav Vanek (See Vanek 1959).

divides economically exceptional goods from standard goods. The former includes:

> scarce raw materials, land exceptionally situated, the work of one peculiarly gifted – particularly an artist or scientific worker of the highest rank, – a secret and at the same time successful process, whereby the persons who have it obtain a preference over others, and, finally, works of human hands, which, on account of their size, or on account of technical difficulties, cannot be repeated.[19]

Wieser defines the latter as those 'goods easily accessible and abundant, or goods whose production can be indefinitely increased'.[20] Examples of the latter, for Wieser, include 'unskilled labour, coal, wood, the common metals, and also land devoted to industrial undertakings where there is no question of any particular advantage in situation'.[21] Wieser argues that the 'value of goods produced under monopoly must, by reason of their small available quantity, stand comparatively high'.[22] Appearing orthodox, Wieser lays out the basics of classical exceptionalism using arguments familiar since Smith, Say, Ricardo and Senior, but he is not satisfied with the classical price theory.

> Monopoly goods have often received a quite peculiar position in theory. Ricardo, for example, teaches that they owe their value altogether to their scarcity, while all other goods receive their value from the labour of producing them. A sufficiently wide consideration, however, shows that monopoly goods come altogether under the ordinary conditions of valuation, and differ from other economic goods only in that they display much more strikingly the character common to all.[23]

Utility is common to both, according to Wieser. And the difference between exceptional goods and cost goods, he argues, is that in the case of the latter only the marginal value counts, whereas in the former, 'they must, on any reasonable valuation, have ascribed to them the full value of the utility which is expected from them'.[24] Hence, he says, a 'starving man will value his last bite at

---

19   Wieser 1893, p. 108.
20   Ibid.
21   Ibid.
22   Wieser 1893, p. 109.
23   Wieser 1893, p. 110.
24   Wieser 1893, p. 22.

its full life-saving value',[25] and only a philistine 'could value the Venus de Milo by the utility of the material of which it is made'.[26]

Wieser overcomes or suppresses the question of economic exceptionalism precisely by diverting our attention to questions of the relative proportion of value of an article that can be attributed to its different factors. The standard example of the French vineyard is given a completely new treatment by Wieser as a result. 'What happens', he asks, 'when some expedient to reduce cost is introduced into a kind of production incapable of further extension – say, the production of wine in a limited area already cultivated to the utmost extent?'[27] It is clear that Wieser frames this question deliberately to sabotage the case for economic exceptionalism, first by introducing the 'expedient' of a technological factor that increases the productivity of labour (thereby reducing the proportion of value derived from the factor labour), and then by raising the possibility of the reduction of costs. Since Wieser argues that the value of wine derives from marginal utility, this reduction of cost does not affect the price of wine produced at all, but it has consequences for production generally (these reduced factors – capital and labour – 'can and will find another employment').[28] Wieser refuses to conclude that the price of the wine might fall as a result of the cost-saving expedient, but also remains silent about the possibility that the price of wine from such a restricted vineyard might be regulated differently from goods that can be reproduced in unlimited numbers to meet demand.

Wieser applies the analysis of factors to the high prices of artworks with the example of an artist making a pewter vessel. He supposes that the vessel commands great admiration because of its perfect form and suggests, for the purpose of the illustration, that the producer is the 'only artist'[29] capable of such fine work, which amplifies Say's theory of the exceptionalism of talented artistic labour. On top of this he adds that this is the only piece of pewter the artist has ever produced, and that no similar vessel has been produced in any other material (gold, silver, wood, clay), simultaneously exaggerating the classical assumption of the absence of competition in supply and reorienting De Quincey's single snuffbox towards the concept of the unique art object. Based on a typical classical example of economic exceptionalism, Wieser makes a neoclassical observation: under such conditions, Wieser says, it would be

---

25   Ibid.
26   Ibid.
27   Wieser 1893, p. 106.
28   Ibid.
29   Wieser 1893, p. 86.

'absolutely impossible to distinguish in the value of the vessel between the value of the labour and that of the material'.[30] We only value the artist's labour as high, Wieser points out, because we compare the value of this fine pewter vessel with other items made in the same material that 'have but a trifling value'.[31] We conclude, therefore, that the factor of the material contributes only a small portion of the value to the vessel and the artist's labour contributes the greatest part of its value. He appears to believe that differentiating the factors in it – material and labour – diffuses its apparent uniqueness because this allows us to compare this pewter artwork with more mundane pewter goods. But locating the difference in price between this pewter vessel and a standard pewter mug in the factor of the artist's labour does not minimise the disparity in prices or explain them.

Neoclassical economists argue that the high prices of artworks are proof that classical economists were wrong about labour being the only source of value. Jevons takes up the classical observation that there are 'high values' of certain goods (he makes his own selection from the familiar list: 'rare ancient books, coins, antiquities, etc.').[32] Like Say and Ricardo, Jevons does not restrict his list of exceptional goods to Smithian natural rarities and includes, among other things, artworks.

> There are some commodities the value of which is determined by their scarcity alone. No labour can increase the quantity of such goods, and therefore the value cannot be lowered by an increased supply. Some rare statues and pictures, scarce books and coins, wines of a peculiar quality, which can be made only from grapes grown on a particular soil, of which there is a very limited quantity, are all of this description.[33]

Rather than follow the established conclusion that such goods are therefore exceptional, he takes these high prices of articles by dead producers as proof that the classical theory was wrong in arguing that 'value depends on labour'.[34] This has since become a standard refutation of both classicism and exceptionalism. If value derives from labour, he muses, then why would the absence of labour bring about an escalation in price? Jevons's critique of the classical labour theory of value is based on a very tendentious reading of it. 'Some economists', he says, believe that 'the labour spent on [gold] is the cause of the

---

30   Ibid.
31   Wieser 1893, p. 87.
32   Jevons 1888, p. 162.
33   Jevons 1888, pp. 162–3.
34   Jevons 1888, p. 163.

high value'. He proves that this is wrong with the example of the work that goes into a book: 'Great labour may be expended in writing, painting and binding a book; but, if nobody wants the book, it is valueless, except as waste paper'.[35] No classical economists ever claimed that commodities derived value from labour even when there is no demand for the product. Jevons chooses examples that are neither standard cases of the labour theory of value nor insightful anomalies indicating the failures of the theory. 'When a shepherd in Australia happens to pick up a nugget of gold on the mountain side', he says, 'it takes no labour worth mentioning to pick it up, yet the gold is just as valuable in proportion to its weight as any other gold'.[36]

No classical economists believed that gold nuggets that are found ought to be given away for free or that slower work was or ought to be paid more than efficient work. The price of a gold nugget, for classical economics, is determined not by the actual individual and contingent amount of labour that happened to go into obtaining it, but by the average social labour *necessary* to obtain or reproduce it. Regardless of the fact that the formula for the labour theory of value found in Smith and Ricardo can be improved, no classical economist had such a foolish working definition of it to be vulnerable to Jevons's critique. Typically, early neoclassical economists wage their campaign against the labour theory of value by referring to valuable goods that are harvested rather than produced, such as the Australian gold nugget. Another example along these lines is given by Jevons to draw the debate to a close. He asks, 'Do men dive for pearls because pearls fetch a high price, or do pearls fetch a high price because men dive in order to get them?'[37] After conceding that pearl diving is hazardous and time-consuming, Jevons presents a two-pronged proof that the value of pearls is not derived from the labour that goes into delivering them from the sea to the jewellery shop. First, he suggests, 'if it were merely a question of labour, a diver might go down anywhere, and, bringing up the first stone or shell he found, insist on selling it for a high price, because he had dived for it'.[38] That is to say, Jevons challenges the 'difficulty of attainment' theory by proposing a method of acquisition that is not so difficult for goods that nobody wants. Goods with no demand command no exchange value, just as goods produced with more than the labour *necessary* to produce them will not command more than goods produced only using up the necessary quantity of labour. Second, Jevons asserts the following: 'The truth is, that pearls are valuable because there are many

35   Jevons 2005, p. 101.
36   Ibid.
37   Jevons 2005, p. 102.
38   Jevons 2005, p. 103.

ladies who have not got pearl necklaces, and who would like to have them; and those who have some pearls would like to get more and finer ones'.[39] In saying this Jevons does not introduce utility, or use value, to economics. Demand and therefore use value was an essential precondition for exchange, as all classical economists knew.

Wicksteed refined the economic calculus of utility, but his argument against the labour theory of value was no more subtle, studious or satisfactory than Jevons's. Wicksteed suggests, kindly, that the 'delusion' of the theory that labour is the source of value is a reversal of causation; it is not that more labour leads to higher prices but that goods which have more utility will be granted more labour. He argues, also, that the labour theory of value must be false because it cannot explain why, if customers want article A twice as much as article B, they will be willing to pay twice as much for A than B even if twice as much labour has been used up in the production of article B. 'Surely you cannot maintain that it *always happens* that the thing that people want twice as much needs exactly twice as much "labour" to produce as the other?'[40] Wicksteed muddles things up here. First, the labour theory of value is not a labour theory of price. Second, if people want milk twice as much as butter, it does not follow that milk will cost twice as much as butter. Third, it would be wrong to assume that prices are set by willingness to pay alone. Fourth, Wicksteed goes on to outline the process by which the quantities of A and B will be adjusted (by producers favouring A over B) until 'both be made in such quantities as to preserve the equilibrium',[41] which eliminates his problem and leaves unanswered the question of the relationship between labour and value. Wicksteed also asks us to puzzle over the example of a single article made for special use that costs considerably more than the labour would command 'generally'. This is an example of economic exceptionalism that Wicksteed challenges the labour theory of value to explain.

Neither Jevons nor Wicksteed produce their critique of the labour theory of value from an analysis of what classical economists actually wrote, or even from the structure of the argument itself. Knowing that classical economics sets aside certain goods as economically exceptional, it is dubious to construct an argument against it entirely by showing that those exceptions cannot be explained through the labour theory of value, as Wicksteed does. The irony is lost, of course, because neoclassical doctrine rejects exceptionalism in the same breath as it rejects the labour theory of value. Mark Blaug ties the 'new theory' to the eradication of the exceptionalist argument, explaining the

---

39   Ibid.

40   Wicksteed 1888, p. 118.

41   Ibid.

superiority of neoclassical economics over its predecessor directly in terms of the elimination of the problem of exceptionalism. 'The new theory', he says, 'encompassed both reproducible and nonreproducible goods'.[42] Buchanan makes the same point:

> Classical analysis was rejected because it contained two separate models, one for reproducible goods, and another for goods in fixed supply. The solution was to claim generality for the single model of exchange value that the classical writers had reserved for the second category. Exchange value is, in all cases, said the marginal-utility theorists, determined by marginal utility, by demand.[43]

Blaug, Buchanan and neoclassical economists in general focus on the apparent consequence that the so-called marginal revolution 'achieved greater generality and economy of argument explaining both factor and product prices on the basis of a single principle'.[44]

Let us examine the basis of this apparently superior theory more closely. The origin for the 'two theories' theory can be traced to Friedrich von Wieser who, in 1889, in the preface to his book *Natural Value*, chastises Smith for giving two theories of value, one philosophical and one empirical. Blaug articulates the distinction between the 'two theories of value' in terms of the difference between industrial goods, on the one hand, which he says were understood in terms of costs of production and the labour theory of value, and the prices of agricultural goods, on the other hand, which Blaug tells us, Ricardo said were affected by the scale of output. He calls this the 'fatal indeterminacy' of classical economics. Both Buchanan and Blaug agree that classical economists have both a supply theory and a demand theory of value, which contradict one another, but the question of whether these two theories are coterminous with the distinction between reproducible and irreproducible goods, or standard and exceptional pricing, is asserted rather than established. The two models that Blaug attends to here are not two competing theories of price, but one theory of price and a separate theory of rent. The distinction between price and rent in classical economics does not coincide with a second difference, that between reproducible and non-reproducible goods. The second distinction, between reproducible and non-reproducible goods, corresponds to the distinction between standard and exceptional goods in classical economics, not the distinction between industry and agriculture, or price and

---

42   Blaug 1969, p. 303.
43   Buchanan 1969, p. 9.
44   Blaug 1969, p. 303.

rent. Neoclassical economics 'resolves' the apparent 'fatal indeterminacy'[45] between price and rent by expanding the classical theory of differential rent to all cases of price formation. Lopping off one of two contenders for a theory is not quite the *aufheben* of Hegelian dialectic, but this resolution of the alleged great internal inconsistency of classical economics is presented as the sign of a superior system. Marginal utility, however, drew directly from classical economics, founding the new theory on a generalisation of the classical analysis of differential rent.[46] Blaug is very clear about this: 'The theory of differential rent is formally identical with the marginal productivity theory, though the marginal increments considered were enormously large instead of being negligibly small, as marginal analysis requires'.[47] He confirms this by saying that 'Ricardo's differential rent theory was generalized to all non-transferable resources, while the postulate that value is determined by production under "the least favorable circumstances"[48] was made the basis for the determination of all prices'.[49]

Wicksteed does not distinguish between goods that are reproducible and goods that are not, nor does he concern himself with goods that sell at higher prices than their 'natural price'. Nevertheless, he makes a passing reference to the concept of 'fancy prices' in discussing the differential pricing structure of water from a medicinal spring. He speculates that 'men of enormous wealth' might pay £50 for a quart, while people with a modest income might value the water 'at not more than ten shillings a quart'.[50] The former he calls fancy prices, but this is not exceptional in a differentiated market. The same principle is discovered to be at work in the theatre. Stalls fetch higher prices than the pit seats and so customers who value the experience of the play according to their own personal utility and pocket, can pay different prices for it.[51] What Wicksteed calls the 'double price' system is also illustrated in 'differential charges of railway companies',[52] the obscure instance of milk being charged at differential rates in London in the nineteenth century 'according to the average

---

45   Ibid.
46   The theory of differential rent is developed simultaneously and independently in 1815 by West, Torrens, Malthus and Ricardo in relation to the 'law of diminishing returns'.
47   Blaug 1969, p. 83.
48   In Ricardian differential rent theory, levels of ground rent are determined by the prices of agricultural goods required for the least fertile land to service average profit, while all land that is more fertile enjoys higher than average profits.
49   Blaug 1969, p. 303.
50   Wicksteed 1888, p. 94.
51   Wicksteed 1888, pp. 107–11.
52   Wicksteed 1888, p. 106.

status (estimated by house rent) of the inhabitants of each street',[53] and the
'case of "reduced terms" at boarding school'.[54] Wicksteed explains the economic rationality of 'reduced rates' in the example of a school that is not full.
In such instances, he says, 'the "reduced" pupils do something towards helping
things along'.[55] Perhaps conscious of the problem of economic exceptionalism, Wicksteed is keen to head off the notion that the higher prices of a double
price system are 'unnaturally high'.[56] He attempts to overcome the perception
of 'fancy prices' here by saying, 'unless some one pays as high as that the ware
cannot be brought into the market at all'.[57] And he even suggests that the seller
who manages to sustain a double price scheme is 'a kind of commercial Robin
Hood, forcing up the price for one class of customers above the level at which
they would naturally[58] be able to obtain their goods, and then lowering it for
others below the paying line'.[59]

Wicksteed says, 'sale by auction is an attempt to escape the law of
indifference',[60] explaining this through the example of a sale of ten old master
paintings. The auctioneer's 'skill consists in getting the man who is most keen[61]
for a specimen to give his full price for the first sold'.[62] When the bidder who
is willing to pay the highest price is satisfied, the auctioneer 'tries to make the
next man give his outside price; and so on'.[63]

---

53   Wicksteed 1888, p. 104.
54   Wicksteed 1888, p. 108.
55   Ibid. That is to say, from the point of view of marginal theory, reduced fees or scholarships
      should not be seen as a net reduction of income, but as a net increase in income, if there
      is not sufficient demand for those places at the full rate. At the same time, the full fee pay-
      ing pupils, for Wicksteed, should neither be thought to be paying over-the-odds, or in fact
      the correct price, but as the price that matches their demand.
56   Wicksteed 1888, p. 106.
57   Wicksteed, 1880, p. 305.
58   The use of the term 'naturally', here, just two sentences after claiming that high-priced
      customers do not pay an 'unnaturally high price', indicates a tension that Wicksteed's
      argument fails to resolve.
59   Wicksteed 1888. p. 307.
60   Wicksteed 1888, p. 102.
61   The description of 'most keen' strikes a false note. Enthusiasm for the work is conflated
      with enthusiasm to purchase it and both are foregrounded while ability to pay is subdued,
      in order to stress the subjective valuation of the work and the basis of prices in marginal
      utility.
62   Wicksteed 1888, p. 102.
63   Ibid.

The bidders...if cool enough, try to form a rough estimate of the marginal utility of the picture, that is to say, of the price which the tenth man will give for a picture when the nine keenest bidders are disposed of, and they know that if they steadily refuse to go above this point there will be one for each of them at that price.[64]

The crucial point, that it is the auction process, not the artwork, that is economically exceptional, is stated immediately after this: 'When the things on sale are such as can be readily got elsewhere, the auctioneer is powerless to evade the law of indifference'.[65] What Wicksteed studiously avoids, of course, is the question of whether, in cases where the things on sale cannot be readily got elsewhere, such goods are economically exceptional.

For neoclassicism, value is independent of labour and costs of production, because the absence of labour to reproduce the antique, work of art and so forth does not result in the absence of value. However, what is neglected in the neoclassical dismissal of economic exceptionalism is the specific role of the absence of labour in the pumping up of the prices of rare and unique goods. Fancy goods are overpriced, according to classical economists, not just because of the *fact* of the absence of labour but because of the *effect* of that absence, namely the impossibility of increasing supply to meet demand. Ricardo had argued that the value of a good depends on the quantity of labour *necessary* to produce it, which should not be conflated with the quantity of labour *actually* used up in its production, or with the labour exerted in the production of products that are non-substitutable, since *necessary labour* can only refer to substitutable labour producing substitutable commodities. Goods that are unique or rare, for which there are no substitutes or for which no labour can produce such substitutes, are not the outcome of substitutable labour. As such, no necessary labour – the quantity of substitutable labour that determines the value of the commodity – can be drawn on to augment supply. What separates the actual quantity of labour used to produce a product and the necessary quantity of labour to produce it, is that the latter refers to what is required to reproduce the good. The absence of labour has the effect of raising prices in the case of exceptional goods precisely because they cannot be reproduced. Strictly speaking, in Ricardo's terms, unique goods that cannot be reproduced have no value at all since value is measured by a quantity that cannot be applied to them. The high prices of artworks and other rare goods is not a reflection of their high value – the quantity of necessary labour required to

---

64   Ibid.
65   Wicksteed 1888, p. 103.

reproduce them. The classical labour theory of value does not apply to works of art, antiques, rare books and other fancy goods. Price is not determined by value in such cases. And this is what is exceptional about them. Neoclassical economists have consistently misinterpreted the labour theory of value since the inauguration of marginal theory and this has led to a sequence of muddled critiques of economic exceptionalism.

Neoclassical economics permits of no economic exceptions of the classical type. Consequently, neoclassical economists tell us, economic exceptionalism belongs to the past of classical doctrine. For neoclassicists, economic exceptionalism is nothing but the result of internal inconsistencies within classical price theory. Once the labour theory of value is jettisoned, it seems, there are no grounds for exceptionalism. It would make a neat story if we could say that the theory of art's economic exceptionalism was confined to the cost of production theory of classical economics and is subsequently ousted by the marginal utility theory of neoclassicism. It must be obvious that any attempt to sustain the case for economic exceptionalism without adjusting its terms of reference for the new theory would be hugely naïve. It is not only the classical formula for exceptionalism that is rejected. Since the classical formula for economic exceptionalism cannot be carried over to neoclassicism, it is assumed that exceptionalism itself has no place within economics after the marginal revolution. Rather than asking whether classical economic exceptionalism persists within neoclassical economics, we need to ask whether there is a case for economic exceptionalism within marginalism itself. The inquiry into neoclassical exceptionalism has to be made independently of the case for classical economic exceptionalism. If artworks and other rare or unique goods remain economically exceptional within the terms of neoclassical economics, then a new formula will have to be developed. Neoclassical economists have not attempted to do so. The rest of this chapter is devoted to the development of a neoclassical formula for economic exceptionalism.

There are some promising candidates within the literature of neoclassical economists. We have already noted, in Chapter One, for instance, that the production of artworks (exemplified but not restricted to paintings and sculptures) differ from standard commodity production by not being perfect substitutes for one another. This absence of substitution in artworks is not to be confused with the standard neoclassical account of elastic and inelastic demand, in which 'goods with close substitutes tend to have more elastic demand because it is easier for consumers to switch from that good to another'.[66] This principle distinguishes between eggs and butter, there being

---

66   Mankiw 2004, p. 90.

no substitute for eggs, but margarine and spreads offer substitutes for butter. However, it is clear that one egg is a perfect substitute for another, just as one pat of butter or margarine is a perfect substitute for another. Mankiw says 'a more narrow category has a more elastic demand... [while] a very narrow category has a very elastic demand'.[67] As such, we need to consider the substitutability of art as such (that is to say, either arguing that art has no substitutes, or that, for instance, popular culture, design[68] or architecture is a substitute for art), and the substitutability of individual artworks, as well perhaps as the substitutability of genres, schools, mediums and so forth. Given, also, that necessities tend to have inelastic demand (consumers purchase them even when prices rise) and luxuries tend to have elastic demand, art would appear to have an elastic demand. However, art would have an inelastic demand if art as such has no substitutes. If purchasers of art substitute art collecting with the collection of design or architecture, then demand for it is elastic, while in the case of an individual artwork, insofar as it is unique and therefore has no substitutes, demand for the work is inelastic. All the mobility within the theory of demand elasticity – shifting between broad and narrow categories, as well as different conceptions of substitution – gives the impression that there must be one kind of demand or another. Neoclassical economists, and especially neoliberal ones, tend to overstate the universality of the price mechanism and the applicability of their own modes of calculation. Anthropologists, on the contrary, are typically more discriminating in their analysis of different kinds of value and different social mechanisms of exchange.

Jacques Maquet, whose anthropology includes the specific study of art and aesthetics, divides art off from the commodity analytically but does so not in order to keep the two kinds of object apart empirically but specifically to trace the metamorphosis between the two. Some objects are intended for exchange as commodities, others are turned into commodities despite originally being produced with entirely different uses in mind, and finally, some objects are originally intended to be commodities but are retrieved from market exchange. Maquet speaks of certain products that are conscientiously protected from market forces and of the processes by which protection is maintained or lost. Nelson Graburn, a leading anthropologist of traditional arts and 'ethnic tourist art', has written extensively about the encounter between traditional ethnic

---

67   Mankiw 2004, p. 91.
68   At a meeting between Charles Esche (the Director of the Van Abbe Museum), and a community of designers, it was suggested by one of the designers that design is for the twenty-first century what art was for the twentieth, and therefore that art has become obsolete at precisely the moment at which design has become essential.

arts and the market, meticulously documenting the difference between several types of transition that take place as a result, including extinction, reintegration, assimilation and commercialisation.[69] Igor Kopytoff drives an analytical wedge between 'singular' and 'homogeneous' products, in which a unique object contrasts with a standardised commodity. 'In every society', Kopytoff says, 'there are things that are publicly precluded from being commoditized', including 'public lands, monuments, state art collections, the paraphernalia of political power, royal residences, chiefly insignia, ritual objects, and so on'.[70] In direct contrast with economics, he says, in no society 'is everything a commodity and exchangeable for everything else within a unitary sphere of exchange'.[71] Art, religion and state garb are linked by Kopytoff with 'heirlooms and old slippers'[72] in a conception of the non-commodity that is at once sacred and mundane. 'To be a non-commodity is to be "priceless" in the full possible sense of the term, ranging from the uniquely valuable to the uniquely worthless'.[73] The key to the non-commodity, he argues, is that 'commodities must be not only produced materially as things, but also culturally marked as being a certain kind of thing'.[74] C.A. Gregory distinguishes between commodities, goods and gifts,[75] originally differentiating the first two according to the division between the classical economic concept of the commodity and the neoclassical concept of a good, and distinguishing them both from the anthropological concept of the gift. In his reconsideration of the difference between the three, Gregory has developed his own alternative theory of goods in opposition to the neoclassical definition. While 'classical political economy has a highly developed labour theory of *commodities*, it has no theory of *goods*', he says, 'neoclassical economics, by way of contrast, has a utility theory of goods but no theory of the commodity'.[76] For Gregory 'a good is a priceless non-commodity'[77] and the difference between a good and a gift is that the former are *kept*.

Without perfect substitution of individual artworks, several key elements of neoclassical doctrine must misfire in the case of art. Since marginalism is based on incremental units of goods, the consumption of unique artworks is

69   See Graburn 1976.
70   Kopytoff in Appadurai 1986, p. 73.
71   Kopytoff in Appadurai 1986, p. 70.
72   Kopytoff in Appadurai 1986, p. 80.
73   Kopytoff in Appadurai 1986, p. 75.
74   Kopytoff in Appadurai 1986, p. 64.
75   Gregory 1997, p. 10.
76   Gregory 1997, p. 127.
77   Gregory 1997, p. 79.

not covered by the standard theory, and this discrepancy could be promising for a neoclassical theory of economic exceptionalism of art. Also, the neoclassical linking of prices to quantities will more than likely apply differently to art than to industrial production and therefore is worth examining more closely, to see if art is economically exceptional specifically in relation to neoclassical price theory. What is more, the theory of decreasing marginal utility needs to be revisited with the consumption patterns of art in mind and art may be exceptional with regard to this neoclassical doctrine, too. Additionally, after outlining the various key components of a neoclassical theory of exceptionalism, I will consider whether artistic production conforms to the doctrine of consumer sovereignty, and if it does not, then the relationship between producer and consumer, and supply and demand, may well vary considerably from that assumed by neoclassical economics.

The indexing of prices to quantities, which is one of the pillars of neoclassical price theory, is a weakness when considering unique articles. Unique commodities were exceptional to classical economics because they prevented competition among producers and could not be equivalents to other goods requiring the same quantity of necessary labour; but unique articles are exceptional to neoclassicism because the prices of one-offs cannot be determined in relation to marginal quantities. No neoclassical equilibrium price can be determined in the absence of perfect substitutes. One does not relate to the unique artwork in the way that Marshall's pre-Raphaelite boy related to blackberries. After consuming the work, there is no other work, no additional unit of consumption, and no incremental increase. Unique objects like artworks 'exhibit an all-or-nothing character on the supply side (supply is either one or nothing)', according to De Marchi, which has the striking consequence that 'there is no final degree of utility. No demand curve, therefore, can be drawn, and certainly not one undergirded by marginal utility thinking'.[78] When the article in question is a unique object, its use of it is indivisible. So it is impossible, strictly speaking, for neoclassical economics to understand the utility of a unique object. We must note that this exception is a new kind of exception.

A rough kind of quantification can be introduced, possibly, by referring for instance to the demand for Cindy Sherman photographs in general, or for specific examples of her 'Untitled Film Stills' series rather than this or that one. Even more generally we might refer to the demand for contemporary photography as a category. However, since no more 'Untitled Film Stills' are being produced and all the existing works within this series are already in the possession of collectors and institutions, the quantities in existence are not to be

---

78   De Marchi and Goodwin 1999, p. 3.

considered as supply. Such works arrive on the market infrequently and in small numbers, usually one at a time. It is therefore of no consequence that twenty collectors are willing to pay $100,000 for one, while another thirty are willing to pay $150,000 per print, if there is only one available and one person is happy to spend $160,000. The problem is not restricted to the auction houses. So long as the number of potential collectors of Cindy Sherman's current work exceeds the number of works produced, then prices will not be set according to neoclassical equilibrium theory. What is more, the commercial gallery system does not function like a standard market, such that many potential clients will not be permitted to collect Sherman's work if her dealer regards their collections as unsuitable or unworthy. There is a waiting list for the most successful commercial contemporary artists and a very limited supply because nobody else can produce Cindy Sherman works.

There is another reason why diminishing marginal utility is inapplicable to an analysis of the consumption and pricing of art. Marshall explains that 'the more good music a man hears, the stronger is his taste for it likely to become'.[79] Neoclassical price theory assumes that satisfaction *diminishes* with the consumption of additional units of the same article, but this is not true for art. Not only are there no additional units of Dexter Dalwood's 2001 painting 'Situationist Apartment May '68', or Ulay and Abramović's 1977 performance 'Imponderabilia', but the satisfaction of experiencing such works does not diminish through the consumption of them. On the contrary, the more an individual engages with art, typically, the more satisfaction they derive from it. This is not only true of art in general – that learning to appreciate art through a limited number of specific works permits the viewer to experience other examples with greater facility, but also that returning to the same work time and time again can generate different and more subtle experiences of it. In the case of standard commodities, Jevons says, 'the degree of utility varies with the quantity of commodity, and ultimately decreases as that quantity increases'.[80] But with goods such as music and art, consumption leads to ever more satisfaction in further consumption. It cannot be assumed that the first novel one reads gives more satisfaction than the tenth or the hundredth or the thousandth. Nor can it be assumed that there is more pleasure in reading a novel for the first time than in re-reading it subsequently. Pleasure in culture increases with additional quantities consumed. The curve does not dip but soars or flies up. If looking at art, listening to music, visiting the theatre and reading literature is the kind of experience in which satisfaction, pleasure and

---

79   Marshall 1997, p. 94.
80   Jevons 1888, p. 53.

critical acumen accumulates, then it is not true of it that 'the last increment is small' or tends towards zero. In art, by contrast, *the last increment tends to be higher than all previous increments.* Wieser is aware that the art collector does not consume according to the standard pattern of diminishing marginal utility. Wieser observes that collectors of books or pictures have an insatiable thirst. 'Every new [item] he acquires serves to stimulate instead of weaken his desire',[81] Wieser says. Wicksteed captures the sense of this exceptionalism in ironically orthodox terms, claiming that a picture yields 'a revenue of enjoyment'.[82] Rather than explore the implications of the evidence of these anomalies, most neoclassical economists continue to peddle the standard doctrine with regard to the decreasing marginal utility without exception. 'No commodity can be named which we continue to desire with the same force, whatever be the quantity already in use or possession',[83] Jevons says, in absolute denial of the *increasing marginal utility* of art, music, literature and so on. Wieser also suppresses the exception, not with a formal condition but an unwarranted assertion. 'Nothing on earth is of such a nature', Wieser says, 'that man can go on enjoying it over and over again, and lose himself in its contemplation'.[84] The doctrine of diminishing marginal utility is so vivid to Wieser, it seems, that it has come to determine his expectations of what the world is like.

Marshall observes that the taste for good music increases the utility of it, but he argues that such increases in utility do not count as exceptions. 'There is however an implicit condition in this law which should be made clear', he says. 'It is that we do not suppose time to be allowed for any alteration in the character or tastes of the man himself'.[85] The law of diminishing marginal utility remains unsullied and art's economic exceptionalism can be denied, according to Marshall, so long as the law is expressed with the assumption that tastes remain constant. The law only stands, therefore, so long as the exceptions to it are excluded in the small print. We can have no objection to scientific laws being formulated with such precision that they require conditions, but if such conditions are prejudicial with regard to the empirical evidence, then the law is likely to be unrealistic. Marshall's condition is not merely a variant on the *exceptis excepiendis* clause used in logical construction; it is a deliberate attempt to set the rules under which the world conforms to the law itself. In other words, there is no exception because the law assumes there is no

81   Wieser 1893, p. 10.

82   Wicksteed 1957, p. 301.

83   Jevons 1888, p. 53.

84   Wieser 1893, p. 10.

85   Marshall 1997, p. 94.

exception, despite empirical evidence that such exceptions exist. Anticipating an exception, however, does not do away with it. What is worse, Marshall's 'implicit condition' is anathema to cultural and aesthetic experience. So long as the law of diminishing marginal utility must contain this condition then it is a law that does not apply to the consumption, production and pricing of art. Presumably, it is some perception of this difficulty that led George Stigler and Gary Becker, in their now classic 1977 essay 'De Gustibus Non Est Disputandum', to argue that Marshall's condition for the exclusion of changing tastes from the law of diminishing marginal utility is unnecessary. The increased demand for good music by virtue of being exposed to it, they argue, is better understood not in terms of changing tastes but as the accumulation of 'music capital' and therefore a reduction in the 'costs' of consuming music. Advertising, likewise, is understood by Stigler and Becker not as aiming to transform the taste of the consumer but as reducing the information costs of purchasing goods, thereby making it more likely that the consumer will purchase the advertised good. However, Stigler and Becker drop the specific difficulty of consuming 'good music' in favour of the effects of advertising, addiction, habit and tradition. As a result they restrict their account to the more standard examples of someone who habitually eats cornflakes for breakfast being more likely to eat cornflakes for breakfast in the future, and therefore fail to explain the specific increasing marginal utility of art.

Stigler and Becker's essay on economics and taste appears routinely on bibliographies and in footnotes to mainstream economic discussions of art. The essay came out of the Chicago School at a time when the neoliberal economic programme was gaining influence and confidence.

> The ambitiousness of our agenda deserves emphasis: we are proposing the hypothesis that widespread and/or persistent human behaviour can be explained by a generalized calculus of utility-maximizing behaviour, without introducing the qualification 'tastes remaining the same'.[86]

Stigler and Becker make a paradoxical claim that Marshall's observation (namely, that the marginal utility of art, culture and heroin 'rise over time because tastes shift in their favor') 'can be explained with some gain in insight by assuming constant tastes'.

---

86   Stigler and Becker 1977, p. 76.

> We take categories of behaviour commonly held to demonstrate changes in tastes or to be explicable only in terms of such changes, and show both that they are reconcilable without assumptions of stable preferences, and that the reformulation is illuminating.[87]

Their assault on the Marshallian intuition that diminishing marginal utility does not strictly apply to the consumption of music, art and so on, is based on 'a recent reformulation of consumer theory' (co-authored by Robert Michael and Becker himself). What Becker and his collaborators claim is that consumption had previously been understood in terms of commodities purchased for utility without factoring in the productive activity of consumption that is added to the goods in any adequate process of consumption. Consumers buy commodities but then go on to consume them only by drawing on 'their own time, their own skills, training and other human capital'. Or, that 'the marginal utility of time allocated to music is increased by an increase in the stock of music capital'.[88] What Stigler and Becker hope to achieve here is the displacement of the exceptionalism of music – and by extension art – by shifting the burden of explanation from output (conventionally understood in terms of utility) to a novel conception of input derived from the consumer (knowledge and skills as music capital). They link the 'accumulation of music capital'[89] to education generally, and therefore, in Becker's terms, 'human capital'. The experience of good music produces 'consumer capital' and an 'increase in music capital increases the productivity of time spent listening to ... music'.[90] Increases in 'music capital', they speculate, means that 'the consumption of music could rise even when the time spent fell'. They provide no empirical evidence for the fall in time music lovers spend listening to music as they increase their 'stock' of music capital. If they can make this speculative argument stick, however, then they can claim that the consumption of music declines precisely because music lovers become more productive at listening.

Like other mainstream economists, Stigler and Becker put art's increased marginal utility under the category of 'addictive goods'. If you take the addiction out of the equation, they say, then you are left with the familiar marginal cost formula. They account for the apparent exceptionalism of addictive consumption – 'a growth in use with exposure'[91] – not in the way that had been

---

87   Stigler and Becker 1977, p. 77.
88   Stigler and Becker 1977, p. 79.
89   Ibid.
90   Stigler and Becker 1977, p. 78.
91   Stigler and Becker 1977, p. 81.

standard since Marshall – by referring to changes in taste – but by arguing that exposure increases the stock of consumer capital that is drawn on in more efficient acts of consumption in the future.

> On this interpretation, the (relative) consumption of music appreciation rises with exposure not because tastes shift in favor of music, but because its shadow price falls as skill and experience in the appreciation of music are acquired with exposure.[92]

With the assumption of stable tastes, 'most irritating to the Austrian subjectivists',[93] as one critical paper puts it, they claim that the whole process can be reduced to rational calculations based on costs. Shadow pricing is a proxy value of a good where price does not reflect the actual value of a good or commodity, or no market value for a good or commodity exists. In this instance, the shadow price of musical appreciation for which there is no price and no market allows economists such as Stigler and Becker to incorporate the music lover's increasing love of music into economic calculation by re-describing increased cultural competence as 'an investment return from producing appreciation'.[94] Listening to good music, for them, does not result in the music lover listening to more good music or spending more time listening to good music, but the accumulation of 'music capital'. If music lovers subsequently listen to less music than they do in their youth then, the hypothesis goes, they will enjoy it more because their consumption is heightened with 'consumer capital'. Consumption of music by those with 'music capital', they claim, costs less (in 'human capital', not cash), and therefore the propensity to consume more music rather than to reach a point of satiety, as the standard downward curve of diminishing marginal utility presumes, can be explained as the result of diminishing 'costs', not changes in taste.

Before proposing 'changes in taste' as his explanation of the consumption of good music, Marshall first identifies the anomaly that listening to good music results in the desire to listen to more good music. In fact, 'De Gustibus . . .' does not argue that 'addictive goods' are, in fact, in some elusive way, standard goods that correspond to the diminishing marginal utility model. In spectacularly dispensing with the condition of changing tastes they also quietly dispense with the framework of diminishing marginal utility. Being content with a formula

---

92   Stigler and Becker 1977, p. 79.

93   West and McKee 1983, p. 1111.

94   Stigler and Becker 1977, p. 79.

that treats of music, art, literature and heroin as subject to generic calculations of cost and price with alternative uses, Stigler and Becker pass over the specific question at hand. Their re-description suppresses the anomaly of *increasing* marginal utility by reimagining it as capital extracted from investment. But 'human capital' is not capital, and the investments, costs and prices they impute, here, are perhaps better understood, for clarity, as metaphors. That is to say, the success of this particular campaign depends on our acceptance of an invitation by Stigler and Becker to substitute terms. Taste disappears from the account if we use the words 'capital investment' for the experience of art, and use the term 'lower price' to describe the difference between a novice and an aesthete in engaging with art. Stigler and Becker recast talk about utility, pleasure and knowledge in the tropes of economics. Deirdre McCloskey's argument that economics is not a science but an art of rhetorical persuasion has never been more apt. But even the rhetorical deployment of economic tropes in the argument is viciously circular. The point of the argument is to incorporate the exceptional consumption of good music (and similar goods and services) into the standard account of consumption by eliminating the condition of changing tastes, but the conclusion is reached in advance through paraphrase. If we substitute market words for taste words then we can eliminate changes in taste from the economic account of art. The preference for the lexicon of economic terminology is never established as necessary, it is just preferable if the conclusion it anticipates is preferable. The terminological substitution is unsuccessful, however, because it does not address the central issue, namely Marshall's observation that the marginal utility of good music does not diminish. Stigler and Becker respond to this observation by speculating that music lovers can listen to music more productively. This dodges the issue. At no point do these Chicago economists actually claim that the consumption of good music follows the pattern of *diminishing* marginal utility. At no point do they directly contradict Marshall's observation; they merely take issue with his explanation. Similarly, how their imputed increase in productivity is to be measured, and whether it offsets increasing marginal utility, is never adequately formulated. Stigler and Becker are so taken by their argument that 'music capital' increases the productivity of consuming music and therefore reduces the costs of music consumption, that they do not bother to demonstrate empirically that seasoned music lovers actually spend less time listening to music than novices. If listening to music, visiting art galleries, reading literature, attending the theatre and so on increases time spent on such activities, not just increasing its productivity or reducing its cost, then Stigler and Becker construct their alternative economic account without explaining the key issue that triggered the debate.

Frank Knight returned from the grave to reply to 'De Gustibus . . .' in an article written by Ross Emmett in 2006 faking Knight's style. In the introduction
to the essay, Emmett explains that he not only adopted the voice of Knight,
but also backdated the essay, thus 'allowing Knight to "predict" (and lament in
advance) the subsequent rise of economic imperialism within the social sciences – a movement directly attributable to the impact Stigler and Becker's
work has had in economics, law, sociology and political science'.[95] Emmett
asks the sort of question that has been common since Ruskin: 'does a scientific
explanation of human behaviour remove that which we understand to be most
human about our behaviour – that unsettledness which keeps us questing for
a better form of life?'[96] This sounds very high minded, but Emmett has something very specific in mind:

> Knight recognized quite early that accepting a methodological assump-
> tion like Stigler and Becker's would allow economics to make forays into
> the explanation of social and political behaviour that he believed were
> not only inappropriate, but in fact dangerous to the future of liberal
> society.[97]

The ventriloquised voice of Knight prefers economics to be realistic rather
than abstractly coherent, arguing that tastes cannot be taken as 'given', but are
always changing; that actual human behaviour is provisional, shifting and contingent; and so on. 'Judgments regarding human action are all in the field of
art, not science, of interpretation, not objective fact',[98] Emmet's Knight says.
Emmett puts Knight's focus on methodological arguments and big philosophical questions, but in the introduction, it is Emmett, not Knight, who hits the
nail (or at least one nail) on the head:

> Stigler and Becker's claim that we can 'usefully treat tastes as stable over
> time and similar among people' poses a problem because it assumes
> away the phenomena that they wish to explain.[99]

Stigler and Becker's attempt to correct the Marshallian reference to taste is not
understood by them as a refutation of exceptionalism because the theory of

---

95   Emmett 2006, p. 102.
96   Ibid.
97   Ibid.
98   Emmett 2006, p. 105.
99   Emmett 2006, p. 102.

exceptionalism has always been limited to classical economics. Marshall never described the anomaly of increasing rather than diminishing marginal utility, nor those who came after, as a specific neoclassical version of exceptionalism. If Marshall's observation is the neoclassical equivalent of being alarmed by 'fancy prices', however, then Stigler and Becker's argument is, in part, a refutation of exceptionalism, or can provide theoretical support for the denial of neoclassical exceptionalism. But as I have shown, and Emmett confirms, the argument 'assumes away the phenomena that they wish to explain', rather than repudiating the evidence that a case for exceptionalism needs answered.

In principle, if art lovers develop a taste for Mondrian then the reduction of prices for works by Paul Klee does not have the effect of increasing demand for Klee and reducing demand for Mondrian. Demand is determined by taste, through non-economic mechanisms, not supply and demand. Becker translates the non-economic mechanisms of taste into the economic language of capital, prices and costs. Someone who already listens to music or attends galleries is 'more likely' to do so in the future. This is widely understood, and is an observation that Becker and Marshall share. The crucial thing is that Becker explains the difference between the likelihood of the established art viewer to view more art in terms of the accumulation of knowledge and experience that makes further experiences 'less costly' in terms of effort, the acquisition of new knowledge and so on. It is 'worth the effort', for Becker, because the additional effort is smaller than the total effort required of a newcomer. This is marginalism applied to units of cultural competence. However, the difficulty at hand is not that people with 'music capital' are 'more likely' to consume further units of music than those without music capital. This is indisputable but is not what needs to be explained. There is nothing exceptional about it. Existing consumers of beef are more likely to be future consumers of beef. But the more that one consumes beef – or the more one has a ready supply of beef in the freezer – the less one is willing to pay for more units of beef. In art, however, it is not only that existing consumers are likely to be future consumers but that, in addition, once the consumer 'gets a taste for it', their consumption of art feeds off itself leading to increasing marginal utility. This is what needs to be explained.

Music appreciation is unlike the consumption of standard goods insofar as it requires knowledge, experience, and so on from the consumer and therefore the consumption of music or art is a combination of the music and one's own ability/capacity to consume it. Becker would say, therefore, that the consumer also consumes their own abilities to produce the good. It is clear that the experience of goods that require human capital can be distinguished from those that do not, like eating apples. But the point of explaining the productive

activity of the consumer in terms of human capital is not merely to establish
the fact that the art viewer brings knowledge and experience to the art object;
the point, for Becker, is to establish that such capital reduces the costs of consumption and that this leads to certain predictable average results. Becker
is not the first to argue that art consumers have knowledge and experience
that contribute significantly to the experience of art. He accepts this widely
observed fact. Becker, however, provides a new economic explanation of the
contribution of the viewer to the experience of art. That is to say, whereas
cultural commentators have typically argued that the art consumer, viewer,
spectator, observer or onlooker needs to be 'adequately sensitive, adequately
informed' and becomes so through serious engagement with art,[100] Becker
argues that the knowledge and experience of art is a form of human capital
which, like economic capital, can be put to work productively, only in this case
it is invested in acts of consumption. The accumulation of human capital leads
to lower 'shadow prices' (time, effort, knowledge acquisition, etc.) in the consumption of art. The problem with the concept of human capital is not that
it fails to resemble adequately the phenomenon it describes. The problem, in
my view, is not descriptive but explanatory: i.e. whether Becker explains what
Marshall and others explain in the idea of 'getting a taste for art'.[101]

True, when T.J. Clark looks again at Manet's 'Olympia', which he has been
studying for half a century, he has a store of knowledge that the tourist seeing

---

100   Wollheim 1987, p. 22.
101   It is interesting to note that Marshall's reference to taste carries none of the elitist over-
       tones of the aesthetic tradition in which taste distinguishes between those with taste
       and those without; nor does it carry any of the normative connotations of the cultivated
       distinction between good and bad taste. Becker, however, who replaces the element of
       'getting a taste for art' in Marshall's account with reference to 'human capital', revives key
       aspects of the elitist version of taste through his understanding of knowledge, experience
       and competence as acquired through restricted social practices. Human capital distin-
       guishes art viewers from philistines just as effectively as good taste once did. Throsby
       dissolves the distinction between those goods that require human capital and those that
       do not in his argument that 'taste' need not be of any concern for the economics of art
       since taste is involved in the consumption of apples and cars – i.e. standard goods – as
       well as art. In doing so Throsby conflates having a taste (a preference) for something with
       getting a taste for something (a growing capacity). Getting a taste for art is not the same
       as having a certain kind of taste – it indicates an acceleration of desire, not a preference.
       What Throsby dissolves, therefore, is the difference between those goods for which mar-
       ginal utility diminishes through incremental increases in consumption and those goods
       for which marginal utility is augmented through incremental increases in consumption.

it for the first time does not have, and Clark's knowledge of 'Olympia', as well as his methodology of art historical inquiry, is not at all useless when he turns his attention to Pollock's 'Blue Poles'. We can re-describe the contrast between Clark and the tourist in terms of shadow costs: it is 'cheaper' for Clark to turn his attention to L.S. Lowry than it would be for a newcomer to start from scratch. But what Becker has to explain is that the 'cheaper' shadow prices incentivise Clark and the relatively higher shadow prices disincentivise the tourist. If (shadow) prices are not (dis)incentives then they are merely descriptive and not explanatory.

Marshall's assumption of constant or stable tastes does not so much eliminate the problem of increasing marginal utility as signal the anomaly. Stigler and Becker appear to recognise the problem and resolve the explicit problem of changing tastes by reformulating the analysis in terms of changing consumer costs. There is no exception for Marshall because he inserts a clause in the law to exclude changing tastes, whereas there is no exception for Stigler and Becker because they can describe the consumption of addictive goods without reference to changing tastes. By eliminating reference to changing tastes, Stigler and Becker appear to assume that the multiple experiences of a single work of art is the same experience time after time, explained by the changing costs of consuming it. If we go back to works of art and see new aspects to them, discover new interpretations, and so forth, if, in short, our relationship to the work is deepened through experience, then it is false to describe the experience of art in terms of the reduction of cost when the only possible means of achieving such a depth of experience is through working harder with the work rather than falling back on previous conclusions. To suppose no alteration of character and taste in the experience of art is to suppose no genuine experience of art at all.

What Stigler and Becker need to overcome in order to banish the economic exceptionalism of the consumption of art is the historical relationship between art and taste. Although the aristocratic version of taste, specifically the concept of 'good taste', emphasised the distinction between those with taste and those without, the bourgeois conception of taste, from Kant onwards, puts the self-transforming subject at the heart of questions of taste, and therefore art. Taste requires judgement and cannot be reduced to rules, principles or objective measures of perfection, hence an active, engaged and reflective subject is a precondition for taste. Kant consistently associates taste with freedom. In fact, Kant's autonomy of aesthetic judgement is free in direct opposition to the decorum, propriety, standards and principles of aristocratic 'good taste'. Schiller says as much when he remarks: 'Art, like science, is emancipated from all that is positive, and all that is humanly conventional; both are completely independent of the arbitrary will of man'.[102] Aesthetic education 'is aimed not so much at particular objects of knowledge as at forming an ethical disposition'.[103] One cannot make a judgement of taste, in the modern sense, without exerting oneself, without making the judgement oneself, and without risking the possibility of failure. This is why Kant calls the aesthetic judgement 'exacting'. Matthew Arnold instrumentalises this self-transformative subject in the notion of 'the development of a "best (i.e., ethical) self" out of the anarchic desires and interests of the "ordinary self"'.[104] Roger Scruton sees the experience of beauty and the development of taste as helping to form character, virtue and order. Brecht devised technical means by which taste and pleasure could be turned against the established order in the production of a revolutionary subject. Neither taste nor art leave us as we are. As such, it is not so much that 'tastes change' or 'tastes are constant', as Stigler and Becker have it, but that the taste changes us. Having preferences and making choices does not capture the full sense of post-Kantian subjectivity. The modern conception of taste does not bring about what economists call 'satisfaction'. Taste is recursive: the individual experiences taste as an active subject who is transformed by the action, leading to the reflective modification of taste. Extracting this dynamism from the conception of taste, especially with regard to art, is brutal and falsifying.

The increasing marginal utility of art is not understood through an economics of addiction, habit and tradition. Addicts, we are told, who begin with soft drugs typically or inevitably advance to hard drugs, and branding can persuade customers to return time and time again to purchase more commodities carrying the same label. The former, we can say, exhibits increasing marginal utility, but the latter conforms to diminishing marginal utility (diminishing marginal utility applies to shirts, we would expect, even when the consumer prefers to purchase shirts from Zara rather than Topshop). What needs to be explained in the case of art is not simply the fact that the consumption of a good affects future consumption, or that certain goods are biologically addictive and therefore must be conscientiously resisted in order to prevent consumption of the good increasing at an accumulative rate. Insofar as the consumption of art transforms the subject, it is likely that consuming art does not only result in the further consumption of art but also the extension of an interest in

---

102   Schiller 1902, p. 30.
103   Lloyd and Thomas 1998, p. 7.
104   Ibid.

literature, music, dance, cinema, theatre, as well, perhaps, as art history, philosophy, psychoanalysis, politics, geography, semiotics and even economics. What is more, what the individual learns in consuming, say, Cubist painting, assists in the consumption of the Conceptualist 'dematerialisation' of the art object. On top of this, the struggle to interpret and judge Minimalism, for instance, can encourage the consumer of art to prefer struggle over enjoyment, and lead to a method of seeking out new, difficult and immediately unappealing works in the future. As such, it cannot be assumed that the increasing marginal utility of art involves a reduction in the 'cost' of consumption. The 'costs' may rise substantially as the consumer of art not only gets a taste for art, so to speak, but gets a taste for more and more difficult processes of interpretation and judgement. The increasing marginal utility of art is not a formula for consuming more of the same.

Neoclassical economists who have taken the trouble to dismiss the theory of art's economic exceptionalism have only gone so far as to demonstrate, from their neoclassical position, that the classical doctrines on which it is based are false. However, if there are forms of consumption that 'grow on what they feed upon', then they are exceptional only to marginal utility theory. The fact that some forms of consumption, art included, increase the capacity for enjoyment rather than diminish it might go unremarked within classical economics and would not be anomalous to its principles and doctrines. Hence, if Stigler and Becker's re-description of changing taste as changing costs is unsuccessful, then the fact that the consumption of art does not conform to the law of diminishing marginal utility is exceptional in a way that neoclassical economics cannot dismiss so easily. Art's increasing marginal utility is a form of exceptionalism native to neoclassicism itself. And if we add to this art's exceptionalism *vis-à-vis* the neoclassical indexing of prices and quantities, and the incremental units of neoclassical marginalism, we begin to develop a vivid picture of art's economic exceptionalism in purely neoclassical terms. And it does not stop there. The inquiry into art's economic exceptionalism in neoclassicism can be extended further. There is a question mark over whether art conforms to the doctrine of 'consumer sovereignty' that is presupposed by neoclassical economics.

The phrase 'consumer sovereignty' is credited to William Hutt in the 1930s.[105] For Hutt, 'consumers' sovereignty is the stimulus to which productive effort is

---

105 He first used the term in 1931 (in an unpublished but circulated article), but he used the term in a published article for the first time in 1934. The credit for the first use of the term, however, is often given for the publication of his book *Economists and the Public: A Study of Competition and Opinion* in 1936.

a response'.[106] Right from the off, the doctrine of consumer sovereignty held that consumption determines the products that it encounters in the market-place. George Hildebrand follows the doctrine to the letter, then, when he says that 'entrepreneurs... are the intermediaries by which consumers achieve their ends'.[107] J.K. Galbraith confirms this: 'In the general view economics is a process by which the individual imposes his will on the producer'.[108] The strange sounding reversal of events (consumption preceding production) was explained very clearly from the outset.

> Consumers' preferences... can be regarded as the 'determining' fac-
> tor... [and] may be said, therefore, to have a logical 'priority' over the
> other elements in the situation – viz., in the sense in which ends can be
> said to be 'prior' to means.[109]

Hence,

> The doctrine of consumers' sovereignty implies, perhaps even entails,
> that preferences on the side of demand are fundamentally and in prin-
> ciple more important than those on the side of supply.[110]

Jevons made a similar point when he said 'industry is essentially prospective, not retrospective'.[111] Adam Smith puts the central idea in long hand:

> Consumption is the sole end and purpose of all production; and the
> interest of the producer ought to be attended to, only so far as it may be
> necessary for promoting that of the consumer.[112]

'Individual consumer sovereignty and the market go together',[113] according to the doctrine, and this is the case even before the revolution of marginal utility. Whereas classical political economists like Smith, Ricardo and Mill understood that capitalist markets made consumption the determining goal of

---

106   Hutt quoted in Fraser 1939, p. 544.
107   Hildebrand 1951, p. 20.
108   Galbraith 1970, p. 473.
109   Frazer 1939, p. 545.
110   Frazer 1939, p. 546.
111   Jevons 1888, p. 164.
112   Smith 1993, p. 625.
113   Hildebrand 1951, p. 31.

production, mainstream economics after the marginalist revolution becomes 'a science of choice'.[114] 'It was not until the subjective utility approach took over economics that a mature conception of the consumer role in resource allocation appeared...to begin a new era in economics'.[115] Neoclassicism is economics in the era of consumer sovereignty. The principle of marginal utility establishes a platform for the consumer that makes consumer sovereignty a compelling doctrine for mainstream economics.

The doctrine of consumer sovereignty always had a normative tinge to it, and nowhere is this more vividly expressed than in the writings of Mises.

> The capitalists, the enterprisers, and the farmers are instrumental in the conduct of economic affairs. They are at the helm and steer the ship. But they are not free to shape its course. They are not supreme, they are steersmen only, bound to obey unconditionally the captain's orders. The captain is the consumer.[116]

Consumers not capitalists, Mises claims, are the 'real bosses' in the 'capitalist system of market economy'.[117]

> They, by their buying and by their abstention from buying, decide who should own the capital and run the plants. They determine what should be produced and in what quantity and quality. Their attitudes result either in profit or in loss for the enterpriser. They make poor men rich and rich men poor.[118]

---

114 Hill and Myatt 2010, p. 9.
115 Bowman 1951, p. 12.
116 Mises 1944, p. 20.
117 Mises 1944, pp. 20–1. Mises's association of consumers with bosses is a flawed image of a classless society that he uses in a direct confrontation with socialism, as is demonstrated in the opening sentences of the preface to his book: 'The main issue in present-day social and political conflicts is whether or not man should give away freedom, private initiative, and individual responsibility and surrender to the guardianship of a gigantic apparatus of compulsion and coercion, the socialist state. Should authoritarian totalitarianism be substituted for individualism and democracy? Should the citizen be transformed into a subject, a subordinate in an all-embracing army of conscripted labor, bound to obey unconditionally the orders of his superiors? Should he be deprived of his most precious privilege to choose means and ends and to shape his own life?' (Mises 1944, p. iii)
118 Mises 1944, p. 21.

Mises develops a cunning argument that makes consumer sovereignty appear to be inevitable within market relations, even when individuals openly flout it. This is illustrated in his famous hypothetical account of an employer who hires a family member rather than take on a more productive rival in the labour market. On the face of it, this act of recruitment contradicts the doctrine of consumer sovereignty because the capitalist is not responding to the demand of consumers (to reduce prices by increasing productivity). Mises overcomes the apparent contradiction of consumer sovereignty by arguing that the employer in this example behaves partly *as a consumer*. The employer consumes the utility of hiring a relative. And, if the employer acts like a consumer in this instance, she is utterly sovereign. Thus, when the employer behaves like a calculating producer, she is behaving according to the doctrine of consumer sovereignty (putting demand first), and when she fails to behave like a calculating producer, she acts according to the doctrine of consumer sovereignty nonetheless, only in this instance the employer is the consumer.

The consumer does not have sovereignty in art. The pioneers of the marginal revolution were aware of the artist's unusual relationship to the consumer as well as to costs and prices generally. Wieser, for instance, remarks on the artist's relationship to the economics of artistic production as anomalous by observing that the artist does not consider the cost of paints and canvas but thinks only of aesthetics. We may be tempted to correct Wieser by pointing out that artists are not always as irrational and fanatical as the Romantic image of the artist suggests, but what is more striking, here, is that Wieser accepts this description of the artist's exceptional economic behaviour without drawing a single economic conclusion from it. Jevons says that 'an artist is usually his own capitalist, for he maintains himself during many months, or even years while he is painting a great picture'.[119] If by 'capitalist', Jevons means nothing more than that the artist funds their own activity, then this is true, but it is not a sufficient condition for a purchaser to become a capitalist. Jevons does nothing here to answer the question of whether the artist produces commodities according to the doctrine of consumer sovereignty as commodities for exchange. Capitalists, we might reasonably assume, are in the business of making profits and therefore almost always abide by the condition of consumer sovereignty, but the fact that an artist supports herself for months or years does not settle this matter in favour of the standard rationale of commodity production in neoclassical economics.

---

119   Jevons 2005, pp. 57–8.

Jevons caps off his anecdote about the artist being his own capitalist with an incentive: 'if he succeeds in doing it excellently well, he can sell the picture for thousands of pounds because there are many rich people who wish to possess good pictures'.[120] This raises a difficulty that Jevons does not discuss, namely, that making paintings 'excellently well' does not guarantee a sale. If the consumer's interpretation of excellence in art determines whether the picture sells, and the artist takes no account of the tastes present in demand, then the picture may well not sell at all. If the artists, in cahoots with critics and curators, decide for themselves what constitutes excellence in art, then there is no guarantee at all that the work will sell. However, if we follow Mises, then the flouting of consumer sovereignty in art is compatible with the standard pattern of consumer sovereignty so long as the artist occupies the place of the consumer rather than the producer. It would be much more elegant, more feasible and more consonant with the facts to understand artists as producers who do not subscribe to the neoclassical doctrine of consumer sovereignty leading to a relationship between producers and consumers that is not guided by consumer sovereignty.

Now, if the production of art does not conform to consumer sovereignty, and the market is a machine for enforcing consumer sovereignty (rewarding producers who meet demand and punishing those who do not), then the artist has a very pragmatic interest in maintaining his or her hostility to the market. In fact, the agenda of the market – to govern the production of commodities according to the effectual demand of consumers – is perhaps the kernel of truth in Llewellyn Smith's opposition of art-value and exchange value, or quality and quantity; which goes some way to providing the material basis for art's commodification without commodification. To submit to the discipline of market forces, for the artist, is to produce works that are demanded by consumers rather than developed according to the artist's own values, principles, taste and knowledge. If an economist complains that artists *ought* to respond to the market instead of their own standards, which has every appearance of a normative economics, we might suggest that the economic theorist ought to write the books that the market wants, and work like a hack, rather than write the pioneering studies that they do. Instead of there being a taboo on money and business in art, therefore, we might say that artists, dealers, curators and critics are acutely aware that art is not produced for exchange – that is, for money and therefore in response to market demand – in the way that capitalist commodities are. Mainstream economists tend to regard such

---

120   Jevons 2005, p. 58.

artists as irrational not because they conscientiously defend the independence of their art practice but because in doing so they risk being poor, having to take lousy 'second jobs' and making no sales. Imagine saying the same thing about a judge, police officer, teacher, political activist or carer.

Commodities, goods and gifts are not different kinds of thing, but different modes of exchange in which things pass.[121] 'A material object', Gregory says, 'is now a *commodity*, now a *gift*, now a *good*, depending upon the specific context of transaction'.[122] Some indication of the contribution that such a distinction can make can be gauged from the following observation: 'capitalist agriculture developed first in a country where land was a good, an inalienable keepsake of elite families who kept their land off the market'.[123] Gregory matches the three types of transaction with three locations between which items move.

> Material objects of use to people, such as land, rice, rupees, dollars, cowries, silver, and gold, are transformed into marked social forms such as gifts, commodities, and goods, and the process through which they acquire these values are institutions such as the Market, the House, and the State.[124]

From this, Gregory can say, '[if] commodities are those values that arise as things pass from House to Market, then gifts are those values that pass between Houses and goods the inalienable keepsakes that are stored within a single House'.[125] (After specifying three locations Gregory uses only two and does not say what metamorphosis occurs when a thing has its origin in, passes through or terminates in the state). Other locations exemplify different theoretical frameworks: 'the location of the imagined source of value has moved from the hoarder's treasury, the landlord's state, then to the factory floor and finally to the supermarket'.[126] The category of the commodity needs to be split to accommodate the difference between 'simple commodities' and 'capitalist commodities', while the category of good needs to be split to accommodate 'neoclassical goods' and 'priceless goods'. The division between both kinds of commodity

---

121   Also see Appadurai 1986, pp. 6–13.
122   Gregory 1997, p. 14.
123   Gregory 1997, p. 120.
124   Gregory 1997, pp. 13–14.
125   Gregory 1997, p. 14.
126   Gregory 1997, p. 23.

on the one hand and both kinds of good on the other corresponds to the distinction between production and consumption: commodities are products produced for exchange,[127] while goods are those items (commodities or not) which consumers are willing and able to obtain through exchange. Gregory suggests that neither the classical theory of commodities, nor the neoclassical theory of goods, provides a satisfactory analysis of the use and circulation of items in society. What is more, the theoretical impasse between classical and neoclassical economics should not, in his view, be resolved with a synthesis of the two but 'to affirm the coevalness of rival value systems'.[128]

In view of this, art's encounters with markets might be understood in terms of the social processes in which enclaved products pass through markets and temporary commodities are withdrawn from exchange, for instance, rather than by insisting that art is commodified once and for all. Anthropology can help to theorise art's non-commodity status even as art evidently is commodified without being commodified. Following Kopytoff's distinction between homogeneous and singular objects, Arjun Appadurai says a line needs to be drawn between a 'standardized steel bar', which is 'indistinguishable in practical terms from any other steel bar',[129] and unique goods such as artworks. Appadurai says there is a qualitative difference not only between a Manet and a Picasso but also between one Manet and another. Appadurai does not argue that singular products cannot be bought and sold as commodities, but that there are social and cultural processes that carry items across the border between commodification and de-commodification: 'whereas enclaving seeks to protect certain things from commoditization, diversion frequently is aimed at drawing protected things into the zone of commoditization'. Scitovsky bases his critique of consumer sovereignty on a case for citizen sovereignty, arguing that 'the sovereignty of the consumer is not at all the same thing as the sovereignty of the individual or the citizen'.[130] Rather than conflate the two types of sovereignty, Scitovsky frames the sovereignty of the consumer within a much broader conception of the individual and a broader conception of sovereignty.

---

127 Simple commodities are not specifically produced for exchange but, in the case of the sale of surplus produce, for instance, consisting of products for private use and commodities for sale (with no qualitative distinction between them), it is the volume of the products as a whole that presupposes that some portion of the product will become commodities.

128 Gregory 1997, p. 7.

129 Appadurai 1986, p. 16.

130 Scitovsky 1962, p. 262.

The consumer is just one facet of the individual – the one that has to do with the consumption of goods sold through the market. The consumer's welfare therefore is only a part of man's welfare and only a part even of his economic welfare.[131]

Thus consumer sovereignty is a narrowing of the concept of sovereignty. We will see in the next chapter how welfare economics developed economic theories that had a much broader conception of sovereignty than consumer sovereignty and that these theories imply yet further examples of art's economic exceptionalism not contained within the classic literature.[132]

---

131   Ibid.
132   Appadurai 1986, p. 26.

CHAPTER 4

Exceptionalism after 1945

David Throsby claims a speech on art and the state presented to the Friends of the City Museum and Art Gallery in Birmingham in 1958 established Lionel Robbins as 'the first British economist of modern times to analyze the economic role of the state in support for the arts in financing public museums and galleries'.[1] Robbins, a Professor of Economics at the London School of Economics, and a leading economic advisor to the British government during the Second World War, was deeply involved in the arts, as a Trustee of the National Gallery between 1953 and 1974. He was also on the board of the Royal Opera Covent Garden between 1955 and 1981, served on the Committee of Management of the Courtauld Institute between the wars, and participated in two governmental commissions. Robbins returned from the First World War a socialist but his study of economics 'completed his disillusionment with socialism'.[2] Immediately following the instigation of the Nazi persecution of the Jews, Robbins and Beveridge established the Academic Freedom Committee that helped Jewish and liberal academics and students to escape from Nazi Germany. Working side by side with John Maynard Keynes during the war, including his 'active support of Keynes' ideas on how to pay for the war',[3] Robbins, as director of the Economic Section, 'was actively committed to planning for a better postwar world'.[4] Robbins put the doctrine of 'opportunity cost' at the heart of his definition of economics and applied this to the arts, saying that we are often faced with a choice between material welfare on the one hand and aesthetic interests on the other and that 'insofar as activity involves the relinquishment of other desired alternatives, it has an economic aspect'.[5] Although expressed in the form of a trade off, Robbins understood that art and economics were at odds: 'Aesthetics is concerned with certain kinds of ends. The beautiful is an end that offers itself for choice in competition, so to speak, with others. Economics is not concerned at all with any ends as such'.[6] Hence, he said, 'both the services of cooks, and the services of opera dancers

---

1 Throsby 1994, p. 2.
2 Howson 2011, p. 3.
3 Howson 2011, p. 4.
4 Ibid.
5 Robbins 1932, p. 17.
6 Robbins 1952, p. 30.

are limited in relation to demand and can be put to alternative uses'[7] which, for him, is decisive in regard to the question of whether art is amenable to economic analysis. Nevertheless, Robbins campaigned for the public purchase of land to extend the National Gallery and called on the government to purchase 'national treasures' to safeguard them from export, among other things. But Robbins did not write a major economic paper on the economics of art. The reports which he authored or signed for the institutions that he served 'reveal a tension', Balisciano and Medema say, 'between respect for the free market on the one hand and a notion that special exception should be made for the arts on the other'.[8] This overt tension between the market and the argument for art as a special case of one sort or another haunts the economics of art in the two or three decades after 1945.

Keynes had played a very significant role in the public funding of art and its institutions over a decade before Robbins gave his talk at the City Museum and Art Gallery in Birmingham, but Throsby overlooks this in his assessment of Robbins's contribution. In 1946 Keynes had even expressed his preeminent role within British art administration by claiming, to a visiting Russian delegate, 'I can almost boast that I am Commissar for Fine Arts in my country',[9] for reasons that will become clear very shortly. Throsby gives Robbins a pivotal role in the formation of cultural economics,[10] not only because of his 'essay', 'Art and the State', published in 1963, but also because Alan Peacock, who, as we will see in the next chapter, is a major figure in the formation of Cultural Economics, had been a junior colleague of Robbins at the LSE, and William Baumol had been Robbins's graduate student at LSE. Both Robbins and Keynes worked closely during the Second World War, including their participation in high-level discussions with William Beveridge on the economic feasibility of introducing universal social security, including family allowances and pensions. Keynes, who was 'in a state of wild enthusiasm'[11] for the general scheme, was certainly the leading economic voice on the committee. The Beveridge Report, *Social Insurance and Allied Services*, which established the blueprint for the British welfare state, incorporated Keynesian fiscal regulation.

The welfare state was conceived, planned and the major elements of it built in the aftermath of the Second World War, but, before the outbreak of the First World War, several European countries had already established

---

7   Robbins 1932, p. 16.
8   Balisciano and Medema in De Marchi and Goodwin 1999, p. 275.
9   Moggridge 1992, p. 705.
10   Throsby 1994, p. 2.
11   Moggridge 1992, p. 706.

some form of what would become the core of the welfare state. Germany led the way, through Bismarck's strategic outflanking of the socialists in the 1880s by guaranteeing national health insurance, a pension, a minimum wage and workplace regulation, vacation, and unemployment insurance. The Bismarckean prototype of the welfare state was followed by Denmark between 1891 and 1907, Sweden between 1891 and 1913 and Britain between 1908 and 1911. Pigou's *Wealth and Welfare*, published in 1912, marks the official birth of welfare economics, but welfare economics would be reborn in the 1930s and was already sketched out in the nineteenth century. Marshall had considered the possibility of state intervention for cheap housing, free meals for children, stabilising employment, and old age pensions (supporting Charles Booth's pension scheme in 1892), as well as fresh air. In an article published in 1907 Marshall argued that the state should be active in 'providing green belts around cities ... by bringing "the beauties of nature and art within the reach of ordinary citizens", and on providing assistance to make everyone ... truly educated'.[12] Pigou examined the limitations of capitalism and various non-market methods for correcting it, focusing on the problems of 'market failure' and what have subsequently been called 'externalities'. Like Marshall before him, Pigou 'thought it necessary that "an authority of wider reach" should step in and "tackle the collective problems of beauty, of air and of light", just as had been done for public utilities such as gas and water'.[13] In the 1930s, the 'New Deal' introduced to American capitalism safeguards and public policies including welfare and jobs creation, which had existed in Europe for some time. The post-war expansion of social security begins in Great Britain during the war, through ambitious plans for reconstruction, leading to the 1942 publication of the Beveridge Report. Alongside recommendations for dealing with poverty, which Beveridge called 'Want', the report called for the integration of social security within a comprehensive universal minimum state provision to combat idleness (that is to say, unemployment), disease, ignorance and squalor. Consequently, 'the voice of Hayek and other opponents to interventionism were largely muffled in the post-war period',[14] while 'Keynes devised forms of intervention that led to his being portrayed as the father of the welfare state and deficit spending'.[15]

It is in this context that the Arts Council of Great Britain established a new relationship between art and the state. But it should not be thought that the

---

12   Groenewegen in Backhouse and Nishiwaza 2010, p. 36.
13   Medema in Backhouse and Nishiwaza 2010, p. 48.
14   Beaud and Dostaler 1997, p. 48.
15   Backhouse and Bateman 2011, p. 131.

public subsidy of the arts is the result of the extension of the welfare state to the funding of culture, as if the Bismarckean welfare state was nothing but a smaller version of the Beveridgean welfare state. Richard Titmuss distinguishes two types of welfare state, one that is restricted (to correcting market failure and assisting deserving groups) and a second that is universalistic and comprehensive.[16] Gøsta Esping-Andersen identifies three distinct but overlapping political economies of the welfare state: one offers only modest guarantees against the effects of the market; another confronts both democracy and the market through the setting up of an elite bureaucratic administration that promotes conservative and traditional social relations; and the third establishes widespread de-commodification through social democracy.[17] In thinking about the economics of art after 1945, in particular how the new provision of state subsidies for the arts transformed the economy (and economics) of art, it is important not to muddle up the various kinds of welfare state into one undifferentiated or vulgar conception of the relationship between the welfare state and the market. It is not a matter of identifying the Arts Council, or public subsidy generally, with one version of the political economy of the welfare state, but to remain alert to the tensions and contradictions entailed in combining rival regimes of conservative, liberal and social democratic state intervention.

At the end of 1939 Lord De La Warr, the President of the Board of Education, approached the Pilgrim Trust with the idea of setting up a committee for the arts. The Committee for the Encouragement of Music and the Arts (CEMA) was soon established and set out to preserve standards in music, theatre and the visual arts. The following year the Committee became a Council when the Treasury got involved. Keynes, who was the most important English economist of his generation, complained to the council that sponsoring tours is more wasteful than guaranteeing companies against loss. Since this contact between CEMA and Keynes led in 1941 to the economist being offered the chairmanship of the Council, the consequences of this correspondence were far-reaching: it gave Keynes his 'first opportunity to shape the domestic post-war world'.[18] Keynes was arguably responsible for the 'revolution' that brought about the birth of macroeconomics. Neoclassical economists before Keynes neglected aggregate data such as GDP, the unemployment rate and the consumer price index, and Keynesian economics effectively replaced the concern with sectors and firms, which had dominated economics before him, with the analysis of

---

16   Titmuss in Pierson and Castles 2006, pp. 40–8.
17   See Esping-Andersen 1990.
18   Moggridge 1992, p. 696.

questions related to growth and employment. Keynes's rejection of *laissez faire* coincided with the Great Depression, which appeared to many as a concrete refutation of the ability of the market to self-regulate. At the time, only Marxism had a theory of capitalist crisis, so Keynes's theory of the limits of unregulated capitalism represented the first mainstream attempt to reflect economically on how capitalism 'is in many ways extremely objectionable',[19] noting that 'the existing system seriously misemploys the factors of production'.[20] However, Keynes argued that '[c]apitalism, wisely managed, can probably be made more efficient for attaining economic ends than any alternative system yet in sight',[21] setting himself against Marxism and neoclassical liberalism at the same time. Or, as Paul Mattick puts it, Keynes's 'purpose was to arrest capitalism's decline and prevent its possible collapse'.[22]

Keynes became the first Chairman of the Arts Council in 1946, preceding the founding of the National Health Service by two years. It provided state funding for the arts in an unprecedented and unparalleled way. Under the stewardship of Keynes, art entered a new phase in its economic history. 'Strange patronage of the arts has crept in',[23] Keynes said. The Keynesian introduction of state subsidy was unprecedented not by virtue of linking art and the state, but rather because it established a new mode of relationship between them. Raymond Williams recognised the nature of this shift by distinguishing between 'cultural policy as display', which embellishes the prevailing social order, and 'cultural policy "proper"'. 'The first sense of cultural policy "proper" is characterized by the system of public patronage of the arts set up in Britain towards the end of the Second World War'.[24]

Before Keynes, there was no such thing as the public funding of the arts strictly speaking. When the state funded art, such as in Prince Albert's Great Exhibition of 1851, it did so for direct instrumental national purposes. When the state paid for the Coronation of Queen Elizabeth II in 1953, too, state funding represents 'the public pomp of a particular social order',[25] as Williams put it, or 'the ritual symbolization of nationhood and state power',[26] as Jim McGuigan says. The Arts Council that Keynes set up may achieve these goals

---

19   Keynes in Medema and Samuels 2003, p. 595.
20   Keynes in Medema and Samuels 2003, p. 606.
21   Keynes in Medema and Samuels 2003, p. 595.
22   Mattick 1980, p. 26.
23   Keynes 1945, p. 31.
24   McGuigan 2004, p. 63.
25   Williams quoted in McGuigan 2004, p. 62.
26   Ibid.

indirectly (not through pomp and the explicit symbolisation of nationhood, but through the development of a national culture, perhaps, or the perception of a vital, innovative national contribution to a world culture), but its principal aim was to support art on its merits. What McGuigan neglects, therefore, when he argues that Williams's concept of 'cultural policy "proper"' was always 'questionable' and 'may now be *passé*', is the distinction between *state* funding for the arts and *public* funding for the arts. The fact that the Arts Council was from the outset biased towards highbrow culture rather than working-class culture suggests that the values underpinning the public subsidy of the arts need to be addressed, not that the public funding of the arts is indistinguishable from the state funding of the arts.

Prior to the seventeenth century there was no public sphere independent of the direct control of the state and church,[27] and between the establishment of the 'bourgeois public sphere' and the founding of the Keynesian welfare state, there was no mechanism for the *public* funding of art according to the values of the public sphere. What the Keynesian architecture of the Arts Council deliberately set out to do was not only secure funding for art but to establish an institutional framework for that funding that coincided neither with the state nor with the market. The state would supply the funds, but would otherwise have no direct say in how the money was to be disbursed. One of the models for Keynes's plan for the Arts Council was the University Grants Committee, which 'acted as a buffer between the government and the academic institutions, allocating public funds in bulk grants to the universities and thereby attempting to remove academic research funding from the political process'.[28] It goes without saying, however, that such a funding structure for the arts was not only removed from the political process, but was protected from the market mechanism too. The quest was to devise a funding structure for the arts that supported the independence of art and the independent assessment of its quality. And if such a quest can be accomplished, the question must be raised as to whether, under these circumstances, we must regard art as economically exceptional in a new way.

The transformation of the relationship between the state and art inaugurated by Keynesianism, in fact, established, for the first time, a distinction between public funding and private funding that not only changed the style of state funding, as Williams understood in his distinction between 'cultural policy as display' and 'cultural policy proper', but established the state as a source of funding unlike any other: public funding. When patronage was the primary

---

27   See Habermas 1961.
28   Upchurch 2004, p. 213.

means by which artists made their living, money was received from the state and the church in exactly the same way as it was received from wealthy individual patrons. It was not possible before Keynes to divide arts funding into three categories, the state, the public and the private. In principle, the difference between private and state, on one side, and public funding, on the other, is that between the arbitrary interests of the sovereign, the sovereign state, and the sovereign consumer, on one side, and the interests of all, on the other. Art collectors had never actually enjoyed this sort of sovereignty in the art market (artists had always found ways to resist the market and remain independent) and the state had never represented the whole of society in an impartial or genuinely universal way. There was a long tradition of markets that dealt with rare and precious objects, including paintings and sculpture, but these were not markets for works produced speculatively by living artists. Between the historical emergence of art and the artist at the end of the fourteenth century, and the development of a market for artworks by living artists in the eighteenth century, the production and circulation of art was controlled by guilds and funded, for the more successful artist, by patrons.

It is important to trace the changing relationship between artists and patrons between the fifteenth century and the middle of the twentieth, not only to take note of the distinctive features of each but also, as we will see below, how Keynes's unprecedented construction of the Arts Council, in fact, had very deep roots in the history of patronage. Ernst Gombrich points out that the 'emergence of a deliberate patronage of "art", such as Vasari celebrates, is impossible without the idea of "art"'.[29] This means that there is no patronage of art prior to the mid-fifteenth century. Before this, patronage existed but was not directed at art or artists, but only at certain kinds of eminent religious projects. The Medici family, for instance, were patrons in this earlier sense before they became patrons of art. Initially, the Medici family became patrons by contributing funds to the construction of religious buildings, and their patronage was organised socially by the church alongside the patronage of the other wealthy families in the town. Patrons in fifteenth-century Italy, Gombrich tells us, were naturally regarded as deserving the full credit for every aspect of the buildings that they funded. Under such circumstances, in which the architects, painters and sculptors who were enlisted to produce the work were credited to the patron, patronage was not a means by which money could be advanced to support the independence of individual producers. To us, and to art historians, the works produced under this form of patronage are attributable to and bear the trace of individual makers. To Florentines at the time, however, the

---

29   Gombrich 1966, p. 36.

phrase 'iste perfecit opus'[30] refers to the patron, not the artist. 'To the fifteenth century this would have been obvious', Gombrich says: 'The work of art is the donor's'.[31] Or, in Michael Baxandall's pithy phrase, 'in the fifteenth century painting was still too important to be left to the painters'.[32] Some artists in fifteenth-century Italy worked for princes who paid them a salary. (Mantegna worked for the Gonzaga Marquises of Mantua for the last 46 years of his life). Most, however, were commissioned to produce individual works according to contracts which, in the first half of the century, specified the subject of the work, the quality of material to be used, and so forth, and in the second half concentrated less on precious pigments and more on pictorial skill.[33] It would be interesting to revisit these issues raised by Baxandall in terms of a more specifically economic analysis of the shift of value in fifteenth-century painting, from paying for precious and rare raw materials to paying for skilled labour and so on. In regard to changing patterns of patronage, however, the emphasis on the skill of the artist, towards the end of the fifteenth century, remains, formally, an assertion of the power of the 'client' but anticipates, in its content, the emerging identification of the artist with his or her art.

'A distinction between "public" and "private" does not fit the functions of fifteenth-century painting very well'.[34] Individual patrons in the fifteenth century funded the works of the parish; hence the utility of such commissions was neither private – residing in the personal interests of the funder – nor public – deriving from the utility of all – but institutional, serving the church and its infrastructure.

> The picture trade was a quite different thing from that in our own late romantic condition, in which painters paint what they think best and then look round for a buyer. We buy our pictures ready-made now; this need not be a matter of our having more respect for the artist's individual talent than fifteenth-century people like Giovanni Rucellai did, so much as of our living in a different sort of commercial society.[35]

---

30   The Latin phrase, meaning 'this one completed the work', is inscribed on the right of Filippo Lippi's 'The Coronation of the Virgin' in the Uffizi. Art historians had assumed for many years that the figure designated by this phrase must be the artist, but now art historians believe that the figure represented in this part of the painting is the patron.

31   Gombrich 1966, p. 40.

32   Baxandall 1972, p. 3.

33   See Baxandall 1972, p. 14.

34   Baxandall 1972, p. 5.

35   Baxandall 1972, p. 3.

'The fifteenth century was a period of bespoke painting',[36] Baxandall says, but 'bespoke', here, refers to something much more than making a one-off, or to the commissioner's personal specifications: the patron was more prominent in the decision-making processes and more prominent in the reception of the work than the artisan who produced it. By the end of the century, the artist had emerged as an economic entity in two ways. The artist became prominent in the visual character and value of the work, and artists became differentiated from one another in the prices that these new skills could fetch.

But while art as a new category of practice – and economic good – is established, and the artist assumes an increasingly prominent role in its intellectual and material production, the two preconditions for the public funding of art are entirely missing. First, the artwork is not produced as a commodity (a 'ready-made' in Baxandall's terms), and second, there is no public for art in any substantial sense. Without the first precondition, the public funding of art would only be able to take the form of the public commissioning of art. Without the second precondition, funding for art that derives its funds from the state can only be state funding. The first precondition is brought about by the introduction of a market for artworks by living artists. The second, that we will come to shortly, is inaugurated by the establishment a public for art itself, rather than the institutions which art had previously served.

At the beginning of the eighteenth century a young painter such as Watteau would be apprenticed to a master (a status assigned by the guild) and would try to attach himself to a patron.[37] By the end of the century, young artists would be educated in academies and through these institutions also establish relations with patrons. Academies of art were 'effective instruments for the central control of education and patronage',[38] and during the eighteenth century there was an enormous growth of these Enlightenment institutions of art. In 1740 there were fewer than forty art academies in the whole of Europe but before the end of the century there were more than a hundred.[39] The role of the patron was changing. No longer the commissioner of bespoke works, the patron of the eighteenth century maintains artists primarily through the purchases of works. Although it is not the dominant economic form through which artists make their living or artworks are exchanged, a market for artworks was developing and artists produced pictures for a limited clientele, no longer under the command of an individual commissioning patron.

36   Ibid.
37   See Crow 1985, p. 58.
38   Eitner 1971, p. 29.
39   See Eitner 1971, p. 30.

Art patronage of the type developed in the Renaissance was replaced with new economic relations but, at the same time, art was assuming a public role in society and a value of its own, culminating in the theory of aesthetics. In fact, the public seemed to offer an alternative to patronage and the market for speculative artworks. The new notion of the public in the eighteenth century could be converted into a revenue source, occasionally, when artists exhibited their works publicly and charged an entry fee. William Hogarth was prominent among another kind of artist who issued prints of their paintings to sell to art's new public directly. In fact, Hogarth was instrumental in the passing of an Act of Parliament in 1735, known as 'Hogarth's Act', to protect the copyright of engravers from unauthorised pirate prints.[40] Hogarth's antipathy to patronage is expressed in 'The No Dedication'[41] which was found among his papers after his death, which dedicates his work to 'nobody'. At the same time, academy theorists presented to high society the case for regarding paintings as a suitable subject for polite conversation and art criticism was developed to occupy the place between the experts, connoisseurs and artists, on one side, and the public, society and 'lay critic', on the other. And it is precisely at this time that the notion of a public for art makes its appearance. Thomas Crow tells us, 'the Salon was the first regularly repeated, open, and free display of contemporary art in Europe to be offered in a completely secular setting and for the purpose of encouraging a primarily aesthetic response in large numbers of people'.[42] During the same period in which the academy and the salon became central institutions of art, the art museum was invented and the artist established a new relationship with the art dealer.

Generally speaking, then, the bourgeoisie does not merely make headway in establishing the dominance of the capitalist mode of production but also 'begins to carve out for itself a distinct discursive space' in the eighteenth century, through the establishment of 'social institutions – clubs, journals, coffee houses, periodicals – in which private individuals assemble for the free, equal interchange of reasonable discourse'.[43] The most spectacular gesture

---

40   See Bindman 1981, p. 62.

41   Perhaps written for a published volume, 'The No Dedication' is a parody of the conventional dedications made by artists to their patrons. Hogarth specifically states that his work is not dedicated to various holders of authority, wealth and power before suggesting that his work, instead, is dedicated to 'nobody' which he equates with 'anybody' (see Eitner 1971, p. 105).

42   Crow 1985, p. 3.

43   Eagleton 1984, p. 9.

of a social institution that transformed art from the classic public sphere of princely patronage to the bourgeois public sphere and public ownership occurred in 1793, when the French revolutionary government nationalised the king's art collection and declared the Louvre a public institution. 'As a public space, the museum also made manifest the public it claimed to serve: it could produce it as a visible entity by literally providing and giving it something to do',[44] Carol Duncan explains. Economically, the liberation of information and opinion from 'authoritarian, aristocratic art judgements'[45] was necessary for the free market to operate effectively in art, but the values and institutions of the public sphere were justified on their own terms and for their own sake, creating at the same time, therefore, a mode of social being that contrasted with and could be wielded against the mechanisms of the market.

The freedom of the self-determining artist was established in a variety of ways and with various levels of success throughout the eighteenth century, culminating in the Romantic image of the isolated, sensitive and inspired artist. While institutions were establishing a secular and rational basis for art education, the art market and the relationship between art and the public, for the first time in history artists in the middle of the eighteenth century claimed to be oriented not by god or piety, nor by knowledge and skill, but by their own 'unconscious drives, inspiration and interior vision'.[46] William Blake epitomises the Romantic version of the opposition to courtly patronage. 'I, William Blake, a Mental Prince', he wrote vitriolically against the patronage of art by Louis XIV and Charles I, 'should decollate and Hang their Souls as Guilty of Mental High Treason'.[47] Blake is an advocate of the new relationship between the artist and the public in terms that are more directly economic than most artists: 'Liberality! we want not liberality. We want a Fair Price & Proportionate Value & a General Demand for Art'.[48] But even Thomas Gainsborough 'was most reluctant to paint to the orders of his customers'.[49] Joshua Reynolds founded the Royal Academy specifically to foster the self-government of visual art. This is why the market for artworks, if carefully negotiated, could be seen as an institution for the liberation of the artist. George Morland has been identified

---

44   Duncan 1995, p. 24.
45   Hohendahl 1982, p. 53.
46   Eitner 1971, p. 71.
47   Eitner 1971, p. 108.
48   Ibid.
49   Barrell 1980, p. 95.

as the first painter in England to enjoy 'a new era in artist-client relationship'[50] that corresponds precisely with the now standard case of the commercially successful artist: 'the artist produces works in his own studio, at his own expense as regards materials and time, and sells them through an agent or gallery'.[51] In France, it was a commission from an art dealer that allowed Watteau to free himself from the master to which he was an assistant, but it was only when the dealer acted as a middle man between the artist and a public of connoisseur collectors that Watteau could become independent in a fuller sense. Portrait painters in the eighteenth century could transform 'portrait painting [into] "a kind of manufacture", in which the procedure was standardized to allow for the division of labour and the production of replicas'.[52] There was money in it, but the artist had to work to commission and flatter the sitter, typically but not exclusively in familiar styles and compositions, but nevertheless, exhibiting 'servility'[53] to some extent.

Even before Romanticism demands autonomy for art and the artist in a tone of voice that presupposes the value of subjective judgement, idiosyncratic perception and uncompromising liberty, artists like Morland were 'determined to avoid that contact with his polite customers in which he would be forced to pay for their admiration with his own independence'.[54] This turn inwards, insofar as it continues to shape the relationship between the artist and his or her work, and therefore the relationship between art and its public, including its patrons and collectors, is both the result of the transformation of the economy of art and the basis on which all economic relations of art have been established until the present day. While the art market could help liberate artists from patronage in the eighteenth century, the independence of the artist had already been established by the non-market institution of the academy, tied as it was to aristocratic patronage and authorised by the monarchy. The salon was a different model again, establishing links between the art community and the public at large through a selection process by experts formed into a jury. The public museum was a revolutionary institution that placed whole collections of artworks that had previously been owned and displayed privately by the very wealthiest of individuals. And finally, the Romantic genius, starving or otherwise, was an innovation of the late eighteenth century and early nineteenth century who cherished art's independence above all else. In fact,

50   Thomas 1954, p. 5.
51   Thomas 1954, pp. 5–6.
52   Bindman 1981, p. 125.
53   Bindman 1981, p. 144.
54   Barrell 1980, p. 97.

it is impossible to imagine Keynes's defence of the artist's independent vision without the values of the 'new era' of the eighteenth-century independence of the artist from his or her clients remaining vivid. The Arts Council, therefore, can be understood as a modern cocktail made up of the most emancipatory institutions of art from the Renaissance to the eighteenth century.

The public funding for the arts that Keynes pioneered combines the late eighteenth century insistence on artistic independence and individuality and a new role for the state within a novel economics of patronage. It is based, also, on the conception of the bourgeois public sphere. Historically, the Arts Council model develops as much out of the Humanist tradition of patronage as it does the earlier practice of religious patronage, but it also depends upon the transformation of artistic production that took place through the replacement of patronage with dealers mediating between artists and collectors. The art market is a prerequisite for its apparent opposite, the public funding of art. But the public funding of art is not merely a bastardised form of market relation. Public funding reverses the order of priorities of fifteenth century patronage in which the interests of the church and the patron take precedence over the interests of art and the artist properly administered. Also, the tensions at the heart of the salon in the eighteenth century, in which the interests and values of the public for art is not identical with those of art's clientele, were meant to be resolved by the public funding of the arts, which made funds available to art's public, represented by panels of experts who judge works on their merit.

Keynes focused on infrastructure, advice and finance, saying: 'if with state aid the material frame can be constructed, the public and the artists will do the rest between them'.[55] Public funding for building and running theatres, galleries and concert halls was intended to encourage independent creative endeavour. The Arts Council was intended by Keynes to 'provide facilities, infrastructure, and funding to fledgling and established groups. It would assist artists, not compete with them. It would continue to organize exhibitions for regional tours'.[56] Keynes hoped, among other things, 'to support new artists before their works [were] accepted by the market'.[57] By injecting public funds into the construction of theatres, galleries and concert halls, Keynes believed that the state could encourage the arts, artists and the public for art. 'The purpose of the Arts Council of Great Britain', he said in a BBC broadcast,

55   Keynes 1982, p. 361.
56   Upchurch 2004, p. 215.
57   Upchurch 2004, p. 212.

is to create an environment to breed a spirit, to cultivate an opinion, to offer a stimulus to such purpose that the artist and the public can each sustain and live on the other in that union which has occasionally existed in the past at the great ages of a communal civilized life.[58]

The British state would have to rebuild the economy after the war, and there was a groundswell of opinion that the new Britain should be more equitable, more democratic and more 'modern' than the traditional, elitist Britain that preceded the war. Artists in the Bloomsbury group (to which Keynes belonged) and beyond had been calling for a new Britain since the Vorticist manifesto, and Ruskin, Morris and the Pre-Raphaelite Brotherhood before them. The establishment of the Arts Council of Great Britain brought these two move-ments together in a pragmatic, limited way. First, the arts need premises. The financing of buildings was urgent in the years following the bombardment of Britain during wwii. Second, these institutions need content. Keynes planned to tour national collections and offer grants to individuals. This last was under-played in Keynes's proclamations about the Arts Council but was essential to promoting independence in the production of art, which was the only guar-antee of supporting the best, least conventional and most challenging works.

The Arts Council was an adventure in state intervention in the economy of art that combined innovative economic arrangements with a commitment to the liberty of the artist and the quality of art within a context of the bour-geois public sphere, but it was immediately constrained by the social forma-tion of the state organisation. Senior members of the Arts Council staff were *appointed*, which led to the organisation being run primarily by the British upper class. Williams, not typical of the pool from which the Council was drawn, was a member of the Council for three years, and remained supportive and critical at the same time. He makes the general point vividly:

> The extension of the social services, including education, is an undoubted gain...which must not be underestimated by those who have simply inherited it. But it remains true...that in their actual operation they remain limited by assumptions and regulations belonging not to the new society but the old.[59]

Instead of the original conception of the organisation being a launching pad for increasingly radical conceptions, the Arts Council lost faith in its original

---

58   Keynes quoted in Harrod 1972, p. 619.
59   Williams 1965, pp. 329–30.

vision and withdrew partly from the commitments that set it apart from the officialdom of the art academy and the instrumentalisation of the patronage of art by state and church. The Arts Council started out in a compromise with the establishment and proceeded to become successively more established and more bureaucratic, with an ever increasing focus on institutions rather than artists, and directed more and more by governmental priorities.

Why did the arts require an Arts Council after World War II? Why not just treat the arts as a commercial activity that, if demand happened to be elusive, they would go out of business? Art had survived for centuries without arm's length public funding, and some of the most highly acclaimed art in history had been produced under unpromising economic circumstances, so why could not art make its own way in the world, so to speak? First, capitalism entered a new phase in this period in which the state played an unprecedented pivotal role in the capitalist economy, and so it would be unfair to single out the state's role in art, as opposed to the state's role in industry, commerce and finance generally. Second, art since the 1920s had normalised the modernist and avant-garde antipathy to the tastes of the educated, leading its reception to be characterised by almost universal hostility (apart from an extremely small group of *aficionados*). While the art market had always neglected living artists in favour of old masters and ancient artefacts, the market for the avant-garde was notoriously weak. Left to the market, such work, which had proved in retrospect to be the best art of its day, would have no chance. Third, the Second World War had led to a clamour for a new more equitable society, and the subsequent building of the welfare state provided a rationale for the state funding of living well, in which art found a place. Fourth, the state was already involved in art and therefore the new patronage of the arts merely modified the principles and administration of the state's relationship to art.

What is important about the Keynesian implementation of public subsidy for the arts is that it was an integral part of a new economics that focused on social welfare rather than capital accumulation. Art's economic exceptionalism as a result of the effects of the public subsidy of the arts might, therefore, be understood in terms of Esping-Andersen's concept of 'de-commodification'. The welfare state identifies certain key goods that are not to be allocated according to supply and demand but universally and for free as social rights. 'The outstanding criterion for social rights must be the degree to which they permit people to make their living standards independent of pure market forces'.[60] According to Esping-Andersen, de-commodification is not 'all or nothing': the 'degree of market immunity' is directly proportional

---

60   Esping-Andersen 1990, p. 3.

to 'the strength, scope, and quality of social rights'.[61] While the 'social right' to art never had the urgency, popular appeal or political implications of the universal public provision of 'the core areas of human need',[62] the principal of engineering a degree of market immunity for something prized over and above its economic value is the same. However, it might be necessary to supplement the theory of art's public subsidy not only with the progressive processes of de-commodification but also the conservative defence of 'pre-commodification'.[63] If the production of art had never been fully commodified in the first place, and if art remained economically exceptional even while it functioned anoma-lously within capitalism, then strictly speaking it would be impossible for art to be de-commodified. Public subsidy for the arts could, at best, be described as art's de-commodification without art's de-commodification. The public sub-sidy of the arts after the Second World War, therefore, may be more accurately understood as an example of the preservation, conservation and expansion of a pre-commodified sphere of culture.

The new institutions of the welfare state spurred developments in welfare economics. At the end of the 1950s, Richard Musgrave invented a new term to identify a special kind of good, or 'want' as he put it, which is publicly funded because it has merit. In his book *The Theory of Public Finance* (1959), Musgrave argued that the state had three objectives to budget policy: allocation, distri-bution and stabilisation.[64] This is the broader context in which to understand the concept of merit wants or merit goods, as they have become known. Merit goods are best understood by distinguishing them from public goods. Public goods, according to the doctrine, are non-excludable and non-rival in con-sumption. Clean air is an example of a public good, since everybody benefits equally from its provision. Providing the instruments, manpower and facilities for democratic elections can be included here too. Now, art is a public good if it can be shown to be non-rival and non-excludable. 'Non-rivalry means that the enjoyment of a good by one person does not reduce what is there for oth-ers to enjoy, and non-excludability means it is not possible (at least without

---

61   Esping-Andersen 1990, p. 37.

62   Esping-Andersen 1990, p. 46.

63   See Esping-Andersen 1990, pp. 38–41.

64   Throsby thus confuses two of Musgrave's objectives, allocation and distribution, when he says: 'Distributional questions, too, are an important aspect of the concept of merit goods, providing a rationale for in-kind transfers to the disadvantaged in areas such as housing and education. The arts do not fit comfortably alongside these examples, because they can scarcely be construed as a social or economic necessity, no matter how convinced artists and others might be of the central importance of art in life' (Throsby 1994, p. 24).

excessive expense and difficulty) to stop people gaining access to them',[65] as Towse so concisely puts it. In the first instance, of course, looking at an artwork (or listening to it, reading it, etc.) does not use it up for rival consumers. In the second instance, artworks can be purchased and exhibited or stored in private, preventing others from enjoying them, but this is not what the condition of excludability is based on. Exclusion in economics is a question of private property and scarcity: if I cannot exclude others from consuming a product that they have not paid for, then I have no incentive to purchase it myself. Air, water and sunlight are non-excludable, and that is why classical economists said they could not fetch any sort of price.[66] Art is excludable in a way that air and national defence are not, but if art is a Veblen good (a good bought specifically to display one's wealth and taste), then it is not excludable without failing in at least one of the purchasers' incentives. Musgrave's examples are flood control, sanitary campaigns, the judiciary, and the armed forces. Since there is no way for the market to ensure that those who pay for flood control are protected while those who refuse to pay or cannot pay will not be protected, then social wants of this kind 'cannot be satisfied through the mechanism of the market'.[67]

> Whereas demand schedules for the satisfaction of private wants are revealed in the auction process of the market, such is not the case for the satisfaction of public wants. Since the same amount will be consumed by all, individuals know that they cannot be excluded from the resulting benefits. This being the case they are not forced to reveal their preferences through bidding in the market. The 'exclusion principle', which is essential to exchange, cannot be applied; and the market mechanism does not work.[68]

Therefore, while it is clear that health and education are both excludable and rivalrous – private education and private healthcare are not available to non-fee payers and one fee payer excludes a rival potential fee payer – they cannot be 'public goods' in the strict sense. However, if society believes that education ought to be available for all regardless of ability to pay and regardless of effectual demand, then, Musgrave argues, there is an argument for providing such goods publicly. When we do, the state supplies 'merit wants'. Merit wants are to

---

65   Towse 2010, p. 28.

66   For a critical discussion of art as a Veblen good, see pp. 284–6.

67   Musgrave 1959, p. 9.

68   Musgrave 1957, pp. 334–5.

be supplied by the public purse regardless of ability to pay but also regardless of consumer demand.

Consider an army. If we think of national defence as an expenditure that is non-excludable and non-rival (all citizens benefit from it) then we might regard it as a public good, but if we contrast it with private armies and local militias, then it is a merit good. The difference is not inherent in the good but refers to the *rationale* for public funding. If a good has so much merit that we believe as a society that everyone ought to be able to consume it regardless of ability to pay (and, moreover, regardless of the choice to consume it), then, it will, as a result, be exempted from the economics of supply and demand. That is to say, health and education are not economically exceptional – they can be supplied according to demand on the market and their prices equilibrated – but providing them publicly as merit goods has the consequence that the market no longer applies to them in the standard way. When goods with merit become merit goods through state subsidy, then do they become economically exceptional? Some indication that merit goods are economically exceptional can be gauged from the controversy that the concept has generated among neoliberal advocates of free markets. The controversy over merit goods is tied up with its flouting of consumer sovereignty. Merit goods, which are publicly funded to ensure universal, equal and free consumption, contradict consumer sovereignty. Consumer sovereignty has no part to play in the allocation of merit goods because the decision to produce them for universal consumption is taken by democratic representatives. The suspension of consumer sovereignty that the concept of merit goods requires strongly indicates that another (non-economic) form of sovereignty takes precedence. This is why Musgrave warned very early on that 'the satisfaction of collective wants should be limited because of the compulsion involved'.[69] In his discussion of social wants, Musgrave asks a searching question. 'Since the market mechanism fails to reveal consumer preferences in social wants, it may be asked what mechanism there is'.[70] The answer is the mechanism of democratic collective decision-making, or, as he puts it, voting. Voting reveals preferences that markets cannot. Neither markets nor voting can reveal the preferences (and shared interests and collective decisions!) that fully participatory democracy reveals. What this question of merit goods – and merit generally – refers to, therefore, is the limit of both economics and free markets.

---

69   Musgrave 1941, p. 320.

70   Musgrave 1959, p. 10.

West and McKee suggest that the public supply of merit goods ought to be temporary measures. If, they argue, those who are uneducated are less likely to demand education in the open market, then supplying education services to them will raise their education and, presumably, show them the value of education, leading to an increase in demand for education. And they regard the fact that universal free and compulsory education still exists as proof that the merit want arguments and the policies they have fostered have failed. To make this assessment they first have to convert a hypothesis into a condition. The market, we might speculate, can supply some merit goods, once the state's provision of them as merit goods has created the demand for them. However, subjecting the education of our children to market forces, in which ability to pay and willingness to pay are determining forces, is clearly to give advantage to the wealthy. Even in higher education, which has no claim to be universal, it is wrong from a pedagogical point of view to have candidates for study pre-selected by their ability to pay rather than their ability to excel. The point of recognising and funding merit goods is to ensure that every member of society has access to those benefits that society deems to be universally valuable and should not be restricted to those who can afford them. The argument that merit goods ought to have a shelf life depends on changes actually taking place in society to remedy the situation that public policy was introduced to remedy. If we still have universal mandatory education this is not because merit goods do not work, but because society has not rejected the principle of the provision of free universal education.

There is no economic rationale for the funding of merit goods; the case for public funding derives from norms at large in society, or perhaps that part of society that has effective sway over policy makers. Insofar as neoliberal economists and neoliberal politicians campaign for the reduction of state funding in almost every branch of public finance, it could be argued that they regard almost all publicly funded goods as merit goods. In fact, 'merit goods' might be best understood as a concept that approaches economics from the perspective of non-economic priorities. Economics has no methods to predict such priorities and market mechanisms are incapable of allocating them in the desired magnitudes (that is to say, universally and equally). The question I want to raise, then, is whether merit goods are a previously neglected example of exceptionalism. We have taken note of two categories of exception, one belonging to classical economics and the other belonging to neoclassicism, but if merit goods are exceptional they are exceptional to economics not because they are natural or artificial monopolies, or because of their increasing marginal utility, but because they benefit from a mechanism for allocating resources that is political rather than economic. If art is a merit good, and merit goods are exceptional, then we have another instance from within economics, this time from welfare economics, for arguing that art is exceptional. Interestingly, in this case, art's exceptionalism would have nothing to do with its economic performance (for instance, fancy prices) or anomalous consumption patterns (for instance, increasing marginal utility) but the special status assigned to art socially. The test of whether art is a merit good is simple. First, examine state policy and see if art is publicly funded. If it is, and art does not meet the two conditions of a public good (that is, non-excludable and non-rival), then, so long as the public funding of art is not for the purpose of propping up the national economy or redistributing wealth, then it is (in practice) a merit good. On the two conditions of a public good, then, we can say conclusively that art is non-rival, but we can say only that art is often but not necessarily non-excludable. But if art is not a public good, and yet receives public subsidy, then it is in all likelihood a merit good.

Merit goods are not funded for economic reasons, but due to policy decisions taken by government, so market forces are marginal to their allocation. Like art, as we have seen, merit goods are not governed by consumer sovereignty but an alternative type of sovereignty. If art is a merit good then it is funded publicly for political, social and cultural reasons alone. For this reason we can speculate that merit goods are better understood, perhaps, within the classical concept of 'value in use', rather than marginal utility, because they are isolated from market mechanisms and are meant to be allocated universally, equally and for free. The classical concept of 'value in use' or 'use value' appears to be upgraded in the concept of merit good. While use value is subjective, individual and the precondition for purchasing, the only valid and effective argument against a merit good is that it is not meritorious. Any argument that art ought not to be subsidised, therefore, must address the normative conditions of its subsidy.

By 1960, the year after the publication of Musgrave's book that launched the concept of merit goods, Dorothy Thompson published her article 'Farewell to the Welfare State'. Thompson documents and responds critically to a definite shift in thinking about the state, specifically the welfare state and the role the state might play for the Labour Party in British politics. She felt that she was swimming against the tide when she argued that the left had 'become far too shy in making demands on public funds', that 'the overall policy on social questions had not advanced since 1945 – in fact it had in many ways receded', and that 'a number of the recommendations from the [Beveridge] Report were never put into operation'.[71] Ironically, it was when the momentum of

---

71   Thompson 1960, p. 42.

Keynesianism as a doctrine was running flat in Britain that public funding for the arts was extended in the UK by the Wilson government and the
National Endowment for the Arts (NEA) was established in the United States
of America, introducing state subsidies for the arts. In one sense, the NEA was
the culmination of the period that began with Keynes's founding of the Arts
Council immediately after World War II, because the new settlement between
art, the market and the state was extended to the greatest capitalist society of
the era. In another sense, however, the NEA signals a new chapter in the history
of art's economics, because the NEA triggered a backlash from economists that
contributed to the end of the Keynesian consensus on the legitimacy of public
funding for the arts.

On the cusp of the backlash against public subsidy for the arts, two major
contributions by American economists extended the insights of Keynes and
Musgrave to the economics of art. The first major American economist to
engage with the economics of art was Galbraith, initially in a lecture series at
Harvard in 1963, then in the final contribution of his BBC Reith lecture series
in 1966, expanded in his book published the following year *The New Industrial
State*.[72] Galbraith raises the question of the economics of art within an argument against the one-dimensional dominance of economic calculation across
the whole breadth of lived experience. Galbraith says, 'if we continue to believe
that the goals of the modern industrial system ... are co-ordinate with all of
life ... [w]e will be the mentally indentured servants of the industrial system'.[73]
This argument echoes that of Max Weber's concept of the 'iron cage' of the
rationalised modernity of capitalism but Galbraith proposes an alternative. 'If
industrial goals are not the only goals, other purposes will be pursued' and '[a]
esthetic goals will have pride of place'.[74] This, then, is a critique, in part, of the
dehumanisation brought about by economic rationality, both through anony-
mously incentivised market mechanisms and through the economic logic of
such a system expressed in economic science. Art, along with the aesthetic
organisation of our lived environment, is singled out as 'a special casualty of
the goals and values of the industrial system'.[75] Galbraith identifies three forms
of the conflict between industrial capitalism and art or the aesthetic life. First,
he observes, there is a conflict between 'beauty and industrial efficiency'.[76]
When production is governed by value for money only, then it makes sense 'to

---

72   Galbraith 2007.
73   Galbraith 1966, p. 6.
74   Ibid.
75   Ibid.
76   Galbraith 1966, p. 7.

have highways take the most direct route through countryside or villages ... to allow modern jet aircraft to ignore the tranquillity of those below; to pour industrial refuse into the air and the streams'.[77] Second, Galbraith claims that there is a conflict between the artist and organisations, hence, the 'artist does badly as an organization man; the organization does badly by the artist. So he tends to stand outside the modern industrial system'.[78] Third, Galbraith argues that 'artistic expression requires a framework of order',[79] citing the need to protect the Taj Mahal from being squeezed between two petrol stations. As such, Galbraith mixes the case for art's exceptionalism with a more far-reaching argument for society to be organised according to aesthetic values.

'The remedy, in each case', Galbraith says,

> is to subordinate economic to aesthetic goals—to sacrifice efficiency, including the efficiency of organization, to beauty. Nor must there be any apologetic nonsense about beauty paying in the long run. It need not pay.[80]

Galbraith, therefore, takes a position more antagonistic to business than Keynes and yet provides a level of intellectual validity for the new policy of state funding for the arts in the US. In fact, he cannot imagine a remedy to be executable without 'strong action by the state'[81] because leaving the built environment and culture to the mechanisms of the market place has historically had an aesthetic effect that was 'at best undistinguished and more often ... ghastly'.[82] Galbraith's argument, therefore, goes beyond economic analysis and can be seen as anti-economic, not concerning itself with the allocation of resources but with the clash of values between market forces and artistic quality, siding with the latter. Ruth Towse accuses Galbraith of developing a 'normative economics' of art, saying he

> regarded the arts as 'exceptional' – that is, not like other economic goods – because they are produced by 'artisan' methods rather than being

---

77   Ibid.
78   Ibid.
79   Ibid.
80   Ibid.
81   Ibid.
82   Ibid.

mass-produced by the big business he abhorred and inveighed against in his many writings.[83]

Note, here, the use of the word 'abhorred' and the phrase 'inveighed against' to indicate the normative basis of Galbraith's claims about the relationship between art and economics. If Galbraith does regard the arts as exceptional then it is not normative to say so, nor is it normative to devise economic measures for reproducing the economic preconditions for art. If art is in fact economically exceptional and this fact is dismissed as objectionable, then the imposition of standard market measures on art must be normative. Towse hopes to dispel the case for exceptionalism by showing that Galbraith harbours normative intent, whereas she ought to demonstrate that treating art as exceptional must be normative by proving, through an economic analysis of art, that art is not economically exceptional.

In the same year as Galbraith's Reith lectures, William Baumol, an American economist who taught both economics and sculpture at Princeton, collaborated with William Bowen on a book that set out, at least in part, to establish the economic credentials of the case for state subsidy of the arts. Galbraith's contribution was theoretical while Baumol and Bowen assembled empirical data that they subjected to systematic analysis. Baumol was approached in 1966 by the Twentieth Century Fund, led by August Heckscher and John D. Rockefeller III, to complete a study on the performing arts. Rockefeller belonged to probably the most important family of philanthropists in New York, and he campaigned for increased state support for the arts, was an art collector and founder of the Lincoln Center for the Performing Arts incorporating 12 institutions, including the Metropolitan Opera, the Lincoln Center Theater, the New York Philharmonic and the New York City Ballet. One consequence of this invitation was Baumol and Bowen's pioneering study *Performing Arts: The Economic Dilemma*,[84] funded by Rockefeller under Heckscher's guidance. This book not only provided precisely the kind of argument that the campaign needed, it also changed the relationship between art and the discipline of economics. A handful of economists had made important comments about art or even advised policy makers and others on the funding and administration of the arts before, but Baumol and Bowen brought art under the *methodology* of economic analysis for the first time. Galbraith was an economist who spoke in an informed way about the relationship between art and modern capitalist conditions of production and consumption, but he did not study any empirical

---

83   Towse 2010, p. 14.
84   Baumol and Bowen 1966.

data or focus on any distinct economic factor of art. Baumol and Bowen attempted for the first time to test economically whether the arts had a special need for state funding, and they did this by focusing on one specific case study, namely, the labour costs of the performing arts. Baumol and Bowen's stated conclusions did not veer seriously away from the theoretical case of Galbraith and supported the Keynesian marriage of state and art, but their methods gave this position a new empirical and statistical basis.

Baumol and Bowen's account of the increasing costs and therefore prices of tickets for certain types of art – not unique old masters, but live music and theatrical productions – is due, not to the impossibility of reproducing them through labour, but to the fact that the labour of which they consist cannot be automated or made more efficient through increases in productivity. What they found was that the costs of the performing arts did not benefit from productivity gains and the mechanisation of industry, and, on the contrary, that they suffered increasing costs as a result of efficiencies elsewhere. Unlike other sectors of the economy, the productivity of the performing arts has not increased for centuries. Since the productivity of labour within the performing arts 'cannot hope to match the remarkable record of productivity growth achieved by the economy as a whole',[85] the cost of labour in the performing arts rises relative to the cost of more productive labour elsewhere. Baumol and Bowen dubbed the effect of the static productivity of labour in the performing arts the 'cost disease'. Whereas in industry the division of labour can multiply output per worker and machinery can reduce the number of workers required to produce a given quantity of goods, the performing arts, Baumol and Bowen observe, always require the same number of musicians to play a Beethoven string quartet today as were needed in the nineteenth century. This fact flouts the methodological assumptions of mainstream economics and is not the case in economic and productive activity generally. In short, it is certainly anomalous and perhaps exceptional. The 'productivity lag' identified by Baumol and Bowen means that labour costs rise and revenue lags behind, creating an 'earnings gap'. To fill the gap, they argued, 'increased support from other sources will have to be found if the performing arts are to continue their present role in the cultural life'.[86] Many within the arts community took this to be a justification for public arts subsidy.

Since the 1990s, Baumol has extended the case for the cost disease to include health care, education and much else besides. Although the principles have remained the same, other than the supplementary argument that the

---

85   Baumol and Bowen 1966, p. 165.
86   Baumol and Bowen 1966, p. 502.

cost disease is its own cure and therefore 'yes, we can afford it',[87] the place of the performing arts within the debate has become marginal and the visual arts have not been included. Baumol focuses on sectors that 'require direct, face-to-face interaction between those who provide the service and those who consume it'.[88] So while the manufacturing of watches becomes cheaper, quicker and requires less labour time, the costs of repairing old watches, which requires the time of a skilled technician, cannot keep up because the 'maintenance and repair of products inherently resist automation'.[89] As average costs drop through automation, the costs of those activities that cannot be automated rise year on year in relation to the average.

> The items in the rising-cost group generally have a handicraft element – that is, a human element not readily replaceable by machines – in their production process, which makes it difficult to reduce their labor content.[90]

From a technical point of view, Baumol points out, research and development suffers from the cost disease insofar as 'there seems to be little reason to believe that we have become more proficient at this handicraft activity than Newton, Leibnitz, and Huygens'.[91] It seems plausible that the same could be said for painters, sculptors and other artists who produce artworks in ways that cannot be automated. By 1925 Ford's automated production could produce each day the equivalent of the yearly output that his craftsmen produced in 1908 and at prices that consistently declined. Picasso, working in the same period, worked no faster and his paintings became more expensive. 'If we speed up the work of surgeons, teachers, or musicians, we are likely to get shoddy heart surgery, poorly trained students, or a very strange musical performance'.[92] Relative to the average productivity of workers, artists are lagging behind, like police officers, librarians and hairdressers.

Did Baumol and Bowen's 'cost disease' establish a new case, implicitly or explicitly, for art's economic exceptionalism? I want to separate this question from the argument for or against public subsidy. State funding may be called on in the case of the service sector that suffers from the cost disease and for

---

87   Baumol 2012, pp. 43–68.
88   Baumol 2012, p. 20.
89   Baumol 2012, p. 37.
90   Baumol 2012, p. 19.
91   Baumol 2012, p. 114.
92   Baumol 2012, p. 23.

economically exceptional goods, but the case for exceptionality needs to be formulated independently. The cost disease is not simply another name or another set of criteria for economic exceptionalism. Repairing watches is not economically exceptional in any of the senses that we have amassed so far and I am not claiming it to be exceptional: it is a service offered on the market to consumers at the going rate. However, we might say that non-automated labour is *technologically exceptional* and that this has economic effects. So, while the cost disease is not a new explanation for the fancy prices of famous artworks sold for millions at auction, and nor is it an explanation of the increasing marginal utility of art, it can supplement the account of art's economic exceptionalism with an economic analysis of the escalating costs of the time necessary to make art and to study as an art student, and potentially the escalating costs of the public subsidy of the arts. Not only is art production the kind of handicraft work that cannot be automated, the same necessity for long periods of time for preparation, research and production are needed for curating art history, art criticism, art education, and so on. Insofar as the cost disease derives from the impossibility of automating work that is human and requires direct human engagement, art of all types and its institutions (principally, the art school, the museum and the art magazine) will be vivid examples of such labour. However, since artists, unlike dancers, actors and musicians tend not to be wage labourers, the costs of the cost disease on the visual arts will be more hidden. But if art is economically exceptional (and this continues to be misunderstood and denied) as well as susceptible to the cost disease (which is also misperceived and rejected by a significant proportion of economists), then the economics of art will be beset with obstructions for the foreseeable future. The next chapter will outline the leading objections to treating art as an economic special case.

CHAPTER 5

Exceptionalism after 1966

The standard narrative for the origin of the economics of art asserts that economists had said little or nothing about art before 1966 but that, by the end of the 1970s, a fully fledged field of 'cultural economics' had been established with its own annual international conference, its own journal, an Association and a separate classification in the bibliography of the *Journal of Economic Literature*. In 1994 Throsby, one of the leading practitioners and organisers of cultural economics as a field, wrote, 'it is only relatively recently that serious work has begun to be undertaken in the area that has come to be known as 'cultural economics', or more particularly the economics of the arts'.[1] Throsby says that 'if contemporary cultural economics has a point of origin, it would lie in the pages of a book by William J. Baumol and William Bowen'.[2] It is normal for academic disciplines to trace their origin back to founding texts, but no historian would regard Baumol and Bowen's book, no matter how pioneering or influential, as the source of subsequent events without examining the historical conditions under which the book was formed. These conditions are illuminating not only for understanding the events that led to the publishing of this special book, but also for the academic reaction to it and the eventual founding of cultural economics.

1966, the year that Baumol and Bowen's book was published, is the year that the NEA became active. Formed in 1965, the NEA began direct grants to artists in 1967, including, in its first year, three young artists that were soon to be recognised as leading artists of their generation, Carl Andre, Dan Flavin and Robert Morris. Heckscher had been appointed by John F. Kennedy as a Special Consultant on the Arts and was asked to prepare a report to the President entitled 'The Arts and National Government'. His recommendation, delivered early in 1963, was to establish the Advisory Council on the Arts and the National Arts Foundation to administer grants. Kennedy's interest in culture was not unprecedented in the USA, with the Works Progess Administration (WPA) funding art projects in the Depression era. What is more, some senators had warned Congress to keep up with Soviet arts funding in the 1950s as 'the cold war was opening an aesthetic front'.[3] Kennedy and Heckscher gave

---

1   Throsby 1994, p. 2.
2   Ibid.
3   Kaufman 1990 (unpaginated).

© KONINKLIJKE BRILL NV, LEIDEN, 2015 | DOI 10.1163/9789004288157_007

Federal support for the arts a different agenda. While the Keynesian rationale in Britain had signalled the need to supplement the market with state provision, the American introduction of government assistance to the arts was carefully steered away from interfering with the market and private patronage, which was well established in America. And no wonder: even today more than $6 billion is donated by private and corporate sponsors to art in the USA. In his letter thanking Heckscher for delivering the report, Kennedy reiterated this point, anticipating 'what I am confident will be a new and fruitful relationship between Government and the arts. Government can never take over the role of patronage and support filled by private individuals and groups in our society. But Government surely has a significant part to play in helping establish the conditions under which art can flourish – in encouraging the arts as it encourages science and learning'.[4] All this led, in the financial year 1965–6, to the creation of the NEA.[5] Roger Stevens, described as a 'hard-headed real estate broker…who once bought the Empire State Building',[6] was appointed by President Johnson in 1964 as Special Assistant to the President on the Arts, the first full-time arts advisor. He later became the first chairman of the National Council on the Arts, under which the NEA was eventually established alongside the National Endowment for the Humanities.

Despite the inclusion of state support for artists within the WPA as part of the New Deal in the second half of the 1930s, Congress consistently rejected the development of an arts policy after the dissolution of the WPA in 1938, deploying arguments against curtailing the freedom of artists alongside the argument for *laissez-faire*.[7] 'Prior to the 1960s, the American government made no substantive attempts to institute a national arts policy for the United States'.[8] Before the NEA was made possible in the 1960s, 'a few dedicated arts advocates[9] began laying the foundation in the 1950s for future legislation'.[10] The election of John F. Kennedy as President in 1960 'set in motion an upsurge of interest in

---

4   Kennedy 1963 (unpaginated).

5   For an official government timeline that links Heckscher's report to the founding of the
      NEA see the online document 'The National Endowment for the Arts 1965–2000: A Brief
      Chronology of Federal Support for the Arts', Keith Donohue (ed.), Washington DC, 2000,
      available at http://www.nea.gov/pub/NEAChronWeb.pdf.

6   Library of Congress press release, April 9 2002, available at http://www.loc.gov/today/
      pr/2002/02–049.html.

7   See Binkiewicz 2004, p. 24.

8   Binkiewicz 2004, p. 33.

9   See Binkiewicz 2004, pp. 24–33.

10   Binkiewicz 2004, p. 24.

cultural advance and support for arts policy'[11] framed partly in terms that echo the case against state subsidy in the previous two or three decades. Kennedy advocated state support for the arts on the basis that art itself promoted *laissez-faire* against authoritarianism: art, he said, 'speaks a language without words, and is thus a chief means for proclaiming America's message to the world over the heads of dictators'.[12] Anti-communist liberal pragmatism, particularly in the influential writings of Arthur Schlesinger, 'became an integral part of both Kennedy's and Johnson's political philosophy',[13] which ushered in a new era in the relationship between the American state and the arts. The political forces that pushed through the formation of the NEA were also behind Baumol and Bowen's book. Furthermore, Galbraith, who argued against art as a business activity between 1963–6, was a member of the inner circle of advisors to John F. Kennedy during this period and therefore was attached to Baumol and Bowen's book through their shared relationship to the architects of the so-called 'Great Society'. While the New Deal had been triggered by economic and social crisis, the reforms of the early 1960s were precipitated 'by both newly found affluence and the demands of African Americans'.[14] The context for the birth of the NEA, like the Arts Council of Great Britain before it, was the 'War on Poverty' alongside which

> the Johnson administration inaugurated Keynesian stimulus policies (the 1964 tax cut), legislated Medicaid/Medicare, relaxed eligibility requirements, and passed two major raises in social security benefits (1965 and 1967).[15]

After guiding through the Public Welfare Amendments in 1962, Kennedy had charged the Council of Economic Advisors with the task of proposing legislative reform for 1964. As a result, 'three days before his death Kennedy committed the administration to act on the issue [of poverty] as part of the 1964 legislative agenda'.[16] Johnson exceeded Kennedy's proposals. 'Kennedy's tentative foray into welfare reform became a War on Poverty'.[17]

---

11   Binkiewicz 2004, p. 33.
12   Kennedy quoted in Binkiewicz 2004, p. 35.
13   Binkiewicz 2004, p. 38.
14   Noble 1997, p. 80.
15   Esping-Andersen 1990, p. 175.
16   Noble 1997, p. 92.
17   Noble 1997, p. 93.

Cultural economics is the response to art's new relationship to the state, not a book on the performing arts. What is more, the book itself has not been followed up with a growing body of studies in its own image. While Baumol and Bowen are rightly credited with producing the first detailed empirical economic analysis of art, it is not their conclusions, but a critique of them, that has subsequently been taken up by cultural economists. One of the earliest respondents to Baumol and Bowen's book was Alan Peacock, an economist who studied at the LSE under Robbins alongside Baumol. Peacock reacted to Baumol and Bowen's findings in an article published in 1969 disputing the case for state subsidy to the arts. His essay 'Welfare Economics and Public Subsidies to the Arts' was a neoliberal rejoinder to what he perceived as Baumol and Bowen's call for government funding for the arts. He was, like all the other economists who pioneered the economic analysis of art, personally involved in the arts.[18] Peacock's rebuttal of the cost disease included, amongst other things, the argument that the case for government funding was flawed because it was based partly on the persistence of old 'elitist' forms of consumption, such as live performances of classical music, theatre and the opera, rather than listening to music on records or on the radio. Peacock switched the debate from an inquiry into non-automated production to an inquiry into automated forms of distribution, arguing for live performances to be replaced with recordings and broadcasts. It was Peacock's critique of Baumol and Bowen, specifically, and the case for market mechanisms as the best means by which to fund and distribute the arts generally, that has crystallised in the field of cultural economics, not the arguments set out within the alleged founding text of the economics of art. Either, therefore, it would be more accurate to name Peacock, not Baumol and Bowen, as the founder of the discipline, or it is best to point to the historical circumstance which frames their exchange as the foundation of cultural economics, namely, that it was the advent of state subsidy to the arts in the USA, specifically the NEA, that gave birth to cultural economics.

Since the 1970s there has been considerable effort by mainstream economists, under the hegemony of neoliberalism, to drive out the idea that art is a special case that requires state subsidy. 'Despite the special position that art occupies in the fabric and culture of societies', Clare McAndrew says:

---

18   He was the conductor of the LSE Orchestra, a composer, musician and Chairman of the Scottish Arts Council between 1986 and 1992. In the year in which he published his critique of Baumol and Bowen, Peacock was appointed Chairman of the Arts Council of Great Britain's Enquiry into Orchestral Resources.

the reality is that art is produced, bought, and sold by individuals and institutions working within an economic framework inescapable from material and market constraints. The economic case is clear: the market for works of art functions at least as well as many others (albeit imperfectly and with certain special features), as it allows market transactions by voluntary consent, in which buyers and sellers mutually benefit.[19]

William Grampp, in his prominent contribution to the debate, *Pricing the Priceless*, took a fanatically pro-market position. Suggesting that museums need to charge visitors prices that can be supported by the market to meet their costs, Grampp argued that museums ought to tighten their belts. He also lamented that museums fail to capitalise on the growing value of their collections and ought to sell works to help fund themselves. Grampp contends that there is no economic rationale behind arts subsidies in any form and calls for their full and total abolition. He argues that any values external to the market will necessarily be reflected in prices. Following the standard neoliberal position, he argues the problem with subsidies to the arts is that they do not reflect what people actually want, but what governments think people ought to have.

If the founding of the Arts Council triggered cultural economics by establishing a new bond between art and the state, we might see the transition from the Keynesian cultural settlement to the current neoliberal hegemony as reaching its fruition not so much in the cuts to the Arts Council in 2011, but in the launch of the Association for Business Sponsorship of the Arts in 1976. According to Neil Mulholland, this organisation was established specifically as an alternative to the model of public funding for the arts, and was a calculated 'assault on the related ideologies of culturalism and Keynesian macroeconomics'.[20] The aim was to abolish the Arts Council and all state subsidies of the arts by showing that business sponsorship could replace it without any need for interference in markets, suspension of consumer sovereignty, or universal taxes to pay for minority culture. Nevertheless, the case for business sponsorship of the arts is compatible with the argument for art's economic exceptionalism, even if it is often sold in terms of the benefits to business through association with excellence, innovation, creativity and so on.

After 1966 a new consensus begins to emerge, not immediately and not without struggle, but by the end of the 1970s it became easier within the professional environment of economics to argue that art is an economic good that

---

19   McAndrew 2010a, p. 19.
20   Mulholland 2003, p. 13.

can be explained by economics and harder to argue that it either was not a typical commodity or that economic analysis could not be applied to it in the standard way. Towse notes that Cowen and Tabarrok 'believe markets can be left to work in the cultural sector as they do in other sectors of the economy'.[21] And yet Towse observes some exceptions in art's economy; she lists the assumptions of neoclassical economics (consumers order their preferences, tastes are given and constant, consumers are costlessly informed, relative prices are the main determinant of consumer choice) and then admits:

> These assumptions do not tie up fully with observed behaviour in cultural markets, and, in addition, the theory needs modification in order to apply to cultural goods and services, which in some respects differ from 'ordinary' goods.[22]

'What is different about the arts and culture is that they deal with novelty and new experiences, about which consumers cannot be fully informed',[23] Towse says, significantly underestimating the range of differences between art and standard commodity *production*. She responds to this observation by examining the concept of 'experience goods'. Within the literature she identifies three slightly discrepant definitions of 'experience goods'. The first is that 'enjoyment increases with experience'; the second is that 'experience is required for enjoyment', and the third is that 'you buy the good for the experience it gives you'. Though all three pertain to art and culture generally, only the first pertains to art's exception from the neoclassical theory of diminishing marginal utility. However, Towse puts the emphasis on the second. Fortunately for her case, the problem of information imperfections – knowledge, taste, education and so on – she believes can be cured through good marketing. Another reason why Towse is not alarmed by art's increased marginal utility, is that she believes the problem to have been solved by Stigler and Becker in their famous essay, 'De Gustibus Non Est Disputandum', discussed in the previous chapter.

The tables had turned. Neoliberalism's expansion of market forces was an active agent in challenging the old consensus and constructing a new one, both practically in the policies of privatisation, and theoretically in the application of the calculus of choice to forms of life that had previously been neglected or regarded as taboo (Becker, for instance, infamously wrote an article about children as consumer goods).[24] The rise of a neoliberal agenda for art, however,

---

21   Towse 2010, p. 52.

22   Towse 2010, p. 151.

23   Ibid.

24   Becker 1960.

is best understood, I would argue, not as an intellectual campaign, in which neoliberals won the argument within the discipline of economics, but as an extension of a political campaign on behalf of big business and global finance as a response to very urgent and new economic questions within the changing conditions of art funding. What drew the attention of economists to study art on a significant scale, I would suggest, is the inauguration, implementation and growth of the state funding of the arts. Under this hegemony, the central doctrines of neoliberal economic thought become the horizon for cultural economics, which subsequently sets out to 'prove' that the arts are normal or near normal economic activities and/or goods. One of the decisive events in the struggle between the collective provision of culture and market forces was *The Peacock Report*, commissioned by the Thatcher government in the mid-1980s to review the possibility of subjecting the BBC to advertising, sponsorship or securing income from consumers rather than licence fees. Tim O'Malley demonstrates that Peacock's report 'marked a break'[25] in the history of thinking about broadcasting in the UK in favour of liberal economics, a conservative politics opposed to the welfare state and the 'belief in the moral value of individualism as an organising social principle,[26] because it 'provided a key justification for allowing economics to dominate the framework of broadcasting policy in the UK'.[27] The shift from the economics of subsidy for the arts to the cultural economics of neoliberal doctrine culminates in Tyler Cowen's *In Praise of Commercial Culture* (2000), which is a manifesto for the application of market forces to all culture. The history of cultural economics might be described as the attempt to prove that no economic anomaly exists in art.

This historical trajectory of cultural economics appears retrospectively to ratify Peacock's critique of Baumol and Bowen. Towse, the chief chronicler of cultural economics, sums up the difference between Peacock and the two authors of 'The Economic Dilemma' as follows: '[Peacock] questioned whether the prognosis of the Cost Disease was as "pernicious" as [Baumol and Bowen] claimed and secondly, he thought that the welfare case for public support was weaker than they implied'.[28] However, the fundamental difference between them, she says, 'was essentially the willingness to accept a role for government in the arts: Baumol, tending more to views somewhat left of centre, was more ready to embrace state involvement than Peacock, the classical liberal'.[29] Peacock had a 'classical liberal aversion to "state monopoly" ... [and] the "case

---

25   O'Malley and Jones 2009, p. 7.
26   O'Malley and Jones 2009, p. 8.
27   O'Malley and Jones 2009, p. 9.
28   Towse 2005, p. 264.
29   Towse 2005, p. 265.

for national public action" [which is why] "public finance for the arts should take the form of vouchers so as to maximise consumer sovereignty and reduce government monopoly".[30] Prior to this dispute, Peacock had warned of the increasing burden of public spending on 'retirement pensions... unemployment and sickness benefits, war pensions, and workmen's compensation benefits',[31] as well as the effect that 'if standards of living improve in the private sector... then the standards of provision in hospitals and schools, for example, are bound to be affected'.[32] In other words, if it becomes normal for households to have indoor toilets and central heating, then the public will expect such facilities in hospitals and schools. Peacock proposed, somewhat feebly, that it might be possible to reverse the trend of the increased burden of taxation and welcomed the growing opposition to the 'cult of welfare'.[33] As such, Peacock was primed and ready for an assault on Baumol and Bowen's case for the public subsidy of the arts, and his argument against it was independent of the specific analysis of art and rejected out of hand the argument that art might be economically exceptional. Long after the original exchange, Peacock confirmed that his agenda was less about the public subsidy of the arts in particular and much more concerned with the principles, flawed in his view, of public funding generally, in the article 'Public Financing of the Arts in England'.[34] Peacock argues that art is economically trivial – 'the arts represent less than 1.5 per cent of total government direct expenditure'[35] and that government expenditure on 'the arts, including heritage and cultural programming in broadcasting is "peanuts" alongside the vast "empires" of... defence, law and order, health and education'[36] – but it commands a great deal more attention than this sum would justify. Peacock's beef is with welfare economics. 'The main issue', he says, 'is whether instances of market failure can be identified that provide a rationale for the amount and form of public authorities' expenditure'.[37] After disputing the key pillars of welfare economics, Peacock revives the case for vouchers so that 'reliance [can be] placed on the doctrine

---

30   Ibid.
31   Peacock and Wiseman 1961, p. 144.
32   Ibid.
33   Peacock and Wiseman 1961, p. 148.
34   Peacock 2000.
35   Peacock 2000, p. 172.
36   Peacock 2000, p. 202.
37   Peacock 2000, p. 186.

of consumer sovereignty',[38] and concludes that 'attempts to rectify market failure may be frustrated by "government failure" '.[39] Finally, Peacock announces that 'funding bodies supporting activities as prestigious and elusive as the arts inevitably finish up as "captives" ', which is nothing more than a restatement of the central dogma of 'public choice theory'.[40]

Peacock was hired by the Arts Council of Great Britain in the early 1980s to write a report. It was clear that the commission 'sought and expected detailed confirmation'[41] of the cost disease, but Peacock (collaborating with Eddie Shoesmith and Geoffrey Milner), disappointed them. His report at the time was too neoliberal for a pre-Thatcherite arts body.

> The Arts Council was outraged by the Committee's recommendations and told Peacock and the Committee to revise them or face public rejection. The Arts Council objected to the very idea of using the price system – the 'cash nexus' – to enhance the position of the regional orchestras and to using public subsidy as a lever to achieve policy objectives. This was the reception of what Peacock calls 'a landmark in the discussions of public policy towards music'.[42] As he noted, the 'great and the good' in England, even if not drawn from patrician stock, aspire to it and discussions of money are not 'good form'.[43]

Peacock did not disprove the thesis or show it to be false, but he concluded that the 'cost disease' was not pronounced, and that there were demand side measures that could alleviate it; thus he argued that public subsidy was not supported by this observable trend. James Heilbrun has examined Baumol and Bowen's predictions of the effects of the 'cost disease' within the parameters set by the narrow definition of market failure. He questions the projected earnings gap of firms in the performing arts sector. Heilbrun explains that

---

38   Peacock 2000, p. 189.

39   Peacock 2000, p. 190.

40   Peacock 2000, p. 203. Public choice theory asserts that public bodies are run by individuals who are driven by their own private interests, such as the power and privilege that accrues from disbursing cash to elite institutions.

41   Peacock 2000, p. 197.

42   Peacock 1993, p. 71.

43   Towse 2005, p. 267.

all industries, including the arts, compete to hire workers in a nationally integrated labour market and that 'artists' wages must therefore rise over time by the same proportion as wages in the general economy to enable the arts industry to hire the workers it needs to carry on.[44]

Heilbrun points out that the industries associated with the mass distribution of culture suffer from the cost disease too. However, on the whole, he says,

> dire predictions that productivity lag would lead to a relentlessly increasing earnings gap proved to be incorrect. A number of factors can work to offset the effects of productivity lag. In this instance expenses of performing arts companies did increase more or less as predicted, but earned income rose at an equal or slightly higher rate, so the relative size of the gap began to decline.[45]

The rise in earned income was due, he says, to increases in ticket prices. And he develops an argument against subsidy on the ability of ticket prices to rise in line with rising living standards due to technologically enhanced productivity in other sectors of the economy. Increased ticket prices are the solution to the cost disease, according to Heilbrun, because other sectors are more productive, and therefore 'those higher costs will be absorbed optimally by the economy'.[46]

Later, Peacock went on to complete the first economic analysis of museums and heritage, and was commissioned by the British government to make a study of the finance of broadcasting. This sort of research paved the way for the Thatcherite decimation of public funding for the arts, and he anticipated the controls that the arts council would later impose on its funded individuals and organisations. Peacock suspected that subsidy to the arts was nothing more than the provision of public money for the benefit of 'certain high income people who like drama'.[47] Combining his commitment to public choice theory with his opposition to government funding increasing the tax burden, Peacock, nonetheless, advocates public subsidies to arts education in schools to form the tastes of subsequent generations, 'thus overcoming the Cost Disease income gap by shifting demand in the long run'.[48] This remains

---

44   Heilbrun in Ginsburgh 2006, p. 92.
45   Heilbrun in Ginsburgh 2006, p. 96.
46   Heilbrun in Ginsburgh 2006, p. 100.
47   Tullock 1994, p. 149.
48   Towse 2005, p. 266.

consistent with his aim to displace the difficulties of the production costs of culture by adjusting demand, such as when he argued that the performing arts might improve productivity and cost efficiencies through recordings, and radio and television broadcasts. All of Peacock's 'cures' for the cost disease are on the demand side. Peacock is so allergic to paying subsidies to cultural producers that he fails entirely to investigate the economics of artistic production and therefore has no basis of determining whether art is a form of production that is economically exceptional.

Mainstream economists like Peacock and Towse tend to rearticulate the problem of the public funding of the arts into a set of technical questions about market failure, which is understood as the consequence of one or more of three economic anomalies, namely, monopoly markets, public good, and externalities (all of which, at one time or another, have been ascribed to art). The opponents of subsidy (chiefly but not exclusively neoliberals) subscribe to the most narrow and restrictive definition of market failure, while the proponents of subsidy (primarily heterodox neoclasssicists, neo-Keynesians and social democrats) subscribe to the widest and least restrictive definition. The tightest definition of market failure requires the loosest definition of market success, and vice versa. Market failure is a concept weakened by the very generality of the concept of economics within economics itself. Neoliberals and heterodox economists also disagree on the *extent* of market failure, the former regarding it as rare, while the latter regard it as common. Joseph Stiglitz says, '[a]mong the "commodities" for which markets are most imperfect are those associated with knowledge and information'.[49] Since knowledge in many ways 'is like a public good' – namely, is non-excludable and non-rival – Stiglitz argues that 'firms may have a difficult time appropriating their returns to knowledge'.[50] Stiglitz is concerned with the effects of market failure on developing countries,[51] but the underlying understanding is that market failure is widespread but for a variety of reasons, primarily with relation to 'information imperfections'[52] and the 'quality mix of what is being offered on

---

49   Stiglitz 1989, p. 198.

50   Ibid.

51   'When spillovers of knowledge within one country (as one surely would expect) are less then perfect, then markets will never be perfectly competitive. The first entrant into a market will enjoy monopoly rents' (Stiglitz 1980, p. 198).

52   'One of the results of our research was to show that ... even a small amount of information imperfection could have a profound effect on the nature of the equilibrium. The creators of the neoclassical model, the reigning economic paradigm of the twentieth

the market'.[53] Stiglitz does not argue that every instance of market failure or imperfect competition calls for state intervention, although he says, 'whenever markets are incomplete and information is imperfect – that is, essentially, always – ...there are, in principle, government interventions...which can make some individuals better off without making anyone else worse off'.[54] More importantly, Stiglitz calls into question the doctrinal assumptions of neoliberals like Peacock and Towse who oppose it on principle and not only for the arts. Economists who object to government funded pension schemes and public education are not likely to become converts to public subsidy for the arts, especially if the case for art's economic exceptionalism appears to them as a relic from the era of classical economics and the costs of production theory of value. Peacock's proposal to distribute vouchers to cultural consumers instead of government grants to cultural producers and cultural institutions is a textbook example of a measure that conforms to the doctrinal assumptions of neoliberalism (reducing the role of government, protecting consumer sovereignty, etc.), follows the pattern of demand-side solutions to supply-side anomalies, and fails to differentiate sectors of culture in terms of their specific economic character. Vouchers could be used, for instance, at theatres, concert halls and public museums, albeit imperfectly, but would not be feasible in cases of public sculpture, street theatre, works for which there is no audience (for example, WochenKlauser's 'boat trip'), net art, works in remote locations, etc. In 1994 the art group Wochenklauser sent out experts in the field of drug issues on boat trips across Lake Zurich to discuss their views. After two weeks almost 60 experts had participated, including leading politicians, journalists and police chiefs. The result was a shelter for prostitutes that ran for six years.

Towse backs Peacock's campaign for any necessary or perceived subsidies for the arts to be delivered in the form of vouchers.

> The well-known economic rationale for vouchers is that they achieve equity objectives – redistribution of spending power – without distorting allocative efficiency objectives as is the case with subsidies to producers. Vouchers as a way of delivering arts subsidy have several advantages for the classical liberal: they put the power of deciding what is art in

---

century, ignored the warnings of nineteenth-century and still earlier masters about how information concerns might alter their analyses – perhaps because they could not see how to embrace them in their seemingly precise models' (Stiglitz 2002, p. 461).

53   Stiglitz 1987, p. 2.

54   Stiglitz 1991, p. 138.

the hands of consumers rather than in those of a paternalistic cultural monopoly.[55]

Vouchers might break up the alleged government monopoly on art's funding and put some small measure of power in the hands of cultural consumers, establishing a semblance of market forces where there is currently a distribution of funds based on merit judged by appointed experts, but vouchers are not a solution for the problem that public funding for the arts was set up to solve – that is, the lack of demand for avant-garde, advanced, difficult and challenging contemporary art. State subsidy for the arts remains a hot topic within cultural economics, perhaps because the field of inquiry was formed originally as a response to the trauma of the public funding of the arts and government interference in the market for the arts has not been eliminated. However, the key question is not whether the arts ought to benefit from state subsidies or should be subject to the discipline of market forces. Disagreements about the public subsidy of the arts mask the underlying question about whether or not art is economically exceptional.

Since the classical case for art's economic exceptionalism was based on the theory of 'monopoly prices', it might appear that a case for art's market failure might be developed from the analysis of the artist's monopoly production, but this is not the sort of monopoly that is presupposed in the concept of market failure. There are millions of artists, thousands of galleries and hundreds of museums in the world, all, in principle, competing within the 'market' of the cultural sector. Compared with the market share of the three major soft drinks corporations, Coca-Cola, Pepsi and Schweppes, the claim that monopoly causes market failure in art is a non-starter. Neoclassical monopoly theory, which understands contemporary market conditions as typically that of oligopolies rather than the open competitive markets of early industrial capitalism, is an analysis of the pricing patterns and corporate strategies in markets that contain only a small number of firms. So long as none of the individual firms are 'price makers' and all are 'price takers' then the oligopolistic market is regarded as conforming to 'perfect competition'. Monopoly is therefore regarded as normal within standard neoclassical theory but as not offering any serious challenge to the modified laws of supply and demand. Unique art objects, however, are not bought and sold under the typical conditions of oligopolistic markets. And neoclassical price theory, even with its sophisticated models for understanding fluctuations in price that result from oligopolistic competition, cannot explain the great surges in value of works of art on the

55   Towse 2005, p. 269.

secondary market or the stark rise in prices of famous living artists. This is because the prices of artworks are not determined by oligopolistic competition mechanisms. The kind of monopoly that brings about the high prices of artworks is not the monopoly of firms but the monopoly of individual unique works of art, and as such a special theory of art's 'monopoly price' needs to be developed.

Scores of economists have attempted to argue that art is a public good in various ways, but this concept has taken a battering from neoliberals in recent years and it has become common to propose that there is no such thing, and that all cases of apparent public goods can be re-described more accurately and explained more adequately using other terms. Finally, then, it has been argued that art cannot be properly accounted for within the self-regulated market because of externalities, and this has become the preferred route for thinking about art in terms of market failure in the last couple of decades. For mainstream economists externalities are spillovers from economic activity enjoyed or suffered by individuals who have played no part as suppliers or consumers of the economic good or service. Pollution is a negative externality while an art critic writing a positive review of an artwork you own is a positive externality. The person who benefits from it does not pay for the review, and the people suffering from pollution do not charge the people producing it. Market mechanisms by themselves cannot exact payments for externalities, so when they are identified, and the political will exists to rectify the situation, then regulations such as fines or royalties are introduced. In other words, where there is market failure due to externalities, there are measures that can be taken to make someone pay, or reimburse someone more adequately. In other words, the theory of market failure is nothing but the attempt to discover instances in which the outcomes of markets have to be imposed on practices because the market is incapable of doing it automatically. The concept of market failure was not designed specifically to address the economic conditions of artistic production and consumption. Questions about the economics of art are therefore distorted by cultural economics in two phases. First, the specific economic analysis of art is held off by filtering all questions about art's deviation from standard economic practice into an assessment of whether art conforms to the established generic concept of market failure. Second, the inquiry into art's economic exceptionalism is jeopardised by linking the case for market failure to the advocacy of public subsidy and therefore associating the case for exceptionalism with normative economics and the *political* preference for state intervention over consumer sovereignty. If we are going to provide an adequate economic analysis of art we must go beyond the narrow conception of market failure.

Throsby has argued against art being considered a 'public good'; he has argued against the theory of the 'cost disease', and has disputed the 'apparent' difference between artists and 'economic man'; and, finally, he has taken issue with the public subsidy of the arts, saying, for instance, that 'the benefits of subsidies to encourage artistic activity will almost certainly have a regressive incidence on consumers'.[56] Nevertheless, he says, art 'might be deemed a merit good in Richard Musgrave's original terms, and that, if so, this would provide normative grounds for collective action'.[57] Throsby argues that

> a number of the characteristics that might be ascribed to the arts as a merit good can actually be explained as generalized externalities or social goods. For instance, a belief that the arts are socially beneficial when held by people who do not themselves consume the arts directly, or the acceptance by some individuals of the desirability of others' consumption, can be accounted for in this way.[58]

Externalities do not pose insurmountable problems for neoclassical economics, so Throsby re-describes merit goods as goods with externalities. West and McKee take a slightly different view, separating merit goods from the concept of externalities, saying, 'Musgrave carefully distinguishes the public good-externality case from merit goods', but they draw the same doctrinally predetermined conclusion:

> The former relate to social wants whose satisfaction is subject to the principle of consumer sovereignty … catering for merit wants on the other hand is directed, not to the satisfaction of consumer sovereignty, but to the interference with it.[59]

Musgrave specifically argued that merit goods were those goods which people should be able to consume not only regardless of the ability to pay but also regardless of demand. So, in the case of merit goods, interference with market mechanisms is based on values attributed to a good independent of subjective judgements of utility by consumers at large. In other words, it is the precondition of the concept of merit goods that they do not conform to the standard pattern of neoclassical supply and demand. When Throsby and others criticise

---

56   Throsby 1994, p. 24.
57   Throsby 1994, p. 23.
58   Ibid.
59   West and McKee 1983, p. 1112.

the concept of merit good for failing to uphold these two preconditions for efficient neoclassical free market enterprise, they demonstrate a complete inability to understand the concept at all. What is important, here, is not whether
Throsby persuades us that the concept of merit good can be deleted from the
lexicon of economics, but that, subsequent to arguing that art is a standard or
near standard economic activity, he attempts to clean the board of all suggestions that art might be economically exceptional in some way. Throsby does
not believe, ultimately, that art is a merit good, so there are no grounds for
collective action, and we are left, instead, with market mechanisms. Included
within market mechanisms, interestingly, are non-market mechanisms such
as the Booker Prize that Throsby treats as market-like. Throsby is not alone
among neoclassical economists who knead together market mechanisms
with non-market mechanisms to form an amorphous, undifferentiated blob
of incentives and rewards all leading, ultimately – in the long run – to 'wealth
maximization'.[60] Throsby is a pioneer of the conflation of non-pecuniary and
pecuniary rewards in the economic analysis of art. Another typical example
of Throsby's campaign is to show, despite appearances, that artists operate
in markets or market-like institutions (basically, any system that contains
rewards of any kind), just like everybody else. He is satisfied with *associating*
art with economics, so at no point does he prove that artists are either wage
labourers or entrepreneurs (or any other standard economic actant), nor that
artworks are standard commodities, nor indeed that art's consumers follow
the standard pattern of diminishing marginal utility. In various different texts,
spanning over two decades, Throsby typically constructs an argument that art
is an economic activity and then proceeds to dismiss all attempts to treat art as
anything but a standard industry.

The emphasis on subjective estimations of value after the marginal revolution has resulted in a failure to distinguish between artists who sacrifice
commercial rewards in the interests of their own practice, and artists who
acquisitively pursue nothing but financial rewards. Cowen and Tabarrok confirm the underlying assumptions about economic subjectivity by attending to
'the various factors that will cause an artist to become less market oriented'.[61]
This implies a 'price of satisfaction',[62] which is a typical Chicago neologism
that colonises non-economic behaviour by recoding it in economic terminology, giving the impression that the artist who does not make rational economic
calculations about their practice pays a calculable price in order to pursue art

60   Throsby 1994, p. 15.
61   Cowen and Tabarrok 2000, p. 236.
62   Cowen and Tabarrok 2000, p. 237.

independently. I use the word 'independently' here to differentiate what artists do from what economists think they do. Artists do not necessarily make work according to their subjective tastes, as Cowen and Tabarrok assume, with their liberal assumptions about individuals 'knowing what they want'. Artists do not necessarily know what they want or what they like, but discover convictions, principles and values actively in the productive processes of making work. Also, artists understand the notion of 'working independently' in terms of the best account of artistic practice that they have developed through education and experience. This is an important distinction, because the conception of individual taste fits neatly into the neoliberal economic scheme of things, but the concept of a community of culture with its own discourses, values and criteria, suggests an alternative social system for determining the allocation of resources). This provides a different reading of Cowen and Tabarrok's observation that 'artists and critics share similar tastes in art. Even if artists do not seek fame, their notion of artistic satisfaction corresponds to critical approval'.[63] Like other mainstream economists, they have a technologically determinist notion of the difference between avant-garde or independent culture and popular, mass or commercial culture. Increases in reproductive technology increase the impact of market forces, they say, citing Warhol, who made prints rather than unique paintings, as an example. The long list of artists who have used reproducible forms such as video, photography, mass producible forms such as neon lights and ready-mades, puts this hypothesis to bed. As is typical of cultural economists, they have a very simplistic view of the relationship between markets and professionalism in contemporary art.

> An amateur artist who receives most of his income from labor in the manufacturing sector can afford to produce his own brand of art at little loss in income. A professional artist pays a high price for deviating from market taste. Similarly, the more avant-garde the artist, the higher the price for being a professional.[64]

Here, the gradient leading from amateur to professional is equated with a gradient leading from independence to 'market taste'. This may be true in many fields, but not art, where artists of the highest ambition and esteem go to extreme lengths to protect their independence from the market, often by generating alternative income so that they can practice freely, in a manner that will undoubtedly appear as sharing the economics of an amateur. But when

---

63   Cowen and Tabarrok 2000, p. 244.
64   Cowen and Tabarrok 2000, p. 237.

they analyse the relationship between income, subsidy and markets, they reveal something very important:

> The dependence of artistic satisfaction on government support introduces a possible bias into decision-making. As government support increases, artists turn away from market sales and art wages fall. Thus, as government support increases, the market appears to become more philistine and the argument for government funding appears stronger.[65]

'Painters are neither constrained by high capital costs nor can they greatly increase the size of their market by appealing to mass tastes',[66] as Cowen and Tabarrok said. Their article presents some evidence for a different perspective. 'Artists have rejected market sales in pursuit of the non-pecuniary benefits of high satisfaction art',[67] they say. However, their understanding of the strain between art and economics confirms the impossibility of subjecting art to the rigours of the market while simultaneously confirming the mechanisms of the market to make artists who do so pay a penalty: 'artists must pay a price for successive increments of fulfilling their artistic visions'.[68]

Throsby reignites Stigler and Becker's discussion of quality and taste in the economics of art. 'One of the most intriguing areas waiting to be tackled in the emerging literature on the economics of the arts is the role of quality considerations in the decisions of firms, consumers and funding agencies',[69] Throsby says.

> The neoclassical view of tastes as given and as differing in some systematic but unmeasured way between individuals says nothing in particular about the arts. But theories of demand that consign taste to a residual status shed no light on the formation of tastes or on their profound influence on life-cycle consumption patterns.[70]

The emphasis on 'decisions' and 'decision makers' stems from a professional interest: economists are often employed as advisors, consultants and experts by government agencies, large organisations and other institutions.

65   Cowen and Tabarrok 2000, pp. 238–9.
66   Cowen and Tabarrok 2000, p. 246.
67   Cowen and Tabarrok 2000, p. 234.
68   Cowen and Tabarrok 2000, p. 235.
69   Throsby 1994, p. 65.
70   Throsby 1994, p. 3.

If economists can argue persuasively that they can account for questions of quality, then they can oust the current 'experts' on quality (writers on writing, artists on art, etc.) with their more scientific assessment of quality. 'The area is a mine field for the unwary economist', Throsby says, because 'some artists and arts administrators will harbor an attitude of skepticism bordering even on hostility towards the notion of cultural economics in any form'.[71] Against Stigler and Becker he says, 'theories of demand that consign taste to a residual status shed no light on the formation of tastes or on their profound influence on life-cycle consumption patterns'.[72] Throsby wants to persuade his profession to 'focus on a search for systematic components in individual or group choices in artistic matters as a means of explaining, at least in part, why decision-makers behave as they do'.[73] Tastes, which Stigler and Becker eject from economic analysis (as exogenous factors), are to be converted into data suitable for economic analysis, in Throsby's vision. 'It is clear', he says, 'that the endogenization of tastes in economic models is likely to be essential if any progress is to be made in explaining demand for the arts'.[74] But how are tastes to be 'endogenized', that is to say, made internal to, brought under the spell of, or recuperated by economics? The answer is to treat taste just as economists treat preferences, choices and decisions. Throsby spells this out in the following way:

> the decisions are similar in principle to decisions in a number of other areas; modelling producer and consumer choice in education or health, for example, could not afford to ignore the qualitative dimension. Indeed, economic theory has long postulated demand and supply functions for all sorts of everyday goods and services where subjective or qualitative considerations (the color of a car, the taste of an apple) affect the allocation of resources in production or the utility obtained from consumption.[75]

So, Stigler and Becker respond to Marshall's observation of 'changing taste' by eliminating 'taste' from economic analysis and transposing the element of change in tastes to changes in price; this eliminates the Marshallian anomaly that 'getting the taste for art' *increases* utility in the consumption of art. This means that, for Throsby, taste is as evident in choosing a Granny Smith's rather

---

71   Throsby 1994, p. 65.
72   Throsby 1994, p. 3.
73   Throsby 1994, p. 66.
74   Throsby 1994, p. 3.
75   Throsby 1994, p. 65.

than a Cox's Pippin! In this way, it seems the presence of taste in the economics of art can be fully acknowledged and incorporated without any deviation from standard practices. Consuming art appears normal or almost normal. But Throsby's solution solves the wrong problem.

Like his eminent Chicago predecessors, Throsby solves the problem he inherits by finding a new focus for it. Throsby is not perturbed by the sight of increasing marginal utility for the consumption of art, and this is probably why it is possible for him to reject the elimination of taste from the economic account of consumption. All that Throsby is after is that the behaviour of consumers exhibits patterns that permit of reasonable predictions.

Throsby is happy to supply an extensive list of features that appear to make art economically exceptional.

> They are created only by individuals. Every unit of output is differentiated from every other unit of output, an extreme case of a heterogeneous commodity. For the work of artists no longer living, supply is non-augmentable. Art works can be copied but not reproduced, in the sense that ultimately there is only one unique original of every work of art....At the same time, artworks form part of the cultural capital of a nation or of the world (some more so than others), and thus have, to a greater or lesser degree, public-good characteristics, especially when they are acquired by galleries or collections for public showing.[76]

Elsewhere, also, Throsby says, correctly, that 'there is imperfect substitution in consumption between different sellers [in music], because several mediocre performances do not substitute for one good one'.[77] Significantly, Throsby does not dwell on the economic implications of these exceptional circumstances. At one point Throsby says that 'cultural consumption can be interpreted as a process leading both to present satisfaction and to the accumulation of knowledge and experience affecting future consumption',[78] but he does not appear to understand the implications of this dual process. For Marshall this statement raises the question of how consumption for art differs from the consumption of ordinary commodities. In particular, Marshall is acutely aware of how the process of consuming art is simultaneously a process of gaining 'knowledge and experience' that increases the utility of 'future consumption'. But Throsby overlooks this anomaly in order to treat tastes as economic data.

---

76   Throsby 1994, p. 4.
77   Throsby 1994, p. 20.
78   Throsby 1994, p. 3.

Paintings and sculptures provide clear consumption benefits to purchasers through their utilitarian characteristics as durable private
goods. . . . Because artworks can be resold, and their prices may rise over
time, they have the characteristics of financial assets, and as such may be
sought as a hedge against inflation, as a store of wealth or as a source of
speculative capital gain.[79]

The fact that artworks have 'benefits to purchasers' understood in terms of the
neoclassical concept of utility, appears to overshadow any inkling that the precise pattern of art's utility is exceptional. The fact that the prices of artworks
rise in the secondary market is taken for granted in establishing art as an asset
class, rather than appearing to be a potentially anomalous phenomenon that
requires an economic explanation.

Throsby satisfies himself with the task of demonstrating in principle that
the producers and consumers of art follow patterns that can be tracked and
ultimately predicted. He is not attuned to the possibility that these patterns
might be exceptional. So long as there are patterns of any kind, he believes
that cultural economics is justified in denying art's exceptionalism. Partly this
is due to the fact that Throsby's definition of economic exceptionalism is very
narrow, referring to the rare if not outright absurd possibility of something
not being economic. Throsby says, 'artists and art lovers will argue that the
inconsistencies, spontaneity, and unpredictability in behaviour in the arts
will always defy rational explanation, because these responses derive from
notions of mystery, imagination, and the unfathomable creative impulse'.[80]
Nevertheless, Throsby insists, 'aggregate data suggest otherwise'.[81] And this, we
suspect, is a little victory for Throsby's campaign. He has shown that economics, which is well equipped to analyse the 'aggregate data', has a duty to perform in the scientific examination of art. The incentives for art lovers, artists
and other arts professionals might not be economic in the narrow and direct
sense (pecuniary rewards), but they are, Throsby wants to establish, economic
in the wider and indirect sense (incentivised, calculated, rewarded, and so on).
Hence he tells us that 'peer group reputation' is important to the art world.

Maximizing one's standing among one's peer group, which is clearly easier to achieve when profit maximization is not the sole or main object of
the firm, is, however, not necessarily inconsistent with long-run wealth
maximization, because prestigious awards given by artists to artists (such

---

79   Throsby 1994, p. 4.
80   Ibid.
81   Ibid.

as the Booker Prize and other literary awards that are judged largely by writers) are often treated by consumers as indicators of the quality of the product.[82]

So, like Stigler and Becker, Throsby helps to make his case for art as a standard commodity by simply applying the tropes of economic analysis to processes and judgements that stand outside economics, or, in other words, by projecting possible medium- to long-term economic consequences for non-economic rewards he believes he understands their true economic character.

Economic exceptionalism appears to be a non-starter within neoclassical economics because it redefines exceptionalism as existing outside economics and has a capacious definition of the economic that appears to include everything. Towse applies this expansive version of economics to the arts thus:

> Entry to a national museum may not be charged for, nor is going to school, but these services are not free, because their production takes up resources that have other uses, and therefore the question of how much of them to produce and how much to spend in doing so is an economic one.[83]

Hence, if artists do not exhibit the key features of the entrepreneur in producing commodities to match demand, neoclassical economists, following Mises, simply regard the artist as conforming to principles of the sovereign consumer. Artists appear to behave like consumers in regard to their own production insofar as they often fund production through a second job, make artworks according to their own tastes and values rather than the consumer's, spend more time making art when they 'can afford to', and increase production when they are excited or inquiring into something rather than when there is increased demand for it. Towse explains that when there is a rise in non-arts wages, artists switch to arts work because they can 'afford' to do so once the income constraint has been met. They also do more arts work when arts wages rise, because they are able to earn the basic income they need and do their chosen arts work. That is what Throsby has referred to as 'perverse'.[84] Throsby, for instance, discovered that as soon as artists reach a 'satisficing' level of income, they devote more time to arts work, rather than taking up the opportunity to earn more from doing more hours of non-arts work. In short, artists

---

82   Throsby 1994, p. 14.
83   Towse 2010, p. 7.
84   Throsby quoted in Towse 2010, p. 300.

are economically irrational. Artists trade off income for art.[85] Producers ought to make commodities that match consumer demand in the hope to maximise profits; consumers ought to get the most for what they can afford in the hope of maximising their satisfaction. Artists, however, produce what they like in order to maximise their satisfaction rather than meeting demand to make profits. It is this pattern of economic behaviour among the arts that Throsby refers to as 'perverse'. The artist is a monstrous figure for neoliberal economists, a hybrid: half producer, half consumer. Artists appear to have a consumer's relationship to art not by looking at it but making it, and yet, according to Towse, '[w]hat all artists have in common, though, is that they sell their accumulated skill and intellectual property in one way or another. In general, work is exchanged for payment via the labour market'.[86]

Towse claims that neither the labour market for the arts nor the market for artistic goods need, in principle, to vary much from the standard model of supply and demand. 'The higher demand is in relation to supply', she says with regard to the low income of most artists and the high prices of some works, 'the higher we would expect prices and rates of pay to be'.[87] The facts are not in dispute: rates of pay for most artists are low while the prices of artworks can be staggeringly high (often in the resale market). Supply and demand, according to Towse, explains both. The cheap labour supply of the arts is due to its 'oversupply', while, in the case of works of art, demand appears to far exceed supply, hence the price of Hirst's iconic shark shoots up to $15 million. Orthodoxy appears to be restored, but this is only if we suspend what is usually meant by demand. Demand is high, normally, when the quantity of a certain good that consumers are willing to purchase at a given price exceeds the quantity of goods for sale at that price or lower (typically, in such cases, prices are maintained by augmenting supply, or prices rise to dampen demand). This is not what we mean in the case of sought after artworks. The quantity of the good for sale is one, and the effective demand is the amount that one person is prepared to pay, competing with others. In this instance, demand means simply that one person – perhaps as a result of a bidding war with one or two others – has been willing to pay a monumental sum. Quantities cannot be increased to maintain prices. The mechanism of supply and demand is lopsided. Supply

---

85   Here, the idea that artists make trade-offs gives the appearance of conventional economic
       behaviour vis-à-vis the science of choice, but this appearance can be maintained only by
       suppressing the nature of this alleged trade-off in which artists sacrifice economic value
       for the value ascribed to art.

86   Towse 1996, p. 8.

87   Towse 1996, p. 19.

is fixed and demand, in terms of quantity, is fixed too. All that can be adjusted is price.

Cultural economists tell us that there is an 'oversupply' of artistic labour, and this is one of the key factors that Abbing uses to explain why artists are poor on average. First, it is not at all clear that the generality can be sustained. There might be an 'oversupply' of artistic labour in London and New York (depending on the definition of oversupply), but there is no oversupply of artistic labour in the towns and regions that supply this labour to the big cultural cities. To suggest that there is an oversupply of artistic labour is to point to the bad choices of artists rather than the systemic exceptionalism of art's economy. Towse and cultural economists like her simply see the lack of demand for artistic labour as a clear signal to would-be artists that they have a very low average chance of making a living in art, and therefore might allocate their resources differently. Towse, therefore, advises the Arts Council to allow market forces to bring the supply of artistic labour down. Treat the arts as if they are not economically exceptional, and they will no longer be exceptional, she appears to say, as if the only thing that is exceptional about the arts is their enjoyment of state (and other) subsidies. Towse has made extensive studies of labour in the arts. She focuses on labour markets, including the various forms of investment put into training and education for labour in skilled markets. When it comes to artistic labour, mainstream economists conclude that there is an oversupply of artists not from the conditions of art's labour market, which, depending on the sector of the arts is either extremely unusual or non-existent, but on a secondary measure, namely whether an individual can 'make a living' from their work in the arts. Ignoring Baumol's 'cost disease', then, and putting aside any exceptionalism, we simply conclude, on the basis of economic first principles, that demand lags behind supply. Towse forgets, here, that the 'cost disease' is an explanation of the necessity of increased wage costs regardless of oversupply or demand, but as a result of the lag in technological forms of cost reduction comparative to industry. Insisting that supply and demand are in operation in the arts is to say little or nothing more than art is economic, which remains aloof from the question of whether it is economically exceptional or not.

This leads to errors. Earnings from non-arts work are divided off from arts work or arts-related work. Mainstream economics examines labour in two key senses, as the commodity for sale in the labour market and as the capital input into other commodities. It examines markets for labour, the decisions made by individuals to enter or remain in a given profession, the education and training of specific types of labour, the costs and benefits of labour (both to individuals and to society at large), labour as an input into the value of commodities, the proportion of individuals in a profession who are employed or self-employed, the incentives and disincentives of the market (and various kinds of subsidy) for individuals within a given profession, the division of labour, the enhancement of labour with technology, the productivity of labour, and the allocation of resources required for labour at various magnitudes. Towse is very vague about the distinction between selling the products of labour and selling labour. Nevertheless, she is aware of differences between goods markets and labour markets.

> The difference between goods markets and the labour market ... is that, while goods are purchased for the utility or satisfaction they offer, labour is hired as a factor of production or input into the production of goods and services, and demand depends upon the contribution labour makes to the value of the product.[88]

This is far from true. Towse fails to mention labour as a consumer good itself (for example, domestic servants, hired not as a factor of production, but precisely for the utility or satisfaction they offered). Towse's investigation is better understood not in terms of an analysis of art's labour market in the proper sense, but of the economics of artistic education and training. She wants to know if art education produces value for money, both for the individual student and the economy at large. This presupposes the sale of labour in labour markets, which in the visual arts does not exist, so the demand for the labour as wage labour is non-existent. Effectively, in this case, the decisions made by students to study the arts will be determined as economically rational or not by the demand placed on this labour by the 'consumers' of labour, namely employers.

Towse appears to be at least superficially aware of the significant economic differences between artists of various kinds.

> To speak of artists' labour markets, however, is to imply that there are economic features common to all artistic activities. Is this so? After all, different groups of artists and craftspeople reach the final consumer in different ways, and the timing of work and payment for work varies. Creative artists and craftspeople mostly have to finance the period of production themselves, whereas performing artists are mostly paid as they rehearse and perform.[89]

---

88   Towse 2010, p. 303.
89   Towse 1996, p. 8.

Some artists sell their labour, especially in the performing arts, but others, especially in the visual arts, sell their products instead (in which case they do not exchange work for payment via the labour market), or do not sell either their labour or their products. We will want to revisit the question of art's exceptionalism, perhaps, with a more differentiated conception of art. Towse suppresses the specific economics of the visual arts in which no artist applies for the job of being an artist, no artist is employed in such a job by a firm, and where artists are not paid wages. The fact that there is no labour market for the visual arts is therefore seen as a problem of demand for artistic labour rather than a conspicuous sign of art's economic exceptionalism. The economic analysis of artistic labour cannot be restricted to consideration of the labour market or the funding of art education but must extend to a thoroughgoing examination of the full range of actual processes of labour, paid and unpaid, that artists execute as artists. In Part 2 of the book I will place the anomalous nature of artistic labour at the heart of a new theory of art's economic exceptionalism. In the next chapter I will provide a context in which this reassessment of exceptionalism can take place.

CHAPTER 6

Exceptionalism Reassessed

Towse's generalisations, McAndrew's over confidence, Grampp's dogmatism and Cowen's promotional tone are the result of three decades of hegemonic struggle in which neoliberalism took hold of the emerging discipline of cultural economics. Fine and Milonakis argue that 'economics imperialism' (the extension of economic study into non-economic activities), which was the intellectual background for the growth of cultural economics, suppresses 'the social (or non-rational)'[1] through strategies that 'ignore the problems ... [or] ... accept the social (or non-rational) but take it as at least in part to be exogenous'.[2] However, 'there is a potential let-out clause from these two options ... if the social could be reduced to the individual'.[3] In the previous chapter, the assembled arguments against art as a special case, against art's economic exceptionalism and against the public subsidy of the arts, can be seen as evidence of the effects of economics imperialism on the economics of art by 'reducing the social to (rational) individuals functioning in an "as if" market environment'.[4] At the same time, the market imposed by economists, both theoretically in their 'as if' analogies, and practically in their policy recommendations, was changing.

> With the rise of neoliberalism, government expenditure was perceived to be excessive and government intervention as inducing inefficiency. Far from perfect competition and general equilibrium being the ideal, from which deviations in the form of market imperfections justified state intervention, the ideal of attaining the free market and minimal state gave rise to what Carrier and Miller (1998) refer to as the new economic 'virtualism' – the imperative to remould the world to conform to an imagined ideal, that of perfectly competitive equilibrium.[5]

---

1   Fine and Milonakis 2009a, p. 42.
2   Ibid.
3   Ibid.
4   Fine and Milonakis 2009a, p. 57.
5   Fine and Milonakis 2009a, p. 61.

© KONINKLIJKE BRILL NV, LEIDEN, 2015 | DOI 10.1163/9789004288157_008

The suppression of the case for art's economic exceptionalism needs to be examined in the context of economics imperialism and the powerful neoliberal advocacy for markets free from interference.

Towse appears to reiterate the orthodox account of the historical advent of current economic thinking on art when she says that before 1966 'there was no consensus as to whether the arts are amenable to economic analysis'.[6] But this is misleading. It is true that economists before the 1960s and 1970s said very little about art, but it is not true that there was no consensus amongst them. The current conviction within mainstream economics that art is not economically exceptional is a very recent development within the discipline, but this fact has been suppressed by the active neglect of a history of economic thought on art prior to the current consensus. The received idea, however, is that economists had neglected questions of the economics of art for 200 years and the inauguration of the inquiry produced the 'consensus', as Towse puts it, that art is, in fact, susceptible to economic analysis.

> Apart from the national art galleries and museums that were owned and administered by the central government and their counterpart civic collections, there was no subsidy to the arts in Britain until the Second World War; there was art in schools and there were some specialist institutions training artists and musicians, etc but nothing faintly resembling present-day provision in Britain.[7]

This observation forms part of Towse's rejection of subsidies to the arts (the arts flourished, she says, for most of their history without subsidy). What she neglects to point out is that art flourished for centuries without self-regulated markets, either, and that funding the production of art through commercial sales in the art market is, also, a very recent development. Nevertheless, Towse is right to trace the shift in the relationship between art and the state to 1945, but the heritage of her own position, in which state subsidy of the arts is regarded as economically suspect, is not fully articulated until after 1966.

While early economists raised the question of whether unique and rare objects such as artworks could be explained economically by the same tools and theorems of industrial and agricultural production and consumption, recent economists have asked quite a different question: is art economic? Proving one does not disprove the other. Mainstream economics refuses to restrict itself to an analysis of capitalism and therefore naturalises the laws of

---

6   Towse 2002, p. 152.
7   Ibid.

supply and demand, pointing out that all societies throughout history (including those of the future) must conform to the basic principles of business.

Everything is economic, in this view, insofar as everything either has a cost, 'shadow cost', opportunity cost, or social cost. Consequently, mainstream economics cannot adequately distinguish capitalism from other social systems. This severely limits the ability of mainstream economists in understanding art's economic exceptionalism because it is impossible to think of art as economically exceptional if by this we mean that it somehow is not subject to the kinds of trade-offs that we must make in the choice to do one thing rather than another, or to use up resources in one way or another. Neoclassical economics is, therefore, in a peculiarly weak position for thinking about art's economic exceptionalism.

Baumol revived discussion of art's economic exceptionalism in 1986 by arguing that the value of artworks, especially of noted artists who are dead, 'float more or less aimlessly'.[8] This study of the prices of artworks, entitled, with a tip of the hat to Adam Smith, Say and Ricardo, 'Unnatural Value', is closely aligned with the range of classical arguments for art's economic exceptionalism, combining Senior's interest in the prices of artworks by dead producers with Ricardo's observations about prices being determined by the caprice of buyers and Smith's theory of the prices of rare items veering significantly from their 'natural price'. This is all brought together in the opening sentence of Baumol's article:

> I shall suggest on the basis of a priori considerations and several centuries of price data that in the market for the visual arts, particularly the works of noted creators who are no longer living, there may exist no equilibrium level, so that the prices of such art objects may be strictly unnatural in the classical sense.[9]

Baumol follows the classical economists by explaining that the difference between the art market and markets for manufactured products such as steel bolts is that the key to equilibration in the latter 'is responsiveness of supply'.[10] He adds, as we might expect, that the art market differs from standard markets insofar as the latter 'is made up of a large number of... perfect substitutes for one another'.[11] There can be no doubt that Baumol is an alert student

8   Baumol 1986, p. 10.
9   Ibid.
10   Ibid.
11   Baumol 1986, pp. 10–11.

of exceptionalism when he contrasts this with the case of artworks: 'Widely known paintings and sculptures are unique, and even two works on the same theme by a given artist are imperfect substitutes'.[12] Baumol does not conflate unique goods with monopoly ownership, as classical economists did in using the term 'monopoly goods', so he adds the condition of monopoly as a separate and distinct factor:

> a given stock is held by many individuals who are potentially independent traders on the near perfectly competitive stock market. The owner of a Cranach or a Caravaggio holds what may be interpreted as a monopoly on that work of art.[13]

He also adds the element of time, contrasting the frequent and continuous sales of manufactured goods with the resale of artworks which might occur, he says, once in a century, and the obstacle of secrecy, contrasting the normal situation of prices being 'public information' and the situation in art whereby the prices of works are often known only to the dealer and collector. Finally, he refers to the problem of pricing artworks at all, asking 'who would dare to claim to know the true equilibrium price [of a work of art]?'[14] Baumol revives the classical case for art's economic exceptionalism, giving it the most coherent and precise expression to date.

Baumol's theory of exceptionalism, however, appears to be anathema to most mainstream economists, especially those campaigning against public subsidy for the arts. Rather than tooling economics to make nuanced distinctions between various limits to the laws of supply and demand, and various exceptions to them, mainstream economics has a history of formulating the widest possible definition of its discipline to incorporate all social systems. Backhouse advises that our definition of economics not be restricted to the institutions of market economies such as firms, money and the stock market, arguing that it is better 'to define economics in relation to . . . more fundamental problems, rather than in relation to institutions that exist in some societies but not all'.[15] Most definitions of economics devised by mainstream economists are simultaneously generic enough to apply to all possible social circumstances in history and biased towards specific schools of economic thought. Marshall's capacious definition, '[e]conomics is a study of mankind in the ordinary business of life',[16]

---

12   Baumol 1986, p. 11.
13   Ibid.
14   Ibid.
15   Backhouse 2002, p. 4.
16   Marshall 1997, p. 1.

appears to be far too open but in fact puts a strong emphasis on microeconomics (as well as failing to distinguish adequately between the role of calculation in capitalist society and non-capitalist societies). Robbins's definition,
that economics is 'the science which studies human behaviour as a relationship between ends and scarce means which have alternative uses', for instance,
is carefully constructed to put neoclassical theories of 'marginal utility' and
'opportunity cost' in the driving seat of economics, even though Backhouse
comments that 'Robbins's definition goes a long way towards capturing the
features common to all economic problems'.[17] Backhouse cites 'other definitions' including 'the logic of choice' and 'the study of markets', which have a
clear agenda in directing our attention to the 'subjective theory of value' and
self-regulated markets. There is a clear pattern in the attempt by economists
to define their own field. Taken together, there is an ambiguity at the heart of
the definition of economics that prevents mainstream economics from paying
close attention to the question of art's economic exceptionalism. Current and
canonical definitions of economics could infer either that the study of choice,
markets and the efficient allocation of resources ought to be applied to all societies regardless of whether a society is run according to the mechanisms of the
self-regulated market, or, on the other hand, that economics has to be fundamentally reconfigured to take into account how other societies do not permit
economic activities free rein. This difference is vital for an economics of art but
is repressed by mainstream economics.

A broader framework for the question must be developed. Marxism does
not address the general question of what is or is not *economic*, but whether a
certain type of production corresponds to the capitalist mode of production.
Roman Rosdolsky underscores the importance of Marx's method and aims by
saying,

> [i]n order to understand the prices of production, which appear on the
> surface, we must go back to their hidden cause, value. And those who do
> not agree to this must confine themselves to mere empiricism, and there-
> fore abandon any attempt to give a real explanation of the processes of
> the capitalist economy.[18]

The basis for a Marxist version of art's exceptionalism (not from the economic
in general but from the capitalist mode of production in particular) is spelled
out in the first chapter of *Capital* Volume 1.

---

17   Backhouse 2002, p. 3.
18   Rosdolsky 1977, p. 173.

A thing can be a use value, without having value. This is the case whenever its utility to man is not due to labour. Such are air, virgin soil, natural meadows, &c. A thing can be useful, and the product of human labour, without being a commodity. Whoever directly satisfies his wants with the produce of his own labour, creates, indeed, use values, but not commodities. In order to produce the latter, he must not only produce use values, but use values for others, social use values.[19]

Engels adds a comment and an example for emphasis in the fourth German edition, explaining in a footnote, 'I am inserting the parenthesis because its omission has often given rise to the misunderstanding that every product that is consumed by someone other than its producer is considered by Marx a commodity'.[20] Questions remain about what precisely constitutes capitalist commodity production but the inquiry, even when expressed as briefly as this, is significantly different from the mainstream version of exceptionalism. The technical question of art's exceptionalism within economics should not be isolated from the ensemble of questions about art's absorption of or resistance to the social relations, techniques and structures of modern capitalism.[21] Marx puts the emphasis on production.[22] Let us look at the question of economic exceptionalism, now, therefore, from the side of production.

---

19   Marx 1954, p. 48.
20   Ibid.
21   Seen through the lens of the Marxist inquiry into what constitutes capitalist commodity production, the question of art's economic exceptionalism overlaps with several prominent debates within art theory, including the controversy of art's autonomy, the thesis of art's commodification, disputes about art's alleged elitism, and so on. At the same time, the inquiry into the relationship between art and capitalism, which tends to be addressed in a very generic way, even among Marxists, finds a sharp focus in the specific economic question of art's exceptionalism.
22   Marx's labour theory of value (not the labour theory of price or exchange-value, it is important to stress) appears to be a rather silly error to sophisticated economists informed by neoclassical theory. Joseph Schumpeter, a student of Böhm-Bawerk (who provided the first full-length neoclassical critique of Marx's three volumes of *Capital* in 1896), argues that Marx's labour theory of value is not significantly different from Ricardo's. Schumpeter characterises Marx's labour theory of value as 'the quantity of labour necessary for its production', which is a direct quotation of Ricardo. Böhm-Bawerk, too, said 'the exchange value of commodities', for Marx, 'finds its origin and its measure in the quantity of labor incorporated in the commodities'. What this means, effectively, is that the mainstream critique of Marx's labour theory of value, insofar as it remains indebted to Böhm-Bawerk and Schumpeter, is actually a critique of Ricardo. Blaug's critique is ortho-

Marx, however, understands precisely that artistic production must be classified as outside capitalist commodity production. 'Leaving aside works of art, whose consideration by their very nature is excluded from our discussion', Marx says in *Capital* Volume III, marking off the exceptionalism of art, as we have seen, not from economics in general but from the analysis of capitalist commodity production.[23] And similarly in the *Grundrisse* Marx contrasts 'labour' with 'really free working', with just one example, that of 'composing'.[24] So, Marx belongs on the side of the proponents of art's exceptionalism, but his inquiry goes further in ways that we will develop later. The consumer version of exceptionalism explains things like the prices of art, while the production version explains, for instance, that the artist is not a capitalist commodity producer. Ricardo explains why rare objects such as artworks fetch arbitrarily high prices, but he does this by dividing production into two spheres, goods for which supply can be increased through human industry, and goods that cannot. This distinction between goods that Ricardo provides stands independently of the explanation of high prices. It seems, then, that Ricardo's aim is to answer a question raised within the theory of exceptionalist consumption (why are the prices of rare goods higher than their 'natural price'?) but he

---

dox in this respect, beginning with the characterisation of Marx's labour theory of value as a claim that 'all products exchange in proportion to the labor embodied in their production'. In fact, the critique of Marx's labour theory of value has become standardised, replicating not only the arguments but the phrases of Böhm-Bawerk and Schumpeter as well as Ladislaus von Bortkiewicz and Ian Steedman's theory of inconsistency in Marx's transformation of values into prices. There is, therefore, a systemic failure within mainstream economics to understand the significance of Marx's reformulation of the relationship between labour and value. This is a serious omission. Marx does not formulate the labour theory of value simply as 'the quantity of labour necessary for its production', but, as we have seen, with 'socially necessary average labour time', or as Engels put it, 'socially necessary labour, necessary for the single product, both in relation to other products of the same kind, and also in relation to society's total demand'. Transposing 'necessary' into 'socially necessary' and inserting 'average' between 'necessary' and 'labour' shifts the burden of value production from actual, individual acts of labour on individual products (i.e. concrete labour) to units of labour quantified by their relation to all other equivalent acts (i.e. abstract labour). Presumably, Schumpeter cannot put a cigarette paper between the two formulations because he sees one through the lens of the other. Marx said a great deal more about the labour theory of value than Ricardo, who improved on Smith's theory by insisting on only counting labour that is necessary, but we cannot assume that Ricardo already knew all the things that Marx theorised but Ricardo left unsaid.

23   Marx 1959, p. 759.
24   Marx 1973, p. 611.

answers this question by referring to conditions of production. He straddles the two camps. Baumol confirms the classical case for exceptional prices in a neoclassical study of art sales that float aimlessly, and he has also compiled evidence that the costs of cultural production can be exceptional, too. Baumol, then, sometimes contributes to a consumption theory of exceptionalism and sometimes to a production theory of exceptionalism. By and large, though, mainstream economists from Smith onwards, when they have observed art's economic exceptionalism, have done so with reference to consumption.

When an economist says a 'work of art often arrives on the market because of one of the famous "three D's" (divorce, death, or debt)',[25] it is clear that cultural economics places its emphasis on consumption and the secondary market. From a Marxist point of view it is utterly absurd for a product to 'arrive' on the market without being produced or works arriving on the market not from its producers but its consumers. A Marxist economic analysis of art cannot begin with the arrival of the artwork for resale on the secondary market. Artworks themselves cannot be a given, but must be identified as the object of economic analysis. If we are to address the question of whether an artwork is a commodity or an asset, or a product independent of commodity production, then we need to examine its mode of production, not its patterns of consumption. Following the labour theory of value, we would expect to build our analysis from a study of how art is produced as a commodity from an analysis of artistic production, not by examining the behaviour of its consumers or its systems of distribution and display.

Nobody *produces* an old master, antique or rare book at all. Diamonds and other rare natural goods are not produced: they are 'harvested' through labour. Similarly, although artists, craftsmen and publishers produce the articles that later take on the special quality of being rare antiques, and the like, no worker produces an antique or old master simply by completing the production process of a product. Seen from the point of view of production, the special status of rarity is not a result of labour but of history, or what subsequently happens to the product in circulation, storage, and so on. When old masters and other rare or unique goods enter into exchange, therefore, they do so inadvertently, awkwardly, reluctantly or fortuitously. Since cultural economics puts all its emphasis on demand (particularly insofar as it often proposes demand-side solutions to supply-side anomalies), it is ill-equipped to distinguish between products produced for the market and products produced for other institutional configurations that promote other values. This distinction is especially

25   McAndrew 2010a, p. 20.

difficult to identify when the analysis takes place only after articles reach the market, however circuitously they get there.

The Marxist labour theory of value can help to develop a more far-reaching theory of art's economic exceptionalism, but before any benefit can be drawn from it, the nature of its difference from classical and neoclassical economics will have to be spelled out. Marx begins the first volume of *Capital* by inter-rogating the properties of the commodity. After setting aside various lines of inquiry, Marx begins his study of the commodity in earnest by contrasting 'use value' and 'exchange value'. Unlike his economic predecessors Smith and Ricardo, who also distinguish 'value in use' and 'value in exchange', Marx con-structs the relationship between them not as a binary opposition, but, follow-ing Hegel, as two contrasting elements of a dialectical whole. The commodity, he says, has a 'twofold nature'.[26] Smith presented his distinction between 'value in use' and 'value in exchange' by telling us that 'the *word* value ... has two different meanings', but Marx says 'a commodity present[s] itself to us as a complex of two things – use value and exchange value'.[27] While modern econo-mists insist on the binary distinction, for instance, between 'fact' and 'value', or positive and normative methodologies, Marx's splitting of value into use value and exchange value ties these two forms of value together in the very act of distinguishing them. Despite Schumpeter's claim that what distinguishes Marx from his predecessors is that 'Marx's arguments are merely less polite, more prolix and more "philosophical" in the worst sense of the word',[28] the dia-lectical fusion of use value and exchange value is not merely a philosophical flourish:[29] Marx will continue to insist on their inseparability throughout his critique of political economy. Use value and exchange value constitute a unity. Also, Marx's dialectical pairing of use value and exchange value contrasts sharply with the neoclassical collapsing of value, price and utility in which marginal utility (a concept that collapses use value, in the form of satisfaction, with economic evaluation and exchange) is the basis of price (which in main-stream economics is insufficiently differentiated from value).

Use value is qualitative while exchange value is quantitative. Since quali-ties are specific, use value is necessarily heterogeneous and concrete, such as the varying properties of individual apples. By contrast, since quantity requires

---

26   Marx 1954, p. 48.
27   Ibid (emphasis added).
28   Schumpeter 1943, p. 21.
29   Blaug complains of 'Marx's Hegelian jargon' saying it is 'no more than window dressing' (Blaug 1969, p. 273).

equivalence, exchange value is necessarily homogeneous and abstract, such as the interchangeability of apples in any dozen. These are not arbitrary pairings of opposites. As David Harvey explains, 'you can't cut the commodity in half and say, that's the exchange value, and that's the use value'.[30] All commodities are the site of a conflict between quantity and quality. 'As use values, commodities are, above all, of different qualities, but as exchange values they are merely different quantities, and consequently do not contain an atom of use value'.[31] Marx does not get caught up in the diamond water paradox to navigate the relationship between use value and exchange value. In fact, he refers to a diamond as a use value, alongside iron and corn. Marx does not say that 'things which have the greatest value in use have frequently little or no value in exchange' (as Smith did). He says that the use value of a commodity 'is independent of the amount of labour required to appropriate its useful qualities',[32] but he does not conclude that use value and exchange values are unrelated. First, he goes further than stating that use value is a precondition of exchange value, that the purchaser must 'want', or have use of, a thing in order to exchange money for it, by saying – in 'the form of society that we are about to consider' – that use values 'are, in addition, the material depositories of exchange value'.[33] Second, he dialecticises the classical observation that exchange value depends on use value, by arguing that 'the exchange of commodities is evidently an act characterized by a total abstraction from use value'.[34] Unlike his predecessors who argued that use value was external to economics, or the neoclassical economists who boil down value to 'marginal utility', Marx held together use value and exchange value in a tense dialectical whole that, therefore, registers the internal contradictions of the capitalist system which 'is subject to two different sets of scientific laws'.[35]

---

30   Harvey 2010, p. 23.
31   Marx 1954, p. 45.
32   Marx 1954, p. 44.
33   Ibid.
34   Marx 1954, p. 45.
35   Harman 2009, p. 23. Harman explains: 'On the one side there are the laws of the physical world – of physics, chemistry, biology, geology and so on. It is these which determine the ways in which different things have to be combined to produce goods (the different components of a machine, the material structure of a factory, the techniques used in a surgical operation and so on) and also the usefulness of those goods to those who finally consume them (the nutritional value of food, the warmth provided by fuels and electricity, the number of children who can be accommodated in a school or patients in a hospital, etc.) . . . . On the other side, there is the way things relate to each other as exchange values.

Use values, or useful things, come in quantities – a bottle of wine, dinner for two, a box of paints. However, use value is not calculable. So, while it is reasonable to expect everyone to prefer £10 to £5, it is not reasonable to expect everyone to prefer Joni Mitchell to Tammy Wynette. Markets set both contradictory logics in motion. One is objective and one is subjective. Exchange value is objective – in the sense that it is a measurable, equivalent and calculable magnitude – whereas use value is subjective, not in the marginalist sense of being a calculus of preference, but in the sense of being non-standard, unpredictable, concrete and specific. As such, those critics of Marx's concept of use value as an objective feature of the commodity or as based on a normative concept of 'need' have not really understood the distinction that Marx articulated. 'The utility of a thing makes it a use value', Marx says, which sounds circular but is intended to emphasise two aspects at once, first that use value is 'limited by the physical properties of the commodity',[36] and second that the commodity is 'a thing that by its properties satisfies human wants ... [regardless of] whether, for instance, they spring from the stomach or from fancy'.[37] The subjective uses of a commodity (or wants) are not reducible to a category of objective or normative useful functions (or needs), or indeed any natural, given or imposed universal measure of utility. Use value, therefore, is historical, social and subjective, as well as including those natural wants of the species such as are expressed in the desire for food, shelter, clothing and so on. Use value in Marx has nothing to do with any moral conception of the use in contrast to pleasure, as J.S. Mill puts it. There is no trace, in Marx's discussion of use value and exchange value, of the moralistic tone in which classical economists often spoke of 'superfluities' or 'ornamental luxuries'. Nor is there a special place within the scheme for the Kantian concept of the productive uselessness of the aesthetic. Fancying to wear a diamond or enjoying a painting are no less examples of use value than eating an apple or exhibiting an apple in a Yoko Ono retrospective. A thing becomes a use value only when someone has

---

These often behave in a very different way to use values. The exchange value of something can fall while its use value remains unaltered. This has happened to the price of computers in recent years – the computer I used to write my last book was twice the price of the much more powerful one I am using now. ... The market treats [use values] as exchange values that can be infinitely divided into parts (worth so many pounds, pence, etc.) ... but they have a physical existence that cannot usually be divided in that way' (Harman 2009, pp. 23–4).

36   Marx 1954, p. 44.
37   Marx 1954, p. 43.

an idea about what to do with it. Or, in the words of Marx, use values 'become a reality only by use or consumption'.[38] However, it should not be assumed that the uses of commodities are to be contrasted with misuse or abuse. The use value of a commodity is not restricted to its 'proper' use. Every commodity, or 'useful thing', 'is an assemblage of many properties, and may therefore be of use in various ways'.[39] Wants, and therefore use values, are based on the physical properties of things but are not fixed in advance by them. Duchamp's proposed 'reciprocal readymade', using a Rembrandt as an ironing board, is a vivid illustration of Marx's concept of use value insofar as it discovers a use for the painting based on its material properties but not restricted to its original, best or proper use.

Money, also, can be given surprising use values when its exchange value almost disappears or is no longer legal tender. Paper money, for instance, can be churned up to make papier mâché, or used with vinegar to clean the windows. Use values have material properties but this does not mean it is predetermined that a bottle of water will be used to quench thirst rather than wash a stain from a skirt, drown a wasp, dilute water colour paint, put out a small fire or poured over someone's head as a joke. Since use values have material properties, they can be destroyed as well as produced. In fact, the consumption of commodities often destroys their use value in exactly the moment when the item is attributed its specific use value. However, use value is destroyed, also, during an economic recession, when plant is left idle, raw materials are dumped and buildings are knocked down. Social commentators protest at such times that perfectly good materials that people need are being wasted because it is not profitable temporarily to supply them. The contradiction between exchange value and use value that appears conspicuously during a crisis is permanently present in every commodity according to Marx's dialectic of use value and exchange value, and the crisis only alerts us to it. Marx identifies the root of this contradiction in the following way: 'the commodity only becomes a commodity . . . insofar as its owner does not relate to it as use value'.[40]

Contrast this with the typical neoclassical interpretation of use value as an objective and intrinsic property of a thing. Believing value to be entirely subjective, and regarding the labour theory of value as an objective theory of value, akin to costs of production, neoclassical economists misrepresent use value as also objective because it does not exhibit the sort of subjective characteristics

---

38   Marx 1954, p. 44.
39   Marx 1954, p. 43.
40   Marx 1973, p. 881.

that they are after in their explanation of the fluctuation of satisfactions and prices. 'The concept of usefulness was also objective', Steve Keen says, 'focussing upon the commodity's actual function rather than how it affected the user's feelings of well-being'.[41] On the contrary, for Marx, use value cannot be present in the objective qualities of the thing independent of a person's use of it. 'The use value of a chair was not how comfortable it made you feel', Keen explains, revealing the extent of his ignorance, 'but that you could sit on it'.[42] Mainstream economists, as well as sociologists and others, have caricatured use value as a glaringly refutable assertion of the *intrinsic* value of a commodity. Jean Baudrillard, for instance, said: 'Use value is the expression of a whole metaphysic: that of utility'.[43] The postmodern philosopher attempted to surpass the pairing use value and exchange value with the concept of 'sign value'. Baudrillard, therefore, distinguishes between three kinds of value and three modes, or 'logics', appropriate to them, thus:

1.   The functional logic of use value.
2.   The economic logic of exchange value.
3.   The differential logic of sign value.[44]

Baudrillard mistakenly links Marx's concept of use value with the moral economy of how things ought to be used, and the positivistic notion of the functional. He preferred 'sign value' because he regarded 'use value' as a petit bourgeois concept connected to 'good use' or socially beneficial use. In his book *Debunking Economics*, Keen says that a 'generic definition of value – one which encompasses the several schools of thought in economics which have used the term – is that value is the innate worth of a commodity',[45] and claims that for all classical economists, including Marx, '[v]alue in use was an essential aspect of a commodity'. Roger McCain says, the 'claim that there are non-economic values distinct from economic values implies that the non-economic values are intrinsic or objective in the sense that they are independent of individual preferences'.[46] In his *Treatise*, Say had contrasted financial goods with the goods that they represent by claiming that the latter had 'intrinsic

---

41   Keen 2011, p. 414.
42   Ibid.
43   Baudrillard 2001, p. 70.
44   Baudrillard 2001, p. 60.
45   Keen 2011, p. 414.
46   McCain in McAndrew 2010, p. 150.

value', but he was talking, here, about the economic value of goods, not their use value.[47] Sweezy, whose formulation of the Marxist concept of use value Rosdolsky tells us 'does not differ substantially from that normally found in popularisations of marxist economics',[48] appears to have read Volume I with at least one eye closed: 'Marx excluded use value (or as it would now be called 'utility') from the field of investigation of political economy on the ground that it does not directly embody a social relation'.[49] First, this is not true: Marx did not exclude use value from the critique of political economy, but spoke variously, for instance, of how it is only the use value of labour power that creates value for capital, or of how use values 'constitute the substance of all wealth',[50] and in Volume III, where Marx considers production as a whole, use value re-emerges not as the utility of a single commodity but as the total 'social needs, which are quantitatively circumscribed' and therefore, ultimately, put a limit on commodity production and value production. Second, to translate use value into utility is to transpose it from the context of Marxian economics to the context of neoclassical economics and demonstrates a very lax definition of use value. Third, to argue that use value does not embody a social relation contradicts Marx's argument that the commodity not only presupposes a use value but a 'social use value'.[51]

Exchange value is a 'quantitative relation'[52] between use values (they must be use values or else they will not exchange for anything). A certain quantity of one use value is exchangeable for a certain quantity of another use value. Hence, use values have exchange value. Price is exchange value expressed in the form of money. It would make no sense for two items with the equivalent exchange value to fetch different prices, but the two concepts are not identical, as we can see in the case of inflation, whereby prices rise without any alteration of relative exchange values. The proportions at which they exchange are not determined by how useful they are, but their price on the market. Hence, 'we see in it no longer a table, a house, yarn, or any other useful thing' and

---

47   See Say 2007, p. 25. The passage goes as follows: 'When they further extend its signification to landed securities, bills, notes of hand, and the like, it is evidently because they contain obligations to deliver things possessed of inherent value. In point of fact, wealth can only exist where there are things possessed of real and intrinsic value'.

48   Rosdolsky 1977, p. 75.

49   Sweezy 1946, p. 26.

50   Marx 1954, p. 44.

51   Marx 1954, p. 48.

52   Marx 1954, p. 44.

its 'existence as a material thing is put out of sight'.[53] Despite their concrete differences, two different quantities of different materials, insofar as they are exchangeable, are abstractly equal: they go for the same price. However, the proportions at which commodities are exchangeable with one another, and therefore the prices that they fetch, are not fixed. Seasonal produce, for instance, will exchange for relatively less of another commodity when supplies are abundant and for relatively more when stocks are seasonally diminished. Chicken, which was once an expensive meat is, today, among the cheapest. So, exchange values are necessarily variable magnitudes, as they reflect changes that are not present or visible in the commodity itself but affect the commodity relative to others. Consider those merchant capitalists who, for instance, buy steel when the price drops and store it for months or years until the price rises enough for them to make a profit. The steel is not transformed in any way but its exchange value changes nonetheless. There is nothing in the commodity that corresponds to its exchange value. Marx says that the relations between commodities determine exchange value and that it is this that regulates the individual decisions made by consumers about what the reasonable price of a commodity is. What the steel magnate is after is not just an increase in steel prices, but a favourable differential between steel prices and the prices of most other commodities: that is to say, an increase in the exchange value of steel. The purpose of buying the steel for the capitalist is only realised in its sale. This is because exchange value has an antagonistic relationship to use value. Using up the steel by consuming it will not only destroy the use value but also eradicate its exchange value. Ernest Mandel contrasts the case of the peasant craftsmen who produce only what they need, who therefore only produce use values, with the commodity producer who only produces for exchange, and therefore 'no longer produces anything but exchange values'.[54] Like the steel magnate, the commodity producer 'can live only if he *gets rid* of these products'.[55] So, while products become use values only in the act of consumption, exchange values realise their value only in their sale. Exchange values can only be realised in the sale of commodities that have use value (or else they will be worthless). Nevertheless, the owner of exchange values (in other words, commodities owned *for the purpose of selling them*) is not an owner of use values. These articles become use values only in the act of consumption. If consumption is the final proof that commodities are, in fact, use values, this

---

53   Marx 1954, p. 45.
54   Mandel 1968, p. 58.
55   Ibid.

should not prejudice our understanding of the fact that in the hands of the trader they are nothing but exchange values.

Marx introduces the idea that the value embodied in commodities derives entirely from labour in an abrupt declaration. 'If then we leave out of consideration the use value of commodities', he says, commodities 'have only one common property left, that of being products of labour'.[56] This is the first use of the word 'labour' in *Capital* Volume I and it enters the scene just as the dialectical relationship between use value and exchange value has been articulated. Marx begins with use value, saying that commodities satisfy wants, but commodities are twofold, and also have exchange values. Since exchange value cannot be read off or derived from use values or the physical properties of commodities, another characteristic of commodities has to be brought in. Marx does not merely follow custom by asserting the function of labour in the production of value; he breaks with the generically and eclectically formulated 'costs of production' theory of value in order to give labour an unprecedented place within the theory of economics. Labour is not introduced by Marx as a cost, as wages, but as the productive force that both creates use values and is the 'social substance'[57] that all exchange values have in common. Labour, like value, therefore, has a twofold nature. Labour is useful and concrete but it is also exchangeable and abstract. Concrete labour is 'productive activity of a definite kind',[58] whereas abstract labour is 'the expenditure of human labour in general'.[59] But these are not two types of labour. Every act of wage labour is both. 'Tailoring and weaving, though qualitatively different productive activities, are each ... but two different modes of expending human labour power'.[60]

All concrete acts of labour are different and incomparable, but labour in the abstract is quantifiable in units of time.

> Some people might think that if the value of a commodity is determined by the quantity of labour spent on it, the more idle and unskillful the labourer, the more valuable would his commodity be, because more time would be required in its production. The labour, however, that forms the

---

56   Marx 1954, p. 45.
57   Marx 1954, p. 46.
58   Marx 1954, p. 49.
59   Marx 1954, p. 51.
60   Ibid.

substance of value, is homogeneous human labour, expenditure of one uniform labour power.[61]

The exchange value of goods is not set by the actual labour time taken in the production of a specific article, but the average necessary labour time. If you have a dozen producers all making the same commodity in a competitive market, then the value will be set in equilibrium by the average, not by the most productive or the least productive. The value that is embodied from the labour that produces commodities is 'no more time than is needed on the average, no more than is socially necessary'.[62] Marx presents his labour theory of value five pages into the first chapter of Volume I: 'The labour-time socially necessary is that required to produce an article under the normal conditions of production, and with the average degree of skill and intensity prevalent at the time'.[63] He explains with an example that underlines the relational and differential character of the value attributed to socially necessary labour time. 'The introduction of power-looms into England probably reduced by one-half the labour required to weave a given quantity of yarn into cloth', he says, only to turn his attention to those weavers who did not benefit from such productivity and continued to work with the old technology. 'The hand-loom weavers', he says, 'continued to require the same time as before' and therefore 'the product of one hour of their labour represented after the change only half an hour's social labour and consequently fell to one-half its former value'.[64]

Marx coined the concepts of 'surplus labour' and 'surplus value', which are absent in Ricardo, as well as the concepts of 'living labour' and 'dead labour', and the distinction between 'concrete labour' and 'abstract labour'. Marx finally put the twin concepts of 'productive labour' and 'unproductive labour' into a coherent form, and is the first thinker to point out that the capitalist does not buy labour but *labour power* and that it is the use value of labour power not its exchange value that produces value. Marx also coined the concept of 'unpaid labour' that, for the first time in the history of economics and politics, permits the general theory of exploitation, linking slavery, serfdom and wage labour without taking anything away from the specific social conditions under which they each differently produce wealth for others. 'Without the labour theory of

---

61   Marx 1954, p. 46.
62   Marx 1954, pp. 46–7.
63   Marx 1954, p. 47.
64   Ibid.

value, no theory of surplus value',[65] and we would be left with nothing but an empirical and contingent 'differential' between costs and prices without being able to explain 'the origins of this "differential"'.[66] Marx is very explicit and detailed in his analysis that workers who take longer to produce a given commodity do not thereby add extra value to it, and was clear that no amount of labour can add value to a commodity for which there is no demand. Marx also pointed out that a price tag can be put on goods that have not been produced by labour, such as a person's honour, making it a commodity with exchange value but having no value. For the first time, also, Marx's labour theory of value eliminates the necessity of adding profit to the value of a commodity, which was a clumsy consequence of all previous cost of production theories of value. And Marx's theory was the first to offer one coherent theory of what had previously been the eclectic mix of profit, rent and interest. One of the key improvements in Marx's formulation, then, is that as productivity improves, and therefore what is socially necessary to produce an article changes, then its price falls regardless of the labour that has actually gone into producing a commodity. According to the same principle, if a manufacturer discovers a way of producing a commodity more productively than the average necessary labour of her competitors, then surplus profit will be made. Marx did not only improve on Ricardo's labour theory of value, he transformed it into the lynchpin of a theory of capitalist accumulation, class conflict and capitalist crisis.

Schumpeter makes the standard neoclassical error of interpreting Marx's *labour theory of value* as an erroneous *theory of labour as a factor of price*. If you try to use Marx's theory of value as a neoclassical price theory, then Marx will come up short. But the shortfall is reversible. As soon as you ask neoclassical price theory to explain the formation of value rather than the determination of prices, then it reveals itself to be ill-equipped. Schumpeter also argues that Marx's theory of value 'does not work at all outside of the case of perfect competition'.[67] It is true that Marx assumes equilibrium, but this is because he is tracking the formation of new value, not the fluctuations of price above and below value. Keen follows Schumpeter in attempting to read Marx as a failed neoclassical economist. Keen attempts to show that Marx is inconsistent in his treatment of use value, saying that Marx's discovery that the use value of labour power is the secret of surplus value is later contradicted when Marx says that the means of production must be constant capital – it transfers

---

65   Mandel 1968, p. 710.

66   Mandel 1968, p. 710n.

67   Schumpeter 1943, p. 21.

its value, but cannot be the source of surplus labour on which surplus value depends. For Keen, the error here is that Marx did not permit the possibility that 'their use value cannot exceed their exchange value'.[68] Keen's error, here, derives from misreading 'use value' as an impoverished synonym for 'utility'.[69] 'One defining belief in conventional Marxian economics', Keen says, 'is that labour is the only source of *profit*: while machines are necessary for production, labour alone generates *profit* for the capitalist'.[70] Marx argues that labour is the only source of value, not the only source of profit. We have already noted that new technology, before it is made available to all manufacturers, allows a minority to increase their rate of profit. Profit is explained separately from value in Marx. Price can vary above and below value. The competitive market is meant to discipline prices so that they correspond to value, but the market is not reliable in achieving this. It is important for an economic theory to be able to distinguish price from value, therefore. Also, in ordinary speech we need to be able to describe goods that are overpriced and underpriced. This means judging prices in terms of another measure. This is value.

Profit can be made without adding value. Buying low and selling high, or arbitrage, is the pure form of profiting without adding any new value. That is, 'commodities may be sold at prices deviating from their values, but these deviations are . . . no method for increasing value'.[71] The cost of labour power – which is the source of value – can be purchased cheaply, leading to an increase in profit. Super profits are made by purchasing labour power below the average cost of labour power in the global labour market. Keeping wage costs to a minimum by outsourcing production to countries where the process of

---

68   Keen 2011, p. 436.

69   Rosdolsky argues convincingly that the use value of labour power is necessary for the production of value. Wages alone do not produce value. Labour power cannot just be paid for, it must be used. Capital, as Marx often says, has to be put to work. But the use value of labour can only be understood as the needs or wants of its consumer, namely, the productive capitalist. Therefore, the use value of labour (to the capitalist) is the production of exchange value, and particularly the production of surplus value through surplus labour. Use value is concrete, while exchange value is abstract. Since living labour is the only source of value for Marx, it is concrete labour put to work – labour's use value, that produces value. But this is only true for productive labour. Unproductive labour (i.e. labour that does not produce surplus value – e.g. domestic servants) is concrete labour too, but produces no new value. The condition for producing new value is that living labour is productive wage labour, that is, abstract labour that produces exchange values.

70   Keen 2011, p. 412 (emphasis added).

71   Marx 1954, p. 156.

proletarianisation is still taking place allows capitalists to produce more surplus value. Marx underpins his investigation into labour as the source of value
by proving that value cannot be added in circulation. If a capitalist earns profit
by purchasing goods below their value or by selling over their value, then profit
is derived from another's pocket. Merely putting it into circulation does not
augment the total quantity of value in society. Even if some individuals derive
profit from circulation, this is only because others lose from it. That is, circulation is a zero sum game. Since exchange values are exchanged as equivalents,
then no new value is added by exchanging them whether they go for their correct value or fetch prices above or below value. The analysis of prices, profits
and marginal utility has no means of conceiving of the distinction between
zero sum profits and new value. The best mainstream economists can do is distinguish between nominal and real prices. Exchange value cannot explain the
production of value because it is based on equivalence. Marx, therefore, takes
the startling decision to explain the production of value through consumption and use value instead of production and exchange value. The capitalist,
he says,

> must be so lucky as to find, within the sphere of circulation, in the mar-
> ket, a commodity, whose use value possesses the peculiar property of
> being a source of value, whose actual consumption, therefore, is itself an
> embodiment of labour, and, consequently, a creation of value. The pos-
> sessor of money does find on the market such a special commodity in
> capacity for labour or labour power.[72]

The key to Marx's labour theory of value, therefore, is the consumption of
labour. The consumption of labour power, when it is put to work, is capable of
adding value over and above its costs. Inserting labour and production into the
consideration of value does not, in principle, solve the puzzle of new value. If,
for instance, wages are equal to the value of labour spent, then no new value
is generated over and above what is spent on obtaining it. With a pre-Marxist
classical conception of labour it is impossible to understand the production of
new value, which is the accumulation of value. A capitalist can derive profit
from labour by selling the products of labour at prices higher than the value
embodied in the commodities, but this is not consistent with a labour theory
of value, requiring an additional sum on top of labour to provide the profit.
Smith suggested that labour has two prices, the price it costs and the price it

---

72   Marx 1954, p. 164.

commands. What Smith fails to explain is how such a difference arises, how it is regulated, how the ratio between them is altered and whether this is true of all cases of labour or only applies in specific circumstances. Marx coins the concept of surplus labour to explain the production of new value, called surplus value.

Since the worker in capitalist society is involved in a social division of labour, she does not directly produce the means of subsistence that she must consume in order to live and, therefore, reproduce her capacity for labour, or labour power. Nevertheless, Marx says, the working day can be divided into two portions, one in which the worker produces the value equivalent to their own reproduction and another portion, in which the wage labourer continues to work, now producing value for the reproduction of the capitalist and the capitalist's enterprise. During the first portion of the day, Marx says, the worker engages in 'necessary labour', and in the second portion, 'surplus labour'. The value which surplus labour produces is surplus value. Marx does not equate surplus value with new value, pointing out that the worker must produce new value in order to replace the value equivalent to wages, but the new value created by surplus labour is value added by unpaid labour. 'The rate of surplus value is therefore an exact expression for the degree of exploitation of labour power by capital'.[73] Since profit is income minus all factor costs, not just wages, surplus value is greater than profit, hence the rate of surplus value is always higher than the rate of profit. Although the use value of labour, not its exchange value, is essential to the production of new value, such new value is only realised by converting the use value of labour back into abstract labour, as a specific quantity of labour time. Concrete labour and abstract labour contribute differently to the production of value. Marx explains with the example of spinning cotton into yarn: abstract labour 'adds new value to the values of cotton and the spindle', while only concrete useful labour 'transfers the values of the means of production to the product, and preserves them in the product'.[74] Capital expended on labour power is *variable capital* because it is the only source of new value; all other factors of production, including raw materials, machinery, premises and fuel, constitute the expenditure of *constant capital*. Keen thinks that Marx's argument that the cost of means of production only transfers its values to the product erroneously equates 'depreciation of a machine with its productive capacity'.[75] If you could get surplus labour out of a machine, then it could

---

73   Marx 1954, p. 209.
74   Marx 1954, p. 194.
75   Keen 201, p. 437.

produce surplus value, he thinks. How would you do that? Labour power is priced at cost of reproduction. A day of labour costs however much the necessities for labour to renew itself costs per day. If you can get a labourer to work beyond the time it takes to reproduce him or herself, then the rest of the labour is surplus labour and the rest of the value is surplus labour. How much does it cost to reproduce a machine per day? The amount it costs divided by its life span. To get the machine to produce more than it depreciates, you would have to use it without using it up. Neoclassical economists argue that the cost of machinery is less than the machine can produce. But machines produce nothing on their own. A screwdriver cannot produce value, nor can any tools. Machines are no different from tools in this respect. The means of production have to be brought to life by living labour in order for any new value to be produced at all. When this happens, labour is the source of the value and the machine is the means by which it is produced. We must remember that machines are also the product of labour. Any value that machines contribute to the production of value, as the means of production, is produced by labour. Even if there were a case for machines producing value, then we would have to say that this capacity was produced itself by labour.

Keen's confusion about the apparent contribution of machinery to the production of value derives from the observation that mechanisation – and other improvements in productivity – increase profitability. If a machine can deliver more profit to the capitalist than the machine costs (which, clearly, is the precondition for investing capital in machinery), then it appears to produce value that labour cannot produce without it. It is clear that machinery, as well as other factors, augments the productive power of labourers, both in terms of the production of use values and the production of exchange values. Although in Marxist terms machinery is dead labour, the origin of machinery in labour is not a satisfactory explanation of why labour is the only source of value and machinery only transfers its value to commodities through living labour. And while it is important to point out that a 'machine to which the power of living labour is not applied ... produces no value',[76] this fact is not, by itself, proof that machinery cannot add value. Marx solves Keen's problem in advance through the differentiation of surplus value into two types, *absolute surplus value* and *relative surplus value*. 'The surplus value produced by prolongation of the working day', Marx says, 'I call *absolute surplus value*. On the other hand, the surplus value arising from the ... alteration of the respective lengths

---

76   Mandel 1968, p. 709.

of the two components of the working day, I call *relative surplus value*.[77] Since surplus value depends on the ratio between necessary and surplus labour, absolute surplus value derives from the absolute increase in the quantity of surplus labour to necessary labour, and relative surplus value derives from the increases in the productivity of labour which reduce the quantity of labour required to reproduce the value of labour and therefore increase the quantity of surplus labour to necessary labour without reducing the wage or adding to the quantity of labour spent in a day. Relative surplus value is produced by the division of labour, automation and so forth, which do not produce new value, but increase the proportion of surplus labour to necessary labour, and increase the proportion of surplus value in relation to wages. In other words, relative surplus value is not new value but results from an increase in the rate of exploitation. Insofar as machines make living labour more productive, and insofar as the capitalist takes the entire share of the increased productivity, machines certainly appear to produce value from the point of view of the productive capitalist, but they only increase the ratio of surplus labour in relation to necessary labour.

Blaug fails to understand how surplus value is produced and its relation to surplus labour and surplus value when he says, 'Marx concluded, as did Ricardo, that profits or total surplus value depend on the cost of wage goods'.[78] Neoclassical economists have always misperceived the labour theory of value as a 'cost of wage goods theory of price', which is why there is no neoclassical theory of value capable of distinguishing between profits made in a zero sum circulation and profits derived from the production of new value. Neoclassicism has not improved on the early classical idea that the capitalist places a mark-up on the costs to reach a price that yields profit (regulated by the subjective perception of marginal utility by consumers). As a result, neoclassical economics has a theory of capital that lacks the capacity for self-accumulation and is incapable of distinguishing the capitalist mode of production from other social methods of extracting value from the surplus product, such as in slave-owning economies and landowner economies. If we are going to redefine art's economic exceptionalism in terms of the capitalist mode of production in particular, then we are going to need a suitable theory of capital.

Historically, neoclassicism has defined capital in three ways: as 'stored value', as 'deferred consumption' and as 'assets that yield income'. 'Stored value' is the most common neoclassical definition of capital and it is not significantly

---

77   Marx 1954, p. 299.
78   Blaug 1969, p. 229.

different from classical definitions of capital. Where mainstream economists aim for clarity with regard to capital they focus on what counts as capital. Smith believed that the mercantilists equated money with capital and sought to extend capital to include the whole breadth of wealth embodied in land, houses, stocks of goods, and so on. Mill's version of the idea that capital is stored value is expressed in the phrase 'capital is the result of saving'. This has been theorised in terms of time (see Böhm-Bawerk's notion of 'waiting') or stocks. Although Marshall defines capital as that part of wealth devoted to 'acquiring an income',[79] he furnishes us only with examples of stocks, namely 'machinery, raw material, any food, clothing, and house-room',[80] or again, 'tools, machines, factories, railways, docks, ships, etc'.[81] The emphasis on stocks is based on the idea of stored value, while the emphasis on time, waiting and saving is based on the idea of deferred consumption. Senior is the primary source of the concept of abstention at the heart of the concept of deferred consumption, but the phrase 'deferred consumption' comes from Kenneth Arrow. Coined in the context of raising objections to the term 'social capital' as not being capital in the proper sense at all, Arrow complained that the term 'capital' implies 'a deliberate sacrifice in the present for future benefit'. Senior complained that economists had failed to define the concept of capital,[82] but defines it himself as 'an article of wealth, the result of human exertion, employed in the production or distribution of wealth',[83] which is consistent with the general notion of capital as stored value; however Senior, the son of a vicar, adds the condition of 'abstinence' in which 'some delay of enjoyment must in general have reserved it from unproductive use'.[84] The third short neoclassical definition of capital – 'assets that yield income' – is the now standard definition, formulated by Irving Fisher, one of the founders of monetarism. More frequently, today, mainstream economists refer to capital as a factor of production, however, new theories of capital are still being formulated. Becker applies Fisher's definition to the worker's care for herself in his concept of human capital, but he has to play with language a little to make it stick. To speak of assets in economics is more usually to speak of investments in the form of bonds, shares and so forth. A worker's physique, skills or experience are assets in a colloquial sense but not

79   Marshall 1997, p. 71.
80   Marshall 1997, p. 72.
81   Marshall 1997, p. 75.
82   See Senior 1836, p. 4.
83   Senior 1836, p. 60.
84   Senior 1836, p. 59.

assets in the economic sense. To define human capital in terms of assets that yield income, therefore, is to defend the use of the metaphor by using a pun. Workers have economic self-interest in their own skills and the wages that they might command, but these are not economic assets for the worker, they are capital only to the capitalist. This relationship between capital and labour is heavily repressed by human capital theory. What Becker needs to dodge here is the difficulty of capital investing in other people's labour. The concept of human capital must suppress this relationship to make its case. Giving the impression that human capital may yield financial and other benefits in the future, Becker associates 'investments' in one's own health and wellbeing with owning shares, even though nobody ever earned a living from purchasing private health insurance or visiting museums. If human capital is nothing but a store of human capacities that can be 'sold' on the labour market, then human capital does not 'yield income' but is simply the basis on which the worker's wages are fixed in the marketplace. It is not human capital that yields income for the worker, but labour power sold as a commodity to the employer. Marx, who encountered similar arguments in his day, pointed out that the worker must actually work to earn the 'interest' on her 'investment', whereas the capitalist earns her premium simply by virtue of owning assets. Any theory of capital that fails to distinguish between the capacity to earn (including all forms of benefit and advantage) *through labour* and the capacity to earn *without labour* is therefore seriously deficient.

All three dominant mainstream theories of capital apply to wealth in all economic systems, not just to the capitalist mode of production. From within mainstream economics, this generality is seen as an accomplishment of economic science. Capital exists before capitalism, of course, and therefore no theory of capital would be adequate that was restricted to the capitalist mode of production. However, capital is extended by capitalism not only in extent (the process whereby capital replaces tradition, custom, landownership and so on) but also by adding to the forms of production. That is to say, it is only with the development of capitalism that a labour market for wage labour emerges and therefore that capital takes the form of productive or industrial capital. Markets existed before the industrial revolution but before that, 'no economy has ever existed that, even in principle, was controlled by markets'.[85] Since, 'gain and profit made on exchange never before played an important part in human economy',[86] the existence of capital before capitalism should not distract us

---

85   Polanyi 2001, p. 45.
86   Ibid.

from the transformation of capital that occurs when it becomes the driving force of society. When protectionist laws stiffly regulate trade, customs, institutions, and so on, it is impossible for capital to express itself. Capital before the historical emergence of the self-regulated market was a store of value, necessarily implied deferred consumption and could, in a limited way, be regarded as an asset yielding income (in usury and ground rent, for instance). Capital takes on new forms within capitalism. Insofar as 'the change from regulated to self-regulating markets at the end of the eighteenth century represented a complete transformation in the structure of society',[87] it also transforms capital. 'Up to the end of the eighteenth century, industrial production in Western Europe was a mere accessory to commerce',[88] hence, capital was largely a store of wealth, and was predominantly in the form of merchant capital not productive capital. Early economists such as Smith, Malthus, Sismondi and Say often gave a marginal role to labour other than agricultural work and to forms of capital other than ground rent, merchant profit and interest on financial assets.

'Stored value' is a poor definition of capital because it is indistinguishable from wealth. Marx called an inert store of value a 'hoard'. Capital is not hoarded but put into circulation with the aim of returning with profit or interest. 'Withdrawn from circulation', Marx says, money becomes 'petrified into a hoard, and though [it] remain[s] in that state till doomsday, not a single farthing would accrue to [it]'.[89] If income from a business is spent as money to purchase necessities or luxuries, it is no longer capital. Like 'stored value', the notion of 'deferred income' following a 'deliberate sacrifice' fails to distinguish between capital and hoard. Capital is wealth put into circulation in order to return as an augmented magnitude; therefore capital must be spent on capital goods, assets, or, after the advent of industrial capitalism, in consuming raw material, the means of production and labour power. However, not all consumption uses capital; some consumption uses revenue (which is wealth spent without returns). Consumption for accumulation and consumption for use are economically poles apart. Only when wealth is consumed in processes of self-accumulation do we have capital. Stores of wealth spent unproductively – that is, for use on necessities or luxuries – are not transformed into capital, no matter how many sacrifices were made to save the hoard or how long the consumption is deferred. Deferring consumption itself is not the conversion of wealth into capital. Productive capital accumulates through the consumption

87   Polanyi 2001, p. 74.
88   Polanyi 2001, p. 77.
89   Marx 1954, pp. 149–50.

of the labour of others, including dead labour crystallised in goods. Income earned through labour is not income earned through capital. Capital is a special kind of wealth, distinguished from money, revenue, income, profit and so on. Capital is not merely owned or stored or hoarded but must be put into circulation specifically for the purpose of withdrawing more wealth from circulation. This is expressed in the formula M-M', in which M represents money, the dash represents an unspecified process and the M' represents a sum of money greater than M. Although capitalists may fail in their attempt to make a profit, the expenditure of capital differs from the expenditure of revenue insofar as the value is spent on condition that it returns, and then some.

Marx identified three kinds of capital: productive, merchant and finance capital. Productive capital is expressed in the formula M-C-M'. M represents money, C represents commodities, and M' represents the value originally invested plus an additional sum. Non-capitalist circulation, which Marx expresses with the formula C-M-C, treats money as a measure of value and a means of circulation, with all three 'moments' representing the same quantity of value. C-M-C only makes sense insofar as the two commodities at each end of the circuit are qualitatively different 'and their exchange ultimately satisfies qualitatively different needs'.[90] The circuit M-C-M', on the other hand, does not aim to exchange qualitatively different use values that satisfy qualitatively different needs. 'By contrast, exchanging money for money makes no sense, unless, that is, a quantitative difference arises'.[91] This means that in the formula M-C-M', money is not merely a measure of value or a medium of exchange but also an end in itself. Ordinarily – or according to the logic behind C-M-C – it is hard to imagine an exchange of a sum of money for a greater sum of money, but this happens in the case of loans and other financial products, and the merchant, who buys cheap and sells high (or buys at wholesale and sells at retail), effectively purchases a greater quantity of money with a smaller quantity of money. But Marx does not base his explanation of the circuit M-C-M' on the profits of the merchant capitalist.

The increase in the value of M in M-M' and M-C-M' can be due to interest, rent or merchant's profit, but Marx provides the first explanation of the specific means by which the industrial capitalist converts a smaller sum of money into a larger sum of money. The profits of the industrial capitalist is due to the purchase of a special commodity that produces new value over and above the value that it fetches in the market: labour power. Merchant capital is money

90   Marx 1973, p. 202.
91   Ibid.

advanced in the purchase of commodities for profitable sale, and therefore follows almost the same sequence as productive capital, beginning with M, passing through C, and culminating in an augmented sum of M. However, since merchant capital typically purchases goods from productive capitalists at a discounted rate (known as the wholesale price), its sequence must be expressed differently in the formula 'M-C-M. 'M represents the discounted price of the goods. By selling at the full price a profit is made. The merchant capitalist takes a share of the surplus value produced by labour; the ratio of the share is determined by negotiations over the discount that the productive capitalist agrees with the merchant capitalist. Finance capital is advanced in the form of loans or traded in the form of stocks, shares and bonds. Finance capital requires two formulas because interest and dividends are obtained in one way while profits from the asset market are obtained in another. The formula for the financial profits of interest and dividends is expressed in the formula M-A-M+. The A represents assets. The + represents the sum added to the value of an asset through interest on it or as a dividend paid to shareholders. The formula for assets made through trading, however, does not follow this pattern and is expressed in the formula M-A-'M'. The 'M' symbol represents the losses and profits of the owners of assets. This is because this kind of profit is made in a zero sum game, just taking money out of other capitalists' pockets. No price theory can distinguish between C-M-C and M-C-M, not to mention 'M-C-M, M-A-M+ and M-A-'M'. One of the reasons why neoclassical economists believe that marginal utility price theory is superior to classical costs of production price theory and the labour theory of value is that it is more general, applying indifferently to natural and artificial monopoly goods, agricultural and industrial goods, profit and rent, etc. When it comes to discriminating between different forms of capital, different economic social relations, different economies of labour and consumption, and so on, mainstream economics typically asserts that all these things are economic and therefore can be studied according to standard economic methods. If art is economically exceptional, however, then we cannot proceed by examining its prices and the utility of its consumers.

A Marxist theory of economic exceptionalism must delineate between products produced according to the capitalist mode of production and products produced not in conformity with capitalist commodity production. Andrew Kliman tells us,

> Marx's value theory ... pertains exclusively to commodity production, that is, to cases in which goods and services are 'produced for the purpose of being exchanged', or equivalently, produced as commodities ... if the

products have been produced for a different purpose, that of satisfying the producers' and others' needs and wants, they have not been produced as commodities.... A key reason for distinguishing between commodity production and non-commodity production is that prices or rates of exchange are determined differently in the two cases. When things are not produced as commodities, the rates at which they exchange may depend exclusively upon the demand for them, or upon normative considerations, or ... upon customary rules. It is only when products are produced for the purpose of being exchanged that their costs of production become significant determinants of their prices.[92]

To say that art is a commodity is to say that art is produced for the purpose of being exchanged. If art is not produced as a commodity, but rather to satisfy aesthetic and cultural needs and wants, then art is not a commodity and the Marxist labour theory of value will not apply to it. Or rather, the Marxist labour theory of value will not be able to analyse how art is exchanged as a commodity because 'the rates at which they exchange may depend exclusively upon ... normative considerations or ... customary rules'. The question is not whether art is economic or not, or whether art ought to be publicly funded or subjected to the rigours of the self-regulating market. The fundamental question for an economic analysis of art is whether or not art is economically exceptional. But economic exceptionalism needs to be reassessed. Art is economically exceptional to the standard economic patterns outlined by classical economics, and I have shown that art is economically exceptional with regard to neoclassical theories of price, utility and marginality. Being exceptional to a theory is one thing; being exceptional to a social system is another. The more substantial question, therefore, is whether art is exceptional not to economic doctrine but to economic practice. What I want to turn my attention to in the rest of this book is the question of whether art is economically exceptional to capitalist commodity production. Unlike mainstream economics, Marxism is capable of identifying precisely where, how and why art is economically exceptional to the capitalist mode of production.

---

92   Kliman 2007, pp. 19–20.

PART 2

The Economics of Art

∙∙

CHAPTER 7

On the Absence of a Marxist Economics of Art

Marxism has made an outstanding contribution to the study of art, aesthetics and culture.[1] While one of those 'systems of thought concerned with the nature and direction of society as a whole', Perry Anderson says 'unlike most of its rivals in this field', Marxism has also 'developed an extensive discourse on literature'.[2] Marxist aesthetics has not limited itself to studies of literature but has made vital contributions to our understanding of film, theatre, radio, painting, sculpture, architecture, photomontage, photography, the media and everyday life, as well as the new practices of installation, performance, video, appropriation, net art, the digital image and the new art of encounter. As such, Marxism, which begins as a political and economic tradition that coalesces post-Hegelian philosophy, classical economics and the workers' movement, found itself, in the twentieth and twenty-first century, to be one of the leading discourses on art and aesthetics. How should we explain the extraordinary attraction between Marxism and art? Margaret Rose has unearthed Marx's extensive engagement with art and argued credibly that the aesthetic was all along central to his materialist philosophy:

> Although such passages have received relatively scant attention, the concept of art as serving needs ... is one which has been accepted within the Marxist aesthetic, and has continued to distinguish it from others, but particularly from the Idealist aesthetics of Kant and Schiller, which were still influential in Marx's time.[3]

---

1   The breadth and depth of Marxism's intellectual and practical engagement with culture can be seen in the work of Antonio Gramsci, Mikhail Bakhtin and Andre Breton in the 1920s, Georg Lukács, Ernst Bloch and Sergei Eisenstein in the 1930s, Walter Benjamin, Bertolt Brecht, Max Raphael, Meyer Schapiro and Theodor Adorno in the 1940s, E.P. Thompson, Arnold Hauser, Herbert Marcuse and Jean Paul Sartre in the 1950s, Louis Althusser, Pierre Macherey and Guy Debord in the 1960s, Fredric Jameson, T.J. Clark, Gillian Rose, Eugene Lunn, Stuart Hall, John Berger and Michael Löwy in the 1970s, Terry Eagleton, Margaret Rose, Janet Wolff and John Roberts in the 1980s, Slavoj Žižek, Chantal Mouffe and Alain Badiou in the 1990s, Julian Stallabrass, Steve Edwards, Gail Day, Malcolm Miles and Esther Leslie in the 2000s. Post-Marxists such as Jacques Ranciere and Gerald Raunig have turned to art and aesthetics as one of the agents of the transformation of everyday life, either in terms of the partition of the sensible or the Deleuzean switch to micropolitics.

2   Anderson 1988, p. 10.

3   Rose 1984, p. 75.

David Harvey observes that Marx's three volumes of *Capital* are dripping with allusions to literature, drama, poetry and painting, even claiming that reading these economic works is improved by first reading Balzac, Dickens and others.[4] However, the attraction between Marxism and art is not always cosy. Fredric Jameson acknowledges that the range of insults that Marxists who attend to questions of art, aesthetics and literature receive from more politically- and economically-oriented Marxists, 'run the gamut from neo-Hegelian idealism, simple revisionism, and existentialism to extreme left deviationism and ultra-Bolshevism'.[5] While many Marxists would defend the attention paid to culture by taking issue with the orthodox limitation of Marxism to questions of economic analysis and political strategy, Chantal Mouffe insists that 'artistic practices can play a role in the struggle against capitalist domination'.[6] Anderson argues that Marxism's valuable contribution to the study of culture is a result of political defeat,[7] saying that, in these circumstances, 'the needle of the whole tradition tended to swing increasingly away [from activist politics] towards contemporary bourgeois culture'.[8] Eagleton, facing in the opposite direction so to speak, claims that the bond between culture and Marxism derives from the 'contradictoriness of the aesthetic', which, he says, 'only a dialectical thought of this kind can adequately encompass'.[9]

György Márkus points out that the archetypal Marxist assertion – that the artwork is a commodity – was absent from the Marxist tradition until the 1930s. 'Marx regarded the progressive commodification of all products of human activities as constituting an aspect of capitalist production, which made it "hostile to art and poetry" in general'.[10] Art cannot be commodified, Markus says, because commodification 'can only be applied to products which are socially reproducible' and therefore 'it has no meaning for genuine works of art as strictly individual and irreplaceable objects of human objectivity (characteristics Marx accepts as self-evident)'.[11] Art's economic exceptionalism appears evident in Marx's own view of art as Markus explains it:

---

4   Harvey 2010, p. 2.
5   Jameson 1971, p. xv.
6   Mouffe 2008, p. 101.
7   Anderson 1987, p. 42.
8   Anderson 1987, p. 55.
9   Eagleton 1990, p. 8.
10   Márkus 2001, p. 3.
11   Márkus 2001, pp. 3–4.

The artwork as universal human value can thus have no economic value in the proper sense, only an irrational, both economically and aesthetically, accidental price. And this means that the 'laws' of capitalist commodity production cannot explain the historical evolution of modern art, beyond positing the general conflict between the two.[12]

Márkus goes so far as to say that 'Marx's oeuvre tends to treat artistic production as the prototype of unalienated human activity'.[13] Hence, Marx neither developed an economic analysis of art nor asserted that art is nothing but a commodity. When, from the 1930s onwards, Marxists developed the 'commodity analysis of art',[14] this was based on an extension of Marx's concept of 'commodity fetishism', not the Marxist analysis of capitalist commodity production. So, even when art becomes theorised by Marxists in terms of commodity production, no Marxist economic analysis of art is developed, as we will see.

The 1930s is a watershed period for Marxism, especially with regard to the theory of art. Marxism has two main legacies. In a division coined by Maurice Merleau-Ponty in 1955, we can identify two phases of Marxism with distinctive characteristics, 'Classical Marxism' and 'Western Marxism'.[15] Early Marxism is a philosophical, political and economic critique of capitalism, while the second phase of Marxism begins with a 'cultural turn' in the 1920s, leading to a longstanding, sophisticated and diverse contribution to the understanding and critique of culture and art. Classical Marxism consists of the theory of Marx and Engels, and extends to the economic and political theory of Lenin, Trotsky, Rosa Luxembourg, and others. Western Marxism consists of the more philosophical, aesthetic and cultural writing of Marxism beginning with Georg Lukács, Theodor Adorno, Walter Benjamin, Ernst Bloch, and extending to Fredric Jameson and others today. In assessing the contribution of Marxism to the understanding of art, we need to distinguish these two legacies. Classical Marxism said a great deal about economics and very little about art; Western Marxism said a lot about art and aesthetics but virtually nothing about economics. Marxist economics after the 1920s is separated from philosophical and aesthetic Marxism, although important contributions to economic theory are made by the likes of Ernest Mandel, Paul Sweezy and Robert Brenner.

---

12   Márkus 2001, p. 4.

13   Ibid.

14   Márkus 2001, p. 7.

15   Originally, Classical and Western Marxism were two parts of a triumvirate. The third form of Marxism from which 'Western Marxism' was contemporaneously divided, 'Soviet Marxism', has dropped out of contention altogether (see Merleau-Ponty 1973).

Effectively, the split between Classical and Western Marxism is not temporal but runs through Marxism itself as a bifurcated living tradition, economic Marxists co-existing with cultural Marxists but hardly ever combining their insights. Classical Marxism – and the economically and politically oriented Marxism that remained faithful to it – did not regard art as significant enough economically or politically to warrant attention. Western Marxism did not regard economics as providing the best tools for grasping the nuances of art. Marxists have rightly examined the relationship between art and capitalism, but have typically turned to political and ideological analysis to examine the class character of art and artists, or to establish art's 'incorporation' or 'recuperation' by market forces and the state. Since art is the official or dominant culture of class divided society, Marxists have often – and justifiably – preferred to study its complicity in the state to providing an economic analysis of art's relationship to capital. I want to argue that we might bring the two legacies of Marxism back together. A Marxist economic analysis of art has never been undertaken in the full sense. What we have instead is Marxists, for instance, applying the analysis of the class relations of industrial capitalism to the production, distribution and consumption of art, or the political interpretation of the price of artworks and the wealth or poverty of artists. I want to argue, however, that a full and undiluted Marxist economic analysis of art not only provides the only possible basis for a Marxist politics of art, a Marxist aesthetics and a Marxist social ontology of art, but also the possibility of bringing the two legacies of Marxism back together in a coherent whole.

Marxists have appeared to examine art economically, but have always fallen short of the task that is required of an economics derived from the three volumes of *Capital*. Arnold Hauser's extended study *The Social History of Art* (1951) stands out for bringing the economic to bear on art history, but includes the economic within the social analysis of art. Hauser does not provide an economic *analysis* of art. Hauser weaves the history of art into the fabric of political, social, cultural and economic life. This kind of analysis, I would say, amounts to a sociology of style. Nevertheless, Hauser was too reductivist for many Western Marxists. Andrew Arato, the historian of the Frankfurt School, provides a vivid picture of how Western Marxism regarded the 'problem' of the economics of art, anchored in a negative assessment of the Classical Marxist attitude to culture:

> Marx wrote nothing on 'culture' as such. Indeed, his methodological remarks on the dependence of 'superstructure' on the 'base' (and in particular the forms of consciousness on the contradictory structure of a

mode of production) have generally been interpreted by Marxists as reason enough to disregard the 'epiphenomena' of culture'.[16]

The distinction between vulgar[17] Marxism and Western Marxism, then, is
described by the contrast between a narrow and direct economic reductionism on the one hand, and, on the other, an analysis of culture based on the
understanding that 'the commodity structure had permeated the "material"
upon which the thinker or the artist worked'.[18] Western Marxism's opposition to 'vulgar Marxism' conflates Stalinist Eastern Marxism with the Classical
Marxism of Marx, Engels, Lenin, Luxemburg and others. The height of vulgarity is the uncritical and one-dimensional use of the Marxist theory of the base
and superstructure. Note, however, this much-maligned metaphor describes
the relationship between the economic system and the ideological processes
necessary for its reproduction. If it is vulgar to regard art as an ideological
form connected to the capitalist economy, it must be obscene to study art as
an economic activity itself. A Marxist economic analysis of art, therefore, has
been unlikely if not impossible within the history of Marxism. There is, we
might say, echoing Llewellyn Smith, a missing chapter, or missing book, on the
Marxist economic analysis of art. I want to make the case for an extension of
Marxist economics into the territory of the 'cultural turn' – that is to say, bringing the two legacies together in one theoretical approach rather than seeing
them as antagonistic to each other.

With economics on one side of the divide between these two traditions,
and art on the other, it is not altogether surprising that there has never been a
systematic economic analysis of art within the Marxist tradition. What are the
obstacles and objections to a Marxist economic analysis of art? Marxism has not
simply neglected the economic analysis of art; it has conscientiously avoided
it. Lukács, whose Realist theory of literature launched Western Marxism's
'cultural turn', leant heavily on philosophy, particularly Hegel, as well as the
sociology of Weber, in his Marxist aesthetics. Contemporaries such as Adorno
did much the same, supplementing his more Kantian and Nietzschean philosophy, following Lukács's use of Weber and adding to this the psychoanalysis
of Freud. Horkheimer, Benjamin, Bloch and Marcuse showed little interest in

---

16   Arato and Gebhardt 1978, p. 187.

17   The term 'vulgar Marxism', which is associated with economic determinism, echoes
       Marx's term 'vulgar economics', which he used to denote the bourgeois apology of capi-
       talism through economic science.

18   Buck-Morss 1977, p. 35.

economics, too, fortifying their dialectical philosophy with empirical sociology, myth, utopianism and Freudianism respectively. Outside the Frankfurt School, but still following Lukács, Arnold Hauser did not provide an economic analysis of art but a 'social history' and Gramsci, who was one of the earliest critics of 'economic determinism', developed the idea of cultural hegemony by borrowing from Lukács the explanation of how capitalism reproduces itself (tying culture to political reproduction directly without the need for a specific economic analysis). Andre Breton founded Surrealism by combining a heterodox Freudianism with a political commitment to Communism, but without any economic analysis of art. Merleau-Ponty and Sartre reinforced their Marxism with existential philosophy, turning away from Marxist economics. Jameson combined a Lukácsian weighted reading of the Frankfurt School with the economic theory of Mandel, reintroducing economics back into the Marxist study of art, but he did not provide an economic analysis of art, just a philosophically sophisticated social interpretation of art under changed economic conditions, a new background for culture, late capitalism.

In the inaugural text of Western Marxism, Lukács's book *History and Class Consciousness* from 1923, a new 'immanent', dialectical critique of culture was introduced in 'opposition to the mechanistic, deterministic, "vulgar" Marxism which had dominated the Second International'.[19] 'Instead of reducing bourgeois thought to the economic conditions of its production, Lukács argued that the nature of those conditions could be found within the intellectual phenomena themselves'.[20] In turning its attention to consciousness, culture and aesthetic form, Western Marxism *conscientiously avoided* the methods, tools and aims of Classical Marxism, especially the critique of political economy. Just as Lenin expanded Marxism by focussing on questions of political organisation that Marx and Engels had neglected, Western Marxist philosophers extended Marxist theory into questions neglected by Classical Marxists such as culture, experience and subjectivity. But there is a crisis at the heart of Western Marxism's disavowal of the economic. Perry Anderson says 'the hidden hallmark of Western Marxism [is that it is] a product of *defeat*'[21] on several fronts, including the crushing of the revolutionary movement in Western Europe, the Stalinisation of Marxism in the USSR, and the exile and imprisonment of the leading Marxist intellectuals. While Stalin obliterated heterodoxy within the Communist Parties of the East and West alike, Western Marxists

---

19   Buck-Morss 1977, p. 25. The Second International existed from 1889–1916, from the expulsion of the anarchists to its dissolution in WWI.

20   Buck-Morss 1977, p. 26.

21   Anderson 1987, p. 42.

avoided 'those areas most central to the classical traditions of historical materialism: scrutiny of the economic laws of motion of capitalism as a mode of production, analysis of the political machinery of the bourgeois state, strategy of the class struggle necessary to overthrow it'.[22] Marxist economics and political theory had been commandeered by the Stalinist leaders of the movement and to speak of them brought intellectuals into conflict with the party, which officially pronounced certain artworks or schools to be expressions of class positions (for example, bourgeois literature) which Western Marxists justifiably saw as reductive and 'vulgar'. Art, for Western Marxists, was not reducible to economic exchange or political instrumentalisation and the ideas, feelings and experiences of art, they argued, could not adequately or fully be understood by the theory of ideology. Another reason for the absence of a Marxist economic analysis of art was that the leading figures of Western Marxism were not economists but philosophers. Rather than applying Marx's analysis of capital to culture, Western Marxists typically turned to philosophers such as Hegel, Schiller, Spinoza, Nietzsche, Kant and Heidegger, or writers such as Weber, Freud and Machiavelli, as well as esoteric religion, utopian literature and the avant-garde. Western Marxism was founded on the separation of economics from culture.

However, not all economic analysis is reductionist. It seems to me that the Western Marxist rejection of economic determinism in the interpretation of art, which is legitimate, put a block on the economic analysis of art. Western Marxism used economic concepts to locate art within modern capitalist society, but it did this by applying an already existing economic and sociological analysis of capitalism to art, rather than providing an actual economic analysis of art's mode of production itself. The case for a Marxist economic analysis of art still appears to most Marxist intellectuals as either a futile and ill-informed inquiry or as something already deeply ingrained in the Western Marxist theories of reification, culture industry, commodification and spectacle. For whichever reason, the dismissal of an economic analysis of art is the legacy of Western Marxism, which provided no economic analysis of art but nevertheless integrated a lot of economic-sounding critique into its theories of art and aesthetic philosophy. This remains the template for the sophisticated Marxist analysis of art's relationship to capitalism. Julian Stallabrass's book, *Art Incorporated*, in the author's own words, counters the 'standard view' that 'artworks are only incidentally products that are made, purchased and displayed, being centrally the airy vehicles of ideas and emotions'.[23] Stallabrass's

---

22   Anderson 1987, pp. 44–5.
23   Stallabrass 2004a, p. 8.

conviction that art is to be understood as material practice within social, historical and cultural apparatuses and economies is justified. However, the focus of Stallabrass's book 'is not the panoply of global art production, which is very varied and produced for all kinds of diverse local conditions, but rather what is filtered through the art world system to international prominence'.[24] What this means is that Stallabrass's analysis of art's relationship to economics is based on art that enters the market only. By ruling out all forms of artistic production and consumption that do not correspond to market relations, therefore, Stallabrass ensures the conclusion that art and capital are thoroughly intertwined. In the absence of an economic analysis of art, though, Stallabrass often links art to economics through homology, resemblance and contagion, such as when he says '[t]hrough the 1990s, art and the fashion industry came into increasingly close contact'.[25]

The rejection of the vulgarity of economic determinism, of art as 'mere' superstructure determined by the economic and material base, did not lead to Marxists falling silent on the relationship between art and capitalism or abandoning the terms of Marxist economic analysis – commodity, labour, surplus value, exchange, commodity form, exploitation, etc. – it proceeded, instead, with an economically informed social theory, or an economically charged vocabulary that spoke allegorically, metaphorically, associatively and homologously about art. So, Adorno and Horkheimer say, 'those who succumb to the ideology [that art 'transcends' economics] are precisely those who cover up the contradiction, instead of taking it into the consciousness of their own production'.[26] While this sort of thinking appears to nail the secret but inevitable complicity of art with the commodity form – Ben Watson, for instance, says that Adorno's *Aesthetic Theory* 'is essential reading for anyone seriously concerned with the place of modern art in a commodity society'[27] – we need to make a fundamental distinction, here. Western Marxism theorised the relationship between art and capitalism without first establishing the relationship between art and capital. I want to begin the task of rectifying this by providing an assessment of the economics of Western Marxism's key theories of art. Theories of reification, culture industry, commodification, spectacle and so on all attest to the fact that Western Marxism's theories of art and aesthetics are always *informed* by economic theory. Western Marxism has consistently intertwined aesthetics

24   Stallabrass 2004a, p. 71.
25   Stallabrass 2004a, p. 83.
26   Adorno and Horkheimer 1989, p. 157.
27   Ben Watson, from a text 'performed' at Goldsmiths College, London, on 18 October 1995,
      unpaginated.

with Marxist economic concepts such as commodity fetishism, subsumption, exchange value and the commodity form. Western Marxism applies the economic theories of Classical Marxism to the analysis of art without constructing any economic analysis of art's specific modes of production. Paradoxically, the rejection of vulgar Marxism and the subsequent absence of a Marxist economic analysis of art, has left the possibility wide open for Western Marxism to exaggerate the extent to which art has been commodified, industrialised and incorporated by the market and state. However, Marxist theories of the convergence of art and capital have not been tested by the economic analysis of their claims. We need to assess Western Marxism's claims about art's relationship to capitalism.

Western Marxism has always used every device it can find to associate art with capitalism without having to conduct the economic analysis that could establish such associations as substantial or superficial. Jameson explains that the 'vexed question of determinism'[28] was overcome through dialectical processes of association. In this 'the language of causality gives way to that of analogy or homology, of parallelism'.[29]

> Such thinking is therefore marked by the will to link together in a single figure two incommensurable realities, two independent codes or systems of signs, two heterogeneous and asymmetrical terms: spirit and matter, the date of individual experience and the vaster forms of institutional society, the language of existence and that of history.[30]

This is justified because 'the social situation of the bourgeoisie set a priori limits to its speculative thought'.[31] Since the 'social situation' is understood to be that which corresponds to the capitalist mode of production, the task is to identify the limits to thought and culture that are attributable to capitalism. For Jameson, 'the priority of the political interpretation of literary texts'[32] over the psychoanalytic, mythocritical, stylistic, ethical and structural, is guaranteed by the existence of ideology (specifically according to Marx's theory of ideology 'which is not, as is widely thought, one of false consciousness, but rather one of structural limitation'),[33] as 'the absolute horizon of all reading

---

28   Jameson 1971, p. 6.
29   Jameson 1971, p. 10.
30   Jameson 1971, pp. 6–7.
31   Jameson 1971, p. 345.
32   Jameson 1983, p. 1.
33   Jameson 1983, p. 37.

and all interpretation'.[34] Terry Eagleton interprets the aesthetic in precisely these terms, as 'no more than a name for the political unconscious',[35] or the translation of ideology into sensibility. Art and capitalism cannot be separated, hence the distinction between political art and non-political art is 'worse than an error: namely, a symptom and a reinforcement of the reification and privatization of contemporary life'.[36]

Western Marxists developed sophisticated techniques for drawing out what they considered to be the inevitable but concealed effects of capitalism on the work of art, rejecting 'the simplistic and mechanical model'[37] of direct codification. This is because 'ideology is not something which informs or invests symbolic production; rather the aesthetic act is itself ideological, and production of aesthetic or narrative form is to be seen as an ideological act'.[38] As such, Jameson says, the Marxist analysis of the historical formation of Freudianism 'is not achieved simply by resituating Freud in the Vienna and the Central Europe of his period'.[39]

> The conditions of possibility of psychoanalysis become visible, one would imagine, only when you begin to appreciate the extent of psychic fragmentation since the beginnings of capitalism, with its systematic quantification and rationalization of experience, its instrumental reorganization of the subject just as much as of the outside world.[40]

The relationship between art and capitalism, therefore, must be articulated through its 'mediations'. It is not reductivism or determinism but mediation that serves as the Marxist technique for establishing relationships between, for instance, 'the formal analysis of a work of art and its social ground'.[41] Art is not an expression or reflection of capitalist reality. So, 'modernism and reification are parts of the same immense process which expresses the contradictory inner logic and dynamics of late capitalism'[42] but this does not mean that modernism is nothing but an expression or example of capitalism. 'One can-

---

34   Jameson 1983, p. 1.
35   Eagleton 1990, p. 37.
36   Jameson 1983, p. 4.
37   Jameson 1983, p. 26.
38   Jameson 1983, p. 64.
39   Jameson 1983, p. 47.
40   Ibid.
41   Jameson 1983, p. 24.
42   Jameson 1983, p. 27.

not without intellectual dishonesty assimilate the "production" of texts ... to the production of goods by factory work',[43] Jameson says. Adding that 'writing and thinking are not alienated labor in that sense',[44] Jameson carefully separates the task of interpreting art works from the study of the economic and political relations of the artist, the artwork and the reader.

Nevertheless, the most sophisticated Western Marxists attached art to capitalism directly, too. Adorno and Horkheimer say, 'pure works of art which deny the commodity society by the very fact that they obey their own law were always wares all the same'[45] and Stallabrass says, 'artists are snug in the market's lap'.[46] Adorno also argues that the 'listener is converted, along his line of least resistance, into the acquiescent purchaser'[47] and Stewart Martin says the 'culture industry is archetypal of artistic capitalism in so far as it intimates the incorporation of culture into industrial commodity production'.[48]

Western Marxists invent a string of new terms that incorporate Marxist economics and Weberian sociology into the examination of art without subjecting art to the vulgarity of economic analysis directly. Reification, culture industry, commodification, Ideological State Apparatuses, spectacle and cultural capital are the most important of these. Does a Marxist economic analysis of art confirm these theories of art's incorporation by capitalism? I will start with a detailed economic analysis of Lukács's theory of reification, and then proceed to an analysis of the culture industry and spectacle. Marx used the term reification a handful of times but in a conventional manner and not systematically theorising it or with any stress. Hence, reification within Marxism is a term devised by Lukács, who uses it in a new way that combines Marx's concept of commodity fetishism with Weber's concept of rationalisation. The emphasis on commodity fetishism allows Lukács to base his theory of art's relationship to capitalism in Volume 1 of Marx's *Capital* while at the same time shifting

---

43   Jameson 1983, p. 30.

44   Ibid.

45   Adorno and Horkheimer 1989, p. 157.

46   Stallabrass 2004a, p. 200. Stallabrass also sees a convergence between art and commodity culture when art *thematises* retail, marketing or corporate culture, such as in the work of Andreas Gursky, Vanessa Beecroft and Liam Gillick. Rather than interpreting such works as proof of the subjection, subsumption and incorporation of art under capitalism, as if artworks are commodified simply by depicting commodities or reproducing visual elements of commodity culture within their own visual style, I would suggest that the question of whether art is commodified be settled through an analysis of their economic relations.

47   Adorno in Arato and Gebhardt 1978, p. 273.

48   Martin 2011, p. 489.

the emphasis from economic analysis to the attempt to 'obtain a clear insight into the *ideological* problems of capitalism and its downfall.'[49] Lukács lays out the shift from economics to ideology in the introduction to his chapter on reification:

> the problem of commodities must not be considered in isolation or even regarded as the central problem in economics, but as the central, structural problem of capitalist society in all its aspects. Only in this case can the structure of commodity relations be made to yield a model of all the objective forms of bourgeois society together with all the subjective forms corresponding to them.[50]

Thus, reification is not the name of an economic phenomenon, but of the social, phenomenological and epistemological consequences of the economic organisation of society. This is based on sociology. The shift from Classical Marxism to Western Marxism coincides with the introduction of Weber to supplement Marx, resulting in a social analysis of art. What is more, Weberian Marxists introduced the idea of constructing an analysis of culture's relationship to capitalism on the basis of homologies. These are symptomatic of the move away from economic analysis. Theories of reification, culture industry, commodification, spectacle and so on bring the economic analysis of Marxism *to* art, rather than constructing an economic analysis *of* art itself, often by abstracting or generalising economic findings from other sectors or by drawing on trends identified by sociological theory. As labour undergoes rationalisation, specialisation and 'the progressive elimination of the qualitative, human and individual attributes of the worker',[51] the worker undergoes a corresponding process of rationalisation, alienation and mechanisation. Reification is the name Lukács gives to the effects of capitalism on the 'worker, wholly separated from his total human personality',[52] according to the principle that the 'fragmentation of the object of production necessarily entails the fragmentation of its subject'.[53]

---

49   Lukács 1990, p. 84 (emphasis added).
50   Lukács 1990, p. 83.
51   Lukács 1990, p. 88.
52   Lukács 1990, p. 90.
53   Lukács 1990, p. 89.

Lukács selects passages from Marx that depict the crippling psychological and social effects of the capitalist mode of production, and he argues that Taylorism has 'invaded the psyche'.[54] Weber, however, allows Lukács to go further:

> Bureaucracy implies the adjustment of one's way of life, mode of work and hence of consciousness, to the general socio-economic premises of the capitalist economy, similar to that which we have observed in the case of the worker.[55]

These are not far-fetched claims. And Axel Honneth confirms Lukács's transition from the economic to the psychological and sociological:

> In the constantly expanding sphere of commodity exchange, subjects are compelled to behave as detached observers, rather than as active participants in social life, because their reciprocal calculation of the benefits that others might yield for their own profit demands a purely rational and emotionless stance.[56]

However, Habermas does not entirely go along with the argument that capitalist society as a whole produces the capitalist subjects that it requires through the process of reification, partly because he insists on distinguishing between different processes and different effects of rationalisation. Rationalisation is responsible simultaneously for 'releasing communicative action from traditionally based institutions – that is, from obligations of consensus'[57] and establishes new 'compulsory associations [via money and power]...that uncouple action from processes of reaching understanding'.[58] For Habermas, 'only domains of action that fulfil economic and political functions can be converted over to steering media'.[59] Lukács does not adequately distinguish between such different spheres, preferring the concept of totality, hence 'he interprets all manifestations of Occidental rationalism as symptoms of a process in which the whole of society is rationalized through and through'.[60] This

---

54   Lukács 1990, p. 99.
55   Lukács 1990, p. 98.
56   Honneth 2007, p. 99.
57   Habermas 1984, p. 341.
58   Ibid.
59   Habermas 1987, p. 323.
60   Habermas 1984, p. 360.

poses a problem for establishing the relationship between reification and the capitalist mode of production, since the former is an effect of the latter without passing through its mechanisms. Reification is not restricted to economic activities proper, but becomes a 'second nature'. Lukács argues that reification is a consequence of commodity exchange in general but that it is evident also in circumstances where commodity exchange is absent. This kind of elasticity is not built in to Marx's account of 'commodity fetishism'. Commodity fetishism is an effect of commodity production that distorts perceptions of value. Marx does not argue that commodity fetishism, once established by the capitalist mode of production, distorts all perceptions in society. This is why Weber is so important to the conception of reification. Weber, in effect, provides the social basis of the material analysis of art in capitalism, displacing the economic analysis of art altogether. Despite Lukács's repeated references to Marx and Hegel, it is Weber who provides the model for the short-circuiting of the analysis between lived experience and the social whole. Lukács's conception of reification, we might say, is an economically informed examination of 'class consciousness' or, perhaps, the theory of the subject of capitalism. So, at the same time as giving greater stress to Marxist ideas within the Weberian sociological framework, Lukács adapts Marx's economic analysis of capitalist industry towards a more Weberian sociological understanding of the psychopathologies of culture within capitalist society. In Jameson's words, reification 'describes the way in which, under capitalism, the older traditional forms of human activity are instrumentally reorganized and "taylorized", analytically fragmented and reconstructed according to various rational models of efficiency'.[61]

The social became the qualifying characteristic of Marxist inquiry. Most turned to sociology, sociological economics (beginning with Thorstein Veblen), and social psychology (such as George Mead). Also, Bakhtin and Voloshinov inaugurated social linguistics. From social history and social geography to social anthropology, generations of Marxists would insist on the importance of the social in their political analysis of everything from ecology to fashion. The left's reception of Foucault and Deleuze adds fuel to this social turn in Marxism with their emphasis on apparatuses, discourse and various material flows and structural forces. Even Baudrillard's politically implosive postmodernist philosophy of simulacra found Marxist admirers because it was explicitly social in its reduction of everything to matrices, systems, codes, imaginaries and orders.

---

61   Jameson 1979, p. 130.

The social turn within Marxism that begins with Lukács explains the absence of a Marxist economics of art.

The sociologist of culture, Pierre Bourdieu, has been a constant in Marxist studies of art in recent decades. His work provides the materialist analysis that Marxist theory stripped of economics lacks. The subtitle to one of Bourdieu's most pioneering books, *Distinction*, 'a social critique of the judgement of taste', is a perfect indication of how the left has come to approach art and culture. The social is dominant, here, and economic analysis absent, as it is for Janet Wolff, whose important book *The Social Production of Art*, opens with the unflinching sentence, 'Art is a social product'.[62] This is true, of course, and it is sad to say that at the end of the 1970s and beginning of the 1980s the assertion that art is social had a kind of shock value in art history. However, the difference between an emphasis on the social and an emphasis on economics is vital to Marxism. The social is more flexible than the economic insofar as it grasps relations of race, gender, sexuality, religion and nationality that economic analysis had long been held to miss, but the economic, we would insist, constitutes the specific character of social relations of the capitalist mode of production. Jameson forcefully reminds us of what is at stake in the surge of social theory. In his defence of the concepts 'totality' and 'structure', Jameson argues, 'we can acknowledge the presence of such a concept, provided we understand that there is ... a "mode of production" '.[63] We are back, here, with the economic in its fullest sense, as the ensemble of the means of production and relations of production, and not the kind of economics that Fine and Milonakis confront in their study of how political economy became economics 'through the desocialisation and dehistoricisation of the dismal science, and how this heralded the separation of economics from other social sciences'.[64] But the statement that art is social leaves wide open the question as to whether art is a commodity in Marx's sense, whether it is produced for economic value or for some other, non-economic value or set of values. Art, of course, might be social without being the kind of product that the labour theory of value explains.

Like Benjamin, Adorno and Horkheimer do not take issue with the sociological and philosophical methodology of Lukács's theory of the relationship between art and capitalism. In fact they develop the theory of the culture industry out of Lukács's theory of reification. Lukács's analysis of the *subject* of capitalist rationalisation was applied thoroughly by Adorno and Horkheimer

62   Wolff 1981, p. 1.
63   Jameson 1988, p. 40.
64   Fine and Milonakis 2009b, p. 1.

to culture. As their preferred term indicates, Adorno and Horkheimer put a stronger emphasis than Lukács on the actual encounter between art and the processes of industrialisation, consumption, marketing and the technologies of mass production and mass distribution. The characteristics of Fordist production – namely, standardisation, routinisation, deskilling, volume, branding and advertising – are discovered to have entered the experience of culture itself. The 'culture industry' is culture subjected to standardisation, regulation, calculation, technology, expertise, management and marketing. Adorno and Horkheimer, like Lukács, are alert to the pitfalls of interpreting culture as nothing but a reflection, expression or effect of the 'economic base'. The material precondition for the culture industry is the emergence of technologies of the reproduction and distribution of cultural works. Although they include art in the essay on the culture industry, its emphasis is on 'mass culture', as Adorno points out in 'Culture Industry Reconsidered', where he explains that the authors replaced the expression 'mass culture' in the original text with 'culture industry' in order to indicate that it was not 'the contemporary form of popular art'.[65] Rather, the culture industry is controlled, managed and administered 'from above'.[66] The culture industry 'finds its typical expression in cinema and radio',[67] they say. That this analysis puts its emphasis on the position of the consumer is expressed immediately through a comparison of the telephone and the radio. 'The former', they say, 'still allowed the subscriber to play the role of subject, and was liberal. The latter is democratic: it turns all participants into listeners and authoritatively subjects them to broadcast programs which are all exactly the same'.[68] This is the material basis for their assertion that the 'man with leisure has to accept what the culture manufacturers offer him'.[69]

The concept of the culture industry does not regard culture as the epiphenomena of political economy, nor does it provide an analysis of the economics of art, despite referring constantly to art as a commodity, the art viewer as a consumer and the exhibition of art as a marketplace. And yet, rather than discussing art in terms of the labour theory of value, labour power, surplus value, formal and real subsumption, self-accumulation, relative surplus value and so

---

65   Adorno 1991, p. 85.
66   Ibid.
67   Adorno and Horkheimer 1989, p. xvi.
68   Adorno and Horkheimer 1989, p. 122.
69   Adorno and Horkheimer 1989, p. 124.

on, they complain, typically, 'no scope is left for the imagination'.[70] Adorno explains that

> the expression 'industry' is not to be taken too literally. It refers to the standardization of the thing itself – such as that of the Western, familiar to every movie-goer – and to the rationalization of distribution techniques, but not strictly the production process.[71]

The emphasis on 'hit songs, stars and soap operas' as 'cyclically recurrent and rigidly invariable types'[72] constituted by 'ready-made clichés to be slotted in anywhere',[73] confirms that the concept of culture industry is not a theory of the industrialisation of culture but an account of the culture that exists within industrial society. Adorno is under no illusions about this, saying the culture industry 'is industrial more in a sociological sense ... rather than in the sense of anything really and actually produced by technological rationality'.[74] In Adorno's extension of the argument of culture industry in 'On the Fetish Character in Music and the Regression of Listening', he states not only that 'regressive listening is tied to production by the machinery of distribution, and particularly of advertising'[75] but also that under the conditions of technological rationalisation '[t]hey become vulgarized'.[76] It is indisputable that the technologies of the mass distribution of culture (radio, magazines, cinema, vinyl records and television) transform the reception of culture, not only entering the home and being experienced instantaneously by an entire nation, but also forming a mode of enjoyment devoid of 'sustained thought' amid 'the relentless rush of facts'.[77] Pleasure under the regime of the culture industry 'hardens into boredom because, if it is to remain pleasure, it must not demand any effort'.[78] As such, the products of the culture industry are produced bureaucratically with the aid of experts according to 'formula', 'prearranged harmony', 'false laughter', 'clichés' and 'fashions which appear like epidemics'.[79] Novelty

---

70   Adorno and Horkheimer 1989, p. 127.
71   Adorno 1991, p. 87.
72   Adorno and Horkheimer 1989, p. 125.
73   Ibid.
74   Adorno 1991, p. 87.
75   Adorno 1991, p. 42.
76   Adorno 1991, p. 36.
77   Adorno and Horkheimer 1989, p. 127.
78   Adorno and Horkheimer 1989, p. 137.
79   Adorno and Horkheimer 1989, p. 165.

crowds out risk: 'What is new about the phase of mass culture compared with the late liberal stage is the exclusion of the new'.[80]

The pessimism of Adorno and Horkheimer's conception of culture industry's violence against subjectivity as final, total and complete, along with the apparent bias of their critique, which can be read as an attack on popular culture as inferior to minority culture, particularly Adorno's utter rejection of jazz, leaves Frankfurt School aesthetics vulnerable to the charge that the perceived uniformity of mass culture is projected onto it by unsympathetic commentators rather than imposed by an inflexible system. According to Bernard Gendron, Adorno 'failed to appreciate the fact that . . . I do not buy records like I buy cans of cleanser'.[81] The underlying problem, here, is not Adorno's elitism or even his revolutionary militancy but the methodological decision to focus the analysis of culture's relationship to capitalism on the properties of the works themselves. While each can of Heinz tomato soup is required to taste the same, each film by Pixar and each song by The Rolling Stones is required to be different, so the application of technology and rationalisation to culture uses processes of standardisation to produce goods that exhibit specific or unique qualities. This is underestimated by Adorno and Horkheimer because they seek to associate culture and industry as closely as possible and they do so by scrutinising the properties of cultural goods for signs of the imprint of industrialisation considered as homologies. While Adorno and Horkheimer express their analysis of the culture industry in unforgiving and relentless phrases, they are aware that there are examples of cinema, music and magazines that do not fit the template. Although the production of film, 'the central sector of the culture industry',[82] often 'resembles technical modes of operation in the extensive division of labour, the employment of machines and the separation of the labourers from the means of production',[83] Adorno understands

---

80   Adorno and Horkheimer 1989, p. 134.

81   Gendron in Modleski 1986, p. 28. Gendron challenges Adorno's emphatic assertion of the uniformity of the culture industry by comparing two versions of the song 'Blue Moon', the first a pining nightclub croon and the second an upbeat urban doo-wop cover: 'If we put melody and harmony in the core, and timbre and connotation in the periphery [as Adorno does], we will see a radical sameness' but if we reverse the polarity of core and periphery, giving emphasis to timbre and connotation, then while the melody and harmony may be the same 'the sounds are radically different' (Gendron in Modleski 1986, p. 28).

82   Adorno 1991, p. 87.

83   Ibid.

that 'individual forms of production are nevertheless maintained'.[84] But when Adorno observed distinctions within mass culture, such as the difference between Garbo as a tragic individual and Mickey Rooney as a commercial star, he regarded the worst as displacing its rival as technological rationalisation tightened its grip on culture.

The starkest contrast drawn by Adorno and Horkheimer is not internal to mass culture, though, but between mass culture and avant-garde art. 'Works of art are ascetic and unashamed; the culture industry is pornographic and prudish',[85] they say. While the culture industry 'makes laughter the instrument of the fraud practised on happiness',[86] Baudelaire is 'devoid of humour'.[87] Picasso, Schonberg, Dadaists and Expressionists are all said to have mistrusted style, while 'the untruth of style as such triumphs today in the sung jargon of a crooner, in the carefully contrived elegance of a film star, and even in the admirable expertise of a photography of a peasant's squalid hut'.[88] Attempts to incorporate art into mass culture are seen by Adorno and Horkheimer as violent confrontations in which, for instance, 'a movement from a Beethoven symphony is crudely "adapted" for a film sound-track . . . [or] a Tolstoy novel is garbled in a film script'.[89] Although Adorno and Horkheimer punch heavier against mass culture than art, and they glimpse more hope in avant-gardism than in pop songs and Hollywood movies, they do not conclude that art is the cure for the culture industry or that art is somehow immune from technological rationality. Rather than taking sides within cultural division, they say the 'division itself is the truth'.[90] Nevertheless, Adorno and Horkheimer tie the subjectivity of the Culture Industry to capitalist technology, associate the formal characteristics of cultural goods with the qualities of standardised production, and note resemblances between culture and industrial commodities. Adorno sums up these ideas in the following manner:

> The consciousness of the mass of listeners is adequate to fetishized music. It listens according to formula, and indeed debasement itself

---

84   Ibid.
85   Adorno and Horkheimer 1989, p. 140.
86   Ibid.
87   Adorno and Horkheimer 1989, p. 141.
88   Adorno and Horkheimer 1989, p. 130.
89   Adorno and Horkheimer 1989, p. 122.
90   Adorno and Horkheimer 1989, p. 135.

would not be possible if resistance ensued, if the listeners still had the capacity to make demands beyond the limits of what was supplied.[91]

The precise social mechanism by which cultural objects are reified is never adequately explained either by Adorno alone or in collaboration with Horkheimer. The theory of the culture industry, therefore, never reaches a decision on whether the industrialised production of mass culture is brought about by the reified subject that demands formulaic culture, or whether the debased consumer of culture is an effect of the changes in culture's economy. Since neither is ultimately satisfactory as an explanation, Adorno and Horkheimer play one off against the other. They place the emphasis of their argument not on the transformation of the economic mode of production, which is assumed at the start but not examined. Instead they plot a constellation of technological developments, the reduction or eradication of the role of the subject in the appreciation of culture, and the reduction or elimination of aesthetic qualities and complexity in cultural objects.

Adorno and Horkheimer's emphasis on cultural consumption, seen from the point of view of a Marxist economic analysis, is a weakness and leads to flawed assessments. The power of their critique, in fact, depends upon ambiguities in economic analysis. For instance, they reveal the operations of capital even in the provision of symphony music universally for free:

> No tickets could be bought when Toscanini conducted over the radio; he was heard without charge, and every sound of the symphony was accompanied, as it were, by the sublime puff that the symphony was not interrupted by any advertising: 'This concert is brought to you as a public service'.[92]

The apparent absence of profit and marketing is an illusion, they argue, because the whole thing 'was made possible by the profits of the united automobile and soap manufacturers, whose payments keep the radio stations going'.[93] While it is true that capitalist enterprises expend sums, frequently enormous amounts, on marketing events that are calculated to augment their brand, from an economic point of view we need to distinguish a firm's income from its marketing. When Toscanini is not asked to endorse commodities, unlike

---

91   Adorno 1991, p. 40.
92   Adorno and Horkheimer 1989, pp. 158–9.
93   Adorno and Horkheimer 1989, p. 159.

Hank Williams, for instance, then the two are separated economically. The radio company paid Hank Williams to peddle its sponsors' goods to listeners who tune in to listen to his music (assuming that the sponsors pay more than the radio company pass on to Hank Williams and the crew combined, this is a straightforward case of profiting from labour). When NBC employed Toscanini and built a studio specifically for the NBC Orchestra, this was good business, but if executives or the conductor himself insisted on eliminating advertising from certain symphonic performances, then this would affect their economic performance. Arguing that there is a time lag between the performance and the profit drawn from them is an illusion: if the radio performances are recorded and subsequently albums are sold, then it is only the production and sale of the records that is profitable.

Nevertheless, Jameson reminds us that Adorno thought 'that the very specificity of modern art lay in its confrontation with the commodity form'.[94] What remains unspecified, here, however, is, first, whether the specificity of mass culture is due to its confrontation with commodity form, too, and second, whether art itself must be commodified in order to be transformed by the emergence of capitalist commodity production. Also, what Jameson and Adorno fail to clarify is the difference between simple commodity production and capitalist commodity production. Western Marxism generally has been satisfied with a generic theory of commodification. Commodification is an English term that attempts to translate the German 'zur Ware werden' – to become a commodity.[95] Kommodifizierung, which the Germans use now, is a translation back from the English. Eugene Lunn uses it in 1974 in relation to Brecht and Lukács, Dick Howard puts it in inverted commas in an essay on Habermas the same year, and poet and Marxist cultural thinker Hans Magnus Enzensberger refers to it in 1974 too, in his book inspired by Adorno, *The Consciousness Industry*.[96] As such, commodification is a relative latecomer as a term within the Marxist lexicon, but it can be traced back to Marx's understanding of how capitalism emerges and subsequently develops. Marx and Engels described the process of commodification as a single operation spread over time in the *Communist Manifesto* (1848). The extension of commodification is a contradictory process. Commodification is linked to the technological revolution of the means of production which is integral to capitalism.

---

94   Jameson 1988, p. 118.
95   I am indebted to Esther Leslie for explaining to me the origin of the concept of commodification within Marxist theory.
96   See Enzensberger 1974.

The bourgeoisie cannot exist without constantly revolutionising the instruments of production, and thereby the relations of production, and with them the whole relations of society. Conservation of the old modes of production in unaltered form, was, on the contrary, the first condition of existence for all earlier industrial classes. Constant revolutionising of production, uninterrupted disturbance of all social conditions, everlasting uncertainty and agitation distinguish the bourgeois epoch from all earlier ones. All fixed, fast frozen relations, with their train of ancient and venerable prejudices and opinions, are swept away, all new-formed ones become antiquated before they can ossify. All that is solid melts into air, all that is holy is profaned, and man is at last compelled to face with sober senses his real condition of life and his relations with his kind.[97]

Commodification is also linked to imperialism and globalisation. 'The need of a constantly expanding market for its products chases the bourgeoisie over the entire surface of the globe'.[98]

The term commodification is used very broadly by Marxists to identify a range of practices and processes and, as a result, can appear to be a blunt instrument. We can tighten it up by showing that commodification has three distinct types or stages (which correspond to three historical moments). First, commodification is the process by which products become commodities by being made available on the market for the first time (this can also be divided into two types, one which precedes capitalism, such as when surplus produce is exchanged or sold, and another in which capitalists use the techniques of 'primitive accumulation' to incorporate new commodities into the global marketplace). Second, commodities are geared towards a market (through, for example, Fordist production), which is to say, products are produced specifically to be sold for profit and therefore the volume of production and even the product produced is led by demand. Thirdly and lastly, markets are introduced to previously free or publicly supplied commodities (also known as privatisation), which either commodifies certain products and services for the first time or re-commodifies products and services that have been de-commodified. Examples of recent commodification include childcare and laundry, the professionalisation of amateur sports, the commercial replacement of parlour games with branded games, the development of supervised soft play centres that replace public parks and street corners, and intellectual property,

---

97   Marx and Engels in Panitch and Leys 1998, p. 243.
98   Ibid.

copyright, patent and price tags being placed on information and knowledge. However, commodification is not achieved all at once, rather it develops unevenly in a patchwork that covers some areas but remains absent in others and with different intensities so that some areas are deeply commodified while others are affected only superficially by it or left untouched altogether. This means that commodities exist coevally and in tension with goods, gifts and other non-commodities. This latter point is typically overlooked in Western Marxism, especially in the theory of art's commodification, according to the doctrine that capitalism is a social totality that commmodifies everything.

The commodification of art is often asserted but the assertion is never sufficiently tested through an economic analysis of the process by which art might in principle be commodified. Childcare is a service which historically took place within the domestic economy without passing through the marketplace, apart from the very wealthy who could afford nannies or au pairs. Recently, however, childcare has been commodified in certain parts of the world on an unprecedented scale through the introduction of commercial, self-employed child minders who are hired to take care of children while both parents go out to work. Has art gone through the same kind of transformation?

Paul Wood links commodification to art in a striking way: 'the commodity, the fetish, fashion, and reification form the constellation of terms in which the typical experience of modernity was constituted'.[99] That is to say, since Baudelaire, the poet of modern life, and Manet, the painter of modern life, artists of any seriousness have been, in a fundamental sense, artists *of* capitalist society. Wood describes Manet as 'the painter of a commodified Baudelairean modernity',[100] not on account of the commodities he depicted but insofar as Manet painted 'an increasingly fractured social space, the space of the commodity'.[101] Wood, therefore, connects 'the emergence in Manet's time of the artwork as commodity',[102] with the representation of capitalist modernity and a new kind of pictorial space, effectively diagnosing art as commodified through and through – that is, commodified at every level. However, he remains open to the possibility that Manet and others 'while offering representations of commodification, contain also the possibility of imaginative freedom from its thrall'.[103] In the period of the emergence of modernity in the

---

99   Wood in Nelson and Shiff 1996, p. 392.
100   Ibid.
101   Wood in Nelson and Shiff 1996, p. 393.
102   Ibid.
103   Ibid.

nineteenth century up to the birth of Western Marxism, commodification was a growing tendency, but was not yet complete. Woods asks whether 'the realm of the commodity [is] now seamless and total' and poses the following question: 'can independence from commodification be if not practically, then at least imaginatively, sustained?'[104] If these are not rhetorical questions then the independence from commodification has to be established either through the Lukácsian technique of developing and sustaining a critical consciousness of commodification, or non-market mechanisms and non-economic modes of decision-making need to be acknowledged and sustained in which practices, including but not restricted to art, can be reproduced as non-commodity production for publics rather than markets. Such thinking presumably appears to be fanciful to Wood, as it does to the Western Marxist tradition generally, and to the generation of Conceptual artists in the 1960s and 1970s, to which Wood is aligned, that built its intellectual barricades against political theories of art that appeared to promote having your 'heart in the right place' even if this meant constructing a critical practice out of the confession of complicity.

Martha Rosler, one of the leading critical artists of the period overlapping Conceptualism and postmodernism, formulated the omnipresence of commodification in the strongest terms: 'Commodity fetishism, the giving over of self to the thing, is not a universal trope of the human psyche, it is not even a quirk of character. It is both the inescapable companion and the serviceable pipe dream of capitalist social organization: it is Our Way of Life'.[105] Asserting that the commodification of art is 'inescapable' was not merely an expression of faith in Marxist doctrine in the 1970s, it was the conclusion of decades of failed attempts by the avant-garde to out-manoeuvre commodification. A typical example is the itinerant British art organisation, the Artist Placement Group. Howard Slater has traced how various attempts by APG to avoid, resist or minimise art's commodification were doomed from the outset. For instance, turning to time-based processes rather than object-making on the assumption that producing art objects 'is similar to the creation of manufactured commodities'[106] naively neglects the commodification of services and spectacle. According to Lucy Lippard, writing in the early 1970s, there was a very short period between the time when it was feasible for Conceptual artists to believe that the new approach might de-commodify art, and the time when it is

---

104   Wood in Nelson and Shiff 1996, p. 405.
105   Rosler in Alberro and Stimson 1999, p. 367.
106   Slater 2000, p. 23.

evident that these tactics were not going to de-commodify art at all, but merely add to the stream of novelties required of artistic production in general.

> Hopes that 'conceptual art' would be able to avoid the general commercialization, the destructively 'progressive' approach of modernism were for the most part unfounded. It seemed in 1969 that no one, not even a public greedy for novelty, would actually pay money, or much of it, for a xerox sheet referring to an event past or never directly perceived, a group of photographs documenting an ephemeral situation or condition, a project for work never to be completed, words spoken but not recorded; it seemed that these artists would therefore be forcibly freed from the tyranny of a commodity status and market-orientation. Three years later, the major conceptualists are selling work for substantial sums here and in Europe; they are represented by (and still more unexpected – showing in) the world's most prestigious galleries. Clearly, whatever minor revolutions in communication have been achieved by the process of dematerializing the object (easily mailed work, catalogues and magazine pieces, primarily art that can be shown inexpensively and unobtrusively in infinite locations at one time), art and artist in a capitalist society remain luxuries.[107]

It is not surprising, therefore, that when Wood asserts the commodification of art in more hedged language, he leaves little doubt that no realistic political assessment of art can pretend that commodification is anything but systemically unavoidable. 'Artworks are a special kind of good',[108] he says. But rather than follow up on the implications of art perhaps being a good rather than a commodity, Wood immediately insists, 'this does not mean that they are not produced and exchanged, only that their modes of production and exchange are specialized forms of a more general condition'.[109] The general condition that Wood refers to here is the relationship between labour and capital. So, while 'the labor involved for Malevich in producing a black square, or for Duchamp in nominating a bicycle wheel, does not relate to the exchange value of the resulting object in the same way as, say, the skilled work and technology involved in producing a car',[110] artists nevertheless, Wood suggests,

---

107   Lippard 1973, p. 263.
108   Wood in Nelson and Shiff 1996, p. 388.
109   Ibid.
110   Ibid.

produce *and* exchange, without claiming – or proving – that artists produce *for* exchange, which is a vital difference, as we will see later in this book.

At roughly the same time as certain Conceptualists still erroneously believed that the commodification of art could be overcome through modifications in the art object itself, Guy Debord theorised *spectacle* specifically in terms of an entire culture deranged by commodification. 'The spectacle is the moment when the commodity has attained the total occupation of social life'.[111] Lukács's concept of reification supplies the scaffolding for Debord's theory of the spectacle which, like Adorno and Horkheimer, renames mass culture in terms appropriate to a society in which culture is a business that no longer presents itself as separate from daily, domestic, private and inner life.[112] Debord does not develop a technologically rationalised vision of culture as an industry but incorporates culture at the heart of capitalist society through the concept of the image. Twenty years after Adorno and Horkheimer's essay, Debord's theory is not nailed to actual technological developments or processes of administration, even if advertising, cinema, radio and television are shared starting points. T.J. Clark says the spectacle was 'not a matter of mere cultural and ideological refurbishing but of all-embracing economic change'.[113] Debord said, '[t]he spectacle is capital to such a degree of accumulation that it becomes an image'.[114] So, Jonathan Crary's riposte to Foucault's dismissal of the spectacle, 'I suspect that Foucault did not spend much time watching television or thinking about it',[115] calls for a theory of power to pass through the ubiquitous experience of the image. 'When culture becomes nothing more than a commodity, it must also become the star commodity of the spectacular society'.[116] Politics, including revolutionary politics, is not excluded from Debord's account of spectacle as it is in Adorno and Horkheimer's culture industry, since Debord notes, for instance, 'portents of a second proletarian assault against class society'.[117] Spectacle is conceived in economic terms derived from the Marxist critique of political economy.

---

111   Debord 1983, § 41 (unpaginated).
112   Debord confirms this: 'the spectacle, taken in the limited sense of "mass media" which are its most glaring superficial manifestation, seems to invade society as mere equipment' (Debord 1983, § 24 (unpaginated)).
113   Clark 1984, p. 9.
114   Debord 1983, § 34 (unpaginated).
115   Crary 1989, p. 105.
116   Debord 1983, § 193 (unpaginated).
117   Debord 1983, § 115 (unpaginated).

Debord intertwines the spectacle with the capitalist economy from root to branch: 'The society which rests on modern industry is not accidentally or superficially spectacular, it is fundamentally *spectaclist*.[118] Justification for this can be found in Marx's concept of 'real abstraction', which denotes the strange ontology of money, for instance, as at once empirical and intangible. Insofar as capitalism is organised around value metamorphosing from money to commodities to money, capitalist society is the collective experience of the domination of exchange value over use value. Debord expresses the degree to which abstraction shapes capitalist reality in the following passage:

> One cannot abstractly contrast the spectacle to actual social activity: such a division is itself divided. The spectacle which inverts the real is in fact produced. Lived reality is materially invaded by the contemplation of the spectacle while simultaneously absorbing this spectacular order, giving it positive cohesiveness. Objective reality is present on both sides.[119]

Hence, the spectacle, Debord says, 'is the other side of money: it is the general abstract equivalent of all commodities'.[120] However, although Debord's concept of the spectacle has its roots in Marx's concept of 'real abstraction', he argues, also, that capitalism had undergone a decisive shift. The real abstractions of capitalism have been further abstracted, or the abstract elements of reality have risen to dominance. Hence: 'The spectacle is the money which one only *looks at*'.[121] Going beyond the argument that culture has been industrialised, Debord argues that capitalism is itself best understood as a vast colony of images. Crary sees the spectacle 'as a new kind of power of recuperation and absorption'.[122] This is certainly an aspect of the spectacle, but Debord makes a more ambitious claim than this. Capitalism, he says, operates spectacularly, with a roster of phantoms, fetishes, fictitious entities, speculations and metamorphoses that are not illusions or speech acts.[123] Capitalism requires a concept of 'abstraction not as a mere mask, fantasy or diversion, but as a force operative in the world'.[124] Benjamin Noys backs up the idea of 'real abstraction

---

118   Debord 1983, § 14 (unpaginated).
119   Debord 1983, § 8 (unpaginated).
120   Debord 1983, § 49 (unpaginated).
121   Debord 1983, § 49 (unpaginated).
122   Crary 1989, p. 100.
123   See Searle 1996.
124   Toscano 2008 p. 274.

as the ontology of capital'[125] by listing the techniques, institutions and agencies of financialisation, speculation, digitalisation, dematerialisation and spectralisation. 'The commodity is this factually real illusion', Debord says, 'and the spectacle is its general manifestation'.[126] A commodity, Marx famously wrote in *Capital* Volume I, is 'a mysterious thing'.[127] No amount of scientific or speculative knowledge can dispel the mystery of the commodity since 'no chemist has ever discovered exchange value either in a pearl or a diamond'.[128]

Debord's *Society of the Spectacle* developed out of Lukács's *History and Class Consciousness*, but spectacle is not merely a new name for reification. For Lukács, reification petrifies social relations and processes, converting them into things. It shows its deathly menace most clearly in one particular commodity, namely wage labour, which reduces humanity to 'a pure measurable quantity, a "thing" appended to the machine – a process in which he is stripped of qualitative, human and individual properties'.[129] Debord's spectacle is the theory of a second phase of reification:

> The first phase of the domination of the economy over social life brought into the definition of all human realization the obvious degradation of being into having. The present phase of total occupation leads to a generalized sliding of having into appearing.[130]

Whereas Lukács extends commodity fetishism into every pore of the social fabric partly by attaching it to Weber's sociology of capitalism, particularly the concept of rationalisation, Debord drills down into the concept of reification to bind the concept of commodity fetishism to real abstraction, which is arguably Marx's most important philosophical contribution. This means that Debord can incorporate the capitalist state and the police into a unified theory of spectacle, saying the 'cleavage of the spectacle is inseparable from the modern State',[131] and '[w]herever the concentrated spectacle rules, so does the police'.[132] Clearly, the authority of the political leader and the legitimated violence of the enforcer of law are both real abstractions. Spectacle, therefore, is not a theory

---

125   Noys 2010, p. 10.
126   Debord 1983, § 47 (unpaginated).
127   Marx 1954, p. 77.
128   Marx 1954, p. 87.
129   Löwy 1979, p. 183.
130   Debord 1983, § 17 (unpaginated).
131   Debord 1983, § 24 (unpaginated).
132   Debord 1983, § 64 (unpaginated).

of the industrialisation of culture or of a more general rationalisation but of the viral metastases of real abstraction. Commodity fetishism is a conspicuous form of real abstraction, and as such, the concept of reification carries within it the imperial threat of real abstraction, but whereas the effects of reification are systematically, if clandestinely, rooted in the commodity form in the absence of an economic analysis of different forms of production, the effects of real abstraction do not require economic analysis. Debord, we might say, headed in the opposite direction of writing an economic analysis of art. If Lukács and the Frankfurt School expelled direct economic analysis from art and aesthetics as vulgar and determinist, that is to say, as lacking mediation, Debord simultaneously planted the theory of reification deeper into Marx's analysis of capital and removed it from the actual processes of economic exchange and the mechanisms for the extraction of surplus value. This eventually becomes the basis of Baudrillard's supersession of use value and exchange value with sign value, but its primary and immediate result was to redirect the Marxist analysis of society towards the production of subjectivity through 'a new kind of image and its speed, ubiquity, and simultaneity'.[133]

The case for art's incorporation and recuperation by market forces remains unproven. Despite the theories of commodification and reification, Western Marxists have not shown that artistic labour has become abstract labour under capitalism. Nor has Western Marxism's examination of art and aesthetics determined whether artistic labour is productive or unproductive labour. Artistic production may have incorporated new technology, but its producers are not obliged to introduce technology into the production of art in order to increase productivity, deskill employees or reduce the price of commodities in order to compete in the market. Rather than simply insisting on the blank assertion of reification in art, we would be better examining the consequences of the fact that artists, unlike the proletariat, continue to own their own means of production and continue to own the products they produce but, unlike productive capitalists, do not derive their income from the difference between capital invested and the surplus value produced by wage labourers. Commodification, although it is a Marxist idea coined in relation to art, is not an economic argument. Cultural capital employs a flawed mainstream concept of capital, not the Marxist version. Spectacle ties culture with commodities at the level of the image. Ideological State Apparatuses are not economic institutions. In fact, ISAs are protected from markets. Rancière, Badiou and Lecercle, today, follow this tradition by providing no economics of art but place art or aesthetics at the heart of their politics, as well as politics at the

---

133   Crary 1989, p. 101.

heart of their analysis of art. Western Marxism has generated its theories of art in the absence of an economics of art. Does a Marxist economic analysis of art's relationship to capital confirm the Western Marxist theories of art's relationship to capitalism? We need to test such ideas by examining precisely how far capital has penetrated the production and distribution of art. The shortcut between art and capitalism begins with the concept of reification, but is replicated in theories of the culture industry, commodification, spectacle and others, such as citadel culture.[134] We have plenty of Marxist theories of the relationship between art and capitalism but none, so far, that can explain the relationship between art and capital. Let us do the economic analysis and find out.

---

134   See Werckmeister 1991.

CHAPTER 8

Art and Productive Capital

A compelling case can be made for the transformation of artistic production in parallel with the transformation of production within capitalist industrial production. During the nineteenth and twentieth centuries, art took on the technologies of the mechanical and digital reproduction of imagery, artists have developed practices using the techniques of administration and management, artworks thematise advertising imagery and mimic the protocols of marketing, the big studio factories resemble manufacturing, artists are presented in the media as celebrities and some have brand strategies, artists have become professionalised, and art has been deskilled so that its labour appears less and less like the handicraft practices of the Renaissance. We would not expect artists to be somehow external to capitalist society. The transformation of artistic labour in the era of the capitalist mode of production, which mirrors the industrial dissolution of craft, offers strong circumstantial evidence of the impact of capitalism on art. While it is possible, for instance, for art to enter the market and fetch enormous sums while remaining in all other respects unaffected by the division of labour, mechanisation, etc., it is also possible for the production methods and relations of art to be utterly revolutionised by the division of labour, new technologies and so on, without entering into the capitalist mode of production. There may be social, cultural, psychological, technological, ideological or other forces that cause art to adopt the productive processes of capitalism, but I am interested here in whether art's production is transformed by capitalism by being brought within its economy. The key factor in art's relationship to the capitalist mode of production, rather than capitalist forms of consumption or finance, which we will consider later, is the relationship it establishes with productive capital. The thesis of commodification, namely the conventional formula by which Western Marxism theorises the incorporation of art into capitalist exchange, remains aloof from the question of art's relation to productive capital. Artists are consumers of capitalist commodities and, in their second jobs, are wage labourers, too. When the first video cameras were made cheap enough to be available to consumers rather than just professionals, artists were among the first to purchase them and video art was soon established as a mode of art production alongside painting, sculpture and performance. The fact that the new video technology was specifically designed to extend the market for leisure (including the new market for the video cassettes that fed them) means that video artists were beneficiaries of capitalist R&D.

© KONINKLIJKE BRILL NV, LEIDEN, 2015 | DOI 10.1163/9789004288157_010

What is more, given that technology is never neutral but carries values within it, all attempts by artists to adopt new technology brings art in close proximity to the values and processes of capitalist society. But the social relations thus established between art and capitalism are a misleading measure of art's economic relations with capital.

What Marx says about 'the mist through which the social character of labour appears to us',[1] in his discussion of 'commodity fetishism', is not the preamble to a call for the study of labour in itself. The labour theory of value is also a value theory of labour. Labour is more extensive than value, or economics in the narrow sense, but even labour outside of economic exchange produces values. Use values, if nothing else. We might coin the term 'labour fetishism' to describe any attempt to discuss labour in isolation from the social totality and particularly the isolation of labour from the economic transactions through which it circulates, from which it is derived or from which it escapes. Marx criticises Ferdinando Galiani for saying 'value is a relation between persons' when he ought to have said, according to Marx, that value is a relation between persons expressed as a relation between things. Similarly, labour must be seen dialectically not only as the productive activity that creates things and values but also as mediated and dominated by the things and values it creates. Examining labour processes in their social, historical, cultural, technological and political contexts, from the point of view of Marxist economics, is to miss the really vital question. Let us take the example of housework to illustrate the point. An individual cleaning their own home performs the same labour as the cleaner who is paid by the household to clean their house. Looking at the work does not tell us which one is waged and which unpaid. Furthermore, the cleaner who works for cash directly from the household does not produce surplus value, but takes the full value of the work. Working for an agency, on the contrary, means that the cleaner works part of the day for those who own the agency. The difference between these three economic circumstances (unpaid, wage labour, surplus labour) is central to understanding the social and economic significance of the work, but it is impossible to get the slightest inkling of the difference by looking at the labour alone. It is the social relations of labour that reveal its economic meaning. Capital circulates only in the third instance of our example, when the agency pays the cleaner's wages and takes the payment from the household as the consumer's purchase of the service that they offer through the labour of the cleaner. In the first instance, no money is exchanged at all, and in the second, the disposable income of the household, not capital, is used to pay the cleaner. Since capitalist production is the production of

---

1   Marx 1954, p. 79.

surplus value, we need to attend to labour primarily in its capacity as the source of surplus value for capital. So, it is not by investigating labour that we will understand labour, including artistic labour. We must examine closely the presence and absence of productive capital.

The theory of commodification typically puts the emphasis on the product itself as it is made available for sale on the market. An altarpiece fixed to the walls of a church does not normally circulate in the market for commodities (although, in principle, a certificate for its ownership can pass through many hands). When the altarpiece is removed from the church, however, and sold, we are justified in speaking of its commodification. There is a well documented historical process by which articles circulating independently of the marketplace are sucked in to markets and are subsequently dominated by market forces and become nothing but commodities. Nevertheless, commodities existed and were exchanged long before capitalism. C-M-C, in which commodities are exchanged for equivalent commodities via the 'universal equivalent', money, is not a specifically capitalist transaction. No capital is involved in this exchange whatsoever, but commodities are. M-C-M', on the other hand, in which money is advanced on the condition that it returns as a greater magnitude, is a capitalist transaction in which the commodity, now a capitalist commodity, is the means through which value is added and profit is made. Commodification, therefore, is not the point; the theory of commodification fails to establish the difference between simple commodity production and capitalist commodity production.

What is lost in the theory of commodification is Marx's insight that capitalist commodity production results from the productive capitalist advancing capital in the production of commodities specifically for profit through sales. He describes the process of the subsumption of labour under capital, not the apparent process of the expansion and proliferation of markets and the intensification of market forces. Marx did not use the term commodification, but the process it describes was familiar to him. After 1861 Marx never uses the concept of subsumption in the philosophical sense, in isolation from the specific process by which productive capital colonises and transforms production. Subsumption in Marx's economic analysis is never abstract or general but always refers to the *subsumption of labour*. The question of the incorporation and transformation of particular spheres of production into the capitalist mode of production is described by Marx, in *The Economic Manuscripts* of 1861–3, as well as in an appendix to Volume I written between 1863 and 1864 for the third draft of *Capital*. The process by which products are brought into the capitalist mode of production is accomplished in two phases, the first called *formal subsumption*, and the second called *real subsumption*. What is more, Marx links the concept of the formal subsumption of labour to the concept of absolute surplus value and, correspondingly, connects the concept of the real subsumption of labour to the concept of relative surplus value. It is impossible to extract a greater proportion of surplus value without first having extracted some quantity of surplus value. Marx's explanation of the process puts the emphasis on the role of productive capital. The capitalist mode of production is the generalisation of the production of commodities specifically for exchange with the express purpose of the accumulation of capital. So, the formal subsumption of labour is the process by which the productive capitalist first extracts surplus value from labour, and the real subsumption of labour is the process by which the productive capitalist increases the proportion of surplus value within the process of valorisation. The *formal subsumption of labour* takes place when the capitalist takes financial control of production – principally, owning the means of production and paying wages for labour power, thus extracting surplus labour and surplus value. Capital, as Marx puts it in the third draft of Volume I, 'subsumes the labour process as it finds it, that is to say, it takes over an *existing labour process*'.[2] The *real subsumption* of labour goes further than this, establishing a capitalist mode of production with the division of labour, the employment of machinery, the centralisation and intensification of production on a large scale and the transformation of the production process into a conscious application of science and technology. In short, everything that is implied with the idea of industrialisation. Formal subsumption is presupposed by the real subsumption of labour, but only the latter can be described in terms of what Marx calls the continual revolution of the means of production and relations of production in capitalism. The *real subsumption of labour* establishes a capitalist mode of production with the division of labour, the employment of machinery, the centralisation and intensification of production on a large scale and the transformation of the production process into a conscious application of science and technology.[3] What Braverman describes as the 'degradation of work' is the real subsumption of labour according to the new technological possibilities and new organisational principles of twentieth-century capitalism.

It is to the subsumption of labour that we should look for the process by which art is or is not colonised by capitalism. Markus also explains that, for Marx, 'genuinely artistic (and scientific) activities can never come to the situation of "real subsumption under capital". As he repeatedly stressed, they can be "formally" subsumed under capitalist relations of production only to a limited

2   Marx 1982, p. 1021.
3   See Braverman 1998.

degree'.[4] In order to test this we need to ask the question: what is the relationship between art and *productive capital*? Capital is a special kind of wealth and productive capital is a special kind of capital. If simple circulation is described as selling in order to buy, capitalist circulation is described as buying in order to sell, 'or, more accurately, buying in order to sell dearer',[5] as Marx says. Although capitalists may fail in their attempt to make a profit, the expenditure of capital differs from the expenditure of revenue insofar as the value is spent on condition that it returns, and then some. Productive capital is one of three kinds of capital identified by Marx, the other two being merchant and finance capital. In order to understand what productive capital is and its function within the capitalist mode of production, it is important to differentiate it from other forms of capital, so I will begin my interrogation of the relationship between art and productive capital by outlining all three kinds of capital. Schematically, we can regard the three kinds of capital as sitting at various distances from production. Productive capital is invested in production; merchant capital, one step away, taking production for granted, invests in commodities (often at wholesale prices); and finance capital, remote from production and commodities alike, deals with loans, shares, bonds and the monetary values of stocks and productive forces. What all three kinds of capital have in common is the relationship between investment and return.

Generally speaking, capital is the process by which wealth is invested for return, or, in a word, self-accumulation. The process of wealth returning to itself in an augmented magnitude has two phases, the first in which wealth enters into circulation and the second when it returns. Between the two extremes of this process, after capital has been entered into circulation and before it is taken out of circulation, capital can take many forms. Capital is not money, but constantly changes. Capital, in the normal scheme of things, begins as money, but in being invested in commodities, say, becomes commodity capital, only to be converted at a later stage, when the value of the commodities is realised in exchange or sales, as money capital again. The two phases involve different modalities of capital. Marx shows how productive capital converts money capital into commodity capital (buying raw materials, machinery, paying wages etc.), in its first phase, and converts commodity capital back into money capital, in its second phase (through the sale of the commodities that result from the productive activity of wage labour on raw materials using the means of production). When there is a division of labour among capitalists, and this second phase of circulation is set apart 'as a special function of a

---

4 Markus 2001, p. 4.
5 Marx 1954, p. 153.

special capital'[6] by a 'special group of capitalists', commodity capital becomes commercial capital or merchant's capital. And when there is a further division of labour among capitalists, and the first phase is funded by loans and other financial instruments, then another special group of capitalists, finance capitalists, are set apart, as well as a special kind of capital, finance capital. Commercial capital or merchant capital is a special kind of capital, according to Marx, 'because the merchant advances money capital, which is realised and functions as capital only by serving exclusively to mediate the metamorphosis of commodity capital ... its conversion into money, and it accomplishes this by the continual purchase and sale of commodities'.[7] That is to say, without entering into production of any sort. The first kind of capital is therefore kept within the sphere of production while the second kind of capital is kept continually within the sphere of circulation. There is a third special section of the capitalist class that deals with a third special kind of capital, including 'money dealing capital', 'interest bearing capital' and 'fictitious capital'. Such capital never enters either production or commodity exchange. I will group them together under the heading finance capital. Finance capitalists purchase assets (certificates, promissory notes, bonds, shares, and so on) and sell them on. Finance capital accelerates circulation and reduces the costs of circulation, as well as socialising capital ('[i]t is the abolition of capital as private property within the framework of capitalist production itself').[8] Also, Marx observes, finance capital transforms the 'actually functioning capitalist into a mere manager, administrator of other people's capital, and ... the owner of capital into a mere owner, a mere money capitalist', the dividends they receive being 'mere compensation for owning capital that now is entirely divorced from the function in the actual process of reproduction'.[9]

The interaction between the three kinds of capital, as well as their relations to labour, needs to be spelled out. When commodity capital owned by a productive capitalist is sold, at wholesale prices, to a merchant capitalist, capital has returned to the first capitalist with profit, but the same transaction is an investment by the second capitalist who hopes to see returns at a later date. So far as the productive capitalist is concerned,

> he has realised the value of his [commodity capital] with the merchant's money', but while the 'metamorphosis into money has taken place for

---

6 Marx 1959, p. 267.
7 Marx 1959, p. 273.
8 Marx 1959, p. 436.
9 Marx 1959, pp. 436–7.

him, as producer, it has not yet taken place for the [commodity] itself. It is still on the market, as commodity capital.[10]

If the productive capital had taken out a loan from an investment capitalist, then part of the profit from the sale of commodity capital to the merchant capitalist will be paid to the finance capitalist as a repayment. The three capitalists share the surplus value between themselves in three different ways. The productive capitalist employs wage labourers that add more value than they cost, but not all the surplus goes to the productive capitalist. By selling at wholesale prices, the productive capitalist shares the surplus with the merchant capitalist who makes profit, therefore, only by selling at the full price, no more. And the productive capitalist shares a portion of the surplus by paying interest or dividends to the finance capitalist. It would be a mistake to add the wage labourer to the list of those who share in the surplus. Even wages that are above the average wage rate cannot count as sharing in the surplus, because the surplus is defined as the value of labour minus wages. Nevertheless, wage labourers also come into contact and make transactions with the three types of capitalist and three kinds of capital. Productive capitalists pay wages and both the means of production and the productive capitalist owns the raw materials that the labourer 'works up'. Also, as we have already seen, the productive capitalist is also in charge of the methods of production and has a disciplinary role in relation to labourers. Merchant capitalists also employ wage labourers, including warehouse workers, transport workers and shop assistants, but they are also the owners of the necessities that workers as consumers purchase to live. Wage labourers relate also to finance capitalists when they take out a loan, buy or rent a house, pay towards a pension, purchase a commodity in instalments, or have a bank account or credit card. Since capitalists of all types are also consumers, each comes into contact with the merchant capitalists and finance capitalists not only through business transactions but also through consumption, personal banking and so on. However, as well as noting the many ways in which the various economic actants meet and exchange goods, services and money, we must note two non-relationships. The first concerns the isolation of the productive capitalist (and productive capital) from the sphere of consumption. Neither wage labourers nor capitalists of all kinds have any non-business transactions with productive capitalists, who remain within the sphere of production. The second concerns the isolation of the other two types of capitalist (and capital) from production. Merchant capitalists and finance capitalists do not pay wages to productive labourers, do not own the means of

---

10   Marx 1959, p. 269.

production, and nor do they own the product as a result of owning the means of production.

But we need to test the extent of this general trend in specific sectors, not merely assume that the transformation has taken place everywhere and therefore in art. Let us look at the key transitions that take place when labour is formally subsumed by capital. The productive capitalist converts commodity producers into wage labourers by supplying them with raw materials and paying wages for their labour power to work up the materials into commodities owned by the capitalist who then realises their full value in the marketplace. Marx introduces the concept of formal subsumption by giving the following examples:

> When a peasant who has always produced enough for his needs becomes a day labourer working for a farmer; when the hierarchic order of guild production vanishes making way for the straightforward distinction between the capitalist and the wage labourers he employs; when the former slave-owner engages his former slaves as paid workers, etc., then we find that what is happening is that production processes of varying social provenance have been transformed into capitalist production.[11]

Having illustrated the concept, Marx identifies the key factors at work:

> The relation between master and journeyman vanishes. That relationship was determined by the fact that the former was the master of his craft. He now confronts his journeyman only as the owner of capital, while the journeyman is reduced to being a vendor of labour. Before the process of production they all confront each other as commodity owners and their relations involve nothing but money; within the process of production, as its components personified: the capitalist as 'capital', the immediate producer as 'labour', and their relation is determined by labour as a mere constituent of capital which is valorising itself.[12]

This short passage contains all the essentials of the concept of the formal subsumption of labour. From the point of view of the 'direct producer', the effect of formal subsumption is not commodification, for these labourers produced commodities in pre-capitalist production, but the replacement of the consumer as the source of payment with the capitalist as the source of wages.

---

11   Marx 1982, p. 1020.
12   Ibid.

From the point of view of the capitalist, the effect of formal subsumption is not profiting from the labour of others, which had always existed, but the ownership and control of production itself. As well as commodities existing before capitalism, and therefore not being decisive in the question of subsumption, Marx points out that capital exists before capitalism, too, in the form of usurer's capital and merchant's capital. Capitalists of earlier epochs were neither producers nor employers, except perhaps on a very small scale. The interaction of direct producers with these two forms of capital, like the fact of the production of commodities, does not constitute the formal subsumption of labour or amount to the introduction of the capitalist mode of production. Usurers could charge crippling rates of interest on workers, but they did not pay wages, own the means of production or own the products of labour. Merchants could pay low prices in the provinces and make enormous profits in the city where demand was higher, but again, they did not pay wages, supply raw materials and tools, or own the products of workers. Commodities and capital existed before capitalism; what did not exist before capitalism was productive capital and the subsumption of wage labour under capital.

Marx goes on to say that the means of production and the means of subsistence must confront the wage labourer as capital, 'as monopolised by the buyer of his labour capacity', as a precondition for the relationship between productive capitalist and wage labourer. And it goes without saying that the productive capitalist, not the worker, owns the product produced by wage labour. This is an unprecedented economic phenomenon. Marx explains this in his series of lectures to the German Workingmen's Club in Brussels in 1847, collected in a pamphlet in 1891, 'Wage Labour and Capital':

> Labour power was not always a commodity...Labour was not always wage labour...The slave did not sell his labour power to the slave-owner... The slave, together with his labour power, was sold to his owner once and for all. He is a commodity...but his labour power is not his commodity. The serf sells only a portion of his labour power. It is not he who receives wages from the owner of the land; it is rather the owner of the land who receives a tribute from him.... The free labourer... auctions off eight, 10, 12, 15 hours of his life ... to the highest bidder, to the owner of raw materials, tools, and the means of life – i.e. to the capitalist.[13]

And in an address delivered to the General Council of the First International in June 1865, Marx went into more detail on the matter. Having already argued

---

13   Marx 1891, p. 205.

that the value of wages falls short of the value produced by labour power, and therefore that the labourer works part of the day unpaid, Marx compares the unpaid part of the wage labourer's labour with that of the slave and the serf.

> On the basis of the wages system even the unpaid labour seems to be paid labour. With the slave, on the contrary, even that part of his labour which is paid appears to be unpaid.[14] ... The peasant worked, for example, three days for himself on his own field or the field allotted to him, and the three subsequent days he performed compulsory and gratuitous labour on the estate of his lord. Here, then, the paid and unpaid parts of labour were sensibly separated ... in time and space.[15]

The formal subsumption of labour, therefore, brought about an unprecedented social relationship (between capitalist and wage labourer) and, for the first time, *appeared* to include no unpaid or compulsory labour, while at the same time assigning the whole of the product of labour to the capitalist.

Even before the real subsumption of labour gets to grips with the actual processes of labour, the introduction of productive capital and wage labour has an enormous impact. The productive capitalist does not initially interfere with the methods of production, 'the change indicated does not mean that an essential change takes place from the outset in the real way in which the labour process is carried on', but, 'the labour becomes more intensive, or the duration of the labour process is prolonged ... the labour becomes more continuous and more systematic'. This is because labour has taken on a new abstract form that can be measured in terms of the difference between capital advanced in wages, on one hand, and value embodied in commodity capital, on the other. Capitalists had never before increased the rate of profit by intensifying productivity. Usurers and merchants were only indirectly concerned with productivity because so long as interest was paid and profits were made, it did not matter from where they came. With productive capitalists during the first phase of the subsumption of labour, however, it was the productivity of wage labour above all else that provided their income. Instead of owning large tracts of land, borrowing money at a low rate and lending at a high rate

---

14   Although it is not relevant to the discussion on subsumption, here, Marx provides further analysis of the slave's 'paid' labour: 'Of course, in order to work the slave must live, and one part of his working day goes to replace the value of his own maintenance. But since no bargain is struck between him and his master, and no acts of selling and buying are going on between the two parties, all his labour seems to be given away for nothing'.

15   Marx 1985, p. 37.

of interest, or travelling from marketplace to marketplace, the productive capitalist set labourers to work producing goods, but most of all producing value.
As well as extending the length of the working day, the productive capitalist
increased their total profit by increasing the scale of production by employing more workers to produce more surplus value during their elongated working days. This is why the main distinction between the formal subsumption of
labour and previous productive economies, Marx says, is scale. 'The capitalist
must be the owner or proprietor of the means of production on a *social* scale
and in quantities that beggar comparison with the possible production of the
individual and his family'.[16]

The real subsumption of labour begins when the productive capitalist
organises the process of labour in such a way as to increase the proportion
of unpaid labour and decrease the proportion of paid labour, and to speed
up, intensify and augment labour as much as possible in order to increase the
proportion of output to input. '*The social forces of production* of labour are now
developed, and with large scale production comes the direct application of science and technology'.[17] The application of science and technology, of course, is
not determined by developments within science and technology – capitalism
is not run by and according to knowledge – but rather, science and technology
is used to rationalise production as the production of surplus value. So, 'with
the development of the real subsumption of labour under capital, or the specifically capitalist mode of production, the real lever of the overall labour process is increasingly not the individual worker'.[18] Production is socialised, not
only through the sheer number of workers employed by a single capitalist, but
also by the scale of raw materials, machinery and plant. Each individual capitalist, therefore, is compelled to produce on a 'social scale'.[19] Hence, the real
subsumption of labour leads to 'combined labour' in which one is an unskilled
manual worker, one a skilled labourer, one an intellectual worker, one a manager, others are engineers, technicians, supervisors, and so on. Where the real
subsumption of labour takes hold, converting a pre-capitalist sector of manufacture into the capitalist mode of production, the new economic relationship between capitalist and wage labourer brings about the socialisation of
labour, along with the division of labour, mechanisation, massive increases in
scale. The features of the real subsumption of labour are not items of a menu
from which the capitalist or the economist can pick and choose, because the

---

16   Marx 1982, p. 1035.
17   Ibid.
18   Marx 1982, p. 1040.
19   Marx 1982, p. 1036.

capitalist cannot choose which of the pressures imposed by the competitive market to acknowledge, or which of the opportunities for productivity, efficiency and profitability to exploit. This is because the real subsumption of labour subjects labour to the rigours of capital accumulation, and this means every aspect of labour that can be transformed into the capitalist mode of production will be so transformed.

So, let us apply Marx's analysis of the formal and real subsumption of labour under capital to the case of artistic labour. Fortunately, Marx gets this inquiry underway himself, briefly examining the economics of the seventeenth-century poet John Milton. When writing *Paradise Lost*, Marx says,

> Milton ... was an unproductive worker. In contrast to this, the writer who delivers hackwork for his publisher is a productive worker. Milton produced Paradise Lost in the way that a silkworm produces silk, as the expression of his own nature. Later on he sold the product for £5 and to that extent became a dealer in a commodity.[20]

Unlike the wage labourer, Milton owns the product he has produced. Unlike the capitalist, Milton owns the product of production because he has produced it. Although Milton is both a producer and a seller of his product, Marx does not toy with the idea of describing Milton as a proletarian or an entrepreneur. Not all producers are wage labourers subsumed by the capitalist mode of production, and even though Milton sells his commodity, Marx does not say that Milton thereby becomes a capitalist or merchant. Milton is first an 'unproductive worker' (I will discuss the precise meaning of the term 'unproductive worker' in the next section of this chapter, especially as it relates to art) and then a 'dealer in a commodity'. The case of the hack writer, on the other hand, is a productive worker (that is to say, a wage labourer who not only produces texts but also surplus value for a capitalist). Milton also has dealings with a capitalist, but not one to whom he sells his labour power, but rather one to whom he sells a commodity, the poem. The writer does not own the means of publication and distribution, so sells his product to the capitalist whose class has a monopoly on the machinery needed to reproduce the work in sufficient quantities to take to the marketplace for consumption. Milton trades in his commodity, but he does not belong to either of the two economic groups that the capitalist mode of production establishes, namely the wage labourers and the productive capitalists. In fact, we night go further and say that, although Milton ultimately sells his product for £5, he is not a commodity producer, certainly not a capitalist commodity producer. And even though he sells a commodity, he is not a capitalist

---

20   Marx 1982, p. 1044.

owner of commodities who realises the value of his capital by converting commodity capital into money capital.

It would be a mistake to think that writing is a type of productive activity that is exempt from the capitalist mode of production. As we have already seen with the example of the hack writer, writing can be wage labour. It is the economic relations between capitalist and labourer that determine whether a certain job of work belongs to the category of wage labour, whether a form of ownership and sale corresponds to the category of productive capital, or whether a certain product belongs to the category of the capitalist commodity. Marx brings the economics of Milton's production of *Paradise Lost* into sharper relief by going into a little more detail about the hack writer:

> But the Leipzig literary proletarian who produces books, e.g. compendia on political economy, at the instructions of his publisher is roughly speaking a productive worker, in so far as his production is subsumed under capital and only takes place for the purpose of the latter's valorisation.[21]

The labour of the hack writer is formally subsumed by being paid a wage, while Milton receives his payment of £5 by selling a product. The labour of the hack writer undergoes real subsumption insofar as he is under instructions from a capitalist, whereas Milton writes of his own volition. The hack writer's labour produces, above all, surplus value for the capitalist, whereas Milton produces no surplus value at all because he sells his commodity, not his labour. Marx clarifies this point with another example.

> A singer who sings like a bird is an unproductive worker. If she sells her singing for money, she is to that extent a wage labourer or a commodity dealer. But the same singer, when engaged by an entrepreneur who has her sing in order to make money, is a productive worker, for she directly produces capital.[22]

To be clear, Marx is absolutely right, here, to offer both possibilities of 'wage labourer or a commodity dealer', because the sale of singing can fall into either category depending entirely on the economic transactions involved. If a club owner pays a dollar a day for a harmonica player, then the harmonica player is a wage labourer who produces surplus value for the capitalist club owner, but if the same harmonica player goes out into the street and is paid as a busker

---

21   Ibid.
22   Ibid.

directly by the public, then he is a 'commodity dealer' (but not, I want to stress, a dealer in capitalist commodities).

Milton and the singer are among those examples given by Marx that are economically exceptional to the capitalist mode of production. They are exceptions because their labour has not been subsumed by capital, in either of the two phases of formal and real subsumption. It is of no consequence whether the prices of such commodities are fancy prices or not, and it does not matter, in the Marxist economic analysis, whether the artist is living or dead, whether supply can be augmented or not, and whether the works are offered for sale or resale; what matters, here, is nothing other than the economic circumstances of production. Work of this kind, he says, 'has scarcely reached the stage of being subsumed even formally under capital, and belongs essentially to a transitional stage'.[23] The first test whether labour is economically exceptional to the capitalist mode of production (which is simply another way of talking about labour that has not been subsumed by capital) is this: does the producer sell their labour? If the producer sells a product rather than their labour, then their labour has not been formally subsumed under capital. But there is another possibility to consider. Since capitalists do not sell their labour but necessarily buy and sell commodities, the second test of whether artistic labour has been subsumed under capital (with the artist, this time, in the role of the capitalist rather than the wage labourer), is this: does the artist advance capital to purchase commodities (including wage labour) in order to produce surplus value? We might think that this description applies to certain artists who employ assistants to produce works for the art market. If so, then the subsumption of artistic labour by capital would seem to take place by substituting wage labourers for the productive activity of the artist, with the artist converted into a supervisor or manager. This transformation has a ring of truth to it. Whether this turns out to be the case for artistic labour generally, for a minority of artists, or is even a misrepresentation of the big commercial art studios depends on the answer to some other key questions, which we will address shortly. But if artists are productive capitalists, then it is clear that art is not, or no longer, economically exceptional in the terms spelled out by Marx's concept of the subsumption of labour. We will reconsider the example of the artist as employer and productive capitalist later on.

Nevertheless, we can say that the artistic labour of the artist has not been formally subsumed under capital. If the condition of the subsumption of artistic labour is the separation of the artist from the assistant, the former occupying the place of the productive capitalist and the latter occupying the place of

---

23   Ibid.

the wage labourer, then any artistic labour performed by the artist remains economically exceptional insofar as they do not sell their labour but their products.
When the artist is the artistic labourer, then the producer owns the product,
which is exceptional in the capitalist mode of production since the capitalist
buyer of labour owns the product. When the artist labours on their own work
and they own their own means of production (equipment, materials, studio
rent, etc.), then this is exceptional to the capitalist mode of production in which
the means of production is owned by one class, the capitalists, and the producers belong to another, the proletariat. What is more, artists, including those
who have assistants and those who do not, have not been converted into wage
labourers, employed by a productive capitalist. If artists have become productive capitalists, then artists are not employed by the productive capitalists of
art. Assistants might be trained artists who have their own art practice on their
days off, but they are not the artists of the work that they produce as assistants.
Of course, other capitalists are involved in the art world, too, but the gallerist
does not establish a relationship with the artist along the lines of the capitalist-worker relationship. No gallerist takes ownership of the means of production for art or engages individual artists to operate those means of production,
consequently, the gallerist, unlike the productive capitalist, does not own the
product. There is no labour market for artists, only a market for artworks produced by artistic labour. Collectors purchase commodities off gallerists that,
unusually for merchant capitalists, do not own the works that they sell. Unlike
in the capitalist mode of production, the product of the production of art is
owned by its producer even while it is being traded by the merchant capitalist.

Artists are not wage labourers but there is a chance that some artists have
become productive capitalists by employing assistants as wage labourers to
produce surplus value. The formal subsumption of artistic labour – executed
by assistants rather than artists – is feasible, but the real subsumption of artistic labour is another question. What would the real subsumption of artistic
labour under capital look like? What changes would take place if a productive
capitalist for the purpose of the accumulation of value produced art? Would
artistic labour be broken down into Fordist chunks of unskilled labour? Would
the studio be reorganised according to Taylorist principles? Would the means
of production be constantly revolutionised, employing the latest technology
and scientific knowledge? Would the scale of the workforce and the finished
commodities be increased to the level of social production? If the productive
capitalists act 'as capital', then how would artistic production be reorganised
to be more profitable, more productive (of surplus value)? Would production
be speeded up? Would assistants and technicians be compelled to work longer days? Of course, each industry will subsume labour in different ways. But

the real subsumption of art cannot be detected in the various ways in which artists, for instance, have integrated art with fashion, advertising, design and so on, as Peter Osborne has recently suggested.[24] What Osborne is driving at, here, I think, is that art has adopted the techniques and processes of those design practices that have been subsumed by capital. If art becomes more like design in every respect other than the fact that artistic labour has not become wage labour, then, perhaps, a case could be made for the real subsumption of art without the formal subsumption of art ever having taken place. This is what I think Osborne is suggesting. Real subsumption is a transformation of technique imposed by capital, but borrowing techniques from subsumed labour does not bring about real subsumption. If the real subsumption of artistic labour has taken place then the techniques of art production will have been transformed to increase surplus value for a capitalist. Since productive capitalists have not muscled in on artistic production, converting the old handicraft producers into wage labourers, the only possible agent for the real subsumption of labour in art is the artist who employs assistants. The fact that artist employers can increase their income by taking on assistants does not prove that the artist is a productive capitalist. A merchant capitalist employs shop assistants, but does not become a productive capitalist by that fact, or by the fact that employing them permits the merchant to earn more money than she otherwise could by working alone. What distinguishes a productive capitalist from a merchant capitalist is not that one is an employer and the other is not, but that they each employ different kinds of labour. The artist, who is an owner-producer as well as an employer of assistants, is neither a productive nor a merchant capitalist but belongs to what Marx referred to as a 'transitional stage'.[25]

The question of whether the artist employer converts artistic labour into wage labour productive of surplus value depends upon the Marxist distinction between productive and unproductive labour. In *Capital* Volume II Marx discusses at length the distinction between productive and unproductive labour. Originally, the distinction was formulated by Adam Smith as follows:

> There is one sort of labour which adds to the value of the subject upon which it is bestowed; there is another which has no such effect. The former as it produces value, may be called productive, the latter, unproductive labour... Thus the labour of a manufacturer adds generally to the value of the materials which he works upon, that of his own maintenance, and of his master's profit. The labour of a menial servant, on the

24   Osborne 2013, p. 167.
25   Marx 1982, p. 1044.

contrary, adds to the value of nothing. Though the manufacturer has his wages advanced to him by his master, he in reality costs him no expense, the value of those wages being generally restored, together with a profit, in the improved value of the subject upon which his labour is bestowed. But the maintenance of a menial servant never is restored.[26]

Smith's application of the theory was flawed. The reference to materiality is bogus and the distinction between capital and revenue is imprecise. Marx therefore argued: '[t]hat labourer alone is productive, who produces surplus value for the capitalist'.[27] Therefore, since 'no value is produced in the process of circulation, and therefore no surplus value',[28] even though merchant capitalists employ wage labourers with capital, 'commercial workers are unproductive labourers'.[29] The difference is not embodied in the labour or present in the kind of wealth expended on it. There is no such thing as productive or unproductive labour in itself. Similarly, there is no such thing as productive capital except insofar as it is capital invested in productive labour. Making material things is no more productive than providing services, information or fulfilling the reproduction of the means of production. Productive labour is exchanged with productive capital and unproductive labour is exchanged with either unproductive capital or revenue.

Current Post-Fordist theories of immaterial labour, when based on the *quality* of labour (as information, service, performative, creative or etc.) miss the point completely (see Chapter 11). Marx provides a handy economic analysis of an immaterial labourer in terms of productive and unproductive labour. 'A schoolmaster who instructs others is not a productive worker',[30] he says, not because of the kind of labour he performs, but because of the economic relationship that frames his labour. If the same schoolmaster takes a job with a private school run as a business enterprise, then the economic character of the labour changes even if the teacher delivers exactly the same lectures. Marx explains:

> a schoolmaster who works for wages in an institution along with others, using his own labour to increase the money of the entrepreneur who owns the knowledge-mongering institution, is a productive worker.[31]

---

26   Smith 1993, p. 67.
27   Marx 1954, p. 477.
28   Marx 1959, p. 279.
29   Gough 1972, p. 56.
30   Marx 1982, p. 1044.
31   Ibid.

The key difference in Marx's example of the schoolmaster is the changed economic circumstances signified by the phrase, in the second formula, that the teacher is engaged as a *wage labourer*. But wage labour by itself is not the secret of productive labour. Wage labour is a necessary but not a sufficient condition for productive labour.

Smith's illustration of the contrasting ways in which the capitalist paid two kinds of wages, one to the workers in a business enterprise, and the other to domestic servants in their homes, retains its clarity. Both factory workers and chambermaids sell their labour not their products and both are wage labourers. One adds value and the other consumes value. The buyer of unproductive labour is the final consumer, while the buyer of productive labour invests in a commodity or service that will be sold on to the final consumer. Retail workers are wage labourers, too, and the merchant capitalist profits from their employment insofar as they realise the value of her stock, but they do not add to the value of her stock. If we try to differentiate between productive and unproductive labour by examining different kinds of labour itself, then we will be thwarted; the key is to follow the capital. Productive capital purchases constant capital and variable capital (means of production and living labour) and accumulation is brought about through surplus value in surplus labour. Merchant capital purchases commodity capital, and its share of the surplus value is deducted from the full value of the goods at the point of purchase from the productive capitalist. If retail workers etc. added value then wholesale prices would be unnecessary and the productive capitalist would sell commodities to merchant capitalists at their full value, after which the merchant would raise the price based on the value added by shop workers etc. The wage labourers employed by finance capital (bank clerks, traders, asset managers, etc.), similarly, do not add value to the assets and financial instruments they handle (profits from loans are derived entirely from interest payments by customers, profits from arbitrage trading in shares derives entirely from the pockets of other investors on resale, dividends are paid to shareholders out of the revenue of businesses, etc.). If we know from where added value derives, then we will not be fooled into thinking, for instance, that banks, money markets and commodity markets are wealth creators. Merchant capital and finance capital employ armies of wage labourers without whom these companies would make no profits, but none of this profit is derived from value created by these wage labourers: they are unproductive workers.

Not all wage labourers employed by productive capitalists are productive labourers. Let us say a company hires its own team of maintenance engineers who swiftly repair machinery that breaks down so that production can resume and constantly maintain the machinery of the plant, prolonging its lifespan and thereby adding to profits by both increasing the rate of production and reducing the outlay on the means of production. There is a good business argument for employing these wage labourers because they increase profits, but there is a case for arguing that they are unproductive labourers,[32] contributing to savings in constant capital. Even though the productive capitalist makes profit from the maintenance crew, this is as a result of relative surplus value only. No absolute surplus value can be derived from this labour if the capitalist who pays the wages is also the final consumer of the commodity supplied, namely the service of maintaining the means of production. If, however, the company outsources maintenance by awarding a contract to a separate company (perhaps, initially, on condition that the same workers continue to be employed doing the same work), then the maintenance staff become productive labourers. Their labour becomes the commodity for which the productive capitalist is the final consumer. Insofar as the supplier of this commodity is the employer of the labour which is sold to the productive capitalist, their profit derives from surplus labour (work over and above the value they pay in wages). Also, if the company employs staff to work in a subsidised (loss-making) canteen, then these workers are unproductive, too. If, however, the canteen is a profit-making operation within the business, or is outsourced, then the canteen workers are productive labourers. The premises of the productive capitalist's business need to be cleaned, of course, but if the company pays for this itself, then there is no difference between this economic transaction and a private household paying a cleaner to clean their house: this is the consumption of unproductive labour. Just as the householder does not generate surplus

---

32   There is a counter-argument that, if the labourers who produced the machinery are productive labourers (insofar as they are the living labour that produces the value embodied in constant capital, and that they produce surplus for their employers) then the maintenance workers are their equivalents in the factory. Certainly, the maintenance workers add value (average necessary labour time) to the machines that they maintain to counteract the destruction of value through age and use, but the same could be said for the shop workers that Marx deemed unproductive, who nevertheless preserve the value of the goods that they sell by storing them, cleaning them and handling them well. The question that needs to be addressed here is not whether maintenance workers are wage labourers or whether they are employed by a productive capitalist or even whether their labour contributes to profits or whether their labour time produces value (since value is the equivalent of average necessary labour time, it follows that all labour produces value), but whether the value of the labour creates surplus value for the productive capitalist. A shop worker, remember, works part of the day reproducing her own labour and part of the day for the merchant capitalist, but produces no new value, since the time that she works for the merchant goes towards realising the value of the commodity capital for sale.

value or profit for themselves from paying a cleaner, the productive capitalist does not either. Paying an agency that employs cleaners, on the other hand, means that part of the payment, over and above the amount passed on to the cleaner as wages, is surplus value produced by the cleaner for the capitalist agent through surplus labour. However, the labour that produces raw materials for the productive capitalist is productive labour from which this particular capitalist draws no surplus or profit. It is productive labour because it produces surplus value for another capitalist.

If we retain our focus on artistic labour and its relation to productive capital, not being distracted by the sale of its products in the art market and not jumping to conclusions based on the mere fact that an artist pays wages to assistants, then we can proceed with our analysis of the economics of art informed by the distinction between productive and unproductive labour. Since artists who perform their own artistic labour are not wage labourers employed by capitalists, we are forced to conclude that this artistic labour is unproductive labour even if certain capitalists, such as gallerists, dealers, and, later in the process, investors, earn a profit from trade in the *products* of artistic labour. The less obvious question is whether the work of studio assistants, technicians, fabricators, interns and so on is productive or unproductive. Since the Renaissance, when art separated off from craft, artists have had assistants. Rembrandt's assistants paid the master for the privilege of working with him. Henry Moore had assistants and technicians, and the sculpture of Anish Kapoor and Richard Serra is impossible for one person to produce, so presupposes the employment of assistants. Hirst used assistants to paint his dot paintings, Chris Ofili has assistants painting the laborious backgrounds to his paintings, certain German artists have a dozen or two young artists making work according to certain rules, and Keith Tyson had assistants to produce his drawings. Jeff Koons employs over a hundred technicians to make his works, giving them very precise instructions about what he needs them to do. Julian Opie designs templates for his paintings which are then executed by an assistant without any trace of the handmade or the idiosyncratic. (The assistant, in this example, is a premium quality printing machine. But, of course, the quality derives from the fact that it is made with highly skilled human labour). Fiona Rae has her assistants stretch, prime and prepare her canvases, not make the paintings. Even Marina Abramovic, the performance artist, has assistants. Many of these artists were once assistants to older artists, and many of their assistants have already gone on to be successful artists in their own right. I want, in a moment, to ask whether these assistants are productive or unproductive labourers, but first I will extend the scope slightly.

Fabricators have become widespread in the production of art in recent times. They tend to be arts graduates who are skilled and knowledgeable in the techniques and values of contemporary art production and run their own businesses making artworks according to the designs of artists. These are not wage labourers, even when they sell their labour as a commodity to artists, and artists pay the full price of the commodity without subtracting a proportion for surplus value or a percentage for wholesale. The payment of fabricators is economically equivalent to paying a window cleaner or a cleaner, which can be paid by a household or a business without changing the nature of the economic relation. Interns, however, can be paid or unpaid. If they are paid, then they are economically equivalent to studio assistants, but if they are unpaid, which adds a further complication, then it is unclear whether they are outside the wage system or whether 100 percent of their labour is surplus labour. The answer to this puzzle depends on the outcome of the economic analysis of studio assistants. So, what about assistants and technicians? Having seen that productive capitalists pay wages from which they do not make surplus value, it is not inevitable that surplus value will be extracted by artists who have paid assistants, technicians and other paid producers of their works. Are these paid workers productive labourers for the artist? Before answering this we need to divide assistants into two main categories. First, there are those who are paid to run the studio in the role of a personal assistant, which is a clerical role. This is unproductive labour because the artist is the final consumer of this service. Second, there are those who are paid to execute the work in some way. But there are various kinds of technical assistant. Some, as we have seen, prepare canvases and so on, and do not make the work itself. This is a luxury that happens to save time for the artist to do more productive (profitable) work, but it is, nonetheless, unproductive. Other assistants produce entire works from start to finish based on detailed instructions, designs or templates. If this labour is the source of the value of a work that is subsequently sold in the art market, then this appears to be productive labour. However, since the prices of artworks are not determined by value (average labour time) and in this sense artworks have no value, it is not at all clear how assistants of any kind can be productive of value in the commodities sold in art galleries and through dealers.

The distinguishing feature of productive labour (in contrast with unproductive labour) is the surplus value that it supplies to the capitalist through surplus labour. In the case of productive labour, the productive capitalist is not the final consumer of the product, but goes on to realise the value of this labour (plus its surplus) in the sale of the final product. But there are intricate issues lurking within this seemingly straightforward formula. Abramovic, for instance, sells photographs of her performances, and yet, since she appears in the photographs and the performances, she cannot be the photographer. Nevertheless, the person who took the photograph (perhaps, in the early days, a friend or member of the audience, but nowadays more likely an assistant charged with specific instructions on how the image must look), has not produced the work in the fullest sense. This would be like claiming that sound engineers are the sole productive labourer of every musical recording. Paradoxically, Abramovic's photograph is the final form of a work that the photographer did not produce. Whoever manufactures the bricks that Carl Andre uses in his sculptures is not the producer of the work. Andre is not a dealer in bricks who just happens to get very high prices for a small number of bricks. The labour that goes into the brick is not the source of the value of Andre's works. Likewise, the labour that goes into Abramovic's photographs is not the source of the value of her work. We should not, therefore, reduce the question of productive labour to the production of objects for sale. The anonymous productive labourers who printed Milton's 'Paradise Lost' add some value to the book insofar as receipts are increased by the quantity of books supplied to meet demand, but the £5 paid to Milton indicates that the greater percentage of unpaid labour was the author's. Milton was not a wage labourer, of course, and the printers were, but that does not mean that the source of all the value in the books must derive from the print workers. The point is not that the labour theory of value is wrong in normal capitalist circumstances, but that not all modes of production correspond to the capitalist mode of production and therefore not all value in these exceptional modes of production derives from productive labour.

Let us consider some exceptions. A Russian oligarch who pays the wages of the football team he owns without any serious intention of recouping this through revenue nevertheless sells tickets and receives payment for the product that these unusual wage labourers perform. Other chairmen of football teams take out enormous sums from the club in payments and treat the club as a profit-making enterprise. In these instances, the football players are productive workers. Or consider a businesswoman who has set up a charitable trust. She employs several wage labourers to run the charity. Let us say the charity combines education, consciousness-raising events and the sale of merchandise. Surplus value is produced by charity workers but the surplus is not converted into profit and therefore the self-accumulation of capital does not take place. Studio assistants are not exceptional in the same ways – their employers neither make extravagant losses in paying their wages nor do they pass their surplus on to good causes. In comparison, studio assistants, whether they produce value or not, appear to be a normal labour cost in a business that makes a profit. Assuming prices are temporarily stable, if the artist continues to produce works in the same quantities, only now with assistants rather than doing all the work herself, then she would make a loss (the same sales as before minus the wages of the assistants). This would be true of the productive capitalist investing in industrial production, too, who if she employed just one worker to produce the amount of work that she could produce on her own would make a loss. It is only if the quantities of production are increased that the artist employer earns more money than they otherwise would. Naturally, if demand is high enough then increasing the volume of products beyond what one individual can produce will increase the income of the artist employer. However, the question is not whether the artist benefits financially from the paid work of assistants, it is whether the artist is a productive capitalist within this relationship; and equivalently, whether the assistant is a productive labourer. If the assistant is paid to look after the artist's appointments and so on, then their work is unproductive. If the assistant prepares canvases and does not produce the work to be sold, then their labour contributes to the means of production only (which is the equivalent of hiring maintenance staff), and is arguably unproductive. If the wage labourer produces the works, like Hirst's spot painters and Tyson's drawing assistants, then there is a stronger case for arguing that the assistant is a productive worker and the artist is a productive capitalist, except, as we have already noted, artworks have no value (average labour time) since they cannot be reproduced and therefore it is impossible for surplus value to be created in their production. Nevertheless, the question of the status of labour within artists' studios needs to be resolved not just with a general principle but through an analysis of the economic relations therein.

Technicians can be freelance or wage labourers, and the same is true of assistants. The first question we must ask is whether the artist pays their wages. The second, which is more difficult, is whether these wage labourers provide surplus labour for the artist. What value do assistants add to the artworks they produce within the artist's studio? Consider a successful musician who hires several assistants (one to look after the instruments, one to sort out transport and accommodation, another to be in charge of food supplies and so on). Now, insofar as they can make the musician's 'business' more efficient and productive, the musician deducts their wages from receipts, and will, perhaps, at a certain point decide that earnings have dropped so that one or two of the assistants will have to be let go. However, none of these paid workers produce what the musician sells, and they are not productive labourers in this respect but perform duties that improve the operations of the business without, in fact, contributing surplus value with their surplus labour. The difference between the musician's assistants and the artist's assistants is that the latter in some cases actually make the objects etc. that the artist sells. Is this the difference between productive and unproductive labour that we are trying to nail down here? Consider, for instance, those photographers and designers who have sued Jeff Koons for copyright infringement. Their claims illustrate the difficulty that I am trying to tease out here, I think. Does the artist 'profit' from their work? Should he not be obliged to pay them a percentage of his earnings if he uses their images and designs as part of his work? Let me stress, first, that I am not trying to settle the political issues regarding conflicts between copyright advocates who defend the rights and incomes of creative workers whose products are exploited by others and advocates of the creative commons that maximises sharing to promote creativity and innovation. In an analysis of labour and value in art that appropriates the work of others, one thing to take into account is the fact that the work by Koons can be sold at extremely high prices that do not reflect the value of the work that he appropriates. It would be wrong to think of Koons's appropriation of the work of others as nothing more than purchasing products at a low price and selling them at a higher price, since the higher price of his product is due to the reputation of the artist himself. That is, very few others – and probably nobody except another extremely successful artist – could possibly sell such works at comparable prices. Without crediting the entire difference to the brilliance of the individual artist, or crediting it entirely to the 'system' of art, we can say that the difference in price between the original photograph and the Koons work is not to be understood according to the standard model by which either the productive capitalist profits from wage labour or the merchant capitalist profits from the sale of products. It is more realistic to think of the photographers and designers attempting to 'cash in' on the value of the artwork, rather than Koons exploiting them. By and large the photographers and designers who Koons 'rips off' have already been paid for their work at the going rate; any additional payment they hoped to receive as a result of Koons's work would be a windfall. Asking for an additional payment as a result of the value of the works that Koons exhibits would be like a producer of raw materials asking to receive a second payment after realising that the raw materials were used to produce a luxury rather than a basic necessity. Within an economy in which super-profits can be derived from the creative work and ideas of others without recompense it is understandable that producers campaign for a percentage of resale values, royalties and so forth, but in the example we are considering here I am concerned more with the appearance of exploitation by Koons, which, from the point of view of the analysis of labour and value, is quite otherwise: the appropriation does not suck profit from the original but generates a whole new magnitude of value by recoding it as a leading example of contemporary art.

The issue, here, is not whether one person earns their living from the labour of others. The merchant capitalist, let us say, lives entirely off the labour of their employees, but is not, thereby, a productive capitalist (the merchant capitalist lives off surplus labour, of course, but only by taking a share, through discounted prices, of the surplus value produced by productive labourers for the productive capitalist). The question, then, for the time being, is whether the artist employer is a productive capitalist. This is true only if studio assistants are productive labourers, not if they are luxuries like other unproductive labourers such as domestic servants, window cleaners and so on. The musician's wardrobe assistant and masseur are luxuries of this type, but the studio assistant in some cases makes the product that the artist sells. If the artist is a productive capitalist, then the strongest candidate for the productive labourer is the studio assistant. However, the same applies to the studio assistant as we have seen with the producer of the original photograph appropriated by Koons, namely that the work is worth much less when it is considered as the product of the assistant than it is when it is considered the artwork of the artist who employs the assistant. Even if artists exploit assistants or profit from them, we can say from our analysis that the relationship between artist and assistant does not follow the standard pattern of the relationship between capitalist and wage labourer. Since artists are not wage labourers either, then art production whether involving studio assistants or not does not conform to the capitalist mode of production and is, instead, exceptional to it.

Let me clarify a point I have just made. Asking whether studio assistants add value to artworks is made more complicated by the fact that, typically, the very same labour performed by the very same individuals would fetch much lower prices if sold as their own work than as the work of the artist employer.[33] Normally, the productive capitalist acquires value through the surplus labour performed by wage labourers, which has a value over and above wages. In the case of art, however, such work considered as nothing but the production of certain goods, independent of the artist, would not necessarily fetch the value

---

33   When Elvis Presley's manager, Tom Parker, negotiated with song writers about Elvis recording one of their songs, he would often stipulate that Elvis be included as one of the song writers, taking a portion of the royalties for writing a song that he did not write. The argument Parker used was that the song was worth more if Elvis recorded it, and Elvis should get a share of the extra income generated for the song by his performance, which is a form of 'monopoly rent'. The song writer would tend to agree to these terms knowing that the song would earn more money with Elvis as the singer rather than somebody else, even with some percentage of the royalties foregone. In this instance, rather than ask whether Elvis extracts surplus value from the songwriter, or whether the songwriter extracts surplus value from Elvis, it is preferable to recognise that the productive capitalist-wage-labourer relationship does not structure the economics of mass popular music.

of the wages if sold on the market as produced by the assistant not the artist. If the assistants could earn the same amount by producing their own work for sale, then they would not be assistants in the first place. The artist's labour is worth more than the assistant's labour, and the prices of the artist's commodities reflect the value of the artist's products, not that of their assistants. In fact, the value of the artist's labour will tend to be significantly higher than the wages paid to the assistant, and therefore the artist who employs assistants at a rate higher than they could earn by selling the products of their own labour, simultaneously pays them below the rate that is added to the value of the commodity measured at the rate of the artist's own labour. But there is something odd, here, I think: something exceptional. Although it goes against the spirit of the labour theory of value, which insists that all value is derived from the labour that goes into it, the labour of assistants is not the source of the value of an artist's work. If it was, then the prices of artworks would, in equilibrium, be set by the costs of labour. We know that the labour of studio assistants would neither produce the work of this artist if the assistants made it in their own time, nor fetch the same value, so there is a kind of break between the actual labour and the labour that the value of artworks appears to represent. The actual labour of studio assistants, oddly, is not the source of the value of artworks, because it is the artist's labour that counts. If we add, here, that the artist's labour is not the source of the value of the work either, since the price is not determined by supply and demand in the standard way, then we can say the following: the source of 'value' of the artwork is not the labour of assistants but is determined by the previous sales of the artist's products (not the value of the artist's labour). Strangely, then, we find ourselves back with the observation, familiar in some respects since Ricardo, that artworks are economically exceptional because they cannot be reproduced – or produced – by anyone other than the artist. As such, the inquiry into the relationship between value and labour in art directs us not to productive capital and its capture of surplus value but to the mechanisms of circulation in which the prices of artworks are determined independently of value. It is to the art market and its relationship to merchant capital, therefore, that I will turn to in the next chapter.

CHAPTER 9

Art and Merchant Capital

The gallerist or art dealer is a capitalist. Entering the marketplace of art with capital and leaving the marketplace with profit, the gallerist follows the sequence M-M', which is the formula for capital. But what kind of capitalist is the gallerist? The productive capitalist advances capital on raw materials, machinery, premises and labour power that is realised in the sale of products, but the gallerist is not this kind of capitalist. We have seen in the previous chapter that the gallery/artist relationship is not an instance of the productive capitalist/wage labourer relationship introduced by the capitalist mode of production. The gallerist does not draw profit from artistic labour itself but from the product of artistic labour, hence does not pay wages to artists, and therefore does not formally subsume artistic labour under capital. Nonetheless, the gallerist represents capital in the first stage of art's economic circulation and exchange. Dealers and gallerists are not productive capitalists, they are merchant capitalists. 'The great economists, such as Smith, Ricardo, etc.', Marx said,

> are perplexed over mercantile capital being a special variety, since they consider the basic form of capital, capital as industrial capital, and circulation capital (commodity capital and money capital) solely because it is a phase in the reproduction process of every capital.[1]

Before the historical emergence of the capitalist mode of production proper there were merchants who bought and sold art. This type of art dealer is still around today, making transactions that have not been affected at all by the advent of capitalism. Art is not the only example of production to have escaped direct and fundamental transformation by the capitalist mode of production. We have shown that along with the other non-capitalist forms of production, art is economically exceptional *in its production*. This is why the economic analysis of art cannot proceed on the basis of Marx's analysis of industrial capitalism in *Capital* Volume I. We must examine art in terms of the extension of Marx's analysis of capitalism in Volumes II and III, which provide detailed analysis of the role and function of merchant and finance capital. In Volume II, Marx examines the circulation of capital and the 'metamorphosis' of capital, including the circuit of commodity capital, which is the sphere of merchant capital.

---

1 Marx 1959, p. 342.

This volume also includes Marx's discussion of the relationship between the production of the means of production and the production of articles of consumption, including luxuries. In Volume III, as well as discussing the relation between surplus value and profit and various techniques for increasing relative surplus value such as increasing turnover and the use of technological inventions, Marx deals with the conversion of commodity capital into merchant capital and finance capital. Capital has not penetrated the production of art, which means that artistic production remains, economically, pre-capitalist, but this does not mean that art never encounters capital or capitalism.

The art market appears to be a thoroughly capitalist operation. Does not art simply enter into capitalist exchange at the next phase of the circuit, not in production but circulation? The passage of the artwork through the gallery, and therefore through the hands of the gallerist, is art's first encounter with capital. This is exceptional in the capitalist mode of production, but it does not isolate art completely from capital. Normally, in the capitalist mode of production, commodities have been produced by wage labour funded by a productive capitalist before they enter into circulation, but with art, the first phase of productive capital is absent, so it is the gallerist who embodies the introduction of capital to art. And since there are no productive capitalists in art, the gallerist appears not only as the agent of the conversion of commodity capital into money capital, but as the agent of the conversion of art into capital more generally.

And yet, the gallerist is not a standard merchant capitalist. Whereas the merchant capitalist, typically, purchases commodities from a productive capitalist at a discounted price, the gallerist has no productive capitalist with whom to share surplus value. What is more, the gallerist does not purchase the commodities that the gallery sells on to collectors, neither from a productive capitalist nor from the artist.

> Art dealers internationally are often single-owner shops or small partnerships, with many built around the names and reputations of individuals or a history of art dealing through family businesses. Dealers typically specialize in a few highly defined fields where they have a high level of expertise and develop a strong vertical presence within one specific designation, building personal and institutional knowledge in this area.[2]

---

2   McAndrew 2010b, p. 11.

Gallerists are capitalists insofar as they advance capital on premises, gallery staff wages, advertising, publications, hospitality, transport, storage, accommodation, art fair fees, and all manner of things. Unusually for a merchant capitalist, however, gallerists tend to advance nothing to purchase the commodities that they sell. Gallerists occasionally advance artists money for various expenses, including the production of some especially expensive artworks, but this is quite distinct from the case of the productive capitalist advancing wages or purchasing the works. In all three cases, of course, capital is advanced to fund production of commodities, but that is where the similarity ends. Productive capital pays wages and other costs to produce commodities that the productive capitalist owns, but when the merchant capitalist advances some capital to an artist producer, the product continues to be owned by the artist and all that belongs to the gallerist is the artist's debt. Sometimes the debt is written off, but when it is not, money capital is not converted into commodity capital but remains money capital as it passes from merchant to producer and returns, as money, to the merchant's stock of capital, either directly from the artist's pocket or indirectly by being deducted from the proportion the artist is due from sales. But if the merchant capitalist typically converts commodity capital into money capital first by advancing money capital to purchase commodity capital, then this first phase is missing in the transactions of the gallerist. Marx makes a similar point about the French silk industry and the English hosiery and lace industries in the seventeenth century. The manufacturer, he says, was

> mostly but nominally a manufacturer until the middle of the 19th century. In point of fact, he was merely a merchant, who let the weaver carry on in their old unorganized way and exerted only a merchant's control.[3]

In preparation for converting commodity capital into money capital, the merchant capitalist typically, first, converts money capital into commodity capital, which is to say, she buys a quantity of commodities. It is exceptional that the gallerist, a merchant capitalist, does not purchase goods for sale, but the second phase, in which commodity capital is converted into money capital, is the gallerist's function within the circulation of art, albeit with one or two anomalies that need to be unpicked. Art may fetch higher prices at auction and on the secondary market generally, but art enters the market, and thereby enters circulation as a commodity, and is first exchanged for money, through the gallerist or dealer.

---

3 Marx 1959, p. 334.

The gallerist converts art into money. At the same time, and in the same transaction, the gallerist converts art into a commodity. In standard capitalist production, in which commodities are produced for the market, products are produced as commodities, but art's is a belated commodification. This is significant. For Marxism a commodity is a use value that is produced for exchange, that is to say, for its exchange value. Let's remind ourselves how Marx describes the distinction between commodity production and non-commodity production in the following way:

> A thing can be useful and the product of human labour, without being a commodity . . . Whoever directly satisfies his own needs with the product of his own labour creates, indeed, use values, but not commodities. In order to produce the latter, he must not only produce use values, but use values for others, social use values.[4]

A commodity is produced for exchange. Marx says, in the *Grundrisse*, 'the commodity only becomes a commodity . . . in so far as its owner does not relate to it as use value'.[5] Consider two loaves of bread, one baked at home for use by the household and one baked by a commercial baker for sale. The former loaf is produced as a use value only, while the commercial loaf is produced as a business, for money. Anything produced for its use value and not put into circulation but consumed by oneself or one's friends, family and so on is not a commodity in the Marxist sense. Also, we might add, anything consumed *without exchange* is not a commodity either, so if an artwork is displayed, exhibited, viewed, discussed, interpreted, disputed, acknowledged, and so on, without it changing hands, then it circulates culturally and socially without exchange and without becoming a commodity.

A great deal of art is never exchanged through the market and such work is not to be understood as a commodity, but other work does. It is to art that passes through the market via the gallerist that I now turn. Without changing its material properties in any way, the gallerist converts art into a commodity. No gallerist however has the power to convert artistic production into commodity production. This conversion does not and cannot take place at all. No merchant capitalist can retrospectively determine that artistic production is the production of commodities for sale. Nevertheless, Marx discusses an exceptional circumstance in which products produced outside of the capitalist mode of production, and which are therefore not produced as commodities,

---

4 Marx 1954, p. 48.
5 Marx 1973, p. 881.

are subsequently purchased by capitalists (as raw materials or whatever) and therefore brought into capitalist circulation. When a productive capitalist purchases raw materials that are not themselves commodities they immediately become commodity capital, and when a merchant capitalist purchases non-commodity goods with the express intention of selling them on, they immediately become commodity capital. 'The character of the process of production from which they originate is immaterial. They function as commodities in the market, and as commodities they enter into the circuit of industrial capital'.[6] Since such items are not produced as commodities their supply and demand may be imbalanced and their prices may be far off equilibrium, but as soon as they enter capitalist exchange, they metamorphose into commodities. This sort of metamorphosis is at the heart of the circulation processes of exchange in capitalism. Money turns into capital, commodity capital turns into money capital, commodities turn into use values, labour turns into value, products are turned into raw materials, raw materials are turned into commodities, capital is realised in the consumption of use values, products are used up in the production of exchange values, and so on and so forth. Not only do products and values move around, circulate, flow and pass from hand to hand, in doing so they change from one kind of economic being to another.

One of the weaknesses of the Western Marxist theory of commodification is its complete insensitivity to the metamorphoses of capital and non-capital, commodity and non-commodity in favour of a one-dimensional and uniform ontology of products and services as nothing but, and once and for all, commodities. Already, in the *Grundrisse* Marx returned time and time again to the metamorphoses of forms taken by value, commodities and capital. In *Capital* Volume I, Marx speaks of the 'metamorphosis of the commodity', in which the commodity is converted into money and money into commodity, and also of the metamorphosis of money into capital and capital into money. In *Capital* Volumes II and III, Marx discusses the 'metamorphosis of capital'. In both contexts Marx discusses the coming together of the two circuits C-M-C and M-C-M. The circulation C-M-C, in which, for instance, a worker exchanges labour as a commodity for money in order to purchase commodities to live, is a circuit that contains no capital, but at each transaction this circuit interacts with the circuit of capital, M-C-M', and therefore a metamorphosis occurs. Labour, which in possession of the worker is not capital, confronts the productive capitalist as a factor of production for which she uses money capital in the form of wage payments, to purchase labour power. For the capitalist, therefore, labour is used up in the production of goods or services for sale, and represents

---

6 Marx 1956, p. 63.

nothing but capital. Wages are not capital to the worker but they are paid for by productive capital. And the commodities that the worker consumes are not capital to the worker but were, at the moment of exchange, commodity capital to the merchant capitalist.

When art moves from the studio to the gallery and beyond, it undergoes a metamorphosis, or several metamorphoses. Artworks are not already commodities since their production has not been subsumed by capital and their mode of production is not capitalist. Nevertheless, artworks can metamorphose into commodities through their circulation. However, the artwork does not necessarily and inevitably metamorphose into a commodity, or any other specific form, but might metamorphose into one, or several, depending entirely on the social circulation through which it passes. Perhaps we might say that an artwork that leaves the studio as a gift is converted from a use value to a social use value. If a direct transaction takes place between an artist and an individual who purchases a single work, the transformation of the work is from a use value (a work in the possession of its producer) to a commodity (a piece exchanged for money), and back into a use value again (a work consumed by its owner). If the gallerist enters the scene, however, then the conversion of the artwork into a commodity is simultaneously the metamorphosis of the artwork into capital because the gallerist's portion of the payment for the work is, in part, capital. As well as converting artworks into commodities, therefore, the gallerist also converts art into capital.

Normally, of course, merchant capitalists deal with articles that are already commodities and already capital, insofar as they are commodity capital purchased from a productive capitalist. Artworks metamorphose not only into commodities and capital, however, they might first become a commodity and then metamorphose again, perhaps into a use value or a financial asset. So, regardless of whether artworks are produced as commodities within the capitalist mode of production, they subsequently circulate as commodities because they are put on the market as commodities, bought as commodities and resold as commodities. However, the theory that art is and always is commodity production collapses the result of circulation with its origin, as if the circulation of art and its consequential transformation into a commodity is irrelevant. The metamorphosis is important because it explains how artworks can become commodities even if artistic production is not commodity production. Artworks, therefore, are economically exceptional insofar as they become commodities through the activity not of productive capitalists but merchant capitalists. When and if artworks are converted from non-commodities into commodities, the alchemist is the gallery owner.

Just as artworks are not already commodities, artworks are not already capital. Artworks do not store productive capital in the way that the commodity capital exchanged between the productive capitalist and merchant capitalist normally does. Since no productive capitalist has converted money capital into commodity capital in the production of artworks, the works produced by the artist are not productive capital and not yet merchant capital. If we were to insist that they are capital, nonetheless, then we need to identify what kind of capital artworks in the possession of the artist are. One candidate, common amongst contemporary Marxist accounts of artworks as capital, is that they function as the store of wealth. What they have in mind is the conversion of money capital into commodity capital by the collector who spends perhaps very large sums on artworks which can be redeemed at a later date. The storage of wealth is closer to the hoard than capital. What is missing from such accounts is the proof that the purchase is for the purpose of accumulation, not the consumption of a commodity. Stored consumable goods for later use are not capital. Marx explains that, while a portion of capital must be kept in the form of money, as a hoard, as 'potential money capital', which he describes as 'a reserve of means of purchase, a reserve of means of payment, and idle capital in the form of money waiting to be put to work',[7] capital is not merely the store of wealth. When artworks do in fact function as a store of wealth, and as potential commodity capital that can be converted into money, they lack liquidity. Works in a given collection can be valued as an asset even when the owner has no intention of selling, and such works are, potentially, commodity capital, but capital permanently withdrawn from circulation is not capital except in name. Capital is wealth advanced for the purpose of the accumulation of wealth. Artists and collectors may make money – sometimes lots of it – from the sale of their works, but this fact does not mean that their works were always vessels for storing value. Artworks still in the possession of the artist are not capital in the Marxist sense of the word, just as money out of circulation is not capital. A hoarder, a miser and a collector of money is not a capitalist. A stock of money can be spent on luxuries or invested for returns, so is neither revenue nor capital until it re-enters circulation either through consumer expenditure or the productive consumption of assets or commodity capital. When I buy potatoes, the commodity capital owned by the retailer is converted into a use value, but when my favourite fish and chip shop buys potatoes then they have purchased commodity capital (raw materials) which will not become a use value until they fry the chips and sell them to me. Art may not metamorphose into capital

---

7   Marx 1959, p. 210.

at all if it leaves the studio, enters the gallery and then enters a public collection that is not permitted to sell off its stock of artworks. Art only becomes capital through the agency of the gallerist. That is to say, since capital is self-accumulating wealth in circulation, then art becomes capital only if it passes through the hands of someone with one eye on sale or resale.

We have noted that gallerists and dealers do not typically employ artists as workers. The gallerist does not establish a relationship with the artist along the lines of the capitalist worker relationship. They do not employ them or pay for their time or by piece. Nor does the gallerist tend to own the means of production for art and then engage individual artists to operate those means of production. Consequently, the gallerist, unlike the capitalist, does not own the product. Art production does not correspond to the capitalist mode of production but, nevertheless, commercially successful artists and their dealers make super profits without 'wage labour' and 'surplus value'. The economic analysis of art must fully acknowledge the fact that, unlike the wage labourer, artists own the products that they produce and their own means of production without becoming productive capitalists. No factory or machinery owned by the capitalist has forced the artist to sell his or her labour power and the working day of the artist has not been extended by the capitalist. No productive capitalist has accomplished the real subsumption of art by rationalising production to make art studios more efficient for the extraction of relative surplus value, that is to say, more productive and more profitable. As a result artists are capable of working independently of the capitalist. This is the economic kernel of truth behind the belief that artists are free from exploitation, free from the market and unaffected by money. The freedom from wage labour and the freedom from the rigours of the market may well be the secret to the ideology that artists are free full stop. Artistic autonomy appears to have a material basis in the economics of artistic production. However, artists turn to the capitalist as the owner of the means of circulation (gallery, contacts, collectors etc.) and as the agent of the conversion of artworks into commodities, capital and money. The gallerist derives all their profit (sometimes super profits) from selling the products of labour of others, extracting returns from it in return for advancing capital in the form of rent on gallery premises, advertising, technical and administrative staffing, and so on. None of the expenditure of the gallerist produces surplus value from surplus labour since, as a merchant capitalist, the dealer does not invest in the productive labour that produces the commodity for the market. Nevertheless, insofar as the conversion of the artwork into money entails costs, this expenditure is a capital investment. Since the gallerist does not purchase the products before reselling them, however, as merchant capitalists typically do, not only is art not converted into commodity capital directly by the merchant (but only through their sale of the work to a third party, the collector), but also the gallerist does not speed up the circulation process in the way that merchant capitalists typically realise the value of commodity capital for productive capitalists. In this sense, merchant capital functions anomalously in art, neither exchanging money capital for commodity capital nor funding the continued production of commodities by realising the value of production in advance of their sale to the final consumer. Assuming that the collector is a final consumer rather than an investor, it is possible for art to pass right through the circulation process of the art market without ever being owned by a capitalist.

Sarah Rowles conducted interviews with gallerists in London in 2007. She asked them about how they funded their gallery, what their relationship was to collectors, how they selected works to show, and so on. 'Do you like the work of the artists you represent?', she asked. One replied, 'yes, of course', another said, 'Only. Only. Only'. And in answer to the question, 'do you think the market affects what kind of art is produced?', the replies she received are worth repeating: 'Yes, up to a point; but it won't affect the best artists'; 'it's hard to get inside the minds of artists though and it's hard to know exactly how that influence manifests itself'; 'ultimately the answer is yes no matter how much we may want it to be a non-factor'; 'No it does not affect what kind of art is produced but what kind of art is visible in the art market'. Two years later Andrea Bellini published interviews with gallerists in over twenty cities across five continents.[8] Bellini does not ask such direct questions about art's economics, but sometimes little glimpses of the antagonism between art and capital slip through, as well as a few indications of art merging with business. Chantal Carousel, a gallerist based in Paris, responds to the question, 'tell me what a collector should never do when dealing with you?', with the remark, 'I detest it when a buyer becomes vulgar or cynical about the value of a work when negotiating a reasonable and fair price for an excellent work, especially when he very much wants that work'. Responding to a similar question, Helga de Alvear, based in Madrid, says she is irritated by collectors 'who buy only by hearing and not by seeing'. Daniele Balice, Paris, mentions a gallerist in New York who was a 'ruthless modern art dealer', and everyone talks about keeping overheads down, some say they are businesslike when they need to be but give as much emphasis as they can to showing work that they admire, while others, like Michele Maccarone, say that the thing they 'hate about being a gallerist is MONEY and having to deal with business'. In response to the question, 'what

---

8   See Bellini 2009.

do you think ought to disappear forever from the world of art?', Francesca Pia, from Zurich, said, 'speculation'.

And yet, stories emerge about gallerists and dealers persuading their artists to produce works for which there is demand. The gallerist visits the artists studio and says, 'I can't sell any of this stuff. Nobody wants it. Can you make some drawings, instead?' Or, a different gallerist checks up on an artist who has a solo exhibition in the gallery in a month or two, and says, 'don't make any more of them; make more of them – I can sell *them!*' Another says, 'I'd like to give you a show, but what I'm hearing from the collectors at the moment is that they are not interested anymore in photography, they want large black sculptures. Can you make some large black sculptures?' Some artists will turn to their gallerist for advice on which type of work to focus on for maximum sales in the run up to a show from which they need to generate income for living expenses and continued production. In Gregor Muir's personal guide through the early years of 'young British art', the story of Gary Hume's rejection of his early conceptual abstract painting and development of a new vivid figuration is told in terms of a conflict with his then gallerist, Karsten Schubert, who had taken on the young artist because of the early work, which was selling. Schubert, apparently, told Hume of his dislike of the new work and the artist subsequently issued the gallerist with an ultimatum: 'either the dealer would commit to showing these new works or Hume would go elsewhere'.[9] Hume moved to White Cube. Dealers and artists disagree about works, can have arguments about what should be included in an exhibition or what direction the work should go in and so on. Insofar as the dealer is the gatekeeper to the market, it is possible that the artist can be swayed not so much by the argument as the money behind the argument. At the same time, collectors can alert dealers to things, and these can be passed on to artists. For instance, a collector is being shown round the gallery by the dealer and asks, 'do you think the artist can make one of these in green?', and the dealer says, 'of course'. And if these stories and many others besides are true, they confirm the suspicion that the circulation of artworks and the 'demand' of collectors can precede the production of art, permitting the marketplace for commodities to enter the studio despite the fact that artistic production has not been subsumed by capital.

It is pointless denying that dealers, gallerists and collectors use the power that money affords them in influencing, directing and, sometimes, bullying artists to produce works that they otherwise would not produce. However, it would be a misapplication of the principle of consumer sovereignty to excuse this interference in artistic production on the grounds that the consumer

---

9   Muir 2009, p. 80.

ought to decide what is produced. (It should be noted in this context also that consumer sovereignty, which is ambiguous regarding which interests ought to be secured when sports fans and television companies are both customers of a sport, does not adequately distinguish between ordinary consumers of art and the corporate sponsors of art and its institutions, or, as Marx put it, between two completely different consumers, individual and productive). Consumer sovereignty works through the anonymous mechanisms of market forces, not through direct instructions and argument. But understood as power, money is not restricted just to the influence it has through transactions made in the market. Wealth provides access to goods, services and capital, but also to decision-making, administration, politics and other forms of authority. The economic exceptionalism of artistic production cannot isolate art from what we might call *money power*. With this non-economic effect of money in mind, therefore, art's independence cannot be guaranteed on an economic basis alone. So long as the gallerist is the conduit through which the artist is granted access to money through the art market, then the gallerist is also the conduit through which money power gains access to the artist.

Money power, I am proposing, is a political force that operates through non-economic mechanisms as an expression of wealth. Insofar as the money power of gallerists and collectors is exerted on artists, it is the power of money expressed through the political mechanisms of coercion and persuasion. Whereas the productive capitalist instructs the wage labourer directly to produce certain goods and services in certain ways, including training workers and reskilling them, money power cajoles, suggests, makes offers, reaches an agreement, makes ultimatums, tempts and issues threats. Economics gives way to politics, here, as wealth is converted into power. The distinction between the deployment of capital and money power is vital if we want to understand the relationship between art and capitalism. If, further, we are concerned with the effects that capitalism and capitalists have on art, then our critique as well as our tactics must vary according to whether we are confronted with capital or money power. Resisting money power through a critique of market forces is both dumb and toothless. Also, money power is not revealed through demand curves, aggregate demand, or anything similar, and therefore it is beyond the ken of neoclassical economics. What is more, the agent of money power, as wielded by the collector, is not the power of the capitalist but the power of the consumer. Such a consumer needs a very large hoard of wealth, but as a potential purchaser of artworks, the collector's money power is not always capital but can also be disposable income. Insofar as the collector, say, has an excess of wealth, such that she can wait a considerable amount of time before completing the purchase without running into trouble, the artist, who, let us say, has more immediate need for the sale, is at a disadvantage in negotiations. The gallerist, too, has overheads and ongoing costs which put the collector, again, in an advantageous position in negotiations. If we assume that money power is deployed widely across the art world, then the independence of artists is precarious and constantly under threat, but a well-run gallery will not always be in desperate need of the financial injection that this sale will provide, even though most gallerists will, once in a while, feel the pinch. Money power might have ebbs and flows in its influence over the production of art, being more intense under certain circumstances. Some dealers and some artists might be more resistant or more antagonistic to money power than others, and some might be immune due to their own wealth or other income streams or commitments.

It would be wrong to argue that the real subsumption of art is accomplished through money power. Money power is not capital in disguise. No matter how widespread is the effect of money power in art, it does not and cannot infect art with capital. No capital expenditure whatsoever is required. Money power is not the true face of capitalism shorn of its liberal veneer of free trade, personal liberty and individual choice. Art's encounters with money power do not establish a relationship between art and capitalism, and certainly not with the capitalist mode of production. Money power existed before capitalism and has its own mode of operation. Insofar as money power effectively, if only in patches, achieves its aims in redirecting artistic practice, we can say that art, or some of it, is bent to the interests of the wealthy, but not that artistic labour has therefore been subsumed by capital. Money power does not require the formal or real subsumption of labour to get results. Money capital does not reorganise labour or introduce new technology and new labour processes, so does not initiate or drive through the real subsumption of labour. Money power does not bring about the capitalist mode of production. And yet, it is not restricted, as merchant capital is in its ideal incarnation, to trade only with the products of labour. Money power affects production without owning it, paying wages or revolutionising the mode of production. That is to say, money power neither belongs to nor facilitates the capitalist mode of production. In a certain sense, in fact, money power undermines market forces and the social system based on it, just as aristocracy and monarchy come into conflict with market forces now and again. Nonetheless, since money power is the privilege of the wealthy, and capital belongs to the very same class of people, the tension between money power and capital appears more as a choice between different tools for getting things done. The advocates of market forces have not defended the free market from the unfree forces of money power, and the critique of capitalism has not prepared separate methods and strategies for understanding and resisting money power. In art, at the moment, this is left to individual artists (supported or hampered by their dealers), to either fend off money power or succumb to it. The issue would not arise, however, if art had been transformed by capital into a sector of standard commodity production. Money power in art is, in effect, the last desperate attempt by the capitalist class to assert their power in a field that remains exceptional and therefore aloof from their economic control. It is striking that artists experience the full force of the politics of money by coming into contact neither with productive capitalists nor merchant capitalists but the consumers of art.

The wealthy collector is not the only consumer of art. Art is consumed in a variety of ways. Purchasing art is not necessary for its consumption. In Marxist terms, this means the consumption of art as a use value is independent of its consumption as an exchange value. Unlike standard commodities within capitalism, the use does not depend on prior exchange. Artworks do not only have collectors, they also have viewers, spectators, publics, visitors, critics, audiences, and so on. Some artworks are only viewable within institutions that charge for access, but viewing art in galleries and museums, even when paying an entrance fee, has nothing to do with ownership of the works and comes at a tiny fraction of the full price of purchasing it. Also, the majority of these works can nonetheless be seen in reproduction in books, journals, on the internet and elsewhere. Art is not only consumed in the flesh, so to speak, but also at great distances and in forms that permit large numbers to view the work simultaneously across the world. In the age of mechanical and digital reproduction, as Walter Benjamin was one of the first to point out, you do not always need to travel to view artworks; they come to you. Artworks do not come to you in reproduction as commodities to be purchased and owned; they come to you as use values not exchange values. Artworks are viewed in commercial galleries for free, just like merchandise is viewed for free in shops, with the crucial difference that the use value of commodities in retail outlets is not normally present in its viewing. Artworks are viewed in museums which are funded publicly or privately in the public interest, displaying works for the public either at reduced (non-commercial) rates or for free. Public artworks are also viewed without payment, as are works deliberately and conscientiously distributed to the public free of charge. Net art is typically free, and works that are reproduced on websites are typically available to view for free. Artworks and reproductions of artworks are also available in books that can be read without payment from public libraries. Art magazines increasingly reproduce good quality images of works and exhibitions, and catalogues of exhibitions are also a good source of images. The publishing industry used to lag behind developments in the contemporary art world by ten years or more but this is no longer the case and therefore recent developments as well as historical trajectories are no longer restricted in the way they were.

Stallabrass's book *High Art Lite* is at once a critique of the commercialisation and popularisation of contemporary art, and a product of the new attitude within publishing that allowed books on contemporary art to be aimed not just at the art world elite. Critics, historians and other academics are also viewers who consume art without having to buy it. Mainstream economists will want to point out that all these seemingly free encounters with art have costs and opportunity costs, blurring the distinctions between different kinds of consumption of art, as if viewing art (consuming its use value) is best understood in terms of various kinds of costs (exchange values) borne by society as well as the individual. However, no economics of art is complete or realistic that fails to acknowledge that for most of us consuming art is not purchasing it, is often free or at low costs, and is not restricted to looking at the work in the flesh. Buying artworks at full price as luxury goods accounts for a tiny proportion of the consumption of art. Nevertheless, purchasing art is an aspect of art's exceptional economy that rewards close examination.

Roman Kräussl says,

> Art is a luxury good. If aggregate levels of wealth are high, the demand for art may also be expected to be high, as investors may spend part of this excess of wealth in the arts. Changes in income are therefore likely to have a significant effect on the demand for art and the prices paid for works of art.[10]

Mainstream economics defines luxuries as those commodities for which demand increases more rapidly than increases in wealth. What this refers to is the fact that the wealthy do not increase their consumption of bread and cheese and other necessities proportional to their relative wealth; their consumption of sports cars and designer clothing increases at a greater rate, thereby becoming an increasingly large proportion of their expenditure. Viewing art for free is not a luxury, but the time devoted to looking at art rather than, say, earning income, might be regarded as a luxury in an extended sense (the mainstream definition of luxury requires supplementary clauses to calculate the demand for free consumption 'proportional' to wealth). Whether or not mainstream economists can satisfactorily account for free consumption as a luxury, free luxuries sound like an oxymoron, and are, at the very least, exceptional. It is also worth reconsidering art as an exceptional luxury insofar as no other luxu-

---

10   Kraussl 2010, pp. 83–4.

ries, barring the ownership of land that has open access perhaps, cost so much to purchase when most people experience them for free. Although art is generally consumed (as use values) outside the market (and its exchange values), the art market itself is a vast luxury trade. To be clear, it is not the high price of artworks by itself that puts art in the category of luxuries. Even the introduction of 'Affordable Art Fairs' expands the luxury trade in art. However, if art became universally cheap, then it would take up a reduced proportion of wealth and perhaps might not figure as a luxury according to the mainstream formula. But since the price of artworks increases to staggering amounts, growth in wealth can easily be disproportionally spent on artworks. One more question needs to be clarified, here. Artworks are not luxuries on account of being 'useless' or 'expendable' in any way. Culture more generally is not a luxury. No matter how useless, pointless, relaxing or leisurely culture is, it is only a luxury, in the neoclassical definition, when expenditure on it increases proportional to income. (By way of illustration, consider dwellings. Housing is a necessity so it is not a luxury, but owning a second house is either a store of capital or a luxury. As such, what counts as a luxury has nothing to do with its usefulness or lack thereof.) Visiting the cinema, reading novels, going to galleries, watching TV and so on are not the sort of cultural activities that can be purchased at the kind of rate that the concept of luxury requires. Superstars like Elvis and Michael Jackson were known to hire out the entire cinema, thus converting the cinema experience into a luxury that only very few could afford. Global travel, for instance, which has become very cheap, is not a luxury until it either increases significantly in quantity or it is priced differentially with a luxury service (Business Class, and so forth). Art, we might say, is the luxury end of cultural purchasing. But art, we will see, is an anomalous kind of luxury good.

In *Capital* Volume II, Marx defines luxuries as products that are neither used as instruments of production nor as means of subsistence. Marx distinguishes production into two 'departments', the second of which is divided again into two. This division provides us with three different circuits of productive capital. Department I consists of products involved in the means of production, and Department II concerns the means of consumption which Marx divides into IIa, daily necessities, and IIb, luxuries. Within this schema, if a product is neither consumed by the means of production nor consumed as a necessity, then it is a luxury. (Ernest Mandel adds department III, the means of destruction,[11] or the arms trade, which in Marx's schema is either part of the means of production in an extended sense, or an unusual luxury because its purchaser is the state). Capitalists from Department I buy commodities from

---

11   Mandel 1975, pp. 277–93.

Department II with revenue, while capitalists from Department II buy goods from Department I with capital. Capital invested in Department I can only be realised in Department II (by capitalist commodity producers purchasing the means of production). By distinguishing expenditure on means of production and means of consumption, Marx raises an issue skirted over by the mainstream definition of luxury goods. While it is technically true that the demand for luxuries increases more than proportionally to increases in wealth, another form of expenditure increases disproportionately, too, namely investment in assets, financial investments and the purchase of capital goods. Spending in the two departments, therefore, is split between the expenditure of capital and the expenditure of revenue, the former as productive consumption and the latter as unproductive consumption (where productive simply refers to the self-accumulation of wealth). Whereas the mainstream definition of luxury goods is formal, the Marxist theory of luxuries is social and historical: social, because the distinction between necessities and luxuries is determined by class division; historical, because the line dividing necessities from luxuries shifts according to changes in the forces of production, the balance of powers between classes and the specific changing traditions of a community. Within Department II, a luxury is distinct from what Marx called 'sustenance'. Sustenance consists of the consumption of necessities. But Marx does not give a list of necessities or identify what sort of needs must be fulfilled by them. This is because necessities change from context to context and period to period. Marx is not left with a relativistic definition of necessities and luxuries, however. A necessity is a commodity consumed by workers. 'Articles of luxury', Marx says, 'enter into the consumption of only the capitalist class and therefore can be exchanged only for spent surplus value, which never falls to the share of the labourer'.[12] Necessities are the commodities that are produced to reproduce the class of producers. The wealthy consume necessities, too, although for the most part with higher quality and prices, but they consume other goods in addition to these. Apart from their consumption of items used in production or their purchase of financial instruments, the rest of what is purchased over and above necessities, therefore by the wealthy, are all luxuries.

The circulation of capital within Department II is different for necessities and luxuries. Necessities are produced by productive capitalists employing wage labourers who then purchase necessities to realise the value of commodity capital for their employers. Luxuries, however, are produced by capitalists who do not realise the value of their capital through purchases made by wage labourers. So, all the variable capital (wages) advanced by capitalists IIa

---

12   Marx 1956, p. 407.

returns to them through sales of necessities, but all the variable capital advanced by capitalists 11b does not return to them, but ends up in the pockets of capitalists 11a. And since labourers need more urgently to purchase their necessities, the circulation of variable capital to capitalists in 11a occurs more steadily and quickly (having a shorter turnover) than returns to capital in 11b, which depends on the expenditure of the disposable income of capitalists for commodities of which they have no need and no urgency to purchase. Also, because of this, only the variable prices of commodities in 11a affect the level of wages (since wages are set by the costs of reproducing labour power), while the price of luxuries has no effect on wages. However, the wages of luxury producers must be paid for, ultimately, by the willingness of the capitalist class to purchase luxuries, rather than invest their money as capital for returns. Marx explains:

> it follows that in proportion as the luxury part of the annual product grows, as therefore an increasing share of the labour power is absorbed in the production of luxuries, the reconversion of the variable capital advanced in 11b into money capital functioning anew as the money-form of the variable capital, and thereby the existence and reproduction of the part of the working-class employed in 11b – the supply to them of consumer necessities – depends upon the prodigality of the capitalist class, upon the exchange of a considerable portion of their surplus value for articles of luxury.[13]

Part of this expense is taken up with employing unproductive labour (in Marx's time, chiefly domestic servants, but today we have a panoply of specialists, from PAS and permanently employed medical staff, to personal trainers, dog walkers, interior decorators, chefs, masseurs and gardeners). These luxuries, Marx says, are the first casualties of an economic crisis. Luxuries, thus, fall into two categories depending on whether they involve productive labour or unproductive labour. Luxury commodities are normally produced by productive labour under the conditions of the capitalist mode of production. Luxury services, on the other hand, are normally labour purchased as a commodity by the final consumer, and so involve unproductive labour. Artistic products, which are not produced with productive labour, are luxury goods not luxury services. Normally, unproductive labour does not produce products that are luxury goods; normally the unproductive labour is the luxury itself. Unusually, art is unproductive labour that is not a luxury in itself but produces luxuries.

---

13   Marx 1956, p. 414.

Normally, the high prices of luxuries are determined by the high labour costs and high raw material costs of producing high quality goods. Unlike *haute cuisine, haute couture* or *fine and rare wines*, however, artworks can command extremely high prices without having to exhibit any qualities of the luxury trade in their raw materials, skills, technology, or any other material property. A clear illustration of this can be found in the practice of readymade and appropriation art, which takes objects – Nike trainers, vacuum cleaners, basketballs – which are available as consumer goods, and sells them as art for much higher prices. Note that these new luxuries are not made of better materials, more expensive processes or more detailed and complex skilled labour. What makes these artworks luxuries has nothing to do with the difference between a basic handbag and a designer handbag. Also, consider neon light texts and images by internationally leading artists like Bruce Nauman and Tracey Emin. These objects fetch inflated prices when sold as art and yet are made with *standard materials by commercial companies in the conventional way.* These are not luxury versions of neon lights due to the high quality of the materials used, or the unusually high level of skill and time involved in making them. These are average neon lights which command luxury prices because they are art. The same principle is demonstrated by Mike Kelley, who buys soft toys at the thrift store for a few dollars and sells them as art for thousands of dollars. Here, abandoned goods that were virtually worthless are re-categorised as luxuries by becoming art. The jump in price of these non-luxury goods transformed into art is due to the fact that they have been transplanted into a different circuit of trade in luxury goods. At $15 million, Damien Hirst's stuffed shark is one of the most expensive artworks by a living artist, but it is technically inferior to comparable stuffed animals. One could purchase a *better* stuffed shark at a fraction of the cost of Hirst's. Viewed in terms of their production, raw materials, skills and so on, the production of artworks is not consistent with the pattern of the production of luxuries in other sectors of the economy. Artworks are exceptional luxuries from the point of view of production.

Similarly, artworks do not conform to the conventional economic pattern of the *consumption* of luxury goods. Art is among that group of luxuries that Veblen described in his book *The Theory of the Leisure Class* from 1899, as purchased precisely to display the wealth of the purchaser. As part of his argument that the wealthy engage in 'conspicuous consumption', Veblen argued that 'pecuniary struggle' (gaining status through the exhibition of wealth) and 'pecuniary emulation' (the attempt to equal or surpass the status of other wealthy individuals) were important incentives in the consumption patterns of the very wealthy. Backhouse describes Veblen's economics as a normatively

driven campaign in which 'he satirized the lifestyles and mores of the capitalists of his day'.[14] But a Veblen good has technical features that the category
of luxury good lacks. A Veblen good is like an inverted Giffen good. Giffen
goods are staples like bread which, counter to the normal laws of supply and
demand, respond to price rises with increased demand (since it is necessary to
purchase staples, when their price goes up, more of them are purchased while
other goods are foregone). Increasing the price of a Veblen good also increases
demand but for the opposite reason: it is not a staple but a luxury that exhibits
the owner's wealth. Lowering the price of a Veblen good can therefore reduce
demand, because the consumer loses a portion of the motivation for purchasing it. The consumers of Veblen goods display their wealth through these purchases and therefore extremely high prices are incentives to purchase rather
than, as for ordinary goods, disincentives. Hence, Nic Forrest says:

> the best example of the Veblen effect is the work of Damien Hirst whose
> work appeared to have benefited greatly from the wealthy trophy buyers
> whose prime motivation was prestige and status. Hirst even hedged his
> bets by using copious amounts of diamonds to cover the infamous skull
> and used diamond dust in some of his works. Even if the art wasn't so
> great the diamonds are sure to attract those seeking a way of decorating
> their house with objects that reflect their level of wealth. One could even
> argue that Hirst was specifically catering for the wealthy trophy hunters
> by producing works that they would find highly attractive such as the
> diamond encrusted human skull.[15]

Luxury goods such as sports cars, fine wines, islands in the sun, the Empire
State Building, and exotic pets are purchased, at least in part, to position oneself competitively with other wealthy consumers and to display one's purchasing power. A Veblen good, therefore, is a positional good.

The display of a Veblen good is not equivalent to sharing it. There is, therefore, a necessary disparity between consuming and looking in the act of display. Consuming a sports car generally means driving it, consuming a designer
dress means wearing it, and consuming a yacht means sailing it. Seeing somebody else drive a sports car is not in itself the consumption of the sports
car. Admiring the dress worn by the wealthiest woman in the room is not to

---

14   Backhouse 2002, p. 195.
15   See http://www.artmarketblog.com/2008/12/28/art-and-the-veblen-effect-artmarketblog
      com.

consume the use value of the dress. And gawping at a yacht being skippered by its owner, is not the transferral of use through the act of gawping. Veblen goods are luxury goods that command higher prices because they are perceived to bring credit and status to the purchaser and this bonus is an effect of its public display. Looking at the luxury item is meant to confirm that the viewer is not the owner, and that this is a significant lack. Looking at the luxury good is also meant to confirm that the owner is the user or consumer, and that this is a significant plus. The display of ownership is typically tied up with the absence of ownership in looking, and the presence of the ability to consume use values in the fact of ownership. This is possible because looking at a luxury item is not the same, normally, as consuming it. Artworks are different in this respect. When a non-owner of an artwork looks at it, they are consuming it without purchasing it and without any diminution in the enjoyment of the product. Art collectors continue to treat artworks as Veblen goods, nonetheless, of course, displaying their wealth and taste by loaning the works they own to public museums and important exhibitions. The difference in the case of art is not in the behaviour of the owner, but in the use values afforded the non-owner by the display of the Veblen good. This means that it is possible for an artwork to be a Veblen good, a luxury good and a public good and a merit good all at the same time. Sports cars and jewellery are not public goods or merit goods in addition to being luxury goods. Artworks, on the other hand, even if and when they are luxury goods, are more than luxury goods.

Art's relationship to merchant capital, which I have examined in terms of art's encounter with the gallerist and the collector, neither follows the pattern of the standard commodity nor conforms to any of the three main theories of luxury goods. However, contemporary capitalism poses new specific issues that need to be addressed before we can complete our study of art and merchant capital. Global companies increasingly outsource production and take a larger proportion of the profits than the productive capitalist (often a factory owner in a developing country), who has a client relation to the global corporation. The Marxist analysis of merchant capital, including its relation to art, appears to lose its footing in a stage of capitalism dominated by merchant capital rather than productive capital. Christian Marazzi, spurred on by Giovanni Arrighi,[16] states the point boldly by insisting that we 'stop identifying ... capitalism with industrial capitalism'.[17] Daniel Bell's thesis of the post-industrial society[18] lurks in the background of the critique of 'productivism'. Political

---

16   See Arighi 2007.

17   Marazzi 2011, p. 32.

18   See Bell 1973.

questions and economic ones begin to collide here, as we need to inquire into whether the shift from industrial manufacturing to circulation (of data as well as goods), manages to overcome Marx's argument that surplus cannot be produced by merchant capital, through circulation.

If art encounters capital only as merchant capital, not as productive capital, does this signal the independence of art from capitalist commodity production or the cunning incorporation of art's economic exceptionalism within the new mode of contemporary capitalism? Marazzi refers to the so-called 'consumer as producer phenomenon'[19] as an example of the new methods by which surplus value is extracted without production beyond the factory gates. IKEA, he tells us, 'externalizes the labor of assembling the "Billy" bookshelf'.[20] But while it is true that the consumer of IKEA furniture also produces the furniture through assembling its parts, this does not mean that the consumer produces value. Producing use value is one thing; producing surplus value is another. IKEA does not profit directly from consumers assembling their own bookshelves and it certainly draws no surplus value from the free labour of its customers. However, it profits and extracts surplus value from customers paying extra for a trained IKEA employee to assemble the item in your home. The same error occurs in the suggestion that Web 2.0 businesses such as Facebook, Flickr and MySpace 'valorize user browsing'.[21] If all this means is that these companies make a profit from selling advertising space on their pages or selling data about their users, then this is true and uncontentious, but Marazzi and others claim, rather, that these businesses enjoy 'the extraction of surplus value from the common actions like linking a site, flagging a blog post, modifying software, and so forth'.[22] Web 2.0 companies make profits from our use of social networks, but they do not draw surplus value from our networking activities. Marazzi believes our status updates and tweets are 'the "free labor" in the sphere of consumption'.[23] But the profits for Web 2.0 companies do not derive from productive labour, and certainly not from 'productive consumption'. Let me explain.

A comic strip signed by the artist 'geek' depicts two pigs having a conversation. One says, 'isn't it great? We have to pay nothing for the barn'. The other says, 'yeah, and even the food is free'. Underneath the image are two lines of text. The first reads: 'Facebook and you'. The second reads: 'If you're not paying

19   Marazzi 2011, p. 50.
20   Marazzi 2011, p. 51.
21   Ibid.
22   Marazzi 2011, pp. 51–2.
23   Marazzi 2011, p. 52.

for it, you're not the customer. You're the product being sold'. The pigs, of course, are products. They are commodity capital, in fact, and will realise their value through sale, usually through a merchant capitalist of some sort such as a butcher or supermarket chain, but perhaps also as raw material for the production of a new commodity such as pork pies. The barn and the food are overheads for the farmer who tries to keep such costs to a minimum. The pigs are not the customers of the barn and food, as the comic rightly points out; the farmer is the (productive) consumer and he consumes these commodities by providing them to the pigs. Facebook is free to its users, but its users are not the customers. This, again, the comic gets right, although it phrases it in a way that suggests being paying customers is the best possible relationship we can have with goods and services. Contrast this with the case of a borrower at a public library. Reading books for free and therefore not being the customer of a library as if it were a bookshop is not necessarily preferable to a reader, and it does not mean you are a product. But nobody makes profit from a public library and a great deal of profit is made from Facebook, so we need to examine the source of this profit. Facebook earns 82–98 percent of its income from advertising. The rest comes from selling 'credits' for online games.

In the case of advertising on websites, the users are neither the customers nor the products. The companies that buy advertising space are the customers; the product is the space that they purchase. In fact, we can see Facebook as a machine for passing money from a large number of capitalists to the shareholders of Facebook. It is possible to pass this money from one to the other because Facebook has a monopoly on advertising space on its pages. Companies pay a fee for a certain space over a specific duration of time to the owner of the space. The users of Facebook are neither the consumers nor the products in this profit-making transaction, as the joke has it. Moreover, Facebookers are not, as Marazzi claims, the unpaid labourers who produce the value that Facebook appropriates. The users of Facebook are the addressees and potential customers of the companies who advertise on Facebook. To understand the economics of Facebook, we need to understand the economics of advertising.

From an economic point of view, Facebook is an Edwardian venture. The reign of Edward VII, from 1901–10, was the first era of branded goods. Canning techniques, industrial boxing, printing and the standardisation of products through industrialisation and mechanisation are among the chief reasons for the triumph of branding in this period. Branding was also a means by which productive capital gained an advantage over merchant capital, as part of the expansion of operations from the production of its own raw materials to the control of the product at the point of sale. Branded goods also fetched premium prices because of their guaranteed quality. Branded tea, for instance, marketed itself as a product for which the consumer could have confidence because its quality was assured by the manufacturer. Loose tea in a barrel might be mixed with anything and the quality of the tea could vary from one scoop to another, but Tetley tea, one of the earliest British tea brands, passes through rigorous quality control checks to ensure that it tastes the same every time. Facebook is a brand, of course, but it is Edwardian in another sense. Brands need publicity, and so the Edwardian period was also the era in which advertising became central to the capitalist mode of production. Facebook is a brand that is also a medium through which other brands advertise their products. It is Facebook's reliance on income from advertising that links it economically to the beginning of the twentieth century. Advertising predates branding but is reborn with it. The sale of advertising space is an innovation of industrial capitalism. In June 1836 *La Presse*, a French newspaper, published paid advertisements and began to lower its price to the reader, which extended its market, increased profitability, and put pressure on its competitors. Before the end of the nineteenth century the first advertising agency was founded. Advertising meets the needs of industrial production. Mass production requires mass consumption. Lyle's Golden Syrup was one of the first companies to use branding around 1885 both on packaging and in advertising. Advertising separated the brand from the physical body of the product. Advertising was invented to create familiarity with unfamiliar products and the companies that produced them, to allow industrial producers to compete with familiar local producers, and to heal the rift between the commodity and the community (a relationship sundered by the centralisation of industrial production). Branding is a continuous labour of abstract attachment through mediated familiarity. Branding and advertising, therefore, predate Fordism, even though Ford is itself a brand name. Ford in the period of the invention of the assembly line is a prototypical Edwardian company. In fact, standardisation is one of the essential ingredients of branded goods. Advertising, branding and marketing are the mechanisms for the industrialisation of consumption. There is nothing post-industrial about the semiotic and symbolic circulation of advertising. There is nothing exotic or novel about how Facebook makes profit. The idea that we have entered a new phase of capitalism in which surplus value can be drawn from consumption is not supported by an economic analysis of Facebook or Web 2.0 generally. And these apparently new forms of profit making, therefore, do not transform art's relationship to capital. Some of these issues will resurface in Chapter 11, which explores the theory of post-Fordism, but before I develop these arguments further I need to address directly the relationship between art and finance capital.

CHAPTER 10

Art and Finance Capital

€46.1 billion (or $62.8 billion) was the size of the global art market in 2011, according to a report by The European Fine Art Foundation published in March 2012. This represents a revival of the art market, which after reaching $60 billion in 2007 dropped by 20 percent in 2008 after the credit crunch and lost another 30 percent in 2009. The market is split equally between auction houses and gallery sales, with Sotheby's and Christie's handling around 35 percent of global auction trade between them, with the most dramatic growth in business taking place in China (up 177 percent in 2010, when China finally overtook the United States and the UK 'as the world's largest auction marketplace for Fine Art',[1] and up another 65 percent in 2011 to command as much as 39 percent of the global art market). There were 36.8 million transactions within the art market in 2011, with nearly 70 percent of global trade made up of 'contemporary and modern art' (art made since 1875) by more than 403,000 dealers, galleries and auction houses employing 2.4 million people. The contemporary and modern markets grew from €92 million to €915 million between 2002 and 2008.[2] Dealers make around a third of their income from sales at art fairs, with 41 percent passing through the gallery (the rest, presumably, are made online[3] or through personal communication). Although art is an enormous global market and the bulk of sales consists of 'contemporary and modern art', these are nonetheless largely sales on the secondary market of artists such as 'Picasso, Gustav Klimt, Egon Schiele, Claude Monet, Maurice de Vlaminck and Salvador Dali',[4] sold from collectors to collectors. The primary market, dealing with living artists selling works to collectors, is a very small percentage of total sales,[5] in which 'the price points are often lower than in the secondary market'.[6] Gallerists have started to deal more vigorously

---

1 Ehrmann 2011, p. 6.

2 McAndrew 2010a, p. 17.

3 See Ehrmann 2012, p. 15. He says: 'The sale of artworks online has become an irreversible aspect of the modern art market and the sums involved have already reached into 7 figures'.

4 Ehrmann 2012, p. 10.

5 See McAndrew 2010b, p. 9. The art market, she says, 'operates on a two-tier system made up of primary and secondary markets, with the latter dominating the trade in terms of value and volume'.

6 McAndrew 2010b, p. 9.

© KONINKLIJKE BRILL NV, LEIDEN, 2015 | DOI 10.1163/9789004288157_012

in the art market through an increasing number of art fairs. In 1970 'there were just three main events (Cologne, Basel and the Brussels based Art Actuel)' but today there are 189 international art fairs. The main reason for this, according to Georgina Adam, is 'the need to offer a buy-it-or-you'll-lose-it situation to challenge the auction houses'.[7]

The art market, effectively, is a massive second hand trading network of collectors and dealers, with little or no place for the producers of art. Their works are exchanged between collectors in a world apart, hence artworks in the secondary market are 'irreproducible' in Ricardo's terms regardless of whether the artist is dead or not. The absence of competition among producers and the impossibility of increasing supply to meet demand is the basis for the astronomical prices of a tiny minority of highly sought after artworks. Neoclassical economics claims to be able to treat the sale of artworks as a standard transaction with prices determined entirely by demand and the subjective perception of utility by wealthy purchasers. However, no demand curve can be drawn for a unique object and no incremental units of such an article can be used to gauge a consumer's marginal utility. In fact, the prices of artworks appear to be beyond mainstream economics. While mainstream economists are the experts on markets and prices, the allocation of resources and the calculus of costs and benefits, they cannot provide any explanation of the mechanisms by which prices of artworks are affected. Baumol argued, for instance, that the value of artworks, especially of noted artists who are dead, 'float more or less aimlessly'.[8] This is not an economic explanation of art prices, but a confession of the absence of one. In order to make progress in the economic understanding of art prices we need to extend our analysis beyond art and productive capital and merchant capital. The secondary market for art is one of the theatres in which merchant capital operates, but this is a sphere dominated by finance capital.

Finance capital differs from productive capital and merchant capital insofar as it appears as a commodity.[9] Moreover, finance capital in the form of loans differs from commodity capital with regard to use value:

> In the case of the other commodities the use value is ultimately consumed. Their substance disappears, and with it their value. In contrast,

---

7   Adam 2012 (unpaginated).

8   Baumol 1986, p. 10.

9   See Marx 1959, p. 341. 'A distinction should be made here. We have seen (Book II, Chap. I), and recall briefly at this point, that in the process of circulation capital serves as commodity-capital and money-capital. But in neither form does capital become a commodity as capital'.

[finance as] commodity capital is peculiar in that its value and use value not only remain intact but also increase, through consumption of its use value.[10]

Marx argues that finance capital has a use value which is value itself.[11] Just like 'the buyer of an ordinary commodity buys its use value...the borrower of money buys...its use value as capital'.[12] Financial assets, therefore, have a use value to their purchasers, which is the returns that they can generate. 'Marxist theory analyses bank profits as deriving typically from handling the monetary transactions of enterprises (earning the average rate of profit) as well as from lending to enterprises (earning interest, a part of surplus value)'.[13] There are two main methods by which finance capital accumulates. Advanced as money capital in the form of credit, finance capital earns interest that is guaranteed to various degrees. By purchasing financial assets such as shares, however, finance capital earns dividends – a portion of profit – which is not guaranteed. The productive capitalist ties up large sums of capital in a single enterprise over a long period. Productive capital cannot be withdrawn without selling commodity capital (realising value through sales) or selling the enterprise in part or whole. The shareholder, on the other hand, is a finance capitalist or money capitalist, and can invest separate portions of capital in a range of enterprises, making capital available to several productive capitalists and withdrawing it from any or all at will. Finance capital metamorphoses more readily, more quickly and more often than productive capital. When we think of capital traversing the globe in an instant, we are thinking of finance capital. Stocks in corporations are bought and sold in large numbers and high frequency around the clock in stock markets across the world. The share can be bought and sold in an instant, but what the asset represents, the business into which it is invested, has already been taken out of circulation, converted into commodity capital (raw materials, means of production, labour power). Seen in this perspective, the trading of stocks and shares occurs independently of the capital that they represent, which is not so mobile, fast moving and liquid. Finance capital is capital but the turnover of shares is not a turnover of capital. Capital, therefore, undergoes another of its many metamorphoses when finance capital purchases assets. The sale and purchase of titles to income from profits can itself be a source of profit but is not itself either productive

10   Marx 1959, p. 351.
11   Marx 1959, p. 352.
12   Ibid.
13   Lapavitsas 2009, p. 18.

(of new value) nor capital. The value in the share seems to contain a second capital independent of the first embodied in productive capital. Marx calls this 'fictitious capital'. In relation to productive capital, shares may be defined, in Hilferding's words, as 'a title to income, a creditor's claim upon future production, or claim upon profit'.[14] Profit is therefore anticipated and traded in advance. Fictitious capital draws on future profits. And this is why Hilferding says, 'it is misleading to regard the price of a share as an aliquot part of industrial capital'.[15] Shares represent a portion of the yield only. A loan is an asset, also, insofar as it represents income derived from the interest on the debt rather than the debt itself. Debts are traded on account of the income that is due to them in the future. Despite these similarities, we need to divide finance capital into two broad sections. One type of finance capital takes a share of surplus value from productive capital in the form of dividends, increased share prices, and so on. A second type generates income through interest.

Standard assets are not consumed but stored; they are durable not perishable; their economy is driven by the future; they are traded in large markets; asset markets deal in stocks not flows; asset markets are fast moving; profit opportunities in asset markets are huge but dissipate in seconds; assets put a price on uncertainty; the storage costs for assets are usually negligible; assets are a vehicle for saving for future consumption; asset transactions are impersonal; assets move around a great deal; traders in assets are preoccupied with very short-term gains; traders pay close attention to each other because information is acted on quickly and without disclosure; and, assets pay dividends or interest. Asset markets exchange entitlements, rights, contracts and promises rather than property, goods and services. Productive capital deals with labour, raw materials and the means of production; merchant capital deals with the products of productive capital combined with the premises, labour and tools of selling, marketing and advertising; finance capital has no direct contact with any of these commodities and processes, exchanging items with the virtual properties of ownership, rights and entitlements only. Such virtual transactions can take place without the movement of any material goods from one place to another as the exchange of commodities requires. As a result, assets can be exchanged in an instant. And since assets can be exchanged for money just as quickly as they can be exchanged for other assets, they are extremely liquid. Assets appear to be capital purified of production. Since finance capital is that type of capital that is most remote from labour, neither paying wages nor purchasing its products, it can appear to appreciate without the help of

---

14   Hilferding 1981, p. 110.
15   Hilferding 1981, p. 110.

labour power. Finance capital can take its profits from surplus labour, or derive profit from revenue. In both cases, however, capital appears as a commodity on the market. The use value of this particular commodity, Marx says, 'lies in producing profit'.

Finance capital can take its profits from surplus labour or derive profit from revenue. Finance capital that profits from business, whether as debt financing or equity financing, takes its interest payments from capital, since borrowing and paying for that borrowing is a method of drawing on capital for future accumulation. Interest charged on consumer loans, private insurance, mortgages, pensions, credit cards and hire purchase to ordinary consumers is taken from revenue, not capital. Dividends derive from capital but interest can derive from either capital or revenue. 'The owner of money who desires to enhance his money as interest bearing capital, turns it over to a third person, throws it into circulation, turns it into a commodity as capital; not just capital for himself, but also for others'.[16] Finance capital is peculiar, though, because unlike commodity capital, or money capital used by merchant capitalists or productive capitalists, 'there is no exchange and no equivalent is received'[17] when a finance capitalist loans a sum of money. What is even more peculiar is that '[o]wnership is not relinquished'.[18] The money returned to the finance capitalist already belongs to her. When a bank is permitted to make loans far in excess of the capital it holds, it appears as if profit is being produced out of nothing, like new value, but the interest that it earns derives entirely from the revenue of the customer and no new value is produced. We might say that to the bank this appears to be a miracle because the bank has made money based on capital it does not have, but the money it receives is the result of a rather less than mysterious process, namely the wages of the worker or the surplus value of the capitalist. The miracle, if there is one, is that it ends up in the hands of the bank, not that it appeared at all. The personal loans market is also a zero sum game. Banks, for instance, lend a household a few thousand pounds to do up their house or buy a new car and the money that returns to the bank (the sum plus interest) is taken directly out of the pockets of the householder. No new value is created by interest payments and the profit from domestic credit is not drawn from surplus value. Assets, including loans, either draw their profit from new value or within zero sum games. We can say that one form of finance capital is productive and the other is unproductive. Finance that draws on revenue rather than capital has no relation to surplus value, and

---

16   Marx 1959, p. 343.
17   Marx 1959, p. 347.
18   Ibid.

is unproductive, but finance that draws on capital inevitably derives its income from surplus value and surplus labour, albeit in a mediated and indirect way, so is productive.

Finance capital is always, in a limited sense, productive insofar as it enters circulation for the purpose of augmenting itself. However, consumer credit and similar forms of finance capital derive their profits from revenue, not capital, so it is helpful to describe such transactions as unproductive. That is to say, it is more precise to distinguish productive credit from unproductive credit not according to whether it produces profits, but whether it derives from surplus value. Finance capital can be productive or unproductive, therefore, but productive capital is always productive in this sense of accumulating through surplus value and not just profiting from revenue. 'Loaning money as capital – its alienation on the condition of it being returned after a certain time – presupposes ... that it will be actually employed as capital, and that it actually flows back to its starting-point'.[19] When production is profitable shares yield dividends. It is possible for share ownership to be rewarded by other means, too, but the link between production and income from assets is important to spell out. Productive credit has a peculiar pattern. Capital in the hands of the finance capitalist is handed over to the productive capitalist without changing its form (remaining money capital), and returns to the finance capitalist from the productive capitalist after the production of commodity capital has been realised and re-converted into money capital. One peculiar aspect of finance capital issued as a loan is that the money moves in the opposite direction from normal: 'In an ordinary exchange of commodities money always comes from the buyer's side; but in a loan it comes from the side of the seller'.[20] So, the sequence of this kind of finance capital is M-M-C-M'-M'.[21] 'Money thus loaned has ... a certain similarity with labour power in its relation to the industrial capitalist', Marx says, with the caveat that, 'the latter pays for the value of labour power, whereas he simply pays back the value of the loaned capital'.[22] Marx points out that for finance capital 'the first time M changes hands is by no means a phase either of the commodity metamorphoses, or of reproduction of capital',[23] but needs to be expended twice, so to speak. 'This double outlay of money as capital, of which the first is merely a transfer from

---

19   Marx 1959, p. 349. Loaning money as anything other than capital (e.g. consumer credit) does not presuppose its employment as capital, of course.

20   Marx 1959, p. 352.

21   Marx 1959, p. 340.

22   Marx 1959, p. 351.

23   Marx 1959, p. 340.

A to B, is matched by its double reflux',[24] which is to say after the value of commodity capital produced by the productive capitalist is realised through sales (including surplus value) it is realised for a second time in the repayments of the loan (plus interest). 'To make its reflux complete, B must consequently return it to A. But in addition to the capital, B must also turn over to A a portion of the profit...which he had made with this capital since A had given him the money only as a capital'.[25] In the case of productive finance, therefore, whereby finance capital is advanced to a productive capitalist (instead of the entrepreneur advancing her own capital, for instance, she borrows from a bank or venture capitalist instead), interest payments on credit constitute a share in the surplus value in exactly the same way as the merchant capitalist takes a share of the surplus value through the discounted rate at which commodity capital is purchased. So, despite their virtuality, speed and agility, assets linked to productive capital are fundamentally dependent on production, surplus labour and surplus value. However, one of the difficulties is that assets can appreciate speculatively in advance of the realisation of value. Asset trading, in this respect, can be a form of gambling in which the future performance of an endeavour or a financial package is realised financially before it is realised materially in production and sales. When finance does not draw revenue out of the pockets of customers in a zero sum game, it draws on or anticipates surplus value in production.

Finance capital differs from productive capital and merchant capital but it is also vital to observe that finance capital, productive capital and merchant capital come into conflict with one another. Lenin argued, for instance, that the twentieth century witnessed the growth of power of finance capitalists *vis-à-vis* productive capitalists, leading to a new phase of capitalism with a different class composition. By the end of the nineteenth century a handful of wealthy families, such as the Mellons and Rockefellers, come to own a significant proportion of money wealth and to use their money power effectively to control the conditions under which all other capitalists operate. As a result, ownership is combined with control in the hands of the oligarchs of interest bearing capital.[26] This illustration 'provides the first working definition of finance capital', David Harvey says. Banking capital and credit generally have become the powerhouse of contemporary capitalism. 'Finance capital has created the epoch of monopolies',[27] Lenin said. And these monopolies are also the

---

24   Marx 1959, p. 341.
25   Ibid.
26   Harvey 1982, p. 317.
27   Lenin 1967, p. 23.

basis of another historical shift in the relationship between productive capitalists and merchant capitalists. Branded goods, which are monopoly goods, are the result of a transformation of commodity production in which major corporations outsource production to factories owned by client productive capitalists. The balance of power (and the share of surplus value) is in the favour of these monopolists who are merchant capitalists rather than productive capitalists. Marx argued that joint stock companies were invented as a response to the growth of finance capital, and Lenin argued that the concentration and centralisation of capital ownership and the trans-national movement of finance capital had brought about a new stage of capitalism based not on competition but monopoly and led neither by productive capitalists nor merchant capitalists but bankers, financiers and speculators. In speaking of finance capital, therefore, we are not merely studying a portion of capital or particular species of self-accumulation but also a particular form of money power and a specific class interest, albeit a sub-class of the capitalist class. Just as capitalism is that form of society dominated by capital, we can talk about finance capitalism as that form of capitalism dominated by finance capital. Examining the relationship between art and finance capital, therefore, is both a technical inquiry into art investment and art as an asset class, and, at the same time, an inquiry into the relationship between art and the hegemonic section of the dominant class. Whereas the era of competitive productive capitalism saw great efforts by the capitalist class to eliminate national tariffs on the export of goods, the era of finance capital is accompanied by attacks by the capitalist class on national restrictions on the movement of money capital. Lenin paints a vivid picture of imperial monopoly capitalism in the years before the First World War:

> Monopolist capitalist associations, cartels, syndicates and trusts first divided the home market among themselves and obtained more or less complete possession of the industry in their own country. But under capitalism the home market is inevitably bound up with the foreign market. Capitalism long ago created a world market. As the export of capital increased, and as the foreign and colonial connections and 'spheres of influence' of the big monopolist associations expanded in all ways, things 'naturally' gravitated towards an international agreement among these associations, and towards the formation of international cartels.[28]

Harvey summarises Lenin's argument as a development within capitalism leading to 'an ever more dramatic uneven development of capitalism and a radical re-structuring of class relations [in which a] dominant financial

---

28   Lenin 1967, p. 728.

oligarchy ... buys labour peace in the "core" countries ... while the rest of the
world is driven deeper and deeper into states of dependency, subservience
and rebellion'.[29]

Gérard Duménil and Dominique Lévy argue that neoliberalism is the
'expression of the desire of a class of capitalist owners and the institutions
in which their power is concentrated, which we collectively call "finance", to
restore ... the class's revenue and power'.[30] Fine and Milonakis point out that
finance was not regarded as a *bona fide* sub-discipline of economics until 1955,
since when it 'has leapfrogged into the vanguard'.[31] Deregulation, privatisation,
globalisation, financialisation and debt are the hallmarks of contemporary
capitalism. Capitalism as a whole has been reconfigured according to the dominance of finance, but the effects are felt at the national, local and domestic
level. Costas Lapavitsas points out that the 'personal revenue of workers and
others has been "financialised" ... [through] loans for housing, general consumption, education, health',[32] pensions, store cards and through wages being
paid directly into bank accounts. Profits derived from 'mediating the circuits
of worker revenues', Lapavitsas says, 'constitute a new source of profits'[33] for
the banks. Some of these new profits for finance capital have been the direct
result of neoliberal policies which have systematically reduced 'public provision of key wage goods',[34] forcing workers 'into the arms of private finance',[35]
including predatory lending and over-charging. Banks, however, have not been
the driving force in contemporary financialisation. Lapavitsas argues that 'the
era of financialisation is not dominated by the banks',[36] but by big corporations. The modern multinational corporation 'is "financialised" in the sense
that financial transactions are a substantial part of its activities and profit
making'.[37] Income generated from their financial operations have allowed
multinational corporations 'to boost their profits independently of surplus
value generated by the indifferently performing sphere of production'.[38] The
dominance of finance capital over productive capital is intensified by the neoliberal turn of Reagonomics and Thatcherist monetarism. William Lazonick

---

29   Harvey 1982, p. 289.
30   Duménil and Lévy 2004, pp. 1–2.
31   Fine and Milonakis 2009a, p. 68.
32   Lapavitsas 2009, p. 17.
33   Lapavitsas 2009, p. 19.
34   Ibid.
35   Ibid.
36   Lapavitsas 2009, p. 16.
37   Lapavitsas 2009, p. 15.
38   Lapavitsas 2009, p. 19.

and Mary O'Sullivan summarise the historical context for the emergence of the new financialisation thus:

> by the 1980s the deregulated financial environment and the rise of the institutional investor as a holder of corporate stocks encouraged top managers to align their own interests with external financial interests rather than with the interests of the productive organizations over which they exercised control.[39]

Mutual funds gave shareholders increased power. Corporate business models shifted from 'retain and reinvest' to 'downsize and distribute'. Which is to say, profits are not put back into the business but issued to shareholders. Companies, therefore, orient their activities to finance capital more than productive capital. Moreover, new financial – and financialising – methods have been introduced to facilitate this change of focus. As part of this transformation, 'stock repurchases have now become a systematic feature of the way in which they allocate revenues'.[40] Production in contemporary capitalism has been reconfigured by the doctrine of 'shareholder value' in which 'stock repurchases' or buybacks increase the value of a company's shares and shareholder dividends by spending its profits on reducing the number of shares.

Since finance is the dominant force in contemporary capitalism, we would not expect banks to sit by as the art market grows into a global market worth over €40 billion with 44 million transactions per year. Banks have developed new products and services for the art sector, providing advice to art collectors, financial services to dealers, loans and so on. During the 1980s, banks began to allow dealers to borrow against the value of artworks. Art loans allowed dealers and collectors to leverage their collections to fund new purchases, but also loans secured on artworks were made available to cover debts. Banks can spread out such loans so that the owner receives monthly payments against the value of their collection, which gets round tax obligations that would result from selling the works. After the art crash in the early 90s, some banks were more reluctant to make art loans, but the revival of growth in the global art market has not only brought the banks back into play but attracted the attention of hedge funds. Interest rates for art loans can be as high as 18 percent and most lenders will offer sums amounting to only 50 percent of the full value of the artwork, to safeguard against the risk of works not maintaining their value. Art is also included within investment portfolios, partly because it

39   Lazonick and O'Sullivan 2000, p. 27.
40   Lazonick and O'Sullivan 2000, p. 23.

has a reputation for enormously impressive financial performance, and partly because the art market is not linked with the prices of other assets.

> The main principle of portfolio management is efficient diversification: through finding and combining assets that have low correlation with each other, it is possible to obtain a portfolio risk that is less than that of the component assets considered in isolation.[41]

According to McAndrew, 'the potential to use art for risk diversification in an investment portfolio is undoubtedly its most tangible and attractive feature as an asset class'.[42] The auction houses play an active role in maintaining the value of artworks as assets. Gallerists and dealers also take an active role, purchasing works by their own artists when they come up for auction to maintain their value.

In 1968, in a legendary lecture at the Museum of Modern Art, New York, Leo Steinberg, one of the three 'kings' of art criticism in the 1960s and 1970s, scandalously linked the avant-garde with finance capital:

> Avant-garde art, lately Americanized, is for the first time associated with big money. And this is because its occult aims and uncertain future have been successfully translated into homely terms. For far-out modernism, we can now read 'speculative growth stock'; for apparent quality, 'market attractiveness'; and for an adverse change of taste, 'technical obsolescence'. A feat of language to absolve a change of attitude. Art is not, after all, what we thought it was; in the broadest sense it is hard cash. The whole of art, its growing tip included, is assimilated to familiar values. Another decade, and we shall have mutual funds based on securities in the form of pictures held in bank vaults.[43]

Steinberg combined a love of the Italian Renaissance with a sensitivity to Abstract Expressionism, so the convergence of art and 'big money' is, for him, lamentable. I only say this because since he made these remarks a new generation of writers with a stronger attachment to free markets than to art might well view this convergence as a blessing. Cultural economists might dispute Steinberg's claim that art had become associated with big money for the first time, but Steinberg is referring to avant-garde art's relationship with

---

41   McAndrew 2010b, p. 26.
42   McAndrew 2010b, p. 25.
43   Steinberg quoted in Stallabrass 2004b, p. 70.

finance, and this was unheard of within the tradition of avant-gardism itself. In fact, Steinberg lays it on thick for satirical effect, but in the intervening years his exaggeration has been overshot by events. Art's relationship to finance capital has outstripped Steinberg's worst fears. Not only has art been developed as an asset class, the relationship between art and credit, including the relationship established between art dealers, banking and finance has grown, intensified and diversified.

Art's relationship to finance, however, is not limited to art's encounters with banking, investment funds, loans and auction houses. It is not uncommon for gallerists to have financial 'backers'. One of the most famous was Robert Scull, the wealthy owner of a taxi company in New York, who as well as being a collector in his own right, backed the pioneering Green Gallery which exhibited 'downtown' artists in an uptown location for the first time. Scull was the backer of one of the most important galleries in New York in a vital period that saw the emergence of Color Field painting, Pop Art and Minimalism, all displayed prominently and in groundbreaking exhibitions at Green Gallery. Furthermore, Scull would finance artists directly, providing the funds to Walter De Maria, for instance, to experiment with polished steel. Scull was often the first collector of avant-garde artists in this period, but by backing the Green Gallery he was also instrumental in giving some of the most important artists of the period visibility within the broader art world. Dan Flavin's most important early exhibition of neon light works, which was held at the Green Gallery in 1964, ended without the sale of a single work, priced at only $1000 per piece. This exhibition was so critically important that another commercial gallery, Zwirner and Wirth, restaged it exactly in 2008 by borrowing the works (and therefore, yet again, selling none). By having Scull as a backer, Richard Bellamy, the gallerist, could put together an ambitious programme of exhibitions like this without any pressure to sell. The backer is a cross between a benefactor and a venture capitalist, making funds available for a gallerist to work with artists without having to respond directly or immediately to market demand. Scull bought many key works by upcoming artists in the 1960s including Rauschenberg, Warhol, Walter De Maria, Tom Wesselman and George Segal. In 1964 Scull withdrew as the backer of the Green Gallery. It had never been profitable and Scull had financed the production of works for the gallery and paid advances on sales to artists who did not sell. The next year the gallery closed altogether. After three years of funding the Green Gallery at a loss, in 1963 Scull infamously auctioned 50 works by American artists from his collection, many of them reaching record prices for living artists. The sale made over $2 million, which was a considerable profit on the sums originally paid to the artists. Barbara Rose described Scull's sale 'profit without honor' and the auction house was the target of protestors on the day who blocked the entrance. The whole event was filmed, including a scene in which Rauschenberg makes a statement about artists' royalties, kisses Ethel Scull then confronts Scull, saying, 'I've been working my ass off for you to make that profit'. Rauschenberg's *Thaw*, purchased in 1958 for $900, went for $85,000. Scull replied, 'I've been working for you too' and says that he hoped the artist's works would fetch higher prices as a result of this sale. Scull was right, of course, but the two never spoke again. Of Robert and Ethel Scull, Baruch Kirschenbaum says, 'they bought courageously'.[44] It was not the buying but the selling that rankled the underground art world. It seems that the artists, critics and gallerists in New York at this time were quite happy with an investor who comes away with no profit and a collector who holds on to the works they buy. A collector who sells works at a profit, on the other hand, appears to metamorphose into an investor or speculator preying on artists for financial gain. An art collector can resemble an art investor or predatory speculator because, in art, as we have already noted, commodities and assets are indistinguishable. I will now turn my attention to some of the key features of art as an asset.

Art appreciates. In fact, this was the first observation ever made by economists that led to the classical theory of art's economic exceptionalism. The primary market for art (galleries selling living artists) is big and it is growing, but it pales into insignificance when compared with the volume and value of the secondary market (auction houses and dealers selling blue chip and old master works). It is not only that works are significantly cheaper and collectors are fewer and further between, but the primary market 'can entail a significant degree of risk'.[45] It is not a risk to purchase an artwork that one loves and expects to view on a regular basis. To speak of risk, in this context, is to regard artworks as investments. Risk, then, applies to artworks not as commodities but assets. Accordingly, the higher risks of contemporary art are met with lower prices and the lower risks in works that have proved themselves to appreciate over a period of time are met with higher prices. The relative cheapness and high risk of a work by a lesser-known artist or 'early work' is based on the uncertainty of whether the artist will ever develop a significant career or sales profile. Cultural economics has not managed to explain the factors that determine which works appreciate and which do not, nor has it explained why the value of artworks appreciates at all. As we have already noted, Baumol argues that the values of artworks, especially of noted artists

44   Kirschenbaum 1979, p. 52.
45   McAndrew 2010b, p. 9.

who are dead, 'float more or less aimlessly'.[46] This is how the pricing of art-works appears to an economist who focuses exclusively on the product and its price history rather than on the factors that bring about changes in value. One of the aims of this chapter is to provide an explanation of the apparently wild prices of artworks on the secondary market that is, in fact, anchored. The key is to identify precisely to what art prices are anchored. But first I want to address the more fundamental question: why and how do investments in art appreci-ate in value? Not all second hand goods appreciate in value. Most of them do not. But when they do, like antiques and vintage cars, they appreciate accord-ing to rarity, quality and demand. Regardless of whether antiques or artworks on the secondary market are bought by the final consumer as a use value or by a dealer as commodity capital from which to profit at a later date, the antiques market and the secondary market for art is a zero sum market in which prof-its made by sellers of antiques come directly out of the pockets of buyers of art and antiques. Despite profitability, no surplus value is created at all in the antiques market or the art market, and therefore commodities and money merely pass from hand to hand with some losing and some gaining along the way. The transactions in a zero sum game are all without exception *like for like*. The purchaser pays what the seller receives and vice versa. Information about antiques often permits the expert and the dealer to profit off somebody else's ignorance, buying low to sell high at someone else's expense. Although the same is possible in vintage cars, they are traded mostly by enthusiasts who have similar levels of knowledge but varying tastes and levels of effective demand. One striking feature of the art market is that not all artworks appreci-ate. The vast majority of artworks produced do not enter the market at all, or enter at a very low level and drop out again. Perhaps we could say that not all furniture becomes an antique, and not all cars manufactured become vintage motors, but they typically enter the primary marketplace at any rate, and this is not true of art. Art appreciates on condition that it enters the market (which is rare for art) and that it stays there (which is even rarer).

Art has developed since the 1980s as an asset class, included in investment portfolios, because of this fact. Art asset managers are led by the observation that some artworks appreciate in value well above average share prices. What is more, buying art that appreciates in value and then selling it can resemble the standard trade in assets. But just how do art assets yield returns on invest-ment? Is the process of appreciation 'like other financial assets', as McAndrew intimates, or are art assets economically exceptional? Artworks exhibit very few of the features that are standard for an asset class. Artworks are consumed

---

46   Baumol 1986, p. 10.

as well as stored, and the owners of artworks that appreciate in value can choose to view them not merely store them. Many artworks are durable but there is a growing number of artworks which are temporary and event based. Ironically, perhaps, these artworks which are less like conventional art commodities (paintings, sculpture, prints) take on forms that belong to assets (documents, contracts, certificates). The economy of artworks is not best described as driven by the future but as always determined by the past (in art it is reputation that counts). Some artworks are risky investments because their reputation has not been secured while others appear not to be risky even though changes in the assignment of reputation can certainly impact negatively on the value of an art asset. Even so, risks in art assets are not the kind of risks that we have in mind with assets generally. When an entrepreneur uses someone else's finance capital to start a new venture, the risk is that the business fails, demand is elusive or the competition cuts into profitability. Artworks are not attached to these sorts of risk. Artworks are not traded in large markets but, usually, one at a time in face to face transactions. Artworks are traded in flows (shipping works from one place to another), not in stocks, and the art market is incredibly slow moving. And because 'art trades very infrequently...it is a relatively illiquid asset, compared with stocks, bonds, and other financial instruments'.[47] Artworks are expensive to store, profit opportunities take many years and the information on them is slowly accumulated. The best that can be hoped for in an art asset is long-term gains, if at all, and artworks do not move around a great deal. Finally, holding artworks does not pay dividends or interest. Artworks are not standard assets. The fact that art assets produce no dividends and yet can generate returns needs to be explained. Art appreciates in value, but a Marxist analysis of art, in contrast with a neoclassical one, needs to inquire into the source of that appreciation, and to determine whether it occurs as a result of the production of new value or not. All these anomalies are significant because they are consequences of art's unusual relation to capital.

McAndrew says,

> One of the most interesting features of works of art is that they are dual in nature...on the one hand they are something to consume and enjoy...and on the other, they are capital assets that yield a return from their appreciation in value over time like other financial assets.[48]

47   McAndrew 2010b, p. 18.
48   McAndrew 2010b, p. 17.

What is more interesting is that the two 'features' of artworks as commodities and assets are *indistinguishable* from one another. Normally, the purchase of an asset differs enormously from the purchase of a commodity. Commodities, whether purchased as use values or exchange values, are themselves exchanged. Assets, which are not articles of wealth but are legal claims on wealth, on the contrary, are typically exchanged without the wealth that they represent being displaced in any way. This difference is not apparent in the case of artworks. Collectors and investors in art purchase the works themselves and the works are transported to their property. Purchasing artworks as use values is different from purchasing artworks as investments, but the usual material and institutional differences between markets for goods and markets for assets is absent, hence the two transactions in the case of art are indistinguishable. Art *collectors*, who tend to buy works of art as consumers, are distinct in principle from *speculative collectors* or *investors*, who invest in artworks to achieve financial goals. In general, the two treat artworks differently. Collectors

> are generally averse to selling works that have been purchased. Investors, on the other hand, purchase works of art with distinct collecting goals in mind; however, these include the possibility of divesting and repurchasing over time to help make their collection work for them financially.[49]

But this says nothing more than that collectors collect and investors buy and sell. Whether actual individuals consistently behave according to type is another matter. Collectors sell, too, but not necessarily when it is most profitable; and sometimes investors sell at a loss to offload a bad investment. Normally, of course, an asset is acquired from different kinds of seller than a commodity. In the case of artworks, however, the form of an art commodity is exactly the same as the form of the art asset, and the collector or investor typically turn to the very same intermediaries to purchase their economically different products. In art, then, the difference between art as a commodity and art as an asset is blurred. It is impossible to tell the difference from the transaction itself or from the product exchanged. If a collector purchases art commodities as a consumer and subsequently is fortunate enough that the value of their collection increases, then it can appear that they were investors in assets all along. It is normal for investors to take some risk with their capital, but it is very unusual for consumers to be so fortunate to discover that they have unintentionally bought an asset that has appreciated in value. And, on average, this is not standard for consumers of art, either, but since art commodities are

49   McAndrew 2010b, p. 14.

indistinguishable from art assets, it is inevitable in some cases because, as we have noted, some artworks appreciate in value.

Not all big profits at auction are made by collectors, entrepreneurs and finance capitalists. At the end of 2009 at a contemporary art auction at Sotheby's, a self-portrait that Warhol had given to Cathy Naso, his secretary in the 1960s, went for over $6 million. Naso received this work as a gift, so is neither an investor nor a collector. One does not become an investor retrospectively by being fortunate enough to own something of value that can be sold to raise funds. Warhol, presumably, made the gift partly with the possibility in mind that Naso would one day be able to cash it in and support herself with the proceeds, but Naso purchased nothing, so the artwork was not an asset while it was in her possession since it was not purchased with capital for the purpose of accumulation. Naso's $6 million is a windfall. If Naso had purchased the Warhol self-portrait, either for a nominal amount or at full cost, because, let us say, it was her favourite piece, then the auction sale would still be a windfall. If, however, Naso had had the foresight to take possession of the work, either for free or at a price, with the express aim of converting it into a tidy sum for her retirement, then she would have owned an asset and been, in this regard, a speculative investor. Reselling commodities is not unusual. There is a second hand market for most durables. One does not become an investor by selling off one's old television to make room for a new one, nor does the car one owns turn out to be an asset rather than a commodity because one trades it in to purchase a new one. The difference between a commodity and an asset is not determined by whether or not they are resold, but whether they are purchased with capital or revenue. If we assume that the Sculls purchased their enormous collection of contemporary art with revenue, the resale of those works in the controversial auction does not convert the works into assets, does not convert their original outlay into capital, and nor does it convert the collectors into investors. Ordinarily, of course, reselling commodities on the second hand market realises less than the full amount of the original purchase price, but the principle is no different for reselling commodities that, for whatever reason, fetch higher prices than the original expenditure on them. Given that, as standard disclaimers make perfectly clear, the value of investments can go down as well as up, the actual accomplishment of profit is not, in itself, the determining factor of what counts as an investment.

The value of artworks appreciate on average at around 0.7 percent per year in Baumol's empirical study of the fluctuating prices of artworks over a 300 year time period. This is an indication of the anomalousness of art assets. Although art asset managers claim that art can produce returns of about 30 percent, this is based on their alleged ability to select those artworks that will appreciate and not get lumbered with those artworks which merely hold their value or, heaven forbid, lose value. Seen as a whole, the appreciation of artworks as assets, whether paltry or spectacular, appears to be independent of the production of new value. If the art market grows, as it has over recent decades, is this nothing more than a measure of increasing amounts of revenue being used up in it? Dealers can purchase works relatively cheaply and sell them for enormous sums. The difference in price, as Marx puts it, is 'coaxed out of the pockets' of other capitalists. When a dealer sells a work for £15 million that was purchased a few years earlier for £20,000, the profit derives entirely from the pockets of the new owner of the work. The difference between the relatively cheap art of artworks that have not yet secured a reputation, and the relative expensiveness of the same work later on, is based on the subsequent (and costly) accumulation of non-economic evaluation of the work in academic, critical and theoretical debates, as well as a sequence of exhibitions, reviews, publications and so on. This leads, retrospectively, to the increased rarity of 'early work' that is subsequently re-priced in relation to the prices of the mature work.

When the price of artists' works rise and fall this is due, if we are talking about average prices, to the general state of the art market or, if we are talking about uneven changes, variations in the artist's reputation. I am concerned, here, exclusively with the latter. We can begin to understand the source of the differential prices of artworks by examining the 'lot notes' to sales of art at auction. The lot notes for Christies' sale of Andreas Gursky's photograph 'Rhein II' estimated between £2.5–£3.5 million, but which realised £4.338 million, consisted of over 1700 words derived from the writing and opinions of five academics and two major artists. The lot notes for one of Alexander Calder's mobiles include a passage from Jean-Paul Sartre on Calder and a comment by Duchamp. The 'lot description' of an artwork not only includes details of the work's production and provenance, but a bibliography and a list of exhibitions in which the work has been included. Auction houses write up 'lot descriptions' and 'lot notes' to indicate the reputation of an artist or work by documenting the work's selection by curators and museums and quoting authorities referring to them. 'Lot notes' can be added to Paul Wood's list of the 'support structures of art',[50] which he suggests, following Michael Carter, are 'the source of art's exchange value'.[51] Carter refers to the critical and historical material brought together in 'lot notes' as the 'valorisation of the Art work (and

---

50   Wood in Nelson and Shiff 1996, p. 401.
51   Wood in Nelson and Shiff 1996, p. 402.

of the artist)'.[52] What is important, for Carter, is a specific process, or range of processes, by which scholarship and critical attention are cashed in with the 'transformation of such interest into economic value',[53] analogous to how 'that indeterminate quality "market confidence" is so crucial to the rise and fall of the stock market'.[54] Although this process of transformation establishes a powerful link between scholarship and art's economy, it is also significant that this relationship puts the economic in the hands of the non-economic, and places the market mechanism within a broader social and cultural framework in which non-market mechanisms, including discursive mechanisms, are dominant. Carter consistently gives such discourses causal priority over art's economy, saying 'the complex systems of revalorization ... impinge on the market, creating oscillations in economic value'.[55]

Baudrillard argues that the art auction is an aristocratic mechanism that is organised around 'sign value' rather than 'exchange value', saying 'the auction of the work of art has this notable characteristic: that economic exchange value ... is exchanged there for a pure sign, the painting'.[56] Paying large sums of money for these 'pure signs', according to Baudrillard, the art auction is 'the competitive field of the destruction of economic value for the sake of another type of value'.[57] Forgetting, of course, that the value paid for art is preserved in the artwork, Baudrillard exaggerates the antagonism between exchange value and sign value in order to stress that 'in the art auction, at the moment of bidding, exchange value and use value are no longer correlated according to an economic calculus'.[58] Baudrillard locates the auction and the art it sells 'beyond economics',[59] explaining, 'here it is not a question of the expanded reproduction of capital and the capitalist class; it is a question of the production of a caste by the collective grace of a play of signs'.[60] With 'lot notes' or something very much like them in mind, Baudrillard riffs on the aristocratic theme by claiming that the art auction discriminates its products by reference to their 'pedigree',[61] not restricted to their 'birth' and the artist's signature that testifies to their origin, but also 'the aura of [their] successive

---

52   Carter 1990, p. 105.
53   Ibid.
54   Ibid.
55   Carter 1990, p. 114.
56   Baudrillard 1981, p. 112.
57   Baudrillard 1981, p. 113.
58   Baudrillard 1981, p. 116.
59   Baudrillard 1981, p. 119.
60   Ibid.
61   Baudrillard 1981, p. 120.

transactions'.[62] Baudrillard is presumably aware that pedigree strictly speaking cannot be acquired in the way that artworks accumulate value through a series of purchases, exhibitions, and so forth, but his exaggeration has a distinct purpose: the aristocratic value of pedigree establishes art and its purchase at auction as 'beyond value'.[63]

Baudrillard goes some way towards a theory of the significance of the non-economic in the valorisation of art, but he falls back onto a Western Marxist style argument when he turns his attention to the relationship between art museums and auctions: 'Museums play the role of banks in the political economy of paintings'.[64] Baudrillard does not go beyond analogy in this argument and fails to establish whether the mechanisms by which an art museum selects, purchases and hangs works corresponds to the mechanisms by which the national bank controls the money supply, sets monetary policy, or acts as the lender of last resort. If it is true that 'the museum acts as an agency guaranteeing the universality of painting',[65] what needs to be explained is how this is accomplished, specifically by understanding the mechanisms through which museums either produce or respond to changes in the assessment and judgement of artworks. Museum purchases and exhibitions appear in 'lot notes' because they are evidence of high levels of esteem, expert scrutiny and scholarly attention. In this sense the fact that an artwork has been hosted by a national museum can only serve the purpose of 'lot notes' to secure the place of the work in the discourses and history of art if the museum is seen as a place of scholarly activity not merely as a bank.

In similar fashion, dealers will display books, magazines, catalogues, articles and other material as evidence of the artist's reputation among critics and scholars. Investment groups also refer directly to art historical judgements and other scholarship prominently within their published information on the assets that they hold. Gallerists are very keen for artists in their 'stable' to win awards such as the Turner Prize, the Northern Art Prize, the Creative Time Prize, various Jerwood awards, the Deutsche Borse photography prize, the Leonore Annenberg Prize, and so on. Also gallerists want their artists to be selected for the Venice Biennale, Manifesta, the Berlin Biennial and other biennials and triennials. Being included in a major curated exhibition and to be given solo exhibitions at public, national and international museums is also valued. These accolades are seen as awarded for merit, and therefore provide

---

62   Ibid.
63   Baudrillard 1981, p. 122.
64   Ibid.
65   Ibid.

a measure of judgements of quality about the artist's work and contribution to the field. It is expected that such expressions of professional and expert opinion can be converted into commercial success, increasing prices as well as the quantity of demand for an artist's work. These are the kind of events in the life of an artwork or an artist that Carter refers to as a 'set of mechanisms' through which art is re-interpreted and re-evaluated, explaining that what we call a change in 'taste' 'is in fact these two operations compressed into a single disposition towards the Art of a particular epoch'.[66] If it is true, as Carter argues, that these re-interpretations and re-evaluations 'broaden out to effect the economic value of Art works',[67] then we need to look at the non-economic processes of judging art and the non-market mechanisms of research (in art practice, writing and curating) that bring value (or take it away) from artworks, artists and types of art.

If art's prices have anything to do with labour as the source of value, then the most likely factor to study would be not the living labour of artists and assistants in their studios but the *reproduction* costs of artistic labour. A mature artist with an impressive exhibition history and critical acclaim is, in effect, a costly thing to reproduce. Just as skilled workers are paid more than unskilled workers because this kind of labour costs more to reproduce, the cost of reproducing a successful, mature, reputable, established artist with hundreds of important exhibitions and a bibliography to match is expressed in the price of their works. As the commodity labour power we can understand that an artist with such a career would be able to command higher prices for works or commissions than an artist just starting out, but this is not the whole story. This explanation of the high prices of artworks as reflecting the high reproduction costs of their labour, which can be found partly in Diederichsen, presents an immediate difficulty, which Diederichsen misses. Whereas the increase in the value of skilled labour is determined by training and education undergone by the labourer individually, the success of an artist's career is due to a range of factors outside their control. The forces which determine the increase or decrease in prices of artworks are external to the labour that produces them. The reputation of an artist is not a quality which is contained in their labour or even their training. Prices of artworks fluctuate according to the reputation of the artist. Practitioners and commentators sustain value in artworks through productive practices of producing objects and knowledge. Values in art are not only expressed through the economic consumption of products, but in the activities of learning from them, asking questions of them, reconfiguring them

---

66   Carter 1990, p. 114.
67   Ibid.

in new products, combining them and rejecting them. What I am suggesting here is that the increase or decrease in the price of artworks is not 'a floating crap game', but is determined by the changing circumstances of the artwork itself vis-à-vis the esteem it is held in by the art community. This is not aimless, but it is external to the commodity and also external to the artist. If I am right that prices are set by scholarly and artistic reputation, then individual works are valued economically according to the artistic value attached to it by the art world. The importance of the artist's reputation in the determination of the prices of art is a key factor in explaining the dominance of the secondary market in the economics of art. Works in the primary market tend to be seen for the first time and, therefore, have no bibliography, exhibition history, sales record, or any of the other elements that constitute a work's reputation. If it is reputation that determines prices, then works on the primary market are more risky – since the buyer cannot be certain that such works will gain the right kind of reputation. Artworks for sale at auction, by contrast, typically bring with them a string of critical appraisal by experts and a sequence of high profile and esteemed exhibitions. As such, if the source of the appreciating value of artworks has its source in labour, it is the labour of critics, commentators, art historians, experts, curators, theorists and other artists, not of the individual artist who produced the work.

We arrive, therefore, at a counterintuitive but very interesting novel conclusion for a Marxist economic analysis of the price of artworks. The economics of art must be analysed in two phases. Today's large studio factories of artworks do not require economising measures, and they do not determine the prices of artworks. This, the first phase, is a strong indication that art production, by itself, even when it is produced directly for the art market, is not commodity production according to the labour theory of value. However, we can see in the second phase that the labour of others in the field contributes to the value of a work when they write about it, exhibit it, or are influenced by it. The value of artworks appreciates proportionally to the growth of information and judgement. The value of this intellectual labour does not disappear without being expressed in prices somehow, but the collector or investor does not pay for the labour of those who increase the value of their holdings, hence the capitalist benefits from it *gratis*, and the escalating prices of artworks are not reflected in the incomes of either artists or academics. In neoclassical economics these can be counted among the externalities of art. In Marxist economics, we can say, perhaps, art historians, critics, scholars, academics, curators and other artists produce relative surplus value for art. Art scholarship is a form of consumption of art, as well as a productive industry in itself. It is strange within the labour theory of value to think that an act of consumption added value to a product, but in fact no value is added at all, even though the prices of artworks appreciate. The difference in price is not extracted from labour but, as Marx puts it when talking about trade as a zero sum game, is 'coaxed' out of the pockets of another capitalist. But if I am right that prices are set by scholarly reputation, then individual works are valued according to the value attached to it by the art world. This is not aimless, but it is external to the commodity and also external to the artist. The importance of the artist's reputation in the determination of the prices of art is a key factor, I would argue, in the dominance of the secondary market in the economics of art.

The prices of artworks are seriously affected – perhaps even driven – by the non-purchasing 'consumers' of art, namely academics, commentators and other artists, that determine the general reputation of artworks. If we want to understand the prices of artworks at the marketplace we need to focus our attention on art's evaluative discourses, the production of knowledge, and the practices of producing objects that provide an assessment and legacy for a work or body of work. Values in art are not only expressed through the economic consumption of products, but in the activities of learning from them, asking questions of them, reconfiguring them in new products, combining them and rejecting them. The high prices of art derive from the high status of the work within the discourses of art. We are back, then, with the concept of value in its broadest sense, combining economic value and normative values including aesthetic value and what Llewellyn Smith called 'art value'. Rather than demonstrating art's incorporation into the trading practices of the luxury market, what we find is the opposite: that the luxury trade for art is utterly dependent on the value attributed to art through the non-market mechanisms of art's discourses. Prices are set by scholarship, we might say. At first sight, the suggestion that the prices of artworks are determined by reputation seems unorthodox and fanciful. The labour theory of value is not designed to explain how the value of a product is determined by the esteem that it acquires in the process of its professional consumption by those who do not purchase it in a marketplace, but we must remember that the fluctuations in price that we are trying to explain here do not imply fluctuations in value understood as average necessary labour time. Art scholarship is a form of non-economic consumption of art, as well as a productive industry in itself, that is one of the main sources of art's fluctuating prices, but no value is added at all, even though the prices of artworks appreciate. The difference in price is not extracted from labour but is conjured out of the bank accounts of another capitalist. What we need to explain when faced with the appreciation of artworks are the mechanisms by which this conjuring takes place. The cynic who believes that art's discourses are equivalent to marketing must explain two things. First, why the writers and the like are economically independent from the producers and owners of art rather than employed directly by the interested parties and charged with specific marketing briefs and so on. And second, why writers and so on are willing to increase the value of artworks without being paid to do so by the owners of those goods who benefit from their work. The answer is quite simple: it is a condition of the contribution of art discourse to the inflation of the value of art that it is independent from the economic interests at stake. Paradoxically, the critics and historians of art find themselves much more intimately tied to the economics of art than the immediate economic transactions of their profession would indicate. Value in its fullest sense cannot be excluded from the economic analysis of art if the prices of artworks increase because they are valued as artworks. The main determinant of price in art is opinion: when opinion changes about a work, then its price is affected. The reason that van Gogh's paintings were once almost worthless and now are almost priceless is that van Gogh has come to occupy a pivotal role within the history of art. If art in the future took such a course as to render van Gogh's contribution nullified, then the price of his works would plummet. Value is everything in the pricing of artworks. An economics of art that distances itself from value isolates itself from the mechanisms of pricing in art.

Does the appreciation of value in artworks represent the picking of pockets in a zero sum game or the production of new value derived from surplus labour – perhaps the unpaid labour of the academics, scholars and artists whose reflections on art do so much in increasing its value? Given that artworks are not produced in the first place according to the capitalist mode of production, it is difficult to see how art in the secondary market could appreciate through surplus labour or new value. Certainly, artists exert no additional labour on artworks once they enter the market as commodities, and prices rise considerably more after an artist dies, so it seems highly unlikely that labour can have any part to play in the explanation of the appreciation of art as an asset class. Ruling out artistic labour as the cause of art's appreciation as an asset does not mean concluding that art's prices are the result of nothing but speculation. It is by assuming that speculation takes over that economists come to believe that art prices float about anchorlessly, according to the whims, tastes and determination of collectors. However, I have suggested, here, that we might develop a new anchored explanation of art prices, based on the labour of academics, commentators, artists and scholars who contribute to the reputation of artists and artworks. This does not change the fact that any gains in the art trade must be derived in a zero sum game from the pockets of other collectors since these commentators and taste-makers, even if they are paid to write reviews, catalogue essays and books, do not produce surplus value by being employed by the collectors who benefit from their work. The seller of a £20 million painting who purchased it for £10 million simply pockets £10 million of somebody else's money. The productive capitalist, on the other hand, who advances £10 million on wages and the means of production, and who subsequently pockets £10 from sales of £20 million, can only do so by selling commodities worth £20 million. That is to say, the productive capitalist does not buy cheap and sell dear, but buys labour which produces value over and above its cost in wages. This distinction cannot be drawn by mainstream economics, which rejects the concept of value altogether, dismisses the labour theory of value in particular, and looks at prices as determined by subjective judgements of marginal utility. Without a concept of value, especially of new value, a theory of the pricing of art assets is hampered from the start because art's economic exceptionalism as an asset that appreciates in the way that it does can only be understood in terms of its unusual relationship to value production. We have seen that art is economically exceptional in its production, sales and consumption, and we have seen that it is exceptional as an asset, too. But these findings are at risk if current theories of value production after the alleged demise of Fordism can be ratified. It is therefore to theories of post-Fordism that I now turn.

CHAPTER 11

Art and Post-Fordism

The political and economic theory of post-Fordism typically argues that the analysis of the three volumes of *Capital* has been superseded by events. If it is true then this casts a shadow over the second part of this book and the possibility of a Marxist analysis of the economic exceptionalism of art that I have outlined. Some Marxists and most post-Marxists argue that capitalism is no longer based on industrial production dominated by the economic confrontation between capitalist and proletariat, capital and labour. Assigning emphasis to the mode of production, now pejoratively known as 'productivism', has been superseded by financialisation and post-industrialism, it is argued. Service personnel, creatives and information workers have allegedly become the dominant type of worker in post-Fordist society. This kind of work is not new, of course, but it appears to have taken centre stage in the new economy. Marx has been accused of 'productivism', and the theories of labour, surplus value and the capitalist mode of production that Marx developed have likewise been seen as no longer adequate to the post-Fordist economy. With capitalism becoming cultural, Marx appears to have put undue emphasis on the so-called 'real' economy rather than on the business of circulation and finance that Marx described as 'unproductive' and 'fictitious', respectively. What happens, then, to the Marxist economic analysis of labour, including artistic labour, when the super-profit of global capitalism appears to be independent of surplus labour? If art is economically exceptional because artistic labour has not been subsumed by capital, then does art become more central to the new economy when the productive capitalist extraction of surplus value from productive labour is, or appears to be, marginal to contemporary capitalism? And, if capitalism has become cultural, has art's economic exceptionalism become obsolete?

Since the French Regulationist school of economics set about to divide the history of capitalism into a variety of regimes of capital – short lived modes of regulation that permit a certain level of cohesion within capitalism as a social system – the Marxist theory of capital has come to appear too general (as if an account of one regulation of capitalism is meant to apply to all regulations of capitalism). This approach to the social history of economic systems is as careful to differentiate geographical modes of capitalism, attending to the differences, for instance, between an Anglo-Saxon form of capitalism and a Rhenish-type capitalism. One of the core arguments in this body of thought

© KONINKLIJKE BRILL NV, LEIDEN, 2015 | DOI 10.1163/9789004288157_013

concerns 'the demise of the mode of regulation known as Fordism'.[1] However, the Italian heterodox Marxist theory of post-Fordism has a closer association with the economics of art and culture, so I will focus my attention on that in this chapter. What the heterodox Italian Left in the 1960s and 1970s argued was that the Socialist and Communist parties as well as the unions had underestimated the changes that had taken place within industry. Raniero Panzieri and Mario Tronti established the *Quaderni Rossi* as a platform for setting about the reassessment. 'The existence of a new working class with needs and behaviours no longer commensurate with either those of the labour movement or capital was a theme that ran through nearly all of the major essays published in *Quaderni Rossi*.[2] Antonio Negri joined them for the second issue of the journal, focusing in particular on questions related to machinery which turned out to be essential to the reconfiguration of Marxist economics in post-Fordist thinking.

Many of the debates within *operaismo* were concerned with tactical questions about the struggle of the new working class. Paolo Virno's interpretation of events links the emergence of new social forms to the changing economic circumstances of post-Fordist labour. Negri, writing with Felix Guattari, argues that the traditional left has been superseded within post-Fordism 'by the collective-singular movements which have emerged ... as the bearers of social transformation ... reflected in the increase of marginal and part-time precarious workers, as well as other numerous minorities who reject the status quo'.[3] Precarity becomes the central theme by which to understand the political response to post-Fordism that superseded the traditional left. In retrospect, we can acknowledge that Berardi, Hardt and Virno perceive the new political and economic situation expressed in the Movement of '77 in terms that come to define the politics of precarity.

'What are the principal qualities demanded of wage labourers today?'[4] asks Virno. His answer is an anatomy of precarity: habitual mobility, keeping pace with rapid change, adaptability and flexibility. 'Uprooting', he says, 'constitutes the substance of our contingency and precariousness'.[5] But whereas 'uprooting' may once have been rare, occasional and traumatic, today it is common, frequent and mundane. 'Precariousness is no longer a marginal and provisional characteristic, but it is the general form of the labor relation in a productive,

---

1   Aglietta 1998, p. 44.
2   Wright 2002, p. 46.
3   Guattari and Negri 2010, pp. 39–40.
4   Virno and Hardt 1996, p. 14.
5   Virno and Hardt 1996, p. 31.

digitalized sphere, reticular and recombinant',[6] Bifo says. Precarity appears to be the new condition for the wage labourer, but it is also the condition of the unwaged, the freelance worker, the unemployed, the redundant worker, the intern, the carer and the student. Angela Mitropoulus points out that precarious work, in the form of domestic, affective, care and sex work, is nothing new at all.[7]

Precarity is not new, nor is it restricted to the post-Fordist labour market. Bifo, in fact, regards Fordism as anomalous in securing non-precarious labour for a brief historical period. Before Fordism, and not only after it, precarity is the condition of the majority. 'With the decline in the political force of the workers' movement', Bifo says, 'the natural precariousness and brutality of labor relations in capitalism have re-emerged'.[8] There are two distinct political interpretations of precariousness. One reads precarity as the effect of changes in the post-Fordist economy, while the other sees precarity as the result of the refusal to work. Compare the following two remarks. 'To function effectively as a component of just-in-time production', Mark Fisher says, 'you must develop a capacity to respond to unforeseen events, you must learn to live in conditions of total instability, or "precarity", as the ugly neologism has it'.[9] Virno, by contrast, says precarity was brought about 'when the young labor-power ... chose temporary and part-time work over full-time employment in big corporations ... giving rise to the eclipse of industrial discipline and allowing for the establishing of a certain degree of self-determination'.[10]

'In the sphere of semiotic-capital and cognitive labour', Bifo tells us in his book *Precarious Rhapsody*, 'when a product is consumed, instead of disappearing it remains available, while its value increases the more its use is shared'.[11] Bifo reprises Adam Smith's interest in labour exerted without a vendible product, Say's remarks on immaterial labour and immaterial products, but not as puzzling marginalia to the analysis of wealth production proper; here, the immaterial has ousted material production. Note, however, the ambiguity in the final phrase: value does not appear to refer to 'exchange value' or socially necessary labour time, or any other specific form of value. And yet, value increases, it seems, through a strange kind of accumulation of unpaid use. Since value is allegedly augmented through the free use of information goods that

6   Berardi 2011, p. 88.
7   See Mitropoulus in Berry-Slater 2005, pp. 12–18.
8   Berardi 2011, p. 89.
9   Fisher 2009, p. 34.
10   Virno 2004, p. 70.
11   Berardi 2009b, p. 59.

share the qualities of public goods (see Chapter 4), the exploitation of labour (itself bought and sold as a commodity on the labour market) appears to lose its place within the new economy. It is not production but circulation that is posited as the sphere in which value of an unspecified kind is increased through shared use. 'The analytic separation between the economic sphere and consciousness enjoyed an actual foundation when productive labor was structurally separate from intellectual labor',[12] Bifo explains, before claiming that this division has dissolved. But, if the production of value 'is not to be considered as a purely economic process, governed exclusively by laws of exchange'[13] then capitalism no longer requires wage labour to generate profits and therefore the economic position of the working class becomes ever more precarious. We know that wages have not risen in real terms since the 1970s, that working conditions have not improved, that unions have been attacked, while redundancies, unemployment and outsourcing have become fixtures within the affluent nations. The question is whether this increased precarity is a result of the emergence of semio-capitalism or of more mundane shifts within the capitalist mode of production such as the political programme of neoliberalism and the deregulation of world markets. Regardless of the reasons for it, however, it is evident that precarity has become a conspicuous feature of labour in the last three or four decades. The Italian heterodox left were absolutely right to oppose the strategy of the official left in the 1970s that 'aimed at pitting the workers who have a regular job against the irregular, unemployed, precarious, underpaid young proletarians'.[14] In response to this, Bifo tells us, the young protestors shouted 'we are all precarious'. This is a correct political assessment but it is also economically correct, despite the fact that Fordism had temporarily given the impression that capitalism was capable of providing security for its workforce. However, the joint demand of 'zerowork for income' and 'automate all production'[15] did not resolve the problem of who was to produce the machines to do all the work. Precarity can be welcomed as a condition that corresponds to the 'refusal of work'[16] or rejected as the imposed condition of a working class under attack (see, for instance, the Precarious Workers Brigade's demand for non-precarity), but only an economic rather than a political analysis can determine if it signals an historical shift from Fordism to post-Fordism.

---

12   Berardi 2009b, p. 67.
13   Ibid.
14   Berardi 2009b, p. 23.
15   Berardi 2009b, p. 25.
16   Berardi 2009a, p. 28.

The case for the economic shift from Fordism to post-Fordism is based primarily on transitions in the labour market, the morphology of labour, the ontology of the commodity, the technologies of manufacture, consumption and distribution, the scope of the market, and the geography of production. Tronti locates the transition within the factory itself: 'When the assembly-island replaces the assembly-line in the great automated factory ... we enter the post-Fordist phase'.[17] Robotisation, small expert crews, total quality management, lean manufacturing, just in time delivery, and flexible contracts redefine the workplace. And outside the factory there is, perhaps, an even bigger shift, 'from industry to service, from employment to self-employment, from security to precarity, from the refusal to work to the lack of it'.[18] It is important to understand these oppositions not only as distinguishing current economic practices from those set up by Ford in the beginning of the twentieth century, but also against the analysis of Gramsci who coined the term 'Fordism' within the Italian Marxist context of the 1930s. Italian Marxists coined post-Fordism, therefore, within the specifically Italian Marxist tradition in which Gramsci was somewhat irksome.[19] By the time that Gramsci wrote 'Americanism and Fordism', the standardised mass production of automobiles had already been successfully challenged by a new focus on consumer choice by General Motors. Car production before Fordism was exclusively in the hands of craftsmen trained in the bicycle and carriage shops. Within three months of the introduction of the assembly line in 1914 the production of a Model T had accelerated to ten times the rate of 1908, and by 1925 Ford could produce the yearly output of 1908 in a day. But there was a hitch. Workers hated to work on assembly lines

---

17   Tronti 2010, p. 188.
18   Tronti 2010, pp. 188–9.
19   Negri talks about how Gramsci was said to have 'anticipated' everything the Communist
        Party did. It is not only Fordism that is superseded in post-Fordism but also the economic
        and political horizon of Gramsci's essay 'Americanism and Fordism' from 1934. Fordism
        for Gramsci combined rationalisation, socialisation and organisation of the production
        process with the rationalisation and re-organisation of subjectivity and society. This was a
        complex and contradictory new settlement in which capitalism's tendency to crisis could
        be averted, thus preserving capitalism, but at the same time was opposed to the con-
        tinued existence of the rentier class of landed gentry, clerics and other economic para-
        sites that Gramsci argued were a political and economic obstacle to the development of
        Europe. In place of the irrationalities, mystifications, traditions and hierarchies of pre-
        capitalist society, Fordism appeared to promise planning, co-operation and modernity – a
        prelude to communism. The regulation of private life, including sexual restraint, sobriety
        and physical health are key to Ford's paternalistic and intrusive treatment of his workers,
        but they are also, according to Gramsci, vital elements of any future communist society.

which meant that retention rates for employees at Ford were extremely poor. Ford solved this problem, famously, by introducing a standard wage of $5 for an eight-hour day in 1914. Retaining employees guaranteed uninterrupted production, and so secure employment, which was welcomed by the unions, was precisely the kind of labour relations policy that Fordist production required. Secure employment and decent wages become synonymous with Fordism, and therefore the return to precarity becomes synonymous with post-Fordism. What is more, by the 1930s, Ford's standardised product and his direct planning and control system had been superseded by innovations in marketing and organisation at General Motors under the leadership of Alfred Sloan. Instead of the standardised and uniform production line, Sloan devised a multi-product, or M-form, organisation of a company made up of separate divisions serving distinct product markets. But what contemporary post-Fordist theory has its eye on is not the nascent consumerism of GM but the flexible production system known as Toyotism or lean manufacturing. Stock is purchased little and often; products and parts are produced on demand rather than mass produced and stored. The labour of the Toyota Production System is based on multiskilling, worker flexibility, and nurtures a bond between educated and motivated employees and the company. The key elements of post-Fordist economic theory have their roots here.

The most important contribution of the Italian post-Fordist re-equipment of Marxist economic theory is the concept of 'immaterial labour' established by Maurizio Lazzarato and developed by Negri and Virno. Lazzarato defines immaterial labour as 'labor that produces the informational and cultural content of the commodity'.[20] Negri (alone and in collaboration with Hardt) defines immaterial labour, as Say did, either as that kind of labour that is immaterial (intellectual, affective emotional, informational) or as the labour that produces a kind of product that is immaterial (his list reads: 'knowledge, information, communication, a relationship, or an emotional response').[21] Virno characterises immaterial labour, in deliberately sharp contrast with the deskilled, standardised and anonymous labour of the Fordist factory, as a virtuosic and linguistic performance with no end product, which again has its precedent in Say's observations on the immaterial labour of talented advocates, judges and painters. 'Activities that have been part of leisure time should now be included in the economic sphere', Zravko Kobe tells us, with the example of the dog walker as a post-Fordist immaterial labourer. 'The principle breakthrough in

20   Lazzarato 1996, p. 133.
21   Hardt and Negri 2005, p. 108.

post-Fordism is that it has placed language into the workplace',[22] says Virno. Bifo identifies the post-Fordist worker as the 'cognitarian'. If the unskilled factory worker was the standard bearer of labour in Marxist and Fordist thinking, the new economy pushed a very different character to the fore, namely the educated and highly skilled, perhaps even talented, freelance worker in 'audiovisual production, advertising, fashion, the production of software, photography, cultural activities, and so forth'.[23] While Fordism brought the private life of the worker under the scrutiny, control and organisation of the paternal productive capitalist, actively constructing a productive *character* for the worker, post-Fordism extends work into leisure, spare time, domesticity, intimate interactions and personality, profiting from unpaid work that is impossible to separate from paid work. As Virno says, the dividing line between labour and non-labour disintegrates in post-Fordism. Immaterial labour is not only harder for the capitalist to break down and re-organise, it is harder for the worker to identify and therefore to separate work from everyday life, making it impossible to 'clock off'. This is why, in Tronti's words, 'the changed conditions of contemporary work [are] fragmentation, dispersion, individualization, precarisation'.[24]

Wolfgang Haug doubts whether the concept of immaterial labour can be stretched beyond its original referent to the students who occupied their universities when the heterodox Italian left first identified this movement as the new subject of social change. 'This was the birth-hour of "post-workerism". It declared that students are "immaterial workers" and then expanded this concept to include ever more groups'.[25] This expansion, Haug argues, gets out of hand. Negri, along with other Italian post-workerists, he says, 'never tires of using "immaterial labour" as a collect-all concept for all post-Fordist labour'.[26] It might be politically expedient to call students 'immaterial labourers' (to place students in the place of the working class without them actually – materially – having to become wage labourers) but it is not at all clear that labour can be considered immaterial except as a vague and inaccurate category. Lazzarato, in fact, abandoned the term that he coined precisely because distinguishing between 'the material and the immaterial was a theoretical complication we were never able to resolve'.[27] The concept of immaterial labour appears, in fact, to be an oxymoron. 'Ideas about the specific kinds of work to be included

22   Virno 2004, p. 91.
23   Lazzarato 1996, p. 137.
24   Tronti 2010, p. 189.
25   Haug 2009, p. 182.
26   Haug 2009, p. 177.
27   Quoted in Noys 2010, p. 138.

under this concept [immaterial labour] are hazy and shifting',[28] according to
Sean Sayers. Affective labour, which includes hospitality, caring, legal work
and entertainment, is meant to have an immaterial result (manipulating feelings rather than raw materials), but Sayers points out that while none 'of these
activities is primarily aimed at creating a material product...they are formative activities nonetheless'.[29] That is to say, they bring about real changes in the
world, not just changes to the way people think and feel. What is more, Sayers
reminds us, Marx had a dialectical understanding of labour in which

> all 'immaterial' labor necessarily involves material activity [and] all mate-
> rial labor is 'immaterial' in the sense that it alters not only the material
> worked upon but also subjectivity and social relations.[30]

Sayers concludes: 'There is no clear distinction between material and immaterial [labour]'.[31]

The claim that contemporary work is immaterial and the related claim that
Marxist economics and politics (which post-Fordists characterise as having
a 'productivist' bias) needs to be rethought as a result, is not borne out by a
close reading of Marx. Sayers responds to the post-Fordist theory of immaterial labour with a thorough analysis of Marx's differentiated theory of labour.
Sayers identifies four kinds of labour in Marx: direct appropriation (such as
fishing), agriculture (such as breeding animals), craft and industry (including the skilled transformation of raw materials), and 'universal' work (such
as administration). Is immaterial labour an additional type of labour not
included in the four kinds of labour theorised by Marx? Sayers subjects the two
most promising versions of immaterial labour, symbolic and affective labour,
to a Marxist examination. Symbolic labour, which is 'primarily intellectual
or linguistic',[32] does not directly produce an object but it remains material,
according to Sayers, for two strongly related reasons. First, it involves 'making marks on paper, agitating the air and making sounds, creating electronic
impulses in a computer system or whatever'.[33] Second, it is 'formative' and
'has material effects'. Sayers therefore turns the accusation of 'productivism'
against the advocates of immaterial labour, explaining that their error 'is to

---

28   Sayers 2007, p. 444.
29   Sayers 2007, pp. 447–8.
30   Sayers 2007, p. 448.
31   Ibid.
32   Sayers 2007, p. 445.
33   Ibid.

imagine that "immaterial" symbolic work has no material result and that only work which directly creates a tangible material product, like industry or craft, is "formative" activity'.[34]

For Marxist economics, the quality or type of labour does not in itself determine its relation to the mode of production. Intellectual, symbolic, affective and cultural labour is wage labour or not according to the social relations of production. A worker who sells their labour occupies a different place in capitalist social relations from a worker who sells her product. So-called immaterial labour either produces surplus value or not according to whether a capitalist mediates between the consumer and the producer. Lazzarato argues that post-Fordism's immaterial labour in the information economy achieves its aims 'without distinguishing between productive and unproductive [labour]'.[35] Post-Fordist theory, therefore, seeks to 'deconstruct the division [between] productive and non-productive activity'.[36] This overlaps with the feminist critique of Marx's concept of productive labour that casts 'reproductive' domestic labour as unproductive. Marina Vishmidt is among those, like Silvia Federici, who question Marx's analysis by arguing that housework, caring and affective labour was always '*directly* productive insofar as it was producing... labour power, and as such was directly inscribed in the circuits of capitalist value production'.[37] Federici says, 'the body has been for women in capitalist society what the factory has been for male waged workers: the primary ground of their exploitation and resistance'.[38] Federici's study of the transformation of the social relations of production, showing that 'the rise of capitalism was coeval with a war against women... confining women to reproductive work',[39] has made an important contribution to the social history of the transition to capitalism and the politics of labour.

There is no doubt that the material and immaterial labour of rearing children who later become productive wage labourers is necessary for the reproduction of capitalism. Unwaged reproductive labour is not unproductive in every sense of the word. Marx's concept of 'necessary labour' refers to the reproduction of labour, but this is entirely a question of the exchange value of labour's reproduction whereas reproductive labour is best understood as the use value of the reproduction of labour. Insofar as workers appear as use values to

---

34   Ibid.
35   Toscano 2007, p. 77.
36   Diefenbach in Kirn 2010, p. 64.
37   Vishmidt in Kirn 2010, p. 308.
38   Federici 2009, p. 16.
39   Federici 2009, p. 14.

capitalists, mothers can be said to produce use values. But this does not discredit the Marxist division between productive and unproductive labour (which refers exclusively to the production of profit). Children become wage labourers from which surplus value is derived, but they also add to the numbers of the unemployed, to the unproductive labour force of the administration, army, education institutions and so forth. Capitalists have mothers too. No capitalist makes a profit merely from the existence of potential wage labourers, but only, as Marx says, by putting them to work. More importantly, though, regardless of the potential surplus value that might be derived from the products of child rearing, insofar as no capitalist draws surplus value from this activity, it is, in the Marxist sense, unproductive (of profit). When childcare is commercialised and industrialised, so that parents pay professionals to look after their children, then the situation changes. Professional childminders are paid to care for children. If these workers derive their pay directly from the consumers of their labour, then they are also strictly speaking unproductive labourers, but if they are employed by an agency that profits from their labour, then they are productive of profit and are productive labourers. The deconstruction or supersession of the distinction between productive and unproductive labour cannot be achieved by claiming that certain practices are productive of something even if they do not produce surplus value. Nor is so-called immaterial labour somehow independent of the categories of productive and unproductive labour because it is informational or affective. The qualities of the labour are irrelevant to the question of whether it produces surplus value or not. Economically, the introduction of language into the workplace does not alter the relationship between capital, wages and profit.

At the very beginning of the Italian post-Fordist reimagining of the Marxist analysis of contemporary capitalism, Panzieri picked up on a remark made by Marx in Notebooks VI and VII, written in 1858, published in 1953 as the *Grundrisse* and translated into Italian in 1968–70. Marx concludes a short section on the 'contradiction between the foundation of bourgeois production ... and its development. Machines etc.' with the following paragraph:

> Nature builds no machines, no locomotives, railways, electric telegraphs, self-acting mules etc. These are products of human industry; natural material transformed into organs of the human will over nature, or of human participation in nature. They are organs of the human brain, created by the human hand; the power of knowledge, objectified. The development of fixed capital indicates to what degree general social knowledge has become a direct force of production, and to what degree, hence, the conditions of the process of social life itself have come under

the control of the general intellect and been transformed in accordance with it. To what degree the powers of social production have been produced, not only in the form of knowledge, but also as immediate organs of social practice, of the real life process.[40]

Panzieri initiated the post-Fordist fascination with this passage as early as 1961, in which the concept of 'general intellect' is identified with the new form of capitalism and the transition from capitalism to communism. General intellect refers to the exponential increase of the ratio of generally accessible knowledge in social production, for Marx, primarily as it is embodied in machines. But Negri's extensive and detailed reading[41] of the *Grundrisse* in the 1970s, published as *Marx Beyond Marx* in 1991, makes no mention of the general intellect even though it devotes a chapter to the study of 'the fragment on machines'. Although Negri eventually came to characterise post-Fordism as the *regime* of the general intellect, it was not until 1990, in the first issue of 'Luogo Commune', that the Italian heterodox left put the concept at the heart of their project. 'Since then', Haug says, 'the expression "general intellect" has functioned as one of the main identifying terms of post-workerism'.[42] Virno formulates his conception of general intellect in terms of the distinction between 'common places' and 'special places', which he borrows from Aristotle. Virno says the distribution of common and special places has recently been radically reconfigured. Today, he says, 'the "special places" of discourse and of argumentation are perishing and dissolving, while immediate visibility is being gained by the "common places", or by generic logical-linguistic forms which establish the pattern for all forms of discourse'.[43] What this means is that 'the "life of the mind" becomes, in itself, *public*'. Intellectual activity has taken on an 'exterior, collective, social character' and has become 'the true mainspring of the production of wealth'.[44] What Virno envisages is 'a multitude of thinkers'.[45]

Bifo locates the concept of the general intellect alongside and against the theory of the intellectual in Marxist political theory from Lenin through Gramsci to the post-operaists. Lenin, he says, allocated the role of class leadership to the intellectuals in the party, while Gramsci complexified this with his

40   Marx 1973, p. 706.
41   Negri says in an interview that he began reading Marx in 1962 after Panzieri 'insisted' on it (see Casarino and Negri 2008, p. 47).
42   Haug 2010, p. 213.
43   Virno 2004, p. 36.
44   Virno 2004, p. 38.
45   Virno 2004, p. 39.

concept of hegemony that required the seizure of power to engage in a process of the transformation of culture and values. 'But Gramsci remained fundamentally attached to an idea of the intellectual as an unproductive figure', Bifo says, not quite accusing Gramsci of believing that all intellectuals are unproductive *labourers*. For Bifo, the advent of the internet accomplishes a technically decisive shift in the social relations of intellectual labour that Marx had anticipated in the *Grundrisse*, with the concept of 'General Intellect'. Borrowing a phrase from Marazzi, Žižek says, the 'possibility of the privatisation of the general intellect was something Marx never envisaged'.[46] The privatisation of general intellect consists, among other things, of the now familiar phenomenon in which workers individually pay for the cost of training for the benefit of their employers.

> The result is not, as Marx seems to have expected, the self-dissolution of capitalism, but the gradual relative transformation of the profit generated by the exploitation of labour power into rent appropriated through the privatisation of this very 'general intellect'.[47]

In this theory, the general intellect is not simply a component of the means of production, like skill or raw materials, it is a new mode of production itself, what Panzieri called 'neocapitalism', and therefore post-Fordism is the 'epoch of the general intellect', as Giannoli says.[48] Knowledge becomes general at the same time that it becomes central to the economy.[49] Hardt and Negri claim that 'immaterial production has an anti-capitalist character itself, thereby divorcing the new economy's network of "affective relations" from the real subsumption of labour"'.[50] Virno distils this argument about the general intellect in the paradoxical idea of the 'communism of capital'.[51] Thus Virno captures the dialectical character of a concept derived from Marx's speculation about how social production will develop within and beyond capitalism, but applied to capitalism in the era of neoliberalism. Toscano interprets the post-operaist theory of the general intellect as an articulation of the intensification of economic value extraction, referring to the theory as 'an extension of exploita-

---

46   Žižek 2012, p. 9.

47   Žižek 2009, pp. 145–6.

48   Giannoli quoted in Haug 2010, p. 213.

49   The proposal that a certain type of labour can be anti-capitalist demonstrates a remarkable ignorance of the Marxist insight that what constitutes capital is a social relationship.

50   Roberts 2007, p. 214.

51   Virno 2004, p. 111.

tion to the whole social field (in a kind of biopolitical *hyperexploitation*)'.[52] The politics of the general intellect appears to belong to both extremes of optimistic anti-capitalism and pessimistic intensification of exploitation. The key to decoding its politics, and the relationship between art and the general intellect, I want to say, is to be found in an economic analysis.

Marx used the phrase 'general intellect' just once. Nevertheless, Haug traces its use alongside an array of similar terms such as 'general social labour', 'general scientific labour', 'the general productive forces of the human brain', 'general powers of the human head', 'general social knowledge' and 'the general state of science and the progress of technology'.[53] Marx coins the term 'general intellect' within an analysis of the unfolding dialectic of the application of science to capitalist production, which begins as an account of prevailing conditions from which is extrapolated 'the emancipatory potential of general social knowledge and intellect'.[54] Initially, science confronts the worker as an alien power of the machine, but the enormous increase in scientific and technical knowledge, on which the capitalist mode of production depends, proceeds beyond the limit of capitalism. Marx proposes that scientific and technical knowledge will be able to provide 'social wealth' in abundance, in which case surplus labour becomes marginal to social production and the precondition for capitalism dissolves. Mechanisation and automation, which enter the historical stage as the embodiment of the capitalist rationalisation of production at the expense of the subjective element of labour – the degradation of work – also prove to be the enemy of the capitalist (economically, although mechanisation and other measures increase the ratio of profit to wages, thereby increasing relative surplus value, the increased ratio of constant capital to variable capital is the basis of the tendency of the rate of profit to fall) and potentially liberates the worker. 'The Marx of the *Grundrisse* pays attention to tendencies and inquiries into empirical signs on which latent possibilities can be read', says Haug, adding:

> Even if he sees that the scientific-technical deployment of natural processes remains blocked by class-antagonistic strategies and by private strategies that compete against one another in the marketplace, which create a regime of secrecy concerning technical knowledge, and which

---

52   Toscano 2007, p. 74.
53   Haug 2010, p. 209.
54   Haug 2010, p. 210.

exclude others from its use, he also sees therein the objective possibility of a control in the sense of the 'general intellect'.[55]

Capitalism socialises production without socialising ownership and decision-making, and the same obstacle confronts the emergence of the general intellect in which, for instance, knowledge which previously belonged to an elite is embodied in smart technologies.

Digital cameras can produce technically competent images without the user having any expertise in focal length, apertures, shutter speeds and so on which had previously kept photography under the monopoly of a minority of professionals and amateur photography buffs. In the light of this example, the debate over the general intellect, it seems to me, turns on whether digital cameras (1) bring about the communism of photography (and image production in general), (2) multiply the production of imagery by establishing a mass market for the means of production of images, (3) replace individuals (such as photographers paid to take family portraits) with branded goods (Nikon, for instance) that outsource production (the owners of cameras take the pictures themselves), or (4) the technological precondition for the extraction of profits from the circulation of images by social network websites, news corporations, and so on. But there is another theoretical pillar that must be introduced in the discussion of the general intellect.

The standard account of the general intellect today follows Vercellone's three periods of capitalism. In this reading, a period of mercantilist capitalism, in which only formal subsumption is possible, is followed by a second phase, industrial capitalism, in which labour is disciplined, deskilled, routinised and degraded. Fordism is the apogee of the epoch of the real subsumption of labour. The third period Vercellone calls the crisis of the Fordist model that he calls 'cognitive capitalism'. Post-Fordism is the third stage of capitalism in which unskilled manual labour is replaced with the general intellect.[56] This third stage of capitalism is based on a shift, according to Vercellone, from profit to rent. Without distinguishing between ground rent, differential rent and absolute rent, Vercellone contextualises the post-Fordist theory of rent by setting it off from both the labour theory of value and the labour theory of rent. He is particularly critical of the argument that rent is a parasitic, pre-capitalist and unproductive form of profit, which Vercellone ascribes exclusively to

---

55   Haug 2010, p. 212.
56   See Vercellone 2005.

Marx.[57] However, the argument that rent is parasitic derives from Ricardo, not Marx, although Marx appears sometimes to take sides with Ricardo and sometimes to deviate from this position. Gramsci's disapproval of the *rentier* class is probably the displaced signified of the explicit antipathy to Marx's imputed blindness to the productive role of finance. Indeed, Gramsci's hatred of the rentier class is turned on its head by the post-Fordist affirmation of rent as a productive force. Post-Fordist theorists like Vercellone suggest that Marx misperceives rent due to the labour theory of value. It is true that rent produces no new value, but rent has a role within the capitalist mode of production. Even consumptive rent (rent paid by the consumers of goods and services such as homes and cars) converts part of revenue into profit. Productive rent (rent paid by capitalists as an overhead) can reduce start up costs, reduce risk and increase liquidity (cancelling a rental agreement can occur without finding a new purchaser to take goods off your hands). Rental payments are not parasitic and rent as revenue is not parasitic, either. Consumptive rent, which is drawn from revenue, is converted into capital. Although it does not produce new value, it redistributes wealth to landowners (typically, from the poorer to the richer, from the worker to the capitalist), and thereby converts revenue for purchasing necessities into revenue for purchasing luxuries or to be used as capital investment. Not only does rent therefore 'play an important role in stimulating effective demand',[58] but it returns money to the capitalist class.

Vercellone chooses Napoleoni as the source of his definition of rent ('the revenue that the owner of certain goods receives as a consequence of the fact that these goods are, or become, available in scarce quantities'). Marazzi quotes Quesnay's definition of rent and makes a passing reference to Ricardo. He does not invoke Marx's concept of 'differential rent' or Mandel's concepts of 'cartel rent' or 'technological rent'. Vercellone quotes Marx throughout his discussion of rent, but only to show his errors. When he wants to provide a definition of rent or some other reliable information, he quotes others. What both agree is that the 'becoming-rent of profit' is based on a twin crisis of the labour theory of value and the industrial mode of production. Hardt and Negri develop Vercellone's thesis, explaining 'why rent has become the paradigmatic economic instrument of neoliberalism and its regimes of financialisation'[59] by linking rent to externalities. Hardt and Negri illustrate their point with the example of real estate. Since the fluctuating value of real estate depends on

---

57   For a more nuanced account of Marx's relationship to Ricardo's judgement of rent as a parasitism, see Harvey 1982.

58   Harvey 1982, p. 365.

59   Hardt and Negri 2009, p. 258.

externalities, Hardt and Negri argue that they are not the result of productive labour. Rent, they say, is not determined by labour but is 'primarily determined by externalities'.[60] Positive externalities are the labour of others, of course, but they go unremunerated or at least are enjoyed for free by the beneficiary. Hardt and Negri, therefore, claim that externalities are the labour of the commons. It is with the externalities of the commons in mind that Hardt and Negri say, 'in the contemporary networks of biopolitical production, the extraction of value from the common is increasingly accomplished without the capitalist intervening in its production'.[61] But how is Hardt and Negri's rent realised? Who pays the rent? And what is the process by which value is extracted from the privatisation of the general intellect, or the common? How are the use values in their list of positive externalities – playgrounds, cultural institutions, intellectual forums, peaceful social relations, and so on – converted into exchange values or rent?

To what kind of theory of rent do Vercellone, Marazzi, Hardt and Negri, Žižek and others subscribe? What Vercellone appears to believe is that post-Fordist rent can be produced or extracted by itself. Rent separate from production is possible, of course, and consumers regularly pay such rents on houses, cars, bowling alleys, telephone services and so on. If Vercellone is basing his economics of post-Fordism on consumptive rent rather than productive rent, though, then this causes problems for his claim that rent is the new form of value production. Vercellone objects to the idea that rent is pre-capitalist, so we need to distinguish between the pre-capitalist and capitalist versions of consumptive rent. Capitalism introduces new forms of rent but also reconfigures previous forms of rent. In the case of consumptive rent before capitalism, prices are not set by self-regulated competitive markets, but custom, power, and the like. In the case of productive rent before capitalism, agricultural workers who are tenants of the landowner pay rent (either in money, a portion of the harvest, or through working part of the week cultivating products for the landlord) in the form of a surplus which can always be expressed as unpaid labour. Within capitalism, ground rent can be paid, for instance, by a capitalist farmer to a landowner, 'for the right to invest his capital in this specific sphere of production'.[62] Scarcity – though more specifically, monopoly – is a prerequisite of ground rent, but it is not the source of value or rent.

---

60   Hardt and Negri 2009, p. 154.
61   Hardt and Negri 2009, p. 140.
62   Marx 1959, p. 618.

Rent and the value of land 'develops with the market for the products of the soil',[63] Marx says. Although capital is objectified in land through fertilisation and so on, ground rent is not the interest paid on this fixed capital. Since 'the earth is not a product of labour and therefore has no value',[64] the price of land, Marx says, 'is nothing but the capitalized income from the lease of the land'.[65] Ground rent is 'paid for the *use* of the land'.[66] Hence, it is within this argument about the relation between rent and labour that Marx reiterates the classical theory of exceptionalism with the significant innovation that he does not speak of the 'fancy prices' of antiques and works of art, but the fact that they have *no value*.[67] Rent, for Marx, derives principally from things that have no value. In addition, the concept of differential rent explains the process by which super profits can be made through monopolies or structural scarcity in which the highest price of production becomes the average price, therefore allowing the most cost efficient producers to earn profit on top of surplus value. Monopoly rent is the difference between the value and the price of goods that are overpriced due to blockages in competition. Monopoly ownership cannot demand r without having to bother with c+v+s. Monopoly super profits, including 'cartel rent', derive from a blockage on competitiveness in which several formally competing firms agree to unify prices so that the company among them with the lowest productivity can realise the socially average rate of profit. Cartel rent is only one kind of monopoly super profit, though. Single monopolies of specific sectors of the economy and oligopolistic markets, for instance, have their own distinctive mechanisms for generating super profits. Post-Fordist economics puts these differences aside.

As we already noted in Chapter 3, the concept of differential rent, which Ricardo introduced and Marx completed, 'was the point of departure of the marginal theories of value which, in the second half of the nineteenth century,

---

63   Marx 1959, p. 637.
64   Marx 1959, p. 623.
65   Marx 1959, p. 625.
66   Marx 1959, p. 619. (emphasis added).
67   "'Finally, it should be borne in mind in considering the various forms of manifestation of ground-rent, that is, the lease money paid under the heading of ground-rent to the landlord for the use of the land for purposes of production or consumption, that the price of things which have in themselves no value, i.e., are not the product of labour, such a land, or which at least cannot be reproduced by labour, such as antiques and works of art by certain masters, etc., may be determined by many fortuitous combinations. In order to sell a thing, nothing more is required than its capacity to be monopolized and alienated' (Marx 1959, p. 633).

challenged the labour theory of value'.[68] It was a theory of rent that ousted the labour theory of value in the marginal revolution. This event is echoed in the post-Fordist theory of the 'becoming-rent of profit' and therefore carries within it the context of pre-Fordist neoclassicism. The problem is not that the heterodox left might be drawing on 'bourgeois economics', but that they are repeating old mistakes. In effect, the attempt to drive out talk about the relationship between labour and value with a generalised theory of rent is not just an utterly conservative gesture that sits snugly within the mainstream economic tradition; it is a repetition of errors long since diagnosed. Mandel's criticism of marginal theory is eerily prescient to the current discussion: it is a mistake to transform the specific theory of ground rent 'into a general theory of value'.[69] According to Mandel this project is based on two errors. First, 'it leaves out the *special conditions of property in land* which give rise to ground rent';[70] second, 'it leaves out the different institutional conditions that govern ownership of land, ownership of capital and "ownership of labour power", respectively'.[71] These special conditions and differences in forms of ownership must still be taken into account even though, as Mandel says in a footnote (and in a later chapter), 'a mechanism comparable to that of ground rent regulates *monopoly profit* in the present phase [mid-1970s] of capitalism'.[72]

Rent in post-Fordism is the augmented return of money capital to money capital without an active or direct role in production. This theory is not borne out by the economic analysis of cognitive labour. Data workers, speaker labourers, cognitarians, affective workers, immaterial labourers, virtuoso workers and the whole of the precariat is either waged labour paid for by productive capital or it is not. A call centre with a contract for the outsourced customer services department of a bank consists of productive labourers whose aggregate pay is below the agreed fee for the service acquired by the bank. The surplus value of speaker labourers, therefore, is derived according to the same formula as obtains for all productive capital. Any income drawn from the privatisation of digital space is rent paid from advertising budgets. Companies who advertise pay the landlord a rental payment for using a space for a given period of time. Rent is also paid by internet users: charges paid to telephone companies for internet access can be called rent but these monies do not arrive in the accounts of the software companies. The small percentage of a transaction on eBay that goes to the internet host can be called rent, too. However,

---

68   Mandel 1977, p. 298.
69   Ibid.
70   Ibid.
71   Ibid.
72   Mandel 1977, p. 299n.

post-Fordist theory conflates the payments made by companies to advertise on the net with the non-paying and unpaid activities of users, and confuses the unpaid production of IKEA customers in assembling their furniture with the allegedly value-creating activity of someone updating their status on Facebook.

Marazzi says, 'today's rent is subsumable to profit precisely *in virtue* of financialisation processes themselves'.[73] There is no doubt that finance capital and merchant capital have gained considerable advantages over productive capital, but it is, at best, an exaggeration to conclude that capitalism is no longer based on the extraction of value from productive labour. If finance capital and merchant capital take a greater proportion of the surplus value than productive capital from productive labour, including the surplus value used to fund advertising campaigns on Web 2.0 platforms, this in no way undermines the labour theory of value.[74] The tendency for companies to be run according to the principles of 'downsize and distribute' is evidence of a shift in power – partly economic and partly political or ideological – from productive capital to finance capital, embodied in 'shareholder value', but it in no way cancels the value production of workers in companies that now prefer to distribute their surplus value as revenue to shareholders rather than using profits as capital in the 'retain and reinvest' model. Similarly, the separation of ownership and control, in which companies are managed by salaried executives (with stock options) on behalf of shareholders, does not alter the source of surplus value. It is true that 'finance permeates from the beginning to the end the circulation of capital' and also that every 'productive act and every act of consumption is directly or indirectly tied to finance'.[75] It is undeniable that debt and credit have come to 'define the production and exchange of goods according to a *speculative logic*'.[76] But no evidence can be found for asserting that the domination of finance in contemporary capitalism 'transform[s] ... the use value of goods ... in[to] veritable potential financial assets that generate surplus value'.[77] Profits can be made through financial transactions and through circulation, but value cannot be added by either of these forms of capitalist accumulation. More money is withdrawn from circulation than is thrown into it by interest-bearing capital and merchant capital, and in recent decades these have been more profitable than investing in industry, but these facts obscure what is distinctive about capitalism.

---

73   Marazzi 2011, p. 63.
74   See Lapavitsas 2009.
75   Marazzi 2011, p. 107.
76   Ibid.
77   Ibid.

Lazzarato, famous for devising the concept of immaterial labour and then renouncing it, has followed Marazzi's theory of debt. Just as Negri turns to the *Grundrisse* to conjure up a 'Marx Beyond Marx', and the early 'workerists' detected the seeds of post-Fordism within Marx's previously neglected 'fragment on machines', Lazzarato does not confront the three volumes of *Capital* directly in his attempt to surpass them. Like his predecessors, Lazzarato digs up an obscure text by the early Marx that appears to outstrip the mature Marx in its articulation of contemporary themes, challenging the central tenets of Marxist economics by drawing on its periphery. From the *Paris Manuscripts* of 1844, Lazzarato alights on the discussion of credit and debt in Marx's notes on James Mill. What Lazzarato finds in these notes is a Nietzschean-Deleuzean Marx quite at odds with the Marx of *Capital*.[78] 'Debt produces a specific morality', Lazzarato says, therefore the Nietzschean knotting together of economics and morality appears to Lazzarato as a strong methodology for interrogating contemporary capitalism. 'The economy seems to have become Nietzschean'.[79] Which is why, for Lazzarato, it is preferable for Marx to become Nietzschean. Debt is not as anomalous as Lazzarato suggests. Lazzarato exaggerates Marx's interest in the ethics of debt, which takes up a very small proportion of the notes on James Mill, and he proceeds as if the special case of consumer debt can be applied to all forms of credit. In order to make his point, Lazzarato neglects the ethics of labour independent of debt relations (the contemporary version of which is the ideology of the unemployed as shirkers who live off what politicians like to call 'hard working families'). Lazzarato's Nietzschean-Deleuzean-Marx is not as wayward as the sociologist based in Paris would have us believe. In his notes on James Mill Marx distinguishes between two types of credit: credit between two capitalists (which we can call 'productive credit') and credit between a capitalist and a worker (which is an example of consumer credit). Since the former is advanced for interest based on projected profits, the decision to give such loans is based entirely on economic calculations and therefore is not based on the ethical judgement of the debtor. It is only with consumer debt that the reliability and industriousness of the debtor is taken into account. In cases of consumer debt, Marx argues that the personality of the borrower is at stake but for lending between capitalists it is only the finances of the capitalist that are assessed. The development of 'credit scores' has almost eliminated this aspect of consumer debt, but Lazzarato prefers to attach debt to character nonetheless.

Dave Graeber, in his extensive anthropological study of debt, also connects debt with morality but in a richer and more differentiated way than Lazzarato.

---

78   Lazzarato 2012, p. 30.
79   Lazzarato 2012, p. 43.

Debt in precapitalist societies, he says, was indistinguishable from morality insofar as those societies were based on mutual aid. The best way to understand how debt worked in such societies is to think about the unpayable debt owed to a parent or to one's ancestors. Debt, in such circumstances, can never be paid. The idea of calculating what one owes to one's parents and then 'squaring accounts',[80] Graeber says, is tantamount to ending your relationship with them. Payment is the ending of a social relationship. Debt, on the other hand, is the acknowledgement of sociality, mutuality and dependence in the context of primitive communism. Debt is not immoral or synonymous with guilt, Graeber points out, but is the very basis of society and morality. Nietzsche, Deleuze and Guattari and Lazzarato do not adequately recognise the sheer difference of the concept of debt in precapitalist societies compared with debt today. Graeber gives a different picture of pre-market society: 'the refusal to calculate credits and debits can be found through the anthropological literature on egalitarian hunting societies'[81] in which 'the hunter insisted that being truly human meant refusing to make such calculations, refusing to measure or remember who had given what to whom'.[82] Deleuze and Guattari take Marcel Mauss to task using Nietzsche's philosophy to question Mauss's anthropology. 'It all makes perfect sense if you start from Nietzsche's initial premise. The problem is that the premise is insane'.[83] Graeber argues that Nietzsche knew the premise was insane. It was the premise of bourgeois philosophy and political economy. Nietzsche, he says, was showing them their own insanity. This is not what Deleuze and Guattari or Lazzarato do with Nietzsche. Deleuze and Guattari say Nietzsche's *Genealogy* is superior to Mauss 'because it interprets primitive society in terms of debt, in the debtor-creditor relationship by eliminating every consideration of exchange'. Lazzarato, effectively, peddles a version of this argument.

'Money is first of all debt-money', Lazzarato says. Debt, in its capacious and hybrid sense, precedes money. In fact, we might say that debt, as gift exchange within primitive communism, is the form of mutual ownership and communal exchange in which money has no role. Money is introduced for acts of exchange with other groups, not within the community itself, and here, money is not connected with debt but with settling up. Money allows strangers, including enemies, to have no relationship with one another. It ends negotiations, obligations and sociality. In this sense, money is right from the start the

---

80   Graeber 2011, p. 92.
81   Graeber 2011, p. 79.
82   Ibid.
83   Graeber 2011, p. 78.

opposite of debt. Money replaces debt, gift exchange and the commons by paying for goods instantly. Lazzarato does not theorise the relationship between
debt and money in this way. He assumes, rather, that debt always stands in
for money and for the kind of calculable transactions that money serves, even
before money. Debt, is finance from the point of view of the debtor, Lazzarato
claims, while interest is finance from the point of view of creditors. This reads
as a political rationale for a theory of debt in preference to the various current theories of financialisation, and it is welcome on that account, but given
that Lazzarato asserts 'everyone is a debtor', including the *rentiers* living off
interest and dividends, the politics is an empty formal commitment. And, in
fact, Lazzarato repels the critique of finance, financiers and the *rentier* class.
Finance should not be opposed to the so-called 'real economy', he says, taking sides temporarily with neoliberalism against the Keynesians in rejecting
the association of finance with wasteful and dangerous speculation, parasitism and rent. His target is the alleged 'productivism' of the Marxist analysis of
the production of surplus value through the exploitation of surplus labour. In
fact, the theory of finance as parasitic derives from Ricardo and was revived by
Lenin, Gramsci and Keynes. Marx, as Lazzarato concedes despite also accusing
Marx of 'productivism', did not underestimate the function of finance within
the capitalist mode of production. Marx understood that consumer debt puts
wages back in the pockets of capitalists and therefore makes them available as
capital again, and also that producer debt increases the rate of accumulation
and the rate of the reproduction of the means of production. There are serious
flaws in the post-Fordist theory of debt and there is no reason to believe that
the proposed eclipse of the labour theory of value is called for by it. We need
to widen our scope.

Post-Fordism has also developed what is known as the 'social factory' argument. Very early on, in fact, Tronti had drawn on Lukács's concept of reification to establish his theory of the 'social factory', in which life itself undergoes
the process of real subsumption. While this theory follows the pattern set by
Lukács's theory of reification, it appears to be more feasible because of the
apparent economic changes in the post-Fordist era. Reification illicitly applies
the analysis of the real subsumption of labour under capital to non-labour (in
particular to art and culture) but the social factory bases the real subsumption of life on the absence of the real subsumption of labour. Nevertheless, the
process of the real subsumption of life is modelled on the real subsumption of
labour by capital. The idea appears to be that non-labour and non-productive
activities (in fact, everything other than productive labour) have adopted the
techniques, processes and ideology of the factory. In art, of course, artists use
industrial technologies, the division of labour and other measures and artists

take on the subjective mannerisms of entrepreneurs even when their studios are not factories and they do not engage in capitalist commodity production. Households are run efficiently to the clock, families coordinate their activities with an online spreadsheet, precarity describes intimate relations and not just industrial ones, popular nutritional experts instruct individuals to treat their bodies like machines that they must manage, popular music and dance become as rationalised as the robotised workplace and so on and so forth. It is evident that elements of the capitalist mode of production leak out of production and enter social life. If I can assume that my economic critique of reification in particular and Western Marxist theories of art's commodification, culture industry and spectacle generally demonstrated that the cultural associations between art and capitalism do not count as an argument that art has economically been converted to the capitalist mode of production, then I can dispense with the social factory argument swiftly. That is to say, just as Lukács was in error by concluding that reification was the totalisation of the capitalist mode of production, the post-Fordist theorists of the real subsumption of life are in error by concluding that the general adoption of capitalist techniques in non-capitalist activities is, in fact, the extension of capitalism, not just its technologies, processes, materials and knowledge. Art which looks like capitalist production, or consciously imitates it, is not therefore capitalist.

Post-Fordism also argues that new technologies have brought about new modes of value production that Marx did not foresee. Consider Web 2.0. Profits are made from the use of data produced by the users of Facebook and other digital interfaces, but post-Fordist theories of the general intellect wrongly ascribe this profit to rent, overstate the economic novelty of this, exaggerate the negative implications this has for the labour theory of value, and erroneously conclude that users are therefore productive of value in the act of consumption. This last error is behind Vercellone's argument that the general intellect is the 'sublation of the real subsumption of labor to capital'.[84] If rent can be drawn from the consumption activities of the general intellect, then the real subsumption of labour is no longer necessary, the extraction of surplus value from labour power is no longer required and the real subsumption of labour by capital becomes unnecessary. The sublation of real subsumption, found in Vercellone and elsewhere, argues that real subsumption is redundant, whereas the social factory argument claims that real subsumption is everywhere. What both share is the marginalisation or elimination of the significance of the real subsumption of labour under capital. If either of these arguments is justified then it is possible that art's economic exceptionalism, too, is a thing of the past,

---

84   Vercellone 2007, p. 26.

as capitalism has managed to bring everything under its spell. The new model for art's incorporation by capitalism, then, is not capitalist commodity production but the non-productive activity of social and cultural intercourse. Rather than the capitalist mode of production serving as the model for understanding the economics of art, therefore, it seems as if the free labour, precarity and cognitive exchanges of art are being used as a model for understanding how contemporary capitalism produces value. If art is economically exceptional, and moreover if this exceptionalism is understood as artists not being capitalist commodity producers, then it is a poor model for understanding capitalism, albeit of a post-Fordist variety. Art would be a powerful model for understanding non-capitalist production, perhaps, but post-Fordism is not post-capitalism even if it is the 'communism of capital'.

Does the post-Fordist theory of rent challenge the economic exceptionalism of art? If art is exceptional to capitalist commodity production, perhaps it is not exceptional to post-Fordist rent extraction? Is an example of the immaterial becoming rent of profit the $45,500 sale of four sheets of steel accompanied by an authenticating certificate signed by Carl Andre? Seen through the lens of differential rent, and thereby the process through which prices are set at the highest of all competing prices allocating to the more efficient producers the benefit of 'super profits', or profits over and above average surplus value, the fancy prices of artworks might appear to be costs of production plus rent. If so, which kind of rent? Monopoly rent, cartel rent, technology rent, differential rent? Since it is clear that the price of Andre's steel is not set by the highest of his competitors, then it is not cartel rent, at least. And since the sale of the work was made through an auction house, the price does not conform to the standard pattern of monopoly rent in which the seller determines the price independent of market forces. In fact, none of the available specific theories of rent explain the high prices of art works.

If art was economically exceptional between the rise of the industrial revolution and the disintegration of Fordism in the 1960s, there is still a case to be answered whether art remains economically exceptional in the post-Fordist period of alleged 'immaterial labour', the rise of the cognitariat, the replacement of security with precarity and the development of semio-capitalism. For art to remain economically exceptional it would have to separate itself not from the processes of industrialisation, deskilling, automation and the assembly line, but immaterial labour, precarity, cognitive labour and the creative processes of creative capitalism. According to Boltanski and Chiapello, 'the new spirit of capitalism incorporated much of the artistic critique that flourished at the end of the 1960s',[85] which has led to the 'economically rather

---

85   Boltanski and Chiapello 2007, p. 418.

marginal domain of cultural enterprises' not only being brought into commodity production but also becoming the model for a new kind of business in
which managers develop 'skills approximate to those of the artist', using 'intuition' to sniff out opportunities that correspond to 'their own desires'.[86] Pascal
Gielen arrives at the same conclusion from the opposite direction, so to speak,
saying many artists 'can probably identify to a large extent with the . . . immaterial worker'.[87] He explains:

> For the artist too, working hours are not neatly nine-to-five, and constant
> demands are made on forthcoming good ideas, on potential. And since
> the undermining of the craft side of creativity – at least in the contem-
> porary visual arts – the artist has come to depend on communication,
> linguistic virtuosity and the performance of his ideas.[88]

He argues, in fact, that 'the modern art world has been a social laboratory for
immaterial labour, and thus for Post-Fordism'.[89] So, it appears, art is no longer
regarded as the antidote to capitalist accumulation but as a formula for success in business. Artistic labour has gone from being anomalous to capitalism
in its deskilled and alienated Fordist variant, to being the very model of work
for post-Fordist capitalism. Business managers have identified artistic labour
as precisely the kind of labour for which the creative, innovative, dynamic,
committed company yearns. Art and artistic labour, it seems, are no longer
marginal to the most advanced techniques of capitalist production, as they
were when mechanisation prevailed, but epitomise a mode of production that
depends on virtuosity, innovation and autonomy.

How can art be economically exceptional with regard to an economy based
on the model of art? If it is true that the post-Fordist economy is characterised
by flexibility, mobility, language, communication, precarity, information, culture, immaterial labour and virtuosity, then there is certainly a *prima facie* case
for arguing that artistic labour is exemplary of post-Fordism, since artists have
been working under conditions of precarity, virtuosity and mobility for centuries. Artists have almost always lived precariously despite their attachment
to the wealthy and their high social status. Artists are also steeped historically
in the values of communication, inventiveness and immaterial labour that
Virno stresses in his account of how the world works today in the information,
service and cultural economies that are distinctive features of contemporary

---

86   Boltanski and Chiapello 2007, p. 444.
87   Gielen 2009, p. 24.
88   Ibid.
89   Gielen 2009, p. 25.

capitalism. Immaterial labour, like artistic labour, does not stop. Mobile phones, laptops, email, internet and other technologies allow work to extend into spaces and times previously set apart from work. Artists, who have always been advised to carry a sketchbook or notebook with them at all times, are very familiar with the dissolution of the division between work and non-work. Post-Fordism commodifies flexibility, creativity, networking and conviviality, thereby collapsing the critical difference between artistic labour and wage labour. Thus, whereas artists since the Renaissance have insisted that the division between labour and non-labour could not contain their commitment to art, this is not the best way to understand how post-Fordism has developed working practices that colonise everyday life, leisure, the domestic environment, private life and friendship.

Speaking about the technique he used to produce the work 'The Physical Impossibility of Death in the Mind of Someone Living', the shark in formaldehyde from 1991, Damien Hirst sounded like he was reading a script advertising a telephone company.

> The Shark – I got an idea that you can get anything over the phone. That's all there is. It's like a screen to hide behind. When you're on the phone there's just so much missing. I just suddenly thought, Fuck it, you can get anything on the phone. I actually wondered if there was no limit to it. I wanted to do a shark and I thought, No, that's fucking impossible; you can't do that. I didn't go, 'Let's go out and get a big fucking fishing rod and go and catch a shark'. I thought, Shit, you can get it over the phone ... I went down to Billingsgate and I said to the guy, 'Oh, can you get me a shark?' And he said, 'Oh yeah, any size you want'. 'You can get me a twelve-foot shark?' 'Oh yeah'. He told me how much it was per pound an' I thought I'd worked it out.[90]

There is some overlap, here, with post-Fordist technique, specifically the use of language in work, the focus on technology and the opposition between material labour ('Let's go out and get a big fucking fishing rod and go and catch a shark') and immaterial labour ('Shit, you can get it over the phone'). Hirst's technique for this work is directly opposed to what post-Fordist theorists call 'productivism'. Hirst is not the 'producer' of the shark in the sense of the labourer who directly appropriates materials from nature. Hirst, not being the producer, is therefore, in the terms of classical Marxist economic analysis, occupying the role either of the capitalist or consumer (leaving to

---

90   Hirst in Burn 2001, p. 45.

one side, for the moment, subdivisions within such roles like overseer, manager and merchant). Hirst is either the capitalist or consumer, depending on
whether the money he uses is revenue or capital. But this is not a straightforward convergence of conceptual art and cognitive capitalism. While the technology and methods that Hirst uses can be seen throughout the commercial
sector of contemporary capitalism, from cold calling sales teams to telephone
banking, the two processes are not economically the same. Hirst had worked
for a telephone research agency and developed skills during that time which
he later used in his work.[91] He raised money for the 'Freeze' exhibition over
the phone, too. But the difference between working for a research agency and
being commissioned by Charles Saatchi for £50,000 to make an artwork is economically vital. Saatchi is not his employer, but his customer, and Saatchi does
not purchase his labour – either as labour power or service – but the product
of his (and others') labour, the shark. The transactions between Hirst, the shark
catcher, various technicians and assistants, transit specialists and Saatchi do
not belong to cognitive capitalism but to trade, craft, haulage, taxidermy and
the purchase of luxury goods.

Insofar as post-Fordism is characterised by outsourcing production and the
dominance of merchant capital and finance capital over productive capital,
Hirst's telephonic transaction can appear to be a striking example of cognitive
capitalism. Profit is not derived from surplus labour since nobody is paid wages
in any of these transactions, but profit is made in the process of circulation
itself (the shark catcher is paid £4000 out of the £50,000 fund). The difference
between the two prices is not covered entirely by the additional expenditure
on technicians, transit and so on, but by the new status of the product as a work
of art. Stuffed sharks in glass vitrines that are priced in a competitive market
do not cost £50,000 to buy. But the apparent super profits enjoyed by Hirst and
his dealer in this transaction is nothing compared with the $15 million price
tag that the work eventually obtains. Again, the difference between the two
prices of the artwork appears to conform to the description of cognitarians
given by Bifo: 'they process information in order to give birth to goods and
services'[92] or 'the cognitarian is one who produces goods through the act of
language'.[93] The difference between a stuffed shark by Hirst and a stuffed shark
worth a fraction of the amount by anyone else is symbolic, semiotic, authorised, certified. Of course, this particular shark has a shared history with Hirst,
but the difference between this shark and another that has gone through the

---

91   For a brief account of this episode see Muir 2009, pp. 44–5.
92   Berardi 2010, p. 4.
93   Berardi 2009b, p. 143.

same process is not embodied in the product but in the information that accompanies it. We might even deploy another of Vercellone's motifs, saying profit, in this instance, is a form of rent drawn on the property of Hirst's authorship. But all of this amounts to nothing but an *interpretation* of Hirst's transactions according to post-Fordist theory, not an analysis of the economic exchanges in play. We could also 'read' this episode through Greimas's theory of narrative actants, but we would be no closer to understanding the relationship between the artist, the labourer, the collector, the gallerist and the viewer. The point is not to read the production of art through the texts of Marx's three volumes of *Capital*. Such a procedure would in all likelihood lead to the error of describing artworks in terms of the features of capitalist commodity production that Marx subjects to critique. What I have been trying to do, by contrast, is to ascertain whether the production and circulation of art actually conforms to any of the key theories and processes of the capitalist mode of production.

Artists on average struggle to make a living but the precarity of someone who has made sacrifices in order to produce the art that they choose is not equivalent to the precarity of the unskilled labourer holding down two or three part-time jobs just to stay above the bread line. Artists are creative labourers whose personality is performed in a virtuoso display, but this is not equivalent to the fast food worker who is instructed by her employer to add personal details to her uniform because the marketing department believes that this will add to the customer experience. Artists tend to continue with their work in some way when they leave the studio, by visiting galleries, reading theory, attending conferences, hanging out at private views, networking with critics and curators, taking notes, making sketches or taking photographs of things that catch their attention, picking things up that might come in useful and so on, but this is not equivalent to the retail worker who is expected to work beyond their contracted hours in the shop, who is under pressure to retrain in their own time and at their own expense, and who comes up with ideas for products or display from which the shop owner ultimately profits. While artists might justifiably belong to the precariat, a close economic analysis of artistic precarity indicates that there are different levels of precarity, different intensities of precarity and even different modes of precarity. Capitalism is a precarious system. The capitalist who ventures a fortune on a business enterprise can a close economic analysis of artistic precarity ruined by it. By and large, however, capitalists invest money over and above what they need to reproduce their own standard of living, and their precarity is a rather limited one. Some artists can be as poor as church mice, but for other more well-heeled artists, or artists cushioned from necessity by wealthy parents, their precarity, we might say, is more formal than real. Economic and social distinctions must be brought to the idea of precarity.

The apparent convergence of post-Fordist techniques of labour and management with art, artistic labour, artistic practices and the precarious lifestyle of artists has not been adequately scrutinised. The literature does not specify precisely what kind of convergence has taken place. Does art *resemble* key features of the post-Fordist economy or is there a stronger relationship between them? Does art share technical, social, political, economic or cultural characteristics with post-Fordism? Or, more strongly, does post-Fordism make profits from art today in a way that Fordism could not? If post-Fordism generates more profits from circulation and finance, is art more prone to capitalism in the new economy than ever before? Artists live precariously and post-Fordism re-introduces precarity into the labour market. Are these two forms of precarity the same? Artists typically do not draw hard and fast lines between work and non-work, often having a second job which funds their 'work'. Post-Fordist workers are encouraged or pressurised to continue working outside of the specified working day and to feel that their work is not just a job but is fulfilling activity for its own good. Are these forms of eradicating the distinction between work and non-work the same? Artists work flexibly and creatively, training and retraining with new skills, new ideas and new technologies, adapting to changing conditions and responding to the latest developments, and post-Fordism requires the workforce to be flexible, to have ideas, to be open to change and to switch jobs or roles frequently. Most artists do not earn a living from the sale of their work and require second jobs, and post-Fordist workers are employed on temporary, casual contracts and therefore tend to have multiple jobs. Artists travel to distant parts of the world to put on exhibitions, taking opportunities as they arise, and post-Fordist labour is characterised by mobility and immigration, but surely these global movements of labour are not the same. Artists are not employed as wage labourers by productive capitalists, but merchant capitalists and finance capitalists can, nonetheless, make vast profits from the circulation of their works, and the post-Fordist labour market is made more precarious by requiring workers to be self-employed, casual, freelance or even free (in the case of interns), which alienates workers from their rights and gives employers more liberty to hire and fire as the market demands. Each apparent convergence, I would suggest, is as indicative of the gulf between artist and the typical post-Fordist labourer as it signifies the centrality of art to post-Fordist capitalism.

What is dubious about re-describing the cognitive labour of artists as a post-Fordist form of value production through semiotic transformation is that artworks had 'fancy prices' derived from their symbolic status all along. Economically speaking, art is not post-Fordist; it is pre-industrial. The question of whether art remains economically exceptional when Fordism gives way to post-Fordism raises an important issue of periodisation. Insofar as post-Fordism appears to generalise certain features of artistic labour and the social relations of art, and insofar as the economics of artistic production have not changed significantly since the Renaissance in some respects and since the eighteenth century in others, post-Fordism appears to coincide with the pre-industrial. What is more, the argument that post-Fordism calls the Marxist theory of labour into question should not be made on the assumption that Marx theorised Fordist capitalism. Marx did not live that long. The accusation of 'productivism' conveniently glosses over the fact that the precarity of labour was clearly understood by Marx. It is also unacceptable to take the alleged immateriality of production in this way, as we have seen. Since capitalism was established through the mobility of workers and the displacement of agricultural labourers, it seems that post-Fordism could not claim that this was unheard of in Marx's times. Of course, digitalisation, computerisation and robotisation are novel processes, but the economic principles of revolutions in the mode of production through the introduction of machinery and automation were at the heart of Marx's analysis of the capitalist mode of production. So, the case for the eradication of art's economic exceptionalism in post-Fordism due to economic novelties is not at all vivid. Having outlined the classical theory of art's economic exceptionalism, and pieced together several contenders for a neoclassical theory of art's economic exceptionalism, I have now provided a Marxist theory of art's economic exceptionalism from the capitalist mode of production that recent developments of post-Marxist theory, it seems to me, cannot dislodge. In the final chapter of this book I will test the arguments of this book against contemporary theories of art's relationship to economic imperatives that will allow a reconsideration of the conjunction of art and value.

Conclusion

The confrontation between bureaucracy and free markets reappears in the discussion of art's funding time and time again. Abbing, who is a portrait painter and an economics graduate, argues that the art market breeds 'market artists' or 'business artists' while the state breeds 'government artists'.[1] A divide that runs right through art itself separates these two types of artist.

> While many people consider it a struggle between art and money, between aesthetic and economic value, between good and evil, the sacred and the worldly, the spiritual and the vulgar, it is basically the fight between different forms of power. The power to tell what is good and what is bad in the arts competes with purchasing power.[2]

By referring to both human judgements and economic markets as powers,[3] Abbing shies away from discussing the different procedures required for each: judgements arising out of experience, conversation and study appear to be a form of power equivalent to the legislative, coercive and administrative power of the state and the forces unleashed by economic exchanges operating through anonymous market mechanisms. Abbing gives the impression that judgements are alien to individuals because they are social and institutional, whereas economic exchanges are both universal and individual.[4] As such the bureaucratic interference with free markets is extended to appear as the interference with sovereign individuals *per se*. Similarly, the freedom to trade in a self-regulating market is extended to appear as the liberty of individuals *per se*. Such ideal individuals who meet in the marketplace appear to require no regulation, organisation or society whatsoever and, hence, the appearance of so-called 'cultural power' or 'well-educated' opinion is not welcome.

---

1 Abbing 2002, p. 99.

2 Abbing 2002, p. 77.

3 Jürgen Habermas has characterised these two forms of power as existing within a triumvirate of powers, consisting of market, state and the public sphere. Market and state, he says, are 'steering media', which means that collective decisions are made without the participation of individuals, whereas the public sphere consists of communicative action.

4 Against this championing of the market, Michael Lebowitz says, 'determination of fundamental social decisions in accordance with private profits rather than human needs is among the specific reasons that Marxists oppose capitalism' (Lebowitz 2003, p. 1).

© KONINKLIJKE BRILL NV, LEIDEN, 2015 | DOI 10.1163/9789004288157_014

Art and value are cemented together, for Abbing, either through power or money. Abbing does not exclude the whole range of mechanisms through which values are attached to art, but he categorises them according to only two types. Dialogue, persuasion, academic dispute, criticism, appreciation, historical research, philosophical speculation and political critique are lumped together with doctrine, dogma, authorised opinion, promotional guff, jargon, catechism and orthodoxy. The point is not to add just one more category but to indicate a range of specific mechanisms, apparatuses, methods and techniques that have different relations to power and emancipation from power, as well as markets and emancipation from markets. Armed with his dual system for categorising values in art, Abbing turns a deaf ear to what artists actually say about their relationship to markets. Abbing collects a considerable amount of original anecdotal evidence to confirm that artists are suspicious of markets, not incentivised by financial rewards, and that they often make sacrifices, make losses and self-subsidise. He demonstrates that it is more typical for artists not to behave according to the model of rational economic calculations of financial self-interest. However, his interpretation of the data brings us directly back to a conception of the artist as a rational utility maximiser. What artists object to, he says, are the commercially successful artists who 'don't care about art at all, and are only interested in wealth and fame'.[5] Artists do not appear to be opposed to the market as a corrupting influence on themselves, only on their competitors. Abbing assumes that artists are, in fact, rational calculators of self-interest but they lack information which leads to irrational choices. His aim, therefore, is to explain the basics of economics to artists so that they can make more rational choices: 'The first group I had in mind while writing this book is *artists* ... The analysis will hopefully help them to develop a better understanding of their economic situation'.[6] For instance, artists do not calculate their economic benefits in decisions made about the production of art, as producers would in other businesses. Many artists do not make a living from sales of works, and take on a second job to support their production of art. Some of Abbing's own friends are poor artists who 'hardly sell, have lousy second jobs, and yet they carry on. I don't understand why they just don't quit the profession', he says. His book, effectively, is not an attempt to understand the exceptional economic circumstances that make sense of their decision to continue making the art they choose regardless of sales, but to show them

---

5   Abbing 2002, p. 85.
6   Abbing 2002, p. 14.

the error of their ways.[7] There is an oversupply of artists, he argues, and as anyone with a basic understanding of economic 'laws' knows, when supply is greater than demand prices fall. The irrational values of artists result in their own poverty.

Abbing cannot overcome what he calls 'the two-faced character of the economy of the arts'.[8] He likes to say that there are two spheres, the gift sphere and the market sphere, and that they both operate in art. One of the abiding perceptions within and beyond the art world, he says, is that aesthetic value and economic value belong to different spheres.[9] Abbing's spheres are sociological entities. They consist largely of beliefs, attitudes and values, including myths, and they appear to create all manner of mischief. As both an artist and an economist, Abbing finds himself subscribing to both sets of belief. Abbing is split. As a practising artist Abbing subscribes to what he calls the 'mythology' of art, but as a trained economist he cannot accept this mythology as true. Art has a mythology that protects it from money, says Abbing. For instance, he says, there is 'a taboo that prevents an artist-dealer relationship from being a normal business relationship'.[10] So much of Abbing's book consists of ventriloquising the values that belong to the opposing spheres that make claims on art. Instead of examining the different mechanisms of aesthetic value and market value, therefore, Abbing reports the beliefs held by individuals regarding aesthetic value and market value. Abbing typically sets an opinion from one alleged sphere against an opinion from another, the only difference being that one sphere is consistently presented in terms of 'the mythology of art' while the other is consistently presented as the scientific, rational, indisputable, inevitable and empirical sphere of economic exchange. The split between art and economics is both raised and resolved in the same moment, therefore, by characterising one as irrational and the other as scientific. Taking sides in the last analysis with economics, the division between art and economics that

---

7   This appears to be his calling: 'First, when I meet youngsters who are interested in becoming artists, I immediately start to stimulate them. I would not bother if all they wanted to become was a hairdresser or a manager. Only later will I inform them that there are already too many artists and that art might end up disappointing them' (Abbing 2002, p. 24).

8   Abbing 2002, p. 12.

9   In addition, he characterises rival types of contemporary artist as occupying two different spheres, one belongs to the 'traditional (modern) sphere' (Abbing 2002, p. 72) and the other to the avant-garde sphere. At one point Abbing discusses the opposing spheres of art and rationality. Spheres are everywhere in this book, both as a recognition of tensions and as a way of dampening them.

10   Abbing 2002, p. 36.

Abbing lives out in his two roles is not a competition between equals, but the orchestrated confrontation between rationality and irrationality, fact and fiction, reality and delusion. In short, the tale of Abbing's split between economics and art is not a genuine fight, as in a boxing match, but a staged display of right defeating wrong, as in a wrestling bout. Abbing's empirical and anecdotal evidence, that he compiles through conversations with artists, follows the anthropological model of interviewing natives only to treat their testimony as irrational and in need of scientific interpretation.

The subtitle to Abbing's book *Why Are Artists Poor?* is *The Exceptional Economy of the Arts*, but the book is an extended argument against the perceived exceptionalism of art. Art appears to be economically exceptional, for Abbing, because it has been hypnotised by myths which have economic consequences. His explanation for art's economic exceptionalism is that art is 'sacred'.[11] Abbing's acknowledgement that artists appear to be economically exceptional producers does not lead him to examine whether artistic production is itself economically exceptional. Abbing says that art has an 'exceptional economy', not that art is economically exceptional, the difference being that, for him, art itself can be brought into standard economic practice through a simple process of enlightenment. As such, Abbing's negative assessment of the various reports of art's exceptionalism is not based on an examination of the exceptional production of art or the exceptional prices of unique goods. Abbing says that the 'large presence of donations and subsidies in the arts is exceptional'.[12] However, if art is economically exceptional in some respects, receiving subsidies is not one of them.[13] Hardly any industry or economic sphere is left to the market. Abbing says there is a 'taboo'[14] on talking about money in relation to art: 'profit motives are not absent, they

---

11   Abbing 2002, pp. 23–5.

12   Abbing 2002, p. 41.

13   Enormous subsidies are enjoyed by car manufacturers, train companies (£120 million to First Great Western in 2010), agriculture, bus companies (£500 million per year for the newly privatised bus companies in the UK), airline companies (subsidised to the tune of £10 billion in the UK alone), coal pits (£21.7 million to UK Coal in 2001), not to mention the staggering sums that governments around the world handed out to banks during the global bailout of 2009. Mimi Abramovitz calls this 'corporate welfare'. And the neoliberal economist Gordon Tullock estimated that 'if corporate welfare dollars were distributed to the poorest ten percent of American families, each family would receive an additional yearly income of forty-seven thousand dollars'. It is inadequate to argue that these industries receive subsidies as a result of the mythology of jobs, or the mythology of profits. Subsidies for art are not, in themselves, evidence that art is economically exceptional.

14   Abbing 2002, p. 36.

are merely veiled, and publicly the economic aspect of art is denied'.[15] The reference to taboo is a deliberate strategy to associate the antagonism to the market in art with irrationality. When he recounts the values of the art community, he frames them in terms of 'myth',[16] 'taboo', 'ritual'[17] and 'the sacred'. He is convinced of the rationality of the economic, while subscribing to the idea that the arts promote an alternative 'value system'.[18] Art, for him, is in the grip of 'the gift sphere'.[19] The concept of the 'gift sphere' allows Abbing to acknowledge the so-called irrational values of art without them challenging economics and economic value. The fact that the myths attached to art attract subsidies from the state, corporate business and family members only exacerbates the problem, as far as he is concerned. For Abbing, the primary reason why artists are poor is that the myths and sacredness of art attract more practitioners than are economically viable. Economic exceptionalism, in Abbing's eyes, is an illusion akin to religious beliefs which affect behaviour and can have actual social effects, but which can and ought to be modified, rectified or eliminated. In fact, he takes it as significant that 'only reverends and priests receive more income from gifts than artists',[20] and that 'part of art consumption clearly resembles religious consumption'.[21] At the same time, however, the myths of art become embedded in economic exchanges and distort them. 'Anti-market behaviour can be profitable',[22] he says. And if an artist openly rejects the market, perhaps for years, but eventually begins to sell her work, Abbing explains this as a kind of shadow play in which the reality of seeking to sell is masked by claims to the contrary. The possibility that artists are taken on by dealers and acquired by collectors as a result of the quality and independence of their work which results from resisting the market for an extended period is not considered by Abbing as feasible. But it is surely not inconceivable that artists who focus their attention exclusively on questions of value in art rather than on art's market value will eventually be recognised by the market nonetheless. Abbing only brings such resistance to the market to bear on the economics of art insofar as they appear as the expressed beliefs of artists, not as a set of material conditions for the production of art linked to art's discourses and modes of evaluation. Hence, economic value and

---

15   Abbing 2002, p. 47.
16   Abbing 2002, p. 30.
17   Abbing 2002, p. 193.
18   Abbing 2002, p. 47.
19   Abbing 2002, p. 39.
20   Abbing 2002, p. 40.
21   Abbing 2002, p. 24.
22   Abbing 2002, p. 48.

economic rationality, for Abbing, always trump the values of art because he regards economic value as objective and unavoidable, while the values of the arts community are mythological and irrational.

Arjo Klamer takes the opposite view, criticising economics and supplementing it with sociology and anthropology because '[e]conomic theory does not account for relationships and does not recognise a value that is beyond measure'.[23] And the Chicago economist Deirdre McCloskey has gone some way in that direction, inserting ethics into economics by arguing that 'hard nosed economic analysis makes mistakes when it forgets that humans are political animals',[24] in the Aristotelian sense of belonging to a community. The arts only offer an idyllic or utopian alternative to the market, according to Abbing, which is to say, 'artists and the arts have become a symbol of an alternative to the bourgeois lifestyle ... [but this is] a romantic, not a realistic alternative'.[25] Since economic mechanisms cannot be suspended, the laws of supply and demand continue to choreograph the allocation of resources in art, according to Abbing. 'I will not deny that different practices exist in different areas of production' (observing that if the director of Shell dies[26] he can be replaced but when an artist dies then nobody can take their place in the production of their works), he asserts that the 'underlying principles, however, are the same'[27] for all areas of production. This is why art's resistance to market forces can only exist, for him, in the comforting and childish form of beliefs and myths. As such, convictions and values which contradict economics and market forces are not just irrational, for Abbing, they are damaging and dangerous. Economic exceptionalism in art is therefore seen as a lamentable kind of superstition or prejudice, that is to say nothing but a remnant of the enchanted world that the Enlightenment confronted with science, rationality and democracy. And it is these myths about the sacredness of art that Abbing believes explains the operations of the art market. Why else would artists persist for decades in producing works that they cannot sell? In one sense the argument that art is economically exceptional in its production as well as its prices and increasing marginal utility is an attempt to answer this question, central to cultural economics, without assuming that artists are irrational in doing so.

Abbing illustrates his theory of art's myth-driven economic exceptionalism with an account of the purchase of a Mondrian:

---

23   Klamer 1996, p. 24.
24   McClosekey in Klamer 1996, p. 199.
25   Abbing 2002, p. 26.
26   Abbing in Klamer 1996, p. 141.
27   Abbing in Klamer 1996, p. 147.

in 1998 the Dutch government was prepared to pay 36 million Euro (appr. 32 million Dollars) for an unfinished painting by Mondrian... After all, it's just a piece of linen on a wooden frame with some dots of paint on it. Much cheaper copies could easily be produced, which in their appearance could offer almost anything the original offers. Nevertheless, people believe that the original is irreplaceable, because they know that Mondrian made this specific work of art.[28]

Abbing explains this purchase in the sociological or anthropological terms of belief. Note not only the reference to what 'people believe' but also, in a contrast that seals the meaning of belief, the reference to 'it's just' and 'their appearance could offer almost anything the original offers'. The Humean guillotine cuts the painting's social meaning off from its significant material properties and Abbing is left with some linen, wood and paint on one side and a set of beliefs on the other. If this separation can be successfully accomplished then there is a possibility, as he speculates, of simply reproducing the object, hence he says, 'cheaper copies could easily be produced'. Apart from begging the question of why anybody would be interested in reproducing the object divorced from its social meaning as a Mondrian painting, Abbing shows a complete disregard for material history, as if all the evidence of human accomplishment can be replaced with doppelgangers. Moreover, the copy requires a completely different set of skills from those called on to produce innovative artistic forms, such as Mondrian's enormous contribution to modern abstract painting. Value is siphoned off from objects, materials and processes in preparation for the conclusion that values, in the form of myths, are expendable. The positivist re-description of the painting as a piece of linen with some dots painted on it is typical of the way anthropologists describe the physical characteristics of fetish objects or the physical actions involved in a ritual: tearing values away from the facts that instantiate them. The reasons that such a work might be purchased by the Dutch government, in Abbing's account, can only be explained with reference to some apparently irrational belief in 'authenticity' and 'originality'. While Abbing characterises the purchase of the Mondrian in terms of belief, he does not speak of the irrational belief in money, for instance, or the myth that wealth increases happiness.[29] The taboo on public subsidy in neoliberal economics is present in Abbing's study but is

---

28   Abbing 2002, p. 25.

29   Robert Nelson says economic theories 'are rooted in unexamined presuppositions that are more like faith commitments... As such, they can be, and in a certain sense must be, treated in terms that echo classic theological themes and categories' (see Nelson 2001, p. xii).

presented as the result of rational scientific study. And the founding myth that before economic exchange there was barter, is also presented as if it were true.[30] Myths, for Abbing, on the contrary, appear only to exist in his gift sphere. None of this is teased out in Abbing's Humean interpretation. Abbing anticipates no material impoverishment in the cheap copy and looks forward to the prospect of saving some money, like an American holidaymaker in Las Vegas enjoying the best of European tourist sites at a fraction of the price.

What Abbing misses altogether in his hypothetical illustration of the Mondrian copy is an economic analysis of the absence of copies, multiples and quantities in Mondrian's production of art, which is untypical for commodity production but typical for visual art. Abbing raises the possibility of a cheap copy in the attempt to show up the irrationality of believing that art is exceptional, but if there are real and not just imagined differences between the original Mondrian and the cheap copy which are important not just in terms of the quality of the work but the history of the object, then this illustration is very suggestive of art's real economic exceptionalism. Baumol had developed a more nuanced economic analysis of the relationship between original artworks and the production of identical commodities in 1986, arguing that the art market differs from standard markets insofar as the latter 'is made up of a large number of... perfect substitutes for one another',[31] whereas 'paintings and sculptures are unique, and even two works on the same theme by a given artist are imperfect substitutes'.[32] Two Rembrandt self-portraits are not substitutes for one another and a cheap print of a Warhol image bought at a museum shop is not a perfect substitute for the original Warhol. By contrast, a CD or MP3 of a song is a perfect substitute for an identical CD or MP3, and they can therefore be replaced, but a live performance, in principle, has no perfect substitute as the same performer playing the same songs on another night will perform differently (despite the fact that mainstream musical theatre and certain genres of pop music go to extreme lengths to eliminate such differences). Books are printed in large numbers and are therefore perfect substitutes of one another, but a handmade book is not. The reason, therefore, that paintings and sculptures, unlike apples or Range Rovers, do not have perfect substitutes is that they are produced differently – not because we hold irrational beliefs about them. It is the production of art, not its myths, that must be the basis of an account of the seemingly metaphysical distinction between the original

---

30   See Graeber 2011, pp. 21–41.
31   Baumol 1986, pp. 10–11.
32   Baumol 1986, p. 11.

and the copy, and the economic difference between the price of the original and the relatively cheaper copy.

Abbing promotes a version of what Mark Fisher calls 'capitalist realism', in which the market for art is rational and the resistance to the market is romantic. Hickey matches this with his own version of capitalist realism in which the art market promotes beauty and art's own institutions promote academicism. Abbing argues that art's myths are at the root of the economic impoverishment of artists, while Hickey (negligently or provocatively) caricatures art's institutions as geared up 'to neutralize art's power'.[33] The central weakness of Hickey's argument lies in his characterisation of beauty in terms that derive entirely from the commodity. Combining together a concept of beauty tied to the consumer's relationship to commodities, and a conviction that the market is the best mechanism for supplying individuals with their 'own brand of beauty',[34] Hickey appears to believe that all artworks are, or ought to be, commodities like any other, and therefore quarantines art off from the anomalous conditions of art's economic exceptionalism. If this is an oversight that undermines Hickey's entire case for beauty, it is one shared by mainstream economists who reserve no place for art outside commodity production. In Marxist economics, by contrast, not all products are commodities. Commodities are only those products specifically produced for exchange. Products are commodities by virtue of being produced through the process of investing capital in production. If these products are, for whatever reason, not subsequently sold, they remain commodities. However, products not produced for exchange do not become commodities by being sold for whatever reason. The capitalist mode of production is devoted entirely to the production of commodities. Nevertheless, within societies dominated by the capitalist mode of production, many products are produced that are not commodities.

In the capitalist mode of production, commodities are produced for the market with the intention of the self-accumulation of value. However, there are many exceptions. Imagine I bake a loaf of bread with my son during the holidays. This loaf of bread is not a commodity; it is baked for personal consumption not exchange. This loaf does not enter economic circulation, is not exchanged and is not made for the market. No capital is advanced in the production of the loaf of bread, as the ingredients are purchased by the final consumer (which is simply another way of saying that these ingredients are not purchased as raw materials for commodity production intended for sale). When I buy the flour, yeast and so on, I am not a productive capitalist investing

---

33   Hickey 2009, p. 54.
34   Hickey 2009, p. 78.

in the means of production anticipating a future yield of surplus value.[35] I am a consumer purchasing goods that I will combine to produce food to eat (as well as an enjoyable experience that I will share with my son). The production of this loaf of bread, therefore, is non-commodity production. And millions of loaves of bread are made every day without any need for exchange, circulation, sale, purchase or capital accumulation. Making your own clothes, or making clothes for loved ones, is not commodity production either. Growing your own vegetables is not agribusiness. In fact, millions of us produce millions of use values on a daily basis without any of them being a commodity. In this sense, art's economic exceptionalism is exceptional to the dominant mode of production but is not as rare as might at first be assumed.

A transformation of production takes place when the production of use values becomes the production of exchange values. Let us look at what changes when one of the millions of domestic bakers decides to start a business baking and selling bread. The decision to make exchange values rather than use values is the best way to understand Marx's distinction between making use values and making 'social use values'. They are social in several senses: first, the quantity of bread that the commercial baker produces is far in excess of what the individual can possibly consume, so it is a social quantity; second, the use value of the bread is social insofar as the commercial baker makes the bread that others want (that is, if the customers prefer white loaves to brown loaves, then the baker who produces social use values switches production to white loaves); and third, the bread has only social use value insofar as the producer has no use for it. So, when a domestic baker becomes a commercial baker, the quantity of loaves produced increases to match the quantity of loaves that others demand. In addition, however, commodification requires a transformation of production in quality. That is to say, the production of the bread will be henceforth determined by the qualities that match the needs and wants of others. Social use values are made for others to consume and, simultaneously, not for the use of the producer.[36] The commercial baker, even a small artisan

---

35   If somebody arrived at your doorstep asking to buy a loaf of bread from you just as you
      had finished baking a loaf of bread for your family, it would take more than the cost of
      the ingredients plus the labour and a spot of profit to lure it from your possession. The
      price of such a loaf would not be set in the same way as a loaf destined from the outset to
      be sold on the market. Non-commodities are priced differently from commodities. And
      since commodities are priced according to supply and demand running in the ordinary
      way, non-commodities are economically exceptional.

36   Social use values are clearly not 'natural' or 'intrinsic' as neoclassical critics such as
      Sweezy and others assume. However, there is an ambiguity in the term. It is possible, for
      instance, for art to be produced outside of commodity production but for its use value

baker, will not only bake far more bread than they could possibly consume themselves, but may well bake bread for which they personally have no affection, find objectionable and would never eat.

There is an ambiguity in the concept of 'social use values', though. The artist who produces non-commodities, has a use value in the product and continues 'to relate' to it, but nevertheless hopes that others will relate to it, too, without necessarily putting the work on the market. In art, the product can be social without being alienated from the producer or being produced as an exchange value. Now, insofar as artists have a use value for the works in the process of making them (the experimental, exploratory and experiential elements of making are often as important to the artist as the final product) and, insofar as artists continue to have a use value for the works they produce (as materials for reflection, re-examination, reinterpretation and so on), artworks do not exclusively have social use values. However, the use values that artists have of their works are made available to others through exhibition, reproduction, documentation and other forms of display, although the specific use values that others have of the artist's work will differ in quality and content. Are art's use values, therefore, not social use values? If we remember that Marx argued that capitalism socialises production but communism will collectivise production, we might want to choose our words carefully about what sort of use values art has. Perhaps we want to say that in not being restricted to private use value, art has collective use value, communal use value or public use value. At any rate, art does not sit comfortably on either side of the distinction that Marx draws between use value and social use value. Art is neither the product of an individual for their own private use, nor the commodity produced inauthentically for others on account of being produced for money.

---

not to be restricted to the producer and her immediate friends and family. Artworks have social use value, we might say, without meaning to imply that the artist produces them merely for the money that she might receive in exchange for them. The ambiguity, then, turns on whether 'social use value' means use value that is social, communal, shared and so forth, or whether it means, as I think Marx intended it, the use value of others, or use values for others. Social use values in the Marxist definition of the commodity are best understood, I would argue, as alien to the producer in an important sense, in the way that we might speak of somebody doing something for someone else's benefit. Making commodities means making things for others in the way that we think of inauthentic acts as *for others*, and is perhaps best understood, then, in terms of the zenith of self-alienation as making something *for money*. In commodity production, the producer produces products that have use value to the consumer (not to herself), and this, I take it, is what Marx means by social use values. But, if I am right, then a product can have social use values and not be a commodity in the strict sense of being produced for sale.

We cannot assume that artistic production is standard commodity production. Demand determines supply only in the case of commodities produced for exchange in a self-regulated market. Market demand is not the principal source of incentives for art practice. Artworks can be bought and sold, of course, but they are more often produced according to values internal to art, partly as a process of discovery in itself, partly to add to knowledge, partly to make a contribution to ongoing debates, partly, perhaps, to set agendas and change the direction of art history, partly to test the water. When producers are not driven by market demand and are prepared to forego sales for values internal to their practice then market mechanisms do not work in standard ways and the economics of this kind of production cannot be explained by the standard theory. Value plays a significant role in the circumstances that make art economically exceptional, but the serious work of rethinking the economics of art must go beyond debating the pros and cons of those values and examine in close detail the economic preconditions and economic effects of those values. So-called 'failed artists' support their artistic production with other jobs, and many *commercially* unsuccessful artists are, in fact, *critically* successful. Mainstream economists have failed to capitalise on the theory of art's economic exceptionalism buried in its history. However, it is not only mainstream economists who are at fault in overlooking the economic exceptionalism of artistic production and consumption. The failure of Marxists to produce a detailed and accurate economic analysis of art – since Marxists have taken the economics of art for granted (as commodity production) or bypassed economics in a sociological theory of art, augmented with psychoanalysis, ideology, politics and aesthetics – has led to exaggerated claims about art's commodification, incorporation, industrialisation, branding, and so forth. Politically, this has meant that the left have been ill-prepared to defend art against market forces, incapable of distinguishing between those artists who produce commodities for the market, and those who do not, and with inadequate resources to engage accurately in the debates over art's subsidies from the state. What mainstream economists and Marxists have underestimated is the extent to which art has been exempt from market forces by virtue of art's economic relations of production.

A summary of exceptionalism in classical, neoclassical, welfare and Marxist economics reveals varieties within the same concept. Classical economics seeks to explain the observation of 'fancy prices' as 'monopoly prices' of goods for which labour cannot augment supply to meet demand. In the case of goods sold at fancy prices there is no competition among suppliers and therefore increased competition among purchasers. The absence of competition among suppliers is precisely what leads classical economists to explain fancy prices in terms of monopoly, but this is unsatisfactory. Theorising exceptional-ism in terms of natural and artificial monopoly endogenises fancy prices and thereby reduces or eliminates the exception at the heart of exceptionalism. In the case of art, in particular, this is unrealistic. If we disaggregate monopoly price and the augmentation of supply then it is possible to rethink classical exceptionalism as a theory of the limits placed on economic exchange by non-economic conditions. When the quantity of a product cannot be increased to meet demand then labour is no longer what is represented by its price. For Smith and the classical economists, it is this divergence of price and labour that is exceptional. If demand increases for an item that cannot be produced or reproduced, then its price cannot be anchored by the labour required to produce it but overshoots that value with no necessary upper limit. Dead art-ists, unique objects, the impossibility of merely substituting one producer of art for another, the rarity of talented labour, the problem of fakes, forgeries and copies, the limited number of wealthy collectors, the extraordinary lengths to which collectors will go to procure a given work, the fact that collectors (unlike merchants) do not buy in order to sell: these are some of the preconditions for art's fancy prices.

In principle, however, the conditions under which prices are regulated by supply and demand can be deliberately avoided in the production of any goods whatsoever. Manufacturers can artificially create the conditions under which commodities can be sold above their equilibrium price by producing special collectors' limited editions or by eliminating competition by produc-ing branded goods or goods protected by copyright and patents, for instance. Handbags are not economically exceptional goods, but the Louis Vuitton 'Tribute Patchwork Bag', released originally in an edition of only 24 in 2007, sold for $45,000 each, although the bags can be produced for just a few hun-dred dollars. Nothing prevents the manufacturer of Louis Vuitton handbags from increasing supply to meet demand, but the marketplace in which no other company can legally produce the 'Tribute Patchwork Bag' does not incentivise such an increase in production either. Designer handbags replicate some of the effects of economic exceptionalism but the cause of the limit on supply is different. It is not impossible to increase the supply of Louis Vuitton handbags to meet demand; the company decided to compel demand to out-strip supply. Economic exceptionalism applies to goods for which supply can-not be increased to meet demand. The artificial restrictions on supply imposed by manufacturers can be excluded from economic exceptionalism if we under-stand the principle feature of economic exceptionalism to be the presence of *external limitations on production*.

There can be monopolistic conditions placed on the supply of a certain artist's work (organisations have been set up to regulate the supply of works by Rembrandt and Warhol, for instance), but this is not monopoly in the conventional sense of the term. The concept of monopoly prices in the theory of economic exceptionalism refers, instead, to a far more unusual and complicated range of constraints on supply. Monopoly is typically a privilege of property rights (having exclusive ownership of a resource such as land, licences, patents and copyright or dominating a whole market by eliminating the competition) but the limitations on the production of wine in certain French vineyards or the production of paintings by Vermeer are not due to property rights. The vineyard has limits that no amount of capital or labour can extend, and the same is true of Vermeer's capacity to produce a certain quantity of paintings per year. In the case of antiques or artworks by dead artists the apparent monopoly is nothing but a false description of a rarity that is fixed by historical circumstances. Not all fancy prices are the result of economic exceptionalism. Some fancy prices (in the market for luxuries) may be due to artificial monopolies established by brands and independent luxury producers, but the fancy prices of artworks are due to the special conditions of artistic production in which the attempt to augment supply through labour is necessarily undermined by the unsubstitutability of the artist and the irreproducibility of the artwork. Unlike in manufacturing generally, identical work made by another producer is not a perfect substitute in art, and even identical work produced by the same artist at different times does not count as a perfect substitute. The preconditions for the economic exceptionalism of artworks are present in the special conditions for the production of art. That is to say, the conditions of artistic production set limits on the economics of art. Even though these conditions are historical (in the sense that they have not always existed and may pass), no economics of art today (or at any point in the last five hundred years) can claim to be realistic if it avoids, suppresses, wishes away or remains ignorant of the forces constraining the reproduction of artworks by interchangeable producers.

When demand for an artist's work increases (as a result of fame, fashion, critical acclaim or whatever) then, in the case of dead artists, no labour can increase the supply of the artist's work to market. However, when the artist is alive, why could the supply of a certain work not be increased? In industry it is possible for a manufacturer to have a monopoly that prevents other producers from meeting an increase in demand, but it does not mean that such articles are irreproducible. What is more, it is to be expected that living artists will increase output when demand for their work increases. However, in most cases, making a work again, even by the same artist, is to make a new work. If Picasso had made a version of his own iconic work '*Les Demoiselles D'Avignon*' twenty years later, no increase in supply of the painting would result: each painting would necessarily remain unique. Artworks are inseparable from how and when they are produced. Supply of given artworks cannot be increased because the time and the context of their production cannot be reproduced. Differences between works produced together and according to the same principles, can lead to enormous discrepancies in quality and price. Individual works in the same exhibition may, therefore, fetch higher prices than others even though they were produced by the same artist in the same year: each work will be uniquely judged (as art) on its merits, and assessed (economically) on its performance. And the individual works that will take on such value are not determined by the artist. The artist can neither choose nor guess which of their artworks will become the key works. The processes of artworks becoming historically important and coins becoming rare, is out of the hands of producers. Unlike monopoly prices in general, opening the marketplace or introducing legislation to prevent individuals and firms from dominating the sector cannot correct the fancy prices of artworks. What is missing from the classical account of art's economic exceptionalism is an explanation of the non-economic constraints placed on the production of art which prevent artworks from being replicated in the way that standard commodities are.

In connection with the difficulties of reproducing the non-substitutable artwork, it is worth revisiting Rosalind Krauss's agenda-setting essay 'The Originality of the Avant-Garde' through an economic lens. Krauss argues convincingly that modernism is defined by the value it ascribes to originality. It is possible to extend the value of originality in art historically to the Renaissance, certainly insofar as artworks from that time were understood as originating in the unique person of the artist. But Ian Watt's important theory of 'the new' published in 1957 locates the modern concept of originality, specifically the inversion of meaning of 'the term "original" which had meant "having existed from the first" ... [into] a term of praise meaning "novel or fresh in character or style",[37] to the period after Descartes. This art supplants the classical and customary narrative consisting of generic characters existing in generic time, narratives 'whose primary criterion was truth to individual experience ... which is always unique and therefore new'. Also, the effort to distinguish one artist's work from another's, through what later was dubbed a 'signature style', certainly predates modernism. Nevertheless, what is significant about Krauss's essay is her postmodern critique of originality and her support for those artists, such as Agnes Martin and Sherrie Levine, who opt for art practices that

---

37   Watt 1957, p. 14.

prioritise repetition rather than originality. The aesthetic and theoretical points are well taken, but two Agnes Martin paintings are not the same, and two Sherrie Levine works are not substitutes of one another. Artworks that are based on the concept of repetition are not necessarily thereby based on the economic practice of producing perfect substitutes of one another, like quantities of onions or Wrangler jeans. Seth Seigelaub had made a similar point about the reproducibility of text art and Conceptual Art's use of photography and publishing: a photograph of a painting is not a painting, he said, and so catalogues and books documenting such works must be secondary to those works, but catalogues of works that exist originally as text or photography can be reproduced in large numbers without any loss in quality or experience, hence catalogues and other publications can be primary for such works. While this results in the production of self-published books such as Ed Ruscha's *Twentysix Gasoline Stations* and *Every Building on the Sunset Strip*, in which each book is a perfect substitute of all the others in the edition (and, coincidentally, the aesthetic organisation of the work is structured around repetition rather than originality), the fact that such works are *technically* capable of being produced and reproduced as commodities, does not mean that this is followed through economically. The reason for this, I would suggest, is that the art market has been set up to respond to the economic exceptionalism of art with the result that artworks with the technical capacity to be standard commodities are required to adapt to exceptional arrangements.

The economic exceptionalism of art remains somewhat sketchy, however, as the suggestive observations of classical economics have not been built in to either cultural economics or the Western Marxist analysis of art's relationship to capitalism. Neoclassical economics does not refine the classical argument for economic exceptionalism so therefore preserves all the ambiguities and errors that beset the conflation of fancy prices with monopoly prices and the narrow theorisation of the impossibility to augment supply as a variety of natural monopoly. The increasing marginal utility of culture is economically exceptional, as is the absence of additional units in the case of unique works of art. Hence, even though neoclassicism fails to improve the classical formulation of economic exceptionalism, it extends the scope of exceptionalism. Not only does neoclassicism furnish the material for a supplementation of the supply theory of fancy prices with a demand theory of *increasing* marginal utility, neoclassicism develops concepts such as imperfect substitution, externality and the cost disease that provide new tools, pose new problems and suggest new articulations of exceptionalism. The apparent non-relationship between classical exceptionalism and neoclassical exceptions raises the possibility that no single coherent concept of economic exceptionalism can be assembled from the fragments in the literature. A coherent or general theory of economic exceptionalism appears to lose out to an observation of fancy prices that are exceptional to classicism and an observation of two distinct anomalies to neoclassical price theory. Despite the fact that art is exceptional to both, the aspects of art that are exceptional in each case appear to be quite separate. True, unique goods are exceptional to both traditions – the first because they are not subject to competition among suppliers, the second because they cannot be divided into units of supply – but the nature of the two types of exceptionalism have nothing in common. What is more, the exception of quantities of a good not being augmentable through labour has nothing at all to do with the exception of the desire for art increasing through exposure. Art, antiques, diamonds and rare books are exceptional to classical doctrine by failing to reach their equilibrium 'natural price' but are exceptional to neoclassical doctrine because their utility and value is indivisible and incalculable in terms of marginal utility. Rather than thinking of economic exceptionalism in general, therefore, we are tempted to speak of exceptions to classical economic theory and exceptions to neoclassical economic theory. It is more worthwhile, I would suggest, to identify the various aspects of the economics of art – the prices of artworks, the tastes of consumers, the production of quantities, and so on – and combine them in a total theory of art's economic exceptionalism.

It is possible to re-describe some aspects of art's economic exceptionalism within the terms of externalities. When a commercial gallery, for instance, displays works for sale, non-purchasing viewers can enjoy the works for free. This is a positive externality. When, on the other hand, a commissioning body uses private or public funds to pay an artist to produce a publicly sited sculpture, many passers-by who have neither paid for the work nor would have asked for it, have no choice but to be confronted by it. This is a negative externality. There can be either positive or negative externalities for a collector when an art historian is commissioned by a third party to write about an artist, if the writing alters the price that a work might fetch. Also, when an artist is selected by a respected curator, exhibited in a prestigious museum, written about in an esteemed publication or discussed at an important conference, then positive externalities result for the owners of the artist's works and the gallerists or dealers who benefit from increased prices of works without contributing financially to the institutions and events that boost the artist's reputation. Since no bargains or trade-offs take place in the transmission of an externality, economists typically resort to the kinds of techniques that they normally regard as interference in the free activity of individuals in order to endogenise such goods/bads (for instance, suggesting that the government impose a tax on the produc-

tion of negative externalities or advocating intellectual copyright for artists).
Mainstream accounts of externalities understand that, since they are not the
result of exchange but the consequence of the absence of exchange, externalities are not governed by the reciprocity of economic transactions. Externalities
leak out from exchange in the form of consequences. What is suppressed in
mainstream economics, however, is the limit to economics and market forces
that this implies. Externalities exist at the intersection of the economic and
non-economic. Externalities are neither economically exceptional (they exist
in every economic sector from healthcare to real estate and from transport to
the chemical industry), nor an explanation of art's economic exceptionalism.
The economic theory of externalities, therefore, cannot replace the theory of
exceptionalism.

    Economic exceptionalism designates a limit. The range of theories of
exceptionalism, or the variety of economic principles to which art is said to be
exceptional, is not proof that art's economic exceptionalism is incoherent but
reflects a whole set of limits. Adam Smith recognised the natural geological
limits of the special conditions for growing certain vines, while Senior added
the limit imposed on production by the death of certain non-substitutable
producers such as artists. Say regarded the rarity of talent as a limit on the production of great art, and Ricardo, who focused on the absence of labour as the
determination of fancy prices, appears to have been struck by antiques, statues
and other rare goods being limited in their supply not only by what was produced in the past but by what has contingently survived. De Quincey builds his
case for exceptionalism around other contingencies, principally geographical
remoteness, which place local and temporary limits on supply. Exceptionalism
is the result not only of insufficient or monopoly supply but also the insistence
of non-market values acting as incentives that put limits on the power of economic forces. Rather than suppress the exceptionalism of such behaviour it
makes more sense to see the apparently irrational choices of artists as exerting
a force on economic rationality that, without fully extinguishing it perhaps, certainly sets limits on its efficacy. The contrast between the purchase of artworks
and the effort required in experiencing them designates another limit to the
economic. Other limits are placed on market forces through art's exceptional
manner of responding to collectors. When an artist is requested by his dealer
to make an additional painting in green because a collector has expressed an
interest in purchasing one, the artist is not thereby instructed by his boss to
complete a job of work. The economic relationship between the dealer and
artist is such that the dealer can only advise, suggest, persuade, threaten and
seduce the artist. And when an artist adopts the imagery, techniques or values

of capitalist production, trade, marketing or management, this is not because of economic but cultural imperatives. Within capitalism, generally, social forces are, at best, secondary to economic forces but in art, we might say, the economic is wrapped up in social imperatives that distort, deflect and limit the laws of supply and demand. Economic exceptionalism, therefore, results from a range of limits placed on market forces by non-economic forces.

Quality or value is the most conspicuous non-economic consideration that sets limits on the standard operation of supply and demand in the production, circulation and consumption of art. What art is or what experts and art's institutions authorise as good taste or informed opinion does not limit value in art. Having said that, the subjective judgements of art by individuals do not have a monopoly on value. Dialogue on value in art is possible and is necessary, albeit often in a hidden and suppressed way, in the formation of individual judgements. One thing we can say about all judgements of value in art is that they are necessarily non-economic. Both originality and repetition are non-economic values. Also, it is clear that Seigulaub's enthusiasm for reproducible art, which resembles the economic imperative to produce perfect substitutes, is actually a non-economic value attached to Conceptual Art's mobility, lightness and auxiliary status. Beauty is a non-economic value. Even if the free market is efficient at responding to the demand for beauty, the value of beauty is non-economic. Equally, the critique of beauty is a non-economic imperative that can have economic effects. What is more, if the experience of beauty and judgements of taste generally require the exertion of a self-transforming subject, then art is integrally linked to a mode of experience that is not only non-economic in origin but non-economic in a fuller sense: no aggregate or statistical average of such experiences can predict future behaviour. This is not because art viewers are always already emancipated, or that they are especially sensitive. Art value is not reducible to consumer preference but this does not mean that the assessment of art's value is restricted to minorities who have the benefit of education, cultivation and minority tastes. Philistine values might not win over the art establishment but they are values nonetheless. The difference between a preference and a value is not between a socially authorised assessment and an individual assessment, but between judging something according to its merits and judging something in relation to its price. With preferences we cut the coat according to our cloth, but with judgements of value we are not required to trade-off quality for affordability. One can value a Paul Smith suit more highly than a Marks & Spencer suit, even while one expresses a preference for the latter by purchasing it. As such, when artworks are discussed according to their merit we do not have to invoke expert opinion, or reject the subjective in order to speak of 'inherent' value. Preference is not more democratic than value, judgements of quality or questions of merit. Value is ordinary.

Value in art need not be restricted to the kind of judgements of *art as art* that dominated discussions of art and aesthetics in high modernism. The association of art with value, of art as a practice of values, precedes modern autonomy. Gombrich said, 'I go back deliberately to the old meaning of the term "art", when art was identified with skill or mastery – the art of war, the art of love, or whatever else'. Prior to the differentiation of craft and skill, the Italian word for skill, *arte*, designated the common ground for them both. 'For Leonardo, arte was a skill, a know-how applied both to his scientific experiments and to painting.'[38] During the Renaissance, however, the artist began to be distinguished from the artisan. Artisans were skilful but artists had something beyond mere skill. Vasari, for instance, wrote biographies of figures from Cimabue to Michelangelo in mythic terms, as compelled by nature to draw and paint, effortlessly excelling their masters at an early age, and quarrelling with their patrons. Subsequently, talk of the artist's 'talent' or 'genius' first supplemented then replaced talk of skill in art's discourses. Art and value had not converged yet, partly because art did not yet exist as a separate category of practice. Before the eighteenth century, Gombrich said, people 'admired paintings and sculptures, but no one talked about art as such'.[39] There were no artists in the Renaissance, either, just 'painters, sculptors and architects', as the title of Vasari's 'Lives' has it. Nevertheless, Vasari conscientiously avoided using the standard common noun for painters, sculptors and architects, namely 'artisan', preferring the word 'artificer' because this was associated with divine creation. The use of the word art changed from the seventeenth century onwards when, in the words of Raymond Williams, 'an increasingly common specialised application to a group of skills not hitherto formally represented: painting, drawing, engraving and sculpture' became 'dominant'.[40] In this new sense of the word, Gombrich says, art is not linked to skill but value: 'art as something next to religion or science'.[41] Skill was not jettisoned from art altogether, but it was allocated an increasingly minor role, first by describing the acquisition of skill in mysterious terms and then by speaking in terms of 'inspiration'. Between the Renaissance and the eighteenth century, art became more than skill. Value rather than craft, technique and know-how becomes central when the word

38   Gombrich 1996, p. 67.
39   Ibid.
40   Williams 1976, p. 41.
41   Gombrich 1996, p. 67.

'art' stopped meaning skill and started meaning art. Now, for the first time, you could speak of the skills of art without saying something circular.

This surplus originated in hyperbole, perhaps, and it has retained an element of mystification about it, but judging products in terms of the skills that are required to produce them is different from judging them in terms of their cultural or aesthetic value. When judgements of the merit of artworks are disaggregated from judgements of the skill of the artist, the first step is taken towards the non-substitutability of the artist, since an artist of equal or superior skill can no longer replace an artist whose work has certain unique qualities. Advocates of craft against art complain that the rubbish presented in prestigious institutions and fetch enormous sums on the market do not compare favourably with the skills required to produce even the most modest craft goods. The evident shortfall between art and craft, from the point of view of craft skill, results from the surplus coming to exist independently of skill to such an extent that it splits off from skill and, eventually, opposes it. Skill is seen as a limitation on art as a result of art becoming the vessel of the new value of 'human poietic powers', which is the source of one of the key elements of modern identity, *inwardness*, that Charles Taylor says was 'reflected and foreshadowed in the great prestige of the visual and plastic arts in the Italian Renaissance'[42] brought about by 'the new self-consciousness about the depiction of reality' and the separation of the subject no longer 'englobed by what is depicted'.[43] The visual arts played a role in representing space in new ways that established new relationships between objects and subjects, but the new mythic accounts of artists also paved the way for concepts such as creative imagination, authenticity, self-determination, self-expression and so on. Adorno picks up on this trajectory of the myth of the artist in relation to general human personality when he says genius 'becomes an ideology in inverse proportion to the world's becoming a less human one'.[44] The Romantic and early modernist love of the art of children, the insane and the so-called primitive indicates just how deeply certain values about humanity as a species begin to erode the status of skill in art. Modernist and avant-gardist art pressed this home through what T.J. Clark called 'practices of negation', namely 'some form of decisive innovation, in method or materials or imagery, whereby a previously established set of skills . . . are deliberately avoided or travestied',[45] including 'attacks on centred and legible composition', 'broken handling',

---

42 Taylor 1989, p. 200.
43 Taylor 1989, p. 202.
44 Adorno 1997, p. 171.
45 Frascina 1985, p. 55.

'mismatching of colours' and 'deliberate displays of painterly awkwardness'. By the nineteenth century, practices of negation become the technical precondition, according to Clark, for any serious art. Interestingly, Clark introduces the concept of 'practices of negation' to address the following question: [w]hat would it be like, exactly, for art to possess its own values?' Whether the negation of skill in art advances art's resistance to orthodoxy and formula, or makes room within technique for the presence of human identity, personality and expression, it is value that drives out skill in art.

If art and value are as tightly knit as I have suggested, then the concept of a merit good has a peculiarly strong relationship with art. Merit goods are given special economic treatment because they are imbued with value, while art is a practice of values. In fact, art separates itself from craft, and manufacturing generally, precisely by virtue of transposing itself according to the rule of values internal to it, a move that puts art on a collision course with the market. Towse interprets the concept of merit good in line with a different conception of the relationship between art and value, one which is attached to an old elitist sense of the value of high culture. 'What Fry and Keynes shared', she says, 'was the upper-middle class view of art as a merit good'.[46] Towse backdates the concept to refer to a set of judgements about the quality of art and the cultivation required to experience it adequately, with no reference to Musgrave's version of welfare economics or public policy. Rather, for Towse, the concept of art as a merit good appears to derive not from welfare economics at all, but from elitism. She explains why Fry and Keynes regarded art as a merit good by telling us that art, to them, was 'something they believed they understood better ... than the grubby types who were responsible for government'.[47] This culturally high-handed definition of a merit good does not fit as neatly with Musgrave's other merit goods such as education and healthcare, nor is it a necessary concomitant of art as a merit good. Art is a merit good, I would argue, not because cultivated and powerful people like Fry and Keynes manage to impose art on the nation, but simply on the condition that there is a serious difference between examples of it being determined by the market (and consumer preference) and being judged on its merits (independent of consumer sovereignty).

But the concept of merit good presents two obstacles for thinking about the economics of art. First, it appears to assume state funding as a solution to the provision of universal goods, and, second, it remains far too timid in its conception of the tension between the economic and the non-economic.

---

46   Towse 2002, p. 152.
47   Ibid.

The argument that certain goods, including education and healthcare, ought to be available universally and free of direct charge to the user, exerts non-economic constraints on economic activities, replacing market mechanisms with mechanisms that derive, in principle, from collective decision-making, and replacing consumer sovereignty with political sovereignty or citizen sovereignty. The principle of the social provision of healthcare to those who need it rather than those who can afford it, as well as providing education to all regardless of the wealth or inclination of households, can only be sustained by a *political* rationale that is imposed independently of market forces. Adding art to the list of merit goods is controversial because it raises questions about elitism, cultural division, privilege and state patronage, but the central question, it seems to me, revolves around the relationship between art and value. That is to say, if health and education are to be allocated according to merit rather than ability to pay and willingness to pay, then art at least has a *prima facie* case for inclusion in the list of merit goods so long as the argument that art ought to be judged on merit and not only according to consumer preference retains its force. If art is a merit good, however, the theory of art's economic exceptionalism can be deployed to rethink the concept of merit good as a collision between the economic and the non-economic in a more far-reaching way than has been typical of the advocacy of public subsidy for merit goods.

Klamer worries that the concept of merit good is simply a technical way of restating 'the old aristocratic idea'[48] that 'culture-is-good-for-you-whether-you-want-to-know-it-or-not'.[49] Such misgivings take only one aspect of the merit good argument – the flouting of consumer sovereignty – and can see only paternalist imposition on individuals denied their power as consumers. What is missed in such arguments, which cannot be avoided when addressing other merit goods such as healthcare and education, is that universal provision is demanded by society through political mechanisms that override economic mechanisms and therefore, in principle, replace one kind of popular sovereignty with another.

This book has not been a roundabout way of defending public subsidy for the arts. Nor has it been a long-winded rejection of the art market. The opposition between the two is a false dichotomy. What is neglected in this short-circuiting of options, is the full range of the non-economic, in which individuals and groups provide for their own and each other's needs, wants and values without exchanging goods and services through markets or the apparatuses of the state. Goodwin appears to permit only two possibilities,

---

48 Klamer 1996, p. 17.
49 Ibid.

asking whether the free market can 'be counted upon to sustain the arts' and, if not, 'what is the proper role for the state?'[50] What I want to take from the concept of merit goods is not the rivalry between the free market and the state, but the combination of three antagonisms: (1) the confrontation between the economic and the non-economic, (2) the employment of political mechanisms rather than market mechanisms for arriving at collective decisions, and (3) the substitution of preference with value. An extended conception of merit goods, incorporated into a thorough re-articulation of economic exceptionalism, therefore, needs to dovetail with Scitovsky's conceptions of the non-economic and citizen sovereignty, Lebovitz's 'political economy of labour' instead of the 'political economy of capital', Ben Fine's resistance to economics imperialism through the distinction between the economic and the non-economic, Esping-Andersen's concept of de-commodification, and something along the lines of Llewellyn Smith's notion of 'art-value'. Hardt and Negri's concept of the Common Wealth and the commons belongs to this reconstitution of economic relations. According to this constellation of concepts, it is possible to think of art as a merit good and therefore as common, in which art is universal and free rather than a hegemonic minority culture subsidised by the multitude. And finally, although many other contributions could be added to the list, David Harvey's concept of the 'cultural and intellectual commons' is important because it combines art and science under a unified description of 'what should be common knowledge open to all'.[51]

Practically, too, the economics of art cannot hang on one isolated measure, such as state subsidy or the art market. Value in art can neither be conflated with market value nor with expert opinion. If art is to become common property in the fullest sense then judgements of the merits of artworks need to be taken by all. The point is neither to determine artistic production by consumer preference nor democratic mandate (both of which presuppose the steering of art by the social aggregate) but to realise the universality of art in social terms both through the extension of collective decision-making about the consumption of art and collective participation in artistic production. Since collective decision-making needs to be made at all levels, from the studio cooperative and local gallery to the national art school and global biennial, under current conditions the state has an important role to play. Under present conditions, also, the only force strong enough to curb the power of the markets is the state, and therefore the state remains a defensible, albeit compromised and compromising, agent in the struggle to vouchsafe the priority of the non-economic

---

50   Ginsburgh and Throsby 2006, p. 28.
51   Harvey 2012, p. 72.

in art, including judgements of artworks on their merit, which market forces threaten with their calculations and trade-offs. Having said that, however, it is important to remember that, under present conditions, the art market, which is in many ways anomalous as a marketplace, is not to be entirely associated with market forces generally. In many ways the art market does not function according to business principles and the laws of supply and demand, including its resistance to consumer sovereignty. Therefore, the struggle against the determination of art by market value sits precariously within the art market itself, permanently under threat and permanently reasserted. To what extent this resistance to market forces within the art market merely pays lip service to art's non-economic value, or whether the art market genuinely risks profits for the sake of artistic merit, is a moot point. Even if this resistance is merely rhetorical, however, it is evidence of the necessity of non-economic value in art even at the heart of art's commercial exchange.

Walter Benjamin's dashed hopes about how culture might be reconfigured as a result of the introduction of technologies of mechanical reproduction can be reinterpreted as a collision between capitalism and the non-economic, and now needs to be extended further into considerations of art's social relations. On some readings, Benjamin appears to argue that technological developments establish social relations by themselves. Radio, photography, vinyl records and the cinema do not merely express already existing social relations, but they cannot bring about revolutionary new social relations just by dint of their social potential. In fact, it has often been argued that these technologies were perfectly adapted to accelerate the commodification of culture, the massification of the audience and the industrialisation of culture. What Benjamin had in mind was not only the technological transformation of culture but the emergence of new collective forms of cultural production and consumption that would reorient these new technologies towards the revolutionary formation of new cultural relations and new cultural subjects. Benjamin's cultural revolution depends on an expanded conception of a sphere counter to the public and, in view of the analysis of art's economic exceptionalism, this cannot exclude the development of non-market mechanisms for decision-making that rival the official apparatuses of cultural competence and expertise. New technologies cannot revolutionise art without a complete transformation of the preconditions for participation in art, particularly the emancipation of the culturally excluded (who I have previously theorised under the heading of the philistine) from the apparatuses of cultural hegemony that allocates the places within culture for the expert, the connoisseur, the consumer, the manager, the student, and, both within and without, the philistine. Benjamin at his most optimistic is the best guide we have for a completely transformed culture organised around the non-economic, the de-commodified, the political economy of labour and the aesthetic commons. What I think the analysis of the economics of art draws out of Benjamin's cultural utopia is, firstly, that we can achieve the kind of transformation of art that Benjamin indicates only if we pay close attention to the mechanisms by which collective decisions are made, and secondly, that this means establishing the conditions for the universalisation of the philistine both as consumer and producer of art. Our utopia for art must be based on discourse as a non-market mechanism for attributing value to art and this must be democratised not merely by extending existing competences but by subverting the expert with philistine knowledge. The market cannot bring this about.

Bibliography

Abbing, Hans 2002, *Why Are Artists Poor? The Exceptional Economy of the Arts*, Amsterdam: Amsterdam University Press.

Abramovitz, Mimi 1983, 'Everyone is on Welfare: "The Role of Redistribution in Social Policy" Revisited', *Social Work*, 28: 441–5.

———— 2001, 'Everyone is Still on Welfare: The Role of Redistribution in Social Policy', *Social Work*, 46: 297–308.

Adam, Georgina 2012, 'Fair or Foul: more art fairs and bigger brand galleries, but is the model sustainable?', *The Art Newspaper*, Issue 236, http://www.theartnewspaper.com/articles/Fair-or-foul-more-art-fairs-and-bigger-brand-galleries-but-is-the-model-sustainable/26672.

Adorno, Theodor 1997 [1970], *Aesthetic Theory*, edited by Gretel Adorno and Rolf Tiedemann, translated by Robert Hullot-Kentor, London: Continuum.

———— 1991 [1938], *The Culture Industry: Selected essays on mass culture*, edited by J.M. Bernstein, London: Routledge.

Adorno, Theodor and Max Horkheimer 1989 [1944], *Dialectic of Enlightenment*, New York: Verso.

Aglietta, Michel 1998, 'Capitalism at the Turn of the Century: Regulation Theory and the Challenge of Social Change', *New Left Review*, 232: 41–90.

Alberro, Alexander 2004, 'Beauty Knows No Pain', *Art Journal*, 63, 2: 37–43.

Alberro, Alexander and Blake Stimson 1999, *Conceptual Art: a critical anthology*, Cambridge, Massachusetts: MIT Press.

———— 2009, *Institutional Critique: an anthology of artists' writings*, Cambridge, Massachusetts: MIT Press.

Anderson, Perry 1987 [1976], *Considerations on Western Marxism*, London: Verso.

———— 1988 [1983], *In the Tracks of Historical Materialism*, London: Verso.

Appadurai, Arjun 1986, *The Social Life of Things*, Cambridge: Cambridge University Press.

Arato, Andrew 1978, *The Frankfurt School Reader*, edited by Andrew Arato and Eike Gebhardt, Oxford: Basil Blackwell.

Arrighi, Giovanni 2007, *Adam Smith in Beijing: Lineages of the twenty-first century*, London: Verso.

Aston, Trevor Henry and C.H.E. Philpin 1985, *The Brenner Debate: Agrarian Class Structure and Economic Development in Pre-Industrial Europe*, Cambridge: Cambridge University Press.

Backhouse, Roger 2002, *The Penguin History of Economics*, London: Penguin Books.

Backhouse, Roger and Tamotsu Nishizawa 2010, *No Wealth But Life*, Cambridge: Cambridge University Press.

Backhouse, Roger and Bradley Bateman 2011, *Capitalist Revolutionary: John Maynard Keynes*, New York: Harvard University Press.

Balibar, Étienne 1995, *The Philosophy of Marx*, translated by Chris Turner, London: Verso.

Barrell, John 1980, *The Dark Side of the Landscape: the rural poor in English painting 1730–1840*, Cambridge: Cambridge University Press.

—— 1986, *The Political Theory of Painting from Reynolds to Hazlitt*, New York: Yale University Press.

Baumol, William 1971, 'Economics of Athenian Drama: its relevance for the arts in a small city today', *The Quarterly Journal of Economics*, 85, 3: 365–76.

—— 1986, 'Unnatural Value: or Art Investment as a Floating Crap Game', *American Economic Review*, 76, 2: 10–14.

Baumol, William and William Bowen 1965, 'On the Performing Arts: The Anatomy of Their Economic Problems', *The American Economic Review*, 55, 1/2: 495–502.

—— 1966, *Performing Arts: the Economic Dilemma*, New York: Twentieth Century.

Baxandall, Michael 1972, *Painting and Experience in Fifteenth Century Italy*, Oxford: Oxford University Press.

Baudrillard, Jean 1981, *For a Critique of the Political Economy of the Sign*, translated by Charles Levin, New York: Telos Press.

—— 2001, *Jean Baudrillard: Selected Writings*, edited by Mark Poster, Stanford: Stanford University Press.

Beaud, Michel and Gilles Dostaler 1997, *Economic Thought Since Keynes*, translated by Valérie Cauchemez, London: Routledge.

Becker, Gary 1960, 'An Economic Analysis of Fertility', in National Bureau of Economic Research, 'Demographic and Economic Change in Developed Countries', Princeton, 209–40.

—— 1996, *Accounting for Tastes*, Cambridge, Massachusetts: Harvard University Press.

—— 2008, 'Human Capital', *The Concise Encyclopedia of Economics*, Library of Economics and Liberty, http://www.econlib.org/library/Enc/HumanCapital.html

Beckley, Bill and Shapiro, David (eds.) 2001, *Uncontrollable Beauty: Towards a New Aesthetic*, New York: Allworth Press.

Bell, Daniel 1973, *The Coming of Post-Industrial Society: A Venture in Social Forecasting*, New York: Basic Books.

Bellini, Andrea 2009, *Everything You Always Wanted to Know About Gallerists But Were Afraid to Ask*, Zurich: JRP Ringier.

Benjamin, Andrew 2006, *Walter Benjamin and Art*, London: Continuum.

Bennett, Tony 1998, *Culture: A Reformer's Science*, London: Sage.

Berardi, Franco 'Bifo' 2009a, *The Soul at Work: From Alienation to Autonomy*, translated by Franscesca Cadel and Giuseppina Mecchia, Los Angeles: Semiotext(e).

———— 2009b, *Precarious Rhapsody: Semio-capitalism and the pathologies of the post-alpha generation*, London: Minor Compositions.

———— 2010, 'Cognitarian Subjectivation', *e-flux*, 20: 1–8.

———— 2011, *After the Future*, Oakland, California: AK Press.

Berlin, Isaiah 2002, *Liberty: Incorporating Four Essays on Liberty*, edited by Henry Hardy, Oxford: Oxford University Press.

Berry-Slater, Josephine 2005, *The Precarious Reader*, London: Mute.

Beveridge, W.H. 1946, 'Obituary', *The Economic Journal*, 56, 221: 143–7.

Bhaskar, Roy 2008, *A Realist Theory of Science*, London: Routledge.

Bindman, David 1981, *Hogarth*, London: Thames and Hudson.

Binkiewicz, Donna 2004, *Federalizing the Muse: United States Arts Policy and the National Endowment of the Arts 1965–1980*, Chapel Hill, North Carolina: University of North Carolina Press.

Blaug, Mark 1969 [1962], *Economic Theory in Retrospect*, Homewood, Illinois: Richard D. Irwin Inc.

Boal, Iain, T.J. Clark, Joseph Matthews, and Michael Watts 2005, *Afflicted Powers: Capital and Spectacle in a New Age of War*, New York: Verso.

Böhm-Bawerk, Eugen von 1949, *Karl Marx and the Close of His System*, edited by Paul Sweezy, New York: Augustus M Kelley.

Bowman, Mary Jean 1951, 'The Role and Interests of the Consumer: the consumer in the history of economic doctrine', The American Economic Review, Papers and Proceedings of the Sixty-Third Annual Meeting of the American Economic Association, 41, 2: 1–18.

Bourdieu, Pierre 1984, *Distinction: A Social Critique of the Judgement of Taste*, London: Routledge.

———— 1990, *The Logic of Practice*, Stanford: Stanford University Press.

———— 2005, *The Social Structures of the Economy*, London: Polity Press.

Braverman, Harry 1998 [1974], *Labor and Monopoly Capitalism*, New York: Monthly Review Press.

Brenner, Robert 1977, 'The Origins of Capitalist Development: A Critique of Neo-Smithian Marxism', *New Left Review*, 104: 25–92.

Buchanan, James 1969, *Cost and Choice*, Indianapolis, Indiana: Liberty Fund.

Buck-Morss, Susan 1977, *The Origin of Negative Dialectics*, New York: Free Press.

Bürger, Peter 1984, *Theory of the Avant-Garde*, translated by Michael Shaw, Minneapolis: University of Minnesota Press.

Buskirk, Martha 2005, *The Contingent Object of Contemporary Art*, Massachusetts: MIT Press.

Callinicos, Alex and Paul Wood 1992, 'Marxism and Modernism: An Exchange between Alex Callinicos and Paul Wood', *Oxford Art Journal*, 15, 2: 120–5.

Casarino, Cesare and Antonio Negri 2008, *In Praise of the Common: A Conversation on Philosophy and Politics*, Minneapolis: University of Minnesota Press.

Charlesworth, Sarah 1975, 'A Declaration of Dependence', *The Fox*, Volume 1, 1: 1–7.

Cockett, Richard 1995, *Thinking the Unthinkable: Think-Tanks and the Economic Counter-Revolution 1931–1983*, London: Fontana.

Cowen, Tyler 1998, *In Praise of Commercial Culture*, Cambridge, Massachusetts: Harvard University Press.

——— 2006, *Good and Plenty: The Creative Successes of American Arts Funding*, New Jersey: Princeton University Press.

Cowen, Tyler and Alexander Tabarrok 2000, 'An Economic Theory of Avant-Garde and Popular Art, or High and Low Culture', *Southern Economic Journal*, 67, 2: 232–53.

Clark, T.J. 1984, *The Painting of Modern Life: Paris in the Art of Manet and His Followers*, Princeton: Princeton University Press.

Crary, Jonathan 1989, 'Spectacle, Attention, Counter-Memory', *October*, 50: 97–107.

Critchley, Simon 2001, *Continental Philosophy: A Very Short Introduction*, Oxford: Oxford University Press.

Crow, Thomas 1985, *Painters and Public Life in Eighteenth-Century Paris*, New Haven: Yale.

Davenport, Herbert 1968 [1913], *The Economics of Enterprise*, New York: Augustus M. Kelley.

Debord, Guy 1983 [1967], *Society of the Spectacle*, Detroit, Michigan: Black & Red.

De Marchi, Neil and Craufurd D. Goodwin 1999, *Economic Engagements with Art*, Durham: Duke University Press.

De Quincey, Thomas 1863, *Logic of Political Economy and Other Papers*, Edinburgh: Adam and Charles Black.

Diederichsen, Diedrich 2008, *On (Surplus) Value in Art*, translated by James Gussen, Berlin: Sternberg Press.

Dobb, Maurice 1950, *Studies in the Development of Capitalism*, London: Routledge & Kegan Paul.

Duménil, Gérard and Dominique Lévy 2004, *Capital Resurgent: Roots of the Neoliberal Revolution*, Cambridge, Massachusetts: Harvard University Press.

Duncan, Carol 1985, *Civilizing Rituals: Inside the Public Art Museums*, London: Routledge.

Eagleton, Terry 1976, *Marxism and Literary Criticism*, London: Methuen.

——— 1984, *The Function of Criticism*, London: Verso.

——— 1990, *The Ideology of the Aesthetic*, London: Basil Blackwell.

Ehrmann, Thierry (ed.) 2011, *Art Market Trends 2010*, Saint Romain au Mont d'Or: Artprice.

——— (ed.) 2012, *Art Market Trends 2011*, Saint Romain au Mont d'Or: Artprice.

Eigenheer, Marianne 2007, *Curating Critique*, Frankfurt: Archiv für aktuelle Kunst.

Eitner, Lorenz 1971, *Neoclassicism and Romanticism 1750–1850: Sources and Documents Volume 1 Enlightenment/Revolution*, London: Prentice-Hall International.

Elliot, Emory, Louis Freitas Caton, and Jeffrey Rhyne (eds.) 2002, *Aesthetics in a Multicultural Age*, New York: Oxford University Press.

Emmett, Ross 2006, 'De gustibus *est* disputandum: Frank H. Knight's reply to George Stigler and Gary Becker's "De gustibus non est disputandum" with an introductory essay', *Journal of Economic Methodology*, 13, 1: 97–111.

Enzensberger, Hans Magnus 1974, *The Consciousness Industry: On Literature, Politics and the Media*, New York: Seabury Press.

Esping-Andersen, Gøsta 1990, *The Three Worlds of Welfare Capitalism*, Cambridge: Polity.

Federici, Silvia 2009, *Caliban and the Witch*, New York: Autonomedia.

Ferris, David 2008, *The Cambridge Introduction to Walter Benjamin*, Cambridge: Cambridge University Press.

Feyerabend, Paul 2010 [1975], *Against Method*, London: Verso.

Fine, Ben and Dimitris Milonakis 2009a, *From Economic Imperialism to Freakonomics*, London: Routledge.

——— 2009b, *From Political Economy to Economics: Method, the social and the historical in the evolution of economic theory*, London: Routledge.

Frascina, Francis 1985, *Pollock and After*, London: Harper and Row.

Fraser, L.M. 1939, 'Consumer Sovereignty', *The Economic Journal*, 49, 195: 544–8.

Friedman, Milton 1966, 'The Methodology of Positive Economics', *Essays In Positive Economics*, Chicago: University of Chicago Press.

Furedi, Frank 2004, *Where Have all the Intellectuals Gone? – Confronting 21st Century Philistinism*, London: Continuum.

Galbraith, John Kenneth 1966, 'Lecture 6: The Cultural Impact', Reith Lectures, transmitted 18 December, transcript available online at http://downloads.bbc.co.uk/rmhttp/radio4/transcripts/1966_reith6.pdf

——— 1970, 'Economics as a System of Beliefs', *The American Economic Review*, 60, 2: 469–78.

——— 2007 [1967], *The New Industrial State*, Princeton: Princeton University Press.

Gazeley, Ian 2003, *Poverty in Britain, 1900–1965*, London: Palgrave.

Gielen, Pascal 2009, *The Murmuring of the Artistic Multitude: Global Art, Memory and Post-Fordism*, translated by Clare McGregor, Amsterdam: Valiz.

Gillick, Liam and Andrew Renton (eds.) 1991, *Technique Anglaise*, London: Thames and Hudson.

Ginsburgh, Victor and David Throsby (eds.) 2006, *The Handbook of the Economics of Art and Culture*, Amsterdam: North-Holland.

Gombrich, Ernst 1966, *Norm and Form*, London: Phaidon.

———— 1996, 'The Big Picture' interviewed by David Carrier, *Artforum*, Volume 34, 6: 66–9.

Gough, Ian 1972, 'Marx's Theory of Productive and Unproductive Labour', *New Left Review*, 1, 76: 47–72.

Graburn, Nelson 1976, *Ethnic and Tourist Arts: Cultural Expressions for the Fourth World*, Bekeley: University of California Press.

Graeber, David 2011, *Debt: the first 5000 years*, New York: Melville House.

Grampp, William 1989, *Pricing the Priceless*, New York: Basic Books.

Green, David 1894, 'Pain-Cost and Opportunity-Cost', *The Quarterly Journal of Economics*, 8, 2: 218–29.

Guattari, Felix and Antonio Negri 2010, *New Lines of Alliance, New Spaces of Liberty*, edited by Stevphen Shukaitis, translated by Michael Ryan, Jared Becker, Arianna Bove and Noe Le Blanc, New York: Autonomedia.

Habermas, Jürgen 1984, *The Theory of Communicative Action, Volume 2: Lifeworld and System: A Critique of Functionalist Reason*, translated by Thomas McCarthy, Cambridge: Polity Press.

———— 1987, *A Theory of Communicative Action, Volume 1: Reason and the Rationalization of Society*, translated by Thomas McCarthy, Boston: Beacon Press.

———— 1989 [1961], *The Structural Transformation of the Public Sphere*, translated by Thomas Burger, Cambridge, Massachusetts: MIT Press.

———— 1992 [1976], *Legitimation Crisis*, translated by Thomas McCarthy, Cambridge: Polity Press.

———— 1996, *Between Facts and Norms*, Cambridge, Massachusetts: MIT Press.

Hall, Stuart and Martin Jacques (eds.) 1989, *New Times: The Changing Face of Politics in the 1990s*, London: Lawrence and Wishart.

Harman, Chris 2009, *Zombie Capitalism: Global Crisis and the Relevance of Marx*, London: Bookmarks.

Harnecker, Marta 2007, *Rebuilding the Left*, London: Zedbooks.

Harris, Jonathan 2001, *The New Art History: A Critical Introduction*, London: Routledge.

Harrod, Roy 1972, *The Life of John Maynard Keynes*, New York: W.W. Norton & Company.

Harvey, David 1982, *The Limits to Capital*, Oxford: Basil Blackwell.

———— 2010, *A Companion to Marx's Capital*, New York: Verso.

———— 2012, *Rebel Cities*, New York: Verso.

Haug, Wolfgang 2009, 'Immaterial Labour', *Historical Materialism*, 17, 177–85.

———— 2010, 'General Intellect,' *Historical Materialism*, 18, 209–16.

Hauser, Arnold 1992 [1951], *The Social History of Art, Volume II: Renaissance, Mannerism, Baroque*, London: Routledge.

———— 1999 [1951], *The Social History of Art, Volume I: From Prehistorical Times to the Middle Ages*, London: Routledge.

Hickey, Dave 2009 [1993], *The Invisible Dragon: Four Essays on Beauty*, Chicago: University of Chicago Press.

Hildebrand, George 1951, 'Consumer Sovereignty in Modern Times', *The American Economic Review*, 41, 2: 19–33.

Hilferding, Rudolf 1981 [1910], *Finance Capital: A Study of the Latest Phase of Capitalist Development*, London: Routledge & Kegan Paul.

Hill, Rod and Tony Myatt 2010, *The Economics Anti-Textbook: A Critical Thinker's Guide to Microeconomics*, London: Zedbooks.

Hilton, Rodney 1976, *The Transition from Feudalism to Capitalism*, London: Verso.

Honneth, Alex 2007, 'Reification: A Recognition-Theoretical View', *The Tanner Lectures on Human Values*, Oxford: Open University Press.

House, Ernest 2001, 'Unfinished Business: Causes and Values', *American Journal of Evaluation*, 22, 3: 309–15.

Howson, Susan 2011, *Lionel Robbins*, New York: Cambridge University Press.

Huff, Daniel 1993, 'Phantom Welfare: Public Relief for Corporate America', *Social Work* 38: 311–16.

Hume, David 1987 [1888], *A Treatise of Human Nature*, edited by L.A. Selby-Bigge, Oxford: Clarendon Press.

Jameson, Fredric 1971, *Marxism and Form*, New Jersey: Princeton University Press.

―――― 1979, 'Reification and Utopia in Mass Culture', *Social Text*, 1: 130–48.

―――― 1983 [1981], *The Political Unconscious*, London: Routledge.

―――― 1988, *The Cultural Turn*, New York: Verso.

Jevons, William Stanley 1888, *The Theory of Political Economy*, London: Macmillan.

Kaufman, Bill 1990, 'Subsidies to the Arts: Cultivating Mediocrity', *Cato Institute Policy Analysis*, 137.

Keen, Steve 1993, 'Use Value, Exchange Value, and the Demise of Marx's Labor Theory of Value', *Journal of the History of Economic Thought*, 15, 1: 107–21.

―――― 2001, *Debunking Economics: The Naked Emperor of the Social Sciences*, London: Pluto Press.

Kennedy, John F. 1963, Letter Accepting Resignation of August Heckscher as Special Consultant for the Arts, dated 10 June, American Presidency Project, http://www.presidency.ucsb.edu/ws/?pid=9281#ixzz1zwOA041C

Kenny, Michael 1995, *The First New Left: British Intellectuals After Stalin*, London: Lawrence and Wishart.

Kester, Grant 2003, 'The World He Has Lost: Dave Hickey's beauty treatment', *Variant*, 2, 18: 11–12.

Keynes, John Maynard 1945, 'The Arts Council: its Policy and Hopes', *Listener*, 34, 861: 31.

―――― 1982, *The Collected Writings of John Maynard Keynes*, edited by D. Moggridge, London: Macmillan Press.

Kirschenbaum, Baruch 1979, 'The Scull Auction and the Scull Film', *Art Journal*, 39, 1: 50–4.

Klamer, Arjo 1996, *The Value of Culture: On the Relationship between Economics and Art*, Amsterdam: Amsterdam University Press.

Kliman, Andrew 2007, *Reclaiming Marx's 'Capital': A Refutation of the Myth of Inconsistency*, Plymouth: Lexington Books.

Kräussl, Roman 2010, 'Art Prices Indices', in *Fine Art and High Finance*, edited by Clare McAndrew, New York: Bloomberg Press.

Lapavitsas, Costas 1990, 'Financialisation, or the Search for Profits in the Sphere of Circulation', Discussion Paper 10, School of Oriental and African Studies, available online at http://www.soas.ac.uk/rmf/papers/file47508.pdf.

Lazzarato, Maurizio 1996, 'Immaterial Labour', translated by Paul Colilli and Ed Emory, in Paolo Virno and Michael Hardt (eds.), *Radical Thought in Italy*, Minneapolis: University of Minnesota Press.

——— 2012, *The Making of Indebted Man*, Los Angeles: Semiotext(e)

Lebowitz, Michael 2003, *Beyond Capital: Marx's Political Economy of the Working Class*, New York: Palgrave Macmillan.

Lenin, Vladmir I. 1967, 'Imperialism, the Highest Stage of Capitalism', in *V.I. Lenin: Selected Works*, Volume 1, Moscow: Progress Publishers.

Liberate, Tate 2011, *Culture Beyond Oil*, London: Platform.

Lippard, Lucy 1973, *Five Years: The Dematerialization of the Art Object from 1966 to 1972*, New York: Praeger.

Llewellyn Smith, Hubert 1924, *The Economic Laws of Art Production: An Essay towards the Construction of a Missing Chapter on Economics*, London: Oxford University Press.

Lloyd, David and Paul Thomas 1998, *Culture and the State*, New York: London.

Löwy, Michael 1979, *Georg Lukács – From Romanticism to Bolshevism*, London: New Left Books.

Lukács, Georg 1979, *The Meaning of Contemporary Realism*, translated by John and Necke Mander, London: Merlin Press.

——— 1990 [1922], *History and Class Consciousness*, translated by Rodney Livingstone, London: Merlin Press.

McAndrew, Clare 2010a, *The International Art Market 2007–2009: Trends in the Art Trade during Global Recession*, Helvoirt: The European Fine Art Foundation.

——— (ed.) 2010b, *Fine Art and High Finance*, New York: Bloomberg Press.

——— 2011, *The Global Art Market in 2010: crisis and recovery*, Helvoirt: The European Fine Art Foundation.

MacIntyre, Alasdair 1987 [1981], *After Virtue: a study in moral theory*, London: Duckworth.

MacKenzie, Norman 1958, 'The Economics of Prosperity', *Universities and Left Review* 5, Autumn, http://www.amielandmelburn.org.uk/collections/ulr/05_62.pdf

Macherey, Pierre 1978, *A Theory of Literary Production*, translated by Geoffrey Wall, London: Routledge and Kegan Paul.

Malthus, Thomas 1836, *Principles of Political Economy*, London: W. Pickering.

Mandel, Ernest 1975, *Late Capitalism*, translated by Joris De Bres, London: Verso.

Mankiw, N. Gregory 2004, *Principles of Economics*, Mason, Ohio: Thomson South-Western.

Marazzi, Christian 2011, *The Violence of Financial Capitalism*, Los Angeles: Semiotext(e).

Markus, Gyorgy 2001, 'Walter Benjamin or: The Commodity as Phantasmagoria', *New German Critique*, 83: 3–42.

Marsall, Alfred 1997 [1890], *Principles of Economics*, New York: Prometheus Books.

Martin, Stewart 2009, 'Artistic Communism – A Sketch', *Third Text*, 23, 4: 481–94.

Marx, Karl 1954 [1867], *Capital: The Critique of Political Economy Volume I*, translated by Samuel Moore and Edward Aveling, edited by Frederick Engels, London: Lawrence and Wishart.

―――― 1956 [1893], *Capital: The Critique of Political Economy Volume II*, translated by Samuel Moore and Edward Aveling, edited by Frederick Engels, London: Lawrence and Wishart.

―――― 1959 [1894], *Capital: A Critique of Political Economy Volume III*, edited by Frederick Engels, London: Lawrence and Wishart.

―――― 1970 [1859], *Contribution to the Critique of Political Economy*, translated by S.W. Ryazanskaya, London: Lawrence and Wishart.

―――― 1973 [1857–8], *Grundrisse*, translated by Martin Nicolaus, London: Penguin Classics.

―――― 1978 [1891], 'Wage Labour and Capital', in *The Marx-Engels Reader*, edited by Robert Tucker, New York: W.W. Norton & Company.

―――― 1982, *Capital: A Critique of Political Economy Volume One*, translated by Ben Fowkes, London: Penguin.

―――― 1985 [1898], *Wages, Price and Profit*, Moscow: Progress Publishers.

Mattick, Paul 1980 [1969], *Marx and Keynes: The Limits of the Mixed Economy*, London: Merlin Press.

McCloskey, Deirdre 1983, 'The Rhetoric of Economics', Journal of Economic Literature, July XXI: 481–571.

McGuigan, Jim 2004, *Rethinking Cultural Policy*, Maidenhead: Open University Press.

Medema, Steven and Warren Samuels 2003, *The History of Economic Thought: A Reader*, London: Routledge.

Merleau-Ponty, Maurice 1973 [1955], *Adventures of the Dialectic*, translated by Joseph Bien, Evanston, Illinois: Northwest University Press.

Mill, John Stuart 1870 [1848], *Principles of Political Economy with some of their applications to social philosophy*, Volume One, New York: D. Appleton and Company.

———— 1945 [1859], *On Liberty*, London: Watts & Co.

———— 1965, *Collected Works*, Toronto: Toronto University Press.

Mises, Ludwig von 1944, *Bureaucracy*, New Haven: Yale University Press.

Modleski, Tania (ed.) 1986, *Studies in Entertainment*, Indiana: Indiana University Press.

Moggridge, D.E. 1992, *Maynard Keynes: An economist's biography*, London: Routledge.

Montias, John Michael 1989, *Vermeer and His Milieu: A Web of Social History*, New Jersey: Princeton University Press.

Möntmann, Nina 2006, *Art and its Institutions: current conflicts, critique and collaborations*, London: Black Dog Publishing.

Moore, Stephen 2008, 'Leo Steinberg and the Provisionality of Modernist Criticism', *Re:Bus*, 2: 1–22.

Mouffe, Chantal 2008, 'Art and Democracy: Art as an Agonistic Intervention in Public Space' *Open*, 14: 101–7.

Muir, Gregor 2009, *Lucky Kunst: The Rise and Fall of Young British Art*, London: Aurum Press.

Munson, Lynne 2000, *Exhibitionism: Art in an Era of Intolerance*, Chicago: Ivan R. Dee.

Musgrave, Richard 1941, 'The Planning Approach in Public Economy: A Reply', *The Quarterly Journal of Economics*, 55, 2: 319–24.

———— 1957, 'A Multiple Theory of Budget Determination', *Finanzarchiv*, 17, 3: 333–43.

———— 1959, *The Theory of Public Finance*, New York: McGraw-Hill.

Negri, Antonio 1991, *Marx Beyond Marx: Lessons on the Grundrisse*, translated by Harry Cleaver, Michael Ryan and Maurizio Viano, edited by Jim Fleming, New York: Autonomedia/Pluto.

———— 2003, 'N for Negri: Antonio Negri in Conversation with Carles Guerra', *Grey Room*, 11: 86–109.

Nelson, Robert 2001, *Economics as a Religion: From Samuelson to Chicago and Beyond*, Pennsylvania: Pennsylvania State University Press.

Nelson, Robert and Richard Shiff 1996, *Critical Terms for Art History*, Chicago: University of Chicago Press.

Noble, Charles 1997, *Welfare As We Knew It*, New York: Oxford University Press.

Novemsky, Frederick, Nathan Novemsky, Jing Wang, Ravi Dhar, and Stephen Nowlis, 2009, 'Opportunity Cost Neglect', *Journal of Consumer Research*, 36, 4: 553–61.

Noys, Benjamin 2010, *The Persistence of the Negative: A Critique of Contemporary Continental Theory*, Edinburgh: Edinburgh University Press.

O'Malley, Tom and Janet Jones 2009, *The Peacock Committee and UK Broadcasting Policy*, London: Palgrave Macmillan.

Osborne, Peter 2007, 'Living with Contradictions: The Resignation of Chris Gilbert', *Afterall*, 16: 109–13.

———— 2013, *Anywhere or Not at All: Philosophy of Contemporary Art*, London: Verso.

Panitch, Leo and Colin Leys 1998, *The Communist Manifesto Now*, Rendlesham, Suffolk: Merlin Press.

Peacock, Alan 1993, *Paying the Piper: Culture, Music, Money*, Edinburgh: Edinburgh University Press.

———— 2000, 'Public Financing of the Arts in England', *Fiscal Studies*, 21, 2: 171–205.

Peacock, Alan and Jack Wiseman 1961, *The Growth of Public Expenditure in the United Kingdom*, London: Oxford University Press.

Polanyi, Karl 2001 [1944], *The Great Transformation: The Political and Economic Origins of Our Time*, Boston: Beacon Press.

Putnam, Hilary 2002, *The Collapse of the Fact/Value Dichotomy and Other Essays*, Cambridge, Massachusetts: Harvard University Press.

Ramsden, Mel 1975, 'On Practice', *The Fox*, 1, 1: 66–83.

Rectanus, Mark 2002, *Culture Incorporated: museums, artists and corporate sponsorship*, Minnesota: University of Minnesota Press.

Ricardo, David 1821 [1817], *On the Principles of Political Economy and Taxation*, London: John Murray.

Roberts, John 1990, *Postmodernism, Politics and Art*, Manchester: Manchester University Press.

———— 2007, *The Intangibilities of Form: Skill and Deskilling in Art After the Readymade*, London: Verso.

Robbins, Lionel 1932, *An Essay on the Nature and Significance of Economic Science*, New York: New York University Press.

———— 1963, 'Art and the state', in *Politics and Economics: Papers in Political Economy*, London: Macmillan.

Rosdolsky, Roman 1977, *The Making of Marx's 'Capital'*, translated by Pete Burgess, London: Pluto Press.

Rose, Margaret 1984, *Marx's Lost Aesthetic*, Cambridge: Cambridge University Press.

Rubin, Isaac Ilych 1979 [1929], *A History of Economic Thought*, translated and edited by Donald Filzer, London: Ink Links.

Ruskin, John 1985 [1862], *Unto This Last and other writings*, edited by Clive Wilmer, London: Penguin.

Saatchi, Charles 2009, *My Name is Charles Saatchi and I Am An Artoholic*, London: Phaidon.

Say, Jean-Baptiste 2007 [1803], *A Treatise on Political Economy*, translated by C.R. Prinsep, Kitchener, Ontario: Batoche Books.

———— 1967 [1821], *Letters to Mr. Malthus*, translated by John Richter, New York: Cosimo Books.

Schiller, Friedrich 1902, *Aesthetical and Philosophical Essays*, edited by Nathan Haskell Dole, Boston, Massachusetts: Francis A Niccolls.

Scitovsky, Tibor 1962, 'On the Principle of Consumers' Sovereignty', *The American Economic Review*, 52, 2: 262–8.

———— 1992 [1976], *The Joyless Economy: The Psychology of Human Satisfaction*, New York: Oxford University Press.

Searle, John 1996, *The Construction of Social Reality*, London: Penguin.

Senior, Nassau 1836, *An Outline of the Science of Political Economy*, London: W. Clowes and Sons.

Sholette, Greg 2011, *Dark Matter: Art and Politics in the Age of Enterprise Culture*, London: Pluto Press.

Sismondi, Jean Charles Léonard 1847, *Political Economy and the Philosophy of Government*, edited by M. Mignet, London: John Chapman.

Slater, Howard 2000, 'The Art of Governance: The Artist Placement Group 1966–89', *Variant*, 2, 11: 23–4.

Smith, Adam 1993 [1776], *An Inquiry into the Nature and Causes of The Wealth of Nations*, Indianapolis: Hackett Publishing.

Spiller, Stephen 2011, 'Opportunity Cost Consideration', *Journal of Consumer Research*, 38, 4: 595–610.

Stallabrass, Julian 2004a, *Art Incorporated*, Oxford: Oxford University Press.

———— 2004b, *Contemporary Art: A Very Short Introduction*, Oxford: Oxford University Press.

Steedman, Ian 1977, *Marx After Sraffa*, London: New Left Books.

Steinberg, Leo 1972, *Other Criteria: Confrontations with Twentieth-Century Art*, New York: Oxford University Press.

———— 1995, 'Picasso's Endgame', *October*, 74: 105–22.

Stigler, George 1969, 'Opportunity Cost of Marriage: Comment', *Journal of Political Economy*, 77, 5: 863–8.

Stigler, George and Gary Becker 1977, 'De Gustibus Non Est Disputandum', *American Economic Review*, 67, 2: 76–90.

Stiglitz, Joseph 1987, 'The Causes and Consequences of the Dependence of Quality on Price', *Journal of Economic Literature*, 25, 1: 1–48.

———— 1989, 'Markets, Market Failures, and Development', *American Economic Review*, 79, 2: 197–203.

———— 1991, 'Another Century of Economic Science', *The Economic Journal*, 101, 404: 134–41.

———— 2002, 'Information Economics and Paradigm Change', *The American Economic Review*, 92, 3: 460–501.

Stolnitz, Jerome 1961, ' "Beauty": Some Stages in the History of an Idea', *Journal of the History of Ideas*, 22, 2: 185–204.

Strong, Roy 1969, *Tudor and Jacobean Portraits*, London: Her Majesty's Stationery Office.

Sweezy, Paul 1946, *The Theory of Capitalist Development*, London: D. Dobson.

Taylor, Charles 1989, *Sources of the Self: The Making of Modern Identity*, Cambridge: Cambridge University Press.

Thomas, David 1954, *George Morland*, London: Arts Council.

Thompson, Dorothy 1960, 'Farewell to the Welfare State', *New Left Review*, 4: 39–42.

Thompson, E.P. 1995 [1978], *The Poverty of Theory*, London: Merlin Press.

Throsby, David 1994, 'The Production and Consumption of the Arts: A View of Cultural Economics', *Journal of Economic Literature*, 32, 1: 1–29.

Toscano, Alberto 2008, 'The Open Secret of Real Abstraction', *Rethinking Marxism*, 20, 2: 273–87.

Towse, Ruth 1996, *The Economics of Artists' Labour Markets*, London: The Arts Council of England.

———— 2002, 'Art and the Market: Roger Fry on Commerce in Art', *The Economic Journal*, 112, 477: 151–3.

———— 2005, 'Alan Peacock and Cultural Economics', *The Economic Journal*, 115, 504: 262–76.

———— 2010, *A Textbook of Cultural Economics*, Cambridge: Cambridge University Press.

Tullock, Gordon 1994, 'Introduction to Alan Peacock's "Welfare Economics and Public Subsidies to the Arts"', *Journal of Cultural Economics*, 18, 2: 149–50.

Upchurch, Anna 2004, 'John Maynard Keynes, The Bloomsbury Group and the Origins of the Arts Council Movement', *International Journal of Cultural Policy*, 10, 2: 203–17.

Vanek, Jarolsav 1959, 'An Afterthought on the "Real Cost-Opportunity Cost" Dispute and Some Aspects of General Equilibrium Under Conditions of Variable Factor Supplies', *The Review of Economic Studies*, 26, 3: 198–208.

Veblen, Thorstein 1900, 'The Preconceptions of Economic Science', *The Quarterly Journal of Economics*, 14, 2: 240–69.

Velthius, Olav 2007, *Talking Prices: Symbolic Meanings of Prices on the Market for Contemporary Art*, Princeton: Princeton University Press.

Vercellone, Carlo 2007, 'From Formal Subsumption to General Intellect: Elements for a Marxist Reading of the Thesis of Cognitive Capitalism', *Historical Materialism*, 15, 1: 13–36.

Virno, Paolo 2004, *A Grammar of the Multitude: For an Analysis of Contemporary Forms of Life*, translated by Isabella Bertoletti, James Cascaito and Andrea Casson, Los Angeles: Semiotext(e).

Watt, Ian 1957, *The Rise of the Novel*, Los Angeles: University of California Press.

Werckmeister, Otto Karl 1991, *Citadel Culture*, Chicago: University of Chicago Press.

West, Edwin and Michael McKee 1983, 'De Gustibus Est Disputandum: The Phenomenon of "Merit Wants" Revisited', *The American Economic Review*, 73, 5: 1110–21.

Wicksteed, Philip 1888 [1880], *The Alphabet of Economic Science: Elements of the Theory of Value or Worth*, London: Macmillan.

—— 1910, *The Common Sense of Political Economy*, London: Macmillan.

Wieser, Friedrich von 1891, 'The Austrian School and the Theory of Value', *The Economic Journal*, 1, 1: 108–21.

—— 1893, *Natural Value*, London: Macmillan.

Williams, Raymond 1965, *The Long Revolution*, London: Pelican Books.

—— 1976, *Keywords*, London: Fontana.

Wolfe, Tom 1975, *The Painted Word*, New York: Picador.

Wolff, Janet 1981, *The Social Production of Art*, London: Macmillan.

Wollheim, Richard 1987, *Painting as an Art*, London: Thames and Hudson.

Wright, Steve 2002, *Storming Heaven: Class Composition and Struggle in Italian Autonomist Marxism*, London: Pluto Press.

Young, Robert 1981, *Untying the Text: A Post-Structuralist Anthology*, Boston: Routledge and Kegan Paul.

Žižek, Slavoj 2009, *First as Tragedy, then as Farce*, London: Verso.

—— 2012, 'The Revolt of the Salaried Bourgeoisie', *London Review of Books*, 34, 2: 2–10.

Index